# Convergence

# Convergence

*Five Critical Steps toward Integrating Lagging and Leading Areas in the Middle East and North Africa*

 **WORLD BANK GROUP**

# Contents

*Acknowledgments* . . . . . . . . . . . . . . . . . . . . . . . . . . . . . . . . . . . . . . . . . . . . . . . . . . . . . . . . . *xv*

*Memorandum to a Concerned Finance Minister* . . . . . . . . . . . . . . . . . . . . . . . . . . . . . . . . . . *xvii*

*About the Authors* . . . . . . . . . . . . . . . . . . . . . . . . . . . . . . . . . . . . . . . . . . . . . . . . . . . . . . . *xxi*

*Abbreviations* . . . . . . . . . . . . . . . . . . . . . . . . . . . . . . . . . . . . . . . . . . . . . . . . . . . . . . . . . . *xxv*

**Overview** . . . . . . . . . . . . . . . . . . . . . . . . . . . . . . . . . . . . . . . . . . . . . . . . . . . . . . . . . . . . . 1
Why do so many place-based interventions fail? . . . . . . . . . . . . . . . . . . . . . . . . . . . . . . . . . 1
How can the region's countries approach convergence? . . . . . . . . . . . . . . . . . . . . . . . . . 4
Fragmented cities, stuck people, walled-off countries: The symptoms of institutional
    constraints on growth . . . . . . . . . . . . . . . . . . . . . . . . . . . . . . . . . . . . . . . . . . . . . . . . . . . . 5
Place-based and centralized: How national policies and institutions in the Middle East
    and North Africa perpetuate economic inefficiency and spatial inequity . . . . . . . . . . . . . 19
Five transitional steps to reduce institutional inefficiency, speed the Middle East
    and North Africa's economic development, and enable convergent growth . . . . . . . . . . . 25
The prospects for regional integration: Distant yet vital to the Middle East and
    North Africa . . . . . . . . . . . . . . . . . . . . . . . . . . . . . . . . . . . . . . . . . . . . . . . . . . . . . . . . . . . . 29
Notes . . . . . . . . . . . . . . . . . . . . . . . . . . . . . . . . . . . . . . . . . . . . . . . . . . . . . . . . . . . . . . . . . . . 30
References . . . . . . . . . . . . . . . . . . . . . . . . . . . . . . . . . . . . . . . . . . . . . . . . . . . . . . . . . . . . . . . 31

**1 Fragmented Cities, Constrained Growth** . . . . . . . . . . . . . . . . . . . . . . . . . . . . . . . . . . . 33
Rapid urbanization has not brought commensurate economic benefits to the
    Middle East and North Africa . . . . . . . . . . . . . . . . . . . . . . . . . . . . . . . . . . . . . . . . . . . . . . 34
Modernist planning and informality play crucial roles in the fragmented urban fabric . . . . . 38
Concluding remarks . . . . . . . . . . . . . . . . . . . . . . . . . . . . . . . . . . . . . . . . . . . . . . . . . . . . . . . . 52
Annex 1A Methodology for calculating the agglomeration index . . . . . . . . . . . . . . . . . . . . . 52
Annex 1B Methodology for developing indicators of urban form . . . . . . . . . . . . . . . . . . . . . 53

Annex 1C Methodology for analyzing road and intersection densities . . . . . . . . . . . . . . . . . 54
Annex 1D Comparison of Global Human Settlement Layers and
    Global Urban Footprint datasets. . . . . . . . . . . . . . . . . . . . . . . . . . . . . . . . . . . . . . . . 54
Notes . . . . . . . . . . . . . . . . . . . . . . . . . . . . . . . . . . . . . . . . . . . . . . . . . . . . . . . . . . . . . . . 55
References . . . . . . . . . . . . . . . . . . . . . . . . . . . . . . . . . . . . . . . . . . . . . . . . . . . . . . . . . . . 56

**2   Unequal Spaces and Stuck People. . . . . . . . . . . . . . . . . . . . . . . . . . . . . . . . . . . . .59**
High disparities and low migration hinder economic mobility . . . . . . . . . . . . . . . . . . . . . 60
Low migration suppresses labor mobility in the Middle East and North Africa. . . . . . . . . . 69
Credential-oriented education systems offer one explanation for low internal mobility . . . . . 80
Concluding remarks. . . . . . . . . . . . . . . . . . . . . . . . . . . . . . . . . . . . . . . . . . . . . . . . . . . . . 82
Annex 2A Data sources and coverage . . . . . . . . . . . . . . . . . . . . . . . . . . . . . . . . . . . . . . . 83
Notes . . . . . . . . . . . . . . . . . . . . . . . . . . . . . . . . . . . . . . . . . . . . . . . . . . . . . . . . . . . . . . . 85
References . . . . . . . . . . . . . . . . . . . . . . . . . . . . . . . . . . . . . . . . . . . . . . . . . . . . . . . . . . . 86

**3   Walled Urban Economies . . . . . . . . . . . . . . . . . . . . . . . . . . . . . . . . . . . . . . . . . . . . .91**
Large cities will remain important in the Middle East and North Africa landscape . . . . . . . 92
Regional integration can deliver large markets for the Middle East and
    North Africa's cities . . . . . . . . . . . . . . . . . . . . . . . . . . . . . . . . . . . . . . . . . . . . . . . . . .99
Concluding remarks. . . . . . . . . . . . . . . . . . . . . . . . . . . . . . . . . . . . . . . . . . . . . . . . . . . . 114
Annex 3A Methodology for analyzing productivity across regions. . . . . . . . . . . . . . . . . . . 114
Notes . . . . . . . . . . . . . . . . . . . . . . . . . . . . . . . . . . . . . . . . . . . . . . . . . . . . . . . . . . . . . . 115
References . . . . . . . . . . . . . . . . . . . . . . . . . . . . . . . . . . . . . . . . . . . . . . . . . . . . . . . . . . 116

**4   How States Shape Markets through Spatial and Private
     Sector Development Bets . . . . . . . . . . . . . . . . . . . . . . . . . . . . . . . . . . . . . . . . . . .119**
Competition regimes in the Middle East and North Africa: How do
    they differ from other regions, and why? . . . . . . . . . . . . . . . . . . . . . . . . . . . . . . . . . 121
Middle East and North Africa governments intervene in markets to shape economic
    geography . . . . . . . . . . . . . . . . . . . . . . . . . . . . . . . . . . . . . . . . . . . . . . . . . . . . . . . . 126
Government interventions cause varying magnitudes of spatial distortion in
    the Middle East and North Africa . . . . . . . . . . . . . . . . . . . . . . . . . . . . . . . . . . . . . . . 131
Implications and persistence of governments' approach to shaping markets in the
    Middle East and North Africa . . . . . . . . . . . . . . . . . . . . . . . . . . . . . . . . . . . . . . . . . . 145
Annex 4A Disaggregation of government expenditure, by government level, for
    each of the comparator countries . . . . . . . . . . . . . . . . . . . . . . . . . . . . . . . . . . . . . . 148
Annex 4B Disclaimers regarding the classification of government expenditures. . . . . . . . . 149
Annex 4C Classification of the IMF database. . . . . . . . . . . . . . . . . . . . . . . . . . . . . . . . . . 150
Annex 4D Reasons for excluding other Middle East and North Africa countries
    from the spatial analysis of government expenditures . . . . . . . . . . . . . . . . . . . . . . . 152
Notes . . . . . . . . . . . . . . . . . . . . . . . . . . . . . . . . . . . . . . . . . . . . . . . . . . . . . . . . . . . . . . 152
References . . . . . . . . . . . . . . . . . . . . . . . . . . . . . . . . . . . . . . . . . . . . . . . . . . . . . . . . . . 154

**5   Centralized Government: Contributor to Economic Geography . . . . . . . . . . . . . . .157**
What do citizens expect of the state in the Middle East and North Africa? . . . . . . . . . . . . 158
Centralized government responses reinforce spatial bias, undermining instead
    of encouraging convergence . . . . . . . . . . . . . . . . . . . . . . . . . . . . . . . . . . . . . . . . . . 159
Decentralization has complex implications for spatial disparity . . . . . . . . . . . . . . . . . . . . 165
Efforts to move from state-centric to citizen-centric approaches vary across the region. . . . 172
Concluding remarks. . . . . . . . . . . . . . . . . . . . . . . . . . . . . . . . . . . . . . . . . . . . . . . . . . . . 174
Notes . . . . . . . . . . . . . . . . . . . . . . . . . . . . . . . . . . . . . . . . . . . . . . . . . . . . . . . . . . . . . . 175
References . . . . . . . . . . . . . . . . . . . . . . . . . . . . . . . . . . . . . . . . . . . . . . . . . . . . . . . . . . 175

**6    Five Steps for Enabling Growth through Thriving Cities and Towns in the Middle East and North Africa** .......................................**179**
Transitional Step 1: Adopt new, evidence-based criteria to guide spatial interventions .... 180
Transitional Step 2: Devolve greater functional authority and resources for local revenue generation and service provision to local governments ................... 188
Transitional Step 3: Step away from credentialist education and toward schooling that cultivates globally tradable skills ...................................... 192
Transitional Step 4: Renew the focus on nurturing urban agglomerations by streamlining land transfer procedures and relaxing zoning regulations in existing cities, lowering the regulatory barriers to their redevelopment ................... 194
Transitional Step 5: Expand market access for cities by thinning the "thick borders" that inhibit mobility across the Middle East and North Africa for both regional trade and migration ........................................ 196
Concluding remarks ................................................... 205
Notes ............................................................... 207
References ........................................................... 207

**Boxes**
O.1    Place-based policies have not led to spatial convergence ........................... 2
O.2    Economic density and agglomeration effects: The urban advantage .................. 3
O.3    Many signs point to one problem: The Middle East and North Africa's economies are moving insufficiently ...................................... 8
O.4    Drivers and results of high urbanization in the Middle East and North Africa ........ 8
O.5    In the Middle East and North Africa, some cities are more spatially fragmented than others ....................................... 10
O.6    Urban fragmentation as a legacy of conflict: Today's polycentric Beirut ............. 12
O.7    Low spatial mobility—and high public employment—among university graduates suggest that the Middle East and North Africa's higher education systems do not impart tradable skills ................................... 15
O.8    Large cities in the Middle East and North Africa show few spillover benefits from regional trade ..................................... 18
O.9    Middle East and North Africa countries stand out in directing a large share of investment expenditures toward place-based interventions ................ 21
O.10   Place-based investments amount to risky development bets—and the stakes are high ... 22
O.11   How to make successful spatial bets? Build on natural advantage ................. 22
O.12   Remembering the forgotten: Institution-based policies for the urban poor .......... 26
1.1    The impact of conflicts on urbanization in the Middle East and North Africa ....... 35
1.2    The impact of Lebanon's civil war on Beirut's urban form ...................... 46
1.3    Refugee self-sorting and fragmentation in migration to urban areas ............... 51
2.1    The ongoing effects of conflict on people of the Middle East and North Africa ...... 68
2.2    Methodology for calculating the cost of barriers to migration ................... 71
3.1    Economic growth can be contagious—but in the Middle East and North Africa, it is not ....................................... 101
4.1    The process for building a housing unit in Jordan ........................... 129
4.2    The IMF Government Finance Statistics database ........................... 133
4.3    Government expenditure data for a subset of Middle East and North Africa countries ................................... 136
5.1    Comparing Arab Barometer and World Values Survey responses on government's role ........................... 161
5.2    Handling decentralization in fragile environments ........................... 167
5.3    Spatial bias in Egypt's subnational fiscal architecture ........................ 168

5.4 Recent advances in implementing decentralization agendas across the Middle East and North Africa, by region . . . . . . . . . . . . . . . . . . . . . . . . . . . . . 173

6.1 Spatially sensitive "last mile" education provision . . . . . . . . . . . . . . . . . . . . . . . . . 182

6.2 Do cheap land and labor create opportunities for lagging regions? . . . . . . . . . . . . . . 183

6.3 Big bottleneck or big opportunity: Targeted place-based policies in Afghanistan and Morocco. . . . . . . . . . . . . . . . . . . . . . . . . . . . . . . . . . . . . . . . . 185

6.4 Industrial zones in Egypt: Suffering a lack of density and complements . . . . . . . . . . 186

6.5 How the dynamics of large investors can justify government intervention . . . . . . . . 187

6.6 Instruments to improve scale and coordination among local governments. . . . . . . . . 189

6.7 Government-regulated private sector service delivery in the Republic of Yemen and Kenya . . . . . . . . . . . . . . . . . . . . . . . . . . . . . . . . . . . . . . . . . . . . . . 192

6.8 How special economic zones supported China's incremental integration into global markets . . . . . . . . . . . . . . . . . . . . . . . . . . . . . . . . . . . . . . . . . . . . . 197

6.9 Logistics, more than infrastructure, impedes trade in the Middle East and North Africa. . . . . . . . . . . . . . . . . . . . . . . . . . . . . . . . . . . . . . . . . . . . . . . . 200

6.10 Scaffolding for cross-border trade and migration in the Great Lakes Region. . . . . . . 202

## Figures

BO.4.1 The Middle East and North Africa is a highly urbanized region . . . . . . . . . . . . . . . . . . . 9

BO.5.1 Fragmentation varies significantly across urban areas of several capital cities in the Middle East and North Africa. . . . . . . . . . . . . . . . . . . . . . . . . . . . . . . . . . . 10

O.1 Aggregated 1990–2004 urban expansion trends of capital cities in the Mashreq, Maghreb, and GCC subregions show divergent patterns . . . . . . . . . . . . . . . 11

BO.6.1 After decades of conflict, Beirut became a polycentric city . . . . . . . . . . . . . . . . . . . . . 12

O.2 Inequality within most Middle East and North Africa countries exceeds that of global peers . . . . . . . . . . . . . . . . . . . . . . . . . . . . . . . . . . . . . . . . . . . . . . . . . 13

O.3 In the Middle East and North Africa, companies located on the periphery face harsher constraints on business development than those in the capital city . . . . . . . . . 13

O.4 Within-country migration is lower in Middle East and North Africa countries than in the rest of the world. . . . . . . . . . . . . . . . . . . . . . . . . . . . . . . . . . . . . . . . . 14

O.5 Globally, the probability of migration tends to rise with education—but not in the Middle East and North Africa . . . . . . . . . . . . . . . . . . . . . . . . . . . . . . . . . . . . 14

BO.7.1 Human capital in the form of tradable skills increases spatial mobility . . . . . . . . . . . . 15

BO.7.2 In the Middle East and North Africa, tertiary education diplomas are highly valued in the public sector . . . . . . . . . . . . . . . . . . . . . . . . . . . . . . . . . . . . . . . . . 15

O.6 Urban populations in the Mashreq and GCC subregions are highly concentrated in the largest city and even more so in large cities . . . . . . . . . . . . . . . . 16

O.7 Few Middle East and North Africa countries trade electricity . . . . . . . . . . . . . . . . . . . 17

BO.8.1 Spatial economic spillovers to large city economies based on deep trade agreements with neighbors, by region . . . . . . . . . . . . . . . . . . . . . . . . . . . . . . . . . . . 18

BO.8.2 Bangkok's per capita GDP would have shrunk had it experienced the regional economic spillovers of the Middle East and North Africa . . . . . . . . . . . . . . . 18

O.8 Place-based interventions distort urban markets—which then fail. . . . . . . . . . . . . . . . 20

BO.9.1 Government expenditure distribution in selected Middle East and North Africa countries, by spatial category, differs greatly from international comparators . . . . . . . 21

O.9 Respondents in surveyed Middle East and North Africa economies identified jobs enablement—not public service provision or citizen representation—as the most essential function of a democratic state . . . . . . . . . . . . . . . . . . . . . . . . . . . . . . 24

1.1 Urbanization in the Middle East and North Africa is catching up with Europe and Latin America, 1960–2015 . . . . . . . . . . . . . . . . . . . . . . . . . . . . . . . . . . . . . . . . . 34

1.2     Urban population growth rates in the Middle East and North Africa vary
        by subregion, 1990–2016 . . . . . . . . . . . . . . . . . . . . . . . . . . . . . . . . . . . . . . . . . . 36

1.3     The Middle East and North Africa displays the world's highest urban
        concentration as measured by the agglomeration index . . . . . . . . . . . . . . . . . . . . . . 37

1.4     Economic growth per capita has not kept pace with urbanization in the
        Middle East and North Africa, 1990–2016 . . . . . . . . . . . . . . . . . . . . . . . . . . . . . 37

1.5     Cities in the Middle East and North Africa display a lower share of urban
        tradable employment than in other regions of the world. . . . . . . . . . . . . . . . . . . . . 38

1.6     Fragmentation varies significantly across urban areas in several capital cities in
        the Middle East and North Africa . . . . . . . . . . . . . . . . . . . . . . . . . . . . . . . . . . . . 40

1.7     The Middle East and North Africa as a whole displays average interaction
        potential compared with other regions but varies widely by subregion . . . . . . . . . . . 41

1.8     Gulf Cooperation Council countries seem to compensate for their urban
        fragmentation with lower commuting costs . . . . . . . . . . . . . . . . . . . . . . . . . . . . . . 42

B1.2.1  After decades of conflict, Beirut became a polycentric city. . . . . . . . . . . . . . . . . . . . 46

1.9     In the Middle East and North Africa, historic centers and informal
        neighborhoods display higher road and intersection density than modernist
        neighborhoods . . . . . . . . . . . . . . . . . . . . . . . . . . . . . . . . . . . . . . . . . . . . . . . . . . . 47

1.10    Aggregated urban expansion trends in capital cities in the Mashreq,
        Maghreb, and GCC subregions show divergent patterns, 1990–2014 . . . . . . . . . . . . 47

1.11    The urban expansion of Middle East and North Africa capital cities varies
        within subregions, 1990–2014 . . . . . . . . . . . . . . . . . . . . . . . . . . . . . . . . . . . . . . . . 48

2.1     Inequalities within most Middle East and North Africa countries exceed
        those of global peers . . . . . . . . . . . . . . . . . . . . . . . . . . . . . . . . . . . . . . . . . . . . . . . 60

2.2     Access to electricity has converged except in low-income economies of the
        Middle East and North Africa, where the poorest regions remain underserved . . . . . . 62

2.3     Primary school completion remains lower in the poorest regions of the
        Middle East and North Africa, except in the Islamic Republic of Iran. . . . . . . . . . . . . 63

2.4     Projected infrastructure needs and financing in the Middle East and North Africa. . . . 64

2.5     Access to a safe water source lags behind in the poorest regions of the
        Middle East and North Africa. . . . . . . . . . . . . . . . . . . . . . . . . . . . . . . . . . . . . . . . . 65

2.6     Far higher shares of population and economic activity are exposed to high or very
        high water stress in the Middle East and North Africa than in world averages . . . . . . . 65

2.7     Economic losses from inadequate water supply and sanitation in the
        Middle East and North Africa vary by economy . . . . . . . . . . . . . . . . . . . . . . . . . . . 66

2.8     Violent events and water risk are associated with higher spatial inequalities
        in the Middle East and North Africa. . . . . . . . . . . . . . . . . . . . . . . . . . . . . . . . . . . . 67

2.9     Within-country migration is lower in the Middle East and North Africa than
        in the rest of the world. . . . . . . . . . . . . . . . . . . . . . . . . . . . . . . . . . . . . . . . . . . . . . 70

2.10    Net migration flows in Tunisia reflect the movement of people from high-
        poverty to low-poverty regions . . . . . . . . . . . . . . . . . . . . . . . . . . . . . . . . . . . . . . . . 70

B2.2.1  Consumption gap between leading and other regions. . . . . . . . . . . . . . . . . . . . . . . . 72

B2.2.2  Share of the consumption gap explained by endowments . . . . . . . . . . . . . . . . . . . . . 72

B2.2.3  Share of the consumption gap explained by returns to endowments. . . . . . . . . . . . . . 72

2.11    Migration to leading regions could increase consumption potential
        significantly in the Middle East and North Africa . . . . . . . . . . . . . . . . . . . . . . . . . . 73

2.12    Among the bottom 40 percent who migrate to leading regions, the
        migration benefits are restricted to the top . . . . . . . . . . . . . . . . . . . . . . . . . . . . . . . 74

2.13    Consumption gaps between the metropolitan region and others vary across
        countries and are largely explained by differences in returns to endowments . . . . . . . 75

2.14 Morocco shows signs of regional convergence in living standards . . . . . . . . . . . . . . . . . 78

2.15 Poverty rates at origin and destination influence migration in the Middle East and North Africa. . . . . . . . . . . . . . . . . . . . . . . . . . . . . . . . . . . . . . . . 79

2.16 Distribution of occupations among internal migrants and stayers in the Syrian Arab Republic, 2002. . . . . . . . . . . . . . . . . . . . . . . . . . . . . . . . . . . . . . . . . 79

2.17 Internal migration rates are higher among women than men in several Middle East and North Africa countries. . . . . . . . . . . . . . . . . . . . . . . . . . . . . . . . . . 80

2.18 Unemployment rates are higher in the Middle East and North Africa than in upper-middle-income countries of other regions, particularly for educated women. . . . . . . . . . . . . . . . . . . . . . . . . . . . . . . . . . . 80

2.19 In the Middle East and North Africa, female migrants are more likely than male migrants to be employed . . . . . . . . . . . . . . . . . . . . . . . . . . . . . . . . . . . . . 81

2.20 Education has virtually no effect on migration in the Middle East and North Africa, in contrast with the rest of the world . . . . . . . . . . . . . . . . . . . . . . . . . . 81

2.21 Higher education in Middle East and North Africa households is not reflected in daily expenditure as much as in other regions. . . . . . . . . . . . . . . . . . . . . . . . . . 82

2.22 In the Middle East and North Africa, tertiary education diplomas are highly valued in the public sector . . . . . . . . . . . . . . . . . . . . . . . . . . . . . . . . . . . . . . . 82

3.1 Urban primacy rates are high in the Middle East and North Africa, driven mainly by population distributions in the GCC and Mashreq subregions . . . . . . . . . . 92

3.2 Urban population distribution is skewed toward large cities in the GCC and the Mashreq, but concentrations are much lower in the Maghreb . . . . . . . . . . . . . . . . . . 93

3.3 Distribution of the urban population skews toward the largest cities in the Middle East and North Africa . . . . . . . . . . . . . . . . . . . . . . . . . . . . . . . . . . . . . . 94

3.4 High urban concentration in the Middle East and North Africa cannot be explained solely by fuel-export-driven consumption cities . . . . . . . . . . . . . . . . . . . . 96

3.5 In the Middle East and North Africa, firms in the capital city have 6 percent higher productivity than firms on the periphery—the highest location-related effect of any region in the world . . . . . . . . . . . . . . . . . . . . . . . . . . . . . . . . . . . . . 97

3.6 In the Middle East and North Africa, companies on the periphery are likelier than those in the capital city to face major constraints . . . . . . . . . . . . . . . . . . . . . . 97

3.7 Selected countries, including Tunisia, show large gaps in access to public services between the primary city and the other urban areas. . . . . . . . . . . . . . . 98

3.8 Fiscal transfers to local governments in the Middle East and North Africa are among the lowest in the world, only slightly above Sub-Saharan Africa . . . . . . . . . . . 98

3.9 Fiscal decentralization in the Middle East and North Africa reflects larger transfers of fiscal autonomy in the Maghreb than in the GCC and Mashreq subregions . . . . . . . 99

B3.1.1 Sweden would be far poorer under Tunisia's low regional economic spillovers . . . . . . 101

B3.1.2 Spatial spillovers based on deep trade agreements with neighbors, by region. . . . . . . . 102

B3.1.3 Bangkok's per capita GDP would have shrunk had it experienced the Middle East and North Africa's regional economic spillovers. . . . . . . . . . . . . . . . . . . . . . . 102

3.10 Many Middle East and North Africa economies have higher average tariffs than their economic peers in other regions . . . . . . . . . . . . . . . . . . . . . . . . . . . . . 102

3.11 Merchandise trade as a share of GDP in many Middle East and North Africa countries is quite low. . . . . . . . . . . . . . . . . . . . . . . . . . . . . . . . . . . . . . . . . . . 104

3.12 Only a small share of global intraregional merchandise trade occurs within the Middle East and North Africa . . . . . . . . . . . . . . . . . . . . . . . . . . . . . . . . . . 105

3.13 As a share of GDP, the Middle East and North Africa's intraregional service trade is small relative to the size of its economies . . . . . . . . . . . . . . . . . . . . . . . . . . . . 105

3.14    Overall, the Middle East and North Africa has a high degree of capital openness. . . . 107

3.15    FDI inflows to the Middle East and North Africa remain low despite
the region's relatively high capital openness . . . . . . . . . . . . . . . . . . . . . . . . . . . . . . 107

3.16    Remittances are significant contributors to several Middle East and
North Africa economies. . . . . . . . . . . . . . . . . . . . . . . . . . . . . . . . . . . . . . . . . . . . . 109

3.17    Use of digital technologies correlates closely with economic wealth . . . . . . . . . . . . . 112

3.18    Many Middle East and North Africa countries make it hard to visit, and
their citizens also face difficulties traveling elsewhere . . . . . . . . . . . . . . . . . . . . . . . 113

4.1     Middle East and North Africa countries are less competitive than most
countries of comparable income . . . . . . . . . . . . . . . . . . . . . . . . . . . . . . . . . . . . . . 121

4.2     Business regulations in the Middle East and North Africa are rated distant from
good practice with respect to efficiency and quality . . . . . . . . . . . . . . . . . . . . . . . . 122

4.3     The Middle East and North Africa has consistently ranked lower than other
middle- to high-income regions on the Worldwide Governance Indicators, 2007–17 . . . 124

4.4     Private investment has responded less to reforms in the Middle East and
North Africa than in other regions . . . . . . . . . . . . . . . . . . . . . . . . . . . . . . . . . . . . . 125

4.5     Government interventions can create varying degrees of spatial distortion . . . . . . . . . 132

B4.2.1  The public sector and its main components. . . . . . . . . . . . . . . . . . . . . . . . . . . . . . . . 133

4.6     Distribution and changes in government expenditures of comparator
countries reflect priorities through a spatial lens . . . . . . . . . . . . . . . . . . . . . . . . . . . 135

4.7     Government expenditure distribution in selected Middle East and
North Africa countries show priorities through a spatial lens for one year . . . . . . . . 138

4.8     Government expenditure distribution in selected Middle East and North Africa
countries, by spatial category, differs greatly from international comparators . . . . . . 138

4.9     Subsidies made up 23–31 percent of Tunisia's yearly budget, with
the greater share linked to current expenditure, 2013–17. . . . . . . . . . . . . . . . . . . . . 141

4.10    Subsidies on current expenditures, representing 19 percent of Tunisia's total
budget, are mainly for place-based interventions . . . . . . . . . . . . . . . . . . . . . . . . . . 142

4.11    Subsidies on capital expenditures, representing 7 percent of Tunisia's total budget,
are less focused than current expenditures on place-based interventions . . . . . . . . . . 142

4.12    Jordanian current public expenditures, by spatial category, 2018. . . . . . . . . . . . . . . . 145

5.1     Respondents in surveyed Middle East and North Africa economies identified
functions to improve socioeconomic well-being as the most essential
characteristics of democracy . . . . . . . . . . . . . . . . . . . . . . . . . . . . . . . . . . . . . . . . . 158

5.2     Rural respondents were more likely to cite government's role in job creation
and public service provision as essential characteristics of democracy . . . . . . . . . . . . 159

5.3     Across Middle East and North Africa economies, subnational surveys also show
a preference for governments' role in job creation over public service delivery . . . . . . 160

B5.1.1  WVS respondents from most Middle East and North Africa economies
identified economic growth as the country's "most important" goal . . . . . . . . . . . . . . 161

5.4     The subregions of the Middle East and North Africa represent a spectrum in
the degree of decentralization . . . . . . . . . . . . . . . . . . . . . . . . . . . . . . . . . . . . . . . . 164

5.5     The fiscal decentralization of subnational governments in the Middle
East and North Africa remains low compared with OECD countries . . . . . . . . . . . . . 165

6.1     Framework for effective spatial policy in the Middle East and North Africa,
from foundations to final steps . . . . . . . . . . . . . . . . . . . . . . . . . . . . . . . . . . . . . . . 184

B6.9.1  Among the Middle East and North Africa countries, about half improved
their logistics performance between 2010 and 2018 . . . . . . . . . . . . . . . . . . . . . . . . . 201

## Maps

B1.1.1   Massive migration patterns to urban areas in the Mashreq region are visible through nighttime light changes . . . . . . . . . . . . . . . . . . . . . . . . . . . . . . . . . . . . . 35

1.1   Visual representations of urban expansion show the extent of development, by type, in selected Middle East and North Africa capitals, 1990–2014 . . . . . . . . . . . . . . 49

B1.3.1   Refugees are concentrating in three main neighborhoods in Tripoli, Lebanon, 2015 . . . 51

1D.1   Comparison of Global Human Settlement Layers and Global Urban Footprint datasets for Cairo and Casablanca, 2016 . . . . . . . . . . . . . . . . . . . . . . . 55

2.1   Middle East and North Africa populations are concentrated in the areas closest to international markets . . . . . . . . . . . . . . . . . . . . . . . . . . . . . . . . . . . . . . . . . . . . . 61

2.2   Consumption gaps in the Islamic Republic of Iran, by region, 2014 . . . . . . . . . . . . . . . . . 76

2.3   Consumption gaps in Iraq, by governorate, 2012 . . . . . . . . . . . . . . . . . . . . . . . . . . . . . . . 77

B6.8.1   China gradually increased special economic zones from 1980 through the 1990s . . . . 197

## Photos

O.1   In Greater Cairo, recent informal settlements share a basic spatial structure with medieval neighborhoods . . . . . . . . . . . . . . . . . . . . . . . . . . . . . . . . . . . . . . . . . . . . 12

1.1   Developments in or near the capitals of United Arab Emirates and Egypt represent modernist urban planning theory. . . . . . . . . . . . . . . . . . . . . . . . . . . . . . . . . . 44

1.2   Aerial views show that, in density and spatial patterns, recent informal settlements highly resemble historic districts across several cities of the Middle East and North Africa . . . . . . . . . . . . . . . . . . . . . . . . . . . . . . . . . . . . . . . . . . . . 45

## Tables

1C.1   Selected neighborhoods for analysis of road and intersection densities in the Middle East and North Africa . . . . . . . . . . . . . . . . . . . . . . . . . . . . . . . . . . . . . . . . . . . . 54

2.1   Economic activity benefits more from natural geography in the Middle East and North Africa than in Sub-Saharan Africa and Latin America but less so than in other regions . . . . . . . . . . . . . . . . . . . . . . . . . . . . . . . . . . . . . . . . . . . . . . 61

B2.1.1   Violence in four current major crises has affected between one-third and two-thirds of the population . . . . . . . . . . . . . . . . . . . . . . . . . . . . . . . . . . . . . . . . . . . 68

2A.1   Sources and years of global census data, by country . . . . . . . . . . . . . . . . . . . . . . . . . . 84

2A.2   Countries and years of survey data . . . . . . . . . . . . . . . . . . . . . . . . . . . . . . . . . . . . . . . . 85

3.1   City size relative to a country's total urban population is associated with positive or negative effects on economic growth. . . . . . . . . . . . . . . . . . . . . . . . . . . . . . . . . . . . 100

3.2   Trade agreements are fewer and shallower in the Middle East and North Africa than in other regions . . . . . . . . . . . . . . . . . . . . . . . . . . . . . . . . . . . . . . . 103

3.3   The Middle East and North Africa has few agreements with important future markets . . . . . . . . . . . . . . . . . . . . . . . . . . . . . . . . . . . . . . . . . . . . . . 103

3.4   Trade in the Middle East and North Africa is still dependent on natural resources . . . . . . . . . . . . . . . . . . . . . . . . . . . . . . . . . . . . . . . . . . . . . . . . . . . . 104

3.5   The Middle East and North Africa has higher service trade restrictions than any other region. . . . . . . . . . . . . . . . . . . . . . . . . . . . . . . . . . . . . . . . . . . . . . . 106

3.6   Migration in the Middle East and North Africa has been driven by both job seekers and refugees . . . . . . . . . . . . . . . . . . . . . . . . . . . . . . . . . . . . . . . . . 108

3.7   Large migration flows have led to equally large remittance flows in the Middle East and North Africa . . . . . . . . . . . . . . . . . . . . . . . . . . . . . . . . . . 110

3.8   Largest intraregional estimated remittance flows in the Middle East and North Africa, 2016 . . . . . . . . . . . . . . . . . . . . . . . . . . . . . . . . . . . . 110

B4.2.1    Classification of expenditure, by government function,
          within divisions and groups .......................................... 134
4.1       On average, comparator countries invest more in people- and
          institution-based interventions, and less in place-based interventions, than
          do Middle East and North Africa countries ............................... 139
4.2       New cities in Saudi Arabia's development plan and spatial strategy .............. 140
4.3       Spatial classification of Tunisia's Finance Law 2017 ........................ 141
4.4       Concentration shares of indirect subsidies in Tunisia, by income decile, 2010 ...... 143
4.5       Off-budget economic authorities in Egypt are highly spatially distortive ........... 143
4.6       On-budget and off-budget expenditure by economic authorities in Egypt,
          by spatial category ..................................................... 144
4.7       Jordanian public expenditures, by spatial category, 2018 ..................... 144
4A.1      Disaggregation of government expenditure for comparator countries,
          by spatial category ..................................................... 148
4A.2      Distribution and changes in government expenditures by comparator
          countries through a spatial lens ......................................... 149
4A.3      Expenditure distribution in the Middle East and North Africa is highly
          weighted toward spatially distortive policies ............................. 149
4B.1      Difficulties in classification of spatial categories of government expenditures ....... 150
4C.1      Classification of subcategories of the IMF Government Finance
          Statistics (GFS) database into eight spatial categories ...................... 150
4D.1      Estimated shares of public expenditures, by category, in Lebanon, the
          Republic of Yemen, and Iraq ............................................ 152
B6.9.1    Logistics Performance Index (LPI) rankings of Middle East and
          North Africa countries, 2018 ........................................... 200

# Acknowledgments

This report was prepared by a team led by Somik V. Lall, co-led by Ayah Mahgoub, and comprising Paolo Avner, Julie Biau, Alex Chunet, Olivia D'Aoust, Uwe Deichmann, Katrin Heger, Mathilde Lebrand, Sally Murray, Emiko Naomasa, Diana Tello, and Yuan Xiao. Victoria Bruce-Goga supported production throughout. It was initiated and prepared under the guidance of Ayat Soliman and delivered under the guidance of Sameh Wahba and Jaafar Friaa. It benefited from the contributions of Chorching Goh, Ellen Hamilton, Leila Kabalan, Elisa Cascardi, and Paola Cordovez.

The report was commissioned by the Middle East and North Africa (MENA) Office of the Chief Economist, and the team extends many thanks to Shanta Devarajan, Rabah Arezki, and Daniel Lederman for their commitment to shedding light on the nature and drivers of—and ways to address—the core drivers of spatial inequality in the Middle East and North Africa.

The team benefited tremendously from the guidance and pushback of the report advisory group. The team thanks its members: Lamia Boutaleb, Paul Collier, Ishac Diwan, Hedi Larbi, Lant Pritchett, and Tony Venables. The team is also grateful for the thoughtful advice of our peer reviewers: Nabila Assaf, Safaa El-Kogali, and Harris Selod. The report also reflects feedback from participants in various workshops in which we presented intermediate drafts, including the World Bank's MENA Chief Economist seminar, the Sustainable Development Chief Economist seminar, and the Global Solutions Group on Territorial Development seminar.

The report benefited from discussions and thoughtful insights from many colleagues, including Tahir Akbar, Axel Baeumler, Kevin Carey, Tabea Dietrich, Ibrahim Elghandour, Marianne Fay, Nancy Lozano Gracia, Maha Hussein, Hind Kadiri, Julian Lampietti, Guido Licciardi, Augustin Maria, Balakrishna Menon, Mohamed Nada, Noriko Oe, Jean Pesme, Björn Philipp, Salma Rasem, Francesca Recanatini, Jade Salhab, Anastasia Touati, Mohamed Yehia Abd El Karim, and Hoda Youssef.

The report was edited by Communications Development Incorporated. The team thanks Bruce Ross-Larson, Nick Moschovakis, Matt Collins, Sarah Bridges, Ahmad Fakih, and their teams. It was designed by Zephyr Incorporated, and the logo was designed by Greenlines. Jewel McFadden, of the World Bank's Development Economics Strategy and Operations unit, and Mary Fisk and

Deb Appel-Barker, of the World Bank's formal publishing unit, were responsible for managing the book throughout the publications process. Mary Anderson was the copyeditor. The team thanks them all. The team also thanks Kristyn Schrader-King, Andu Shuai Liu, William Stebbins, and Isabelle Poupaert for their communications support. The report was cofinanced by the U.K. Department for International Development through the Multi-Donor Trust Fund for Sustainable Urban Development.

# Memorandum to a Concerned Finance Minister

**Subject: Five critical steps toward integrating lagging and leading areas in your country**

This memo introduces a report that you may find useful and interesting. Focusing on actions that can put countries in the Middle East and North Africa on a path to territorial convergence, it concludes that governments can take the lead by tackling the economic and institutional causes of spatial exclusion.

Rising spatial disparities are threatening economic growth and social inclusion in your country and across the region. This report shows that opportunities for your citizens are shaped by accidents of where they were born—much more so than in any other part of the world. Decision makers in your country and in other parts of the region have taken steps to respond to the needs of people left behind in your cities and across your regions. Even so, spatial disparities either continue to grow or are closing more slowly than would be expected given the volume of investment you have directed to those locations.

Why is territorial convergence so difficult? First, most lagging areas in your country are limited by an inability to leverage the full returns to their endowments. The business environment in many cities and towns restricts new firms from entering and growing, and the lack of complementary infrastructure investments hobbles local economies. Second, most residents in your lagging areas are stuck in place, unable to take full advantage of jobs that vibrant urban economies can offer. So, what do your cities need for more vibrancy and private sector jobs? They need larger markets—often beyond national borders—to increase the demand for goods and services, to increase the demand for human capital, and to create fulfilling jobs for young people.

How then, can you start building a *convergence machine* for your lagging areas?

You can reduce territorial disparities more immediately and effectively by taking five steps:

1. **Strengthen coordination and complementarities across sectoral interventions.** Efforts to enhance job prospects in places left behind should operate across and address multiple development axes simultaneously. Development strategies are more likely to succeed if they are multidimensional—including access to energy, transport, land, and markets in the same place, whether sequentially

or concurrently. Because starting anew is extremely difficult, there is little value in single-sector interventions. A good place to start is by anchoring investments around cities, which have many of the missing complements. Complementary reforms that help get the prices right—for energy and for land—can go a long way toward creating the conditions for job creation in lagging areas. The good news is that you don't have to pay more to see better results, because spatial coordination will generate cost savings in the medium to longer term.

2. **Redistribute roles and responsibilities across tiers of government.** Citizens in different parts of the country have varying needs, and local conditions require flexible service delivery models. Devolving responsibilities for local revenue generation and service provision to local governments can make them better equipped and more accountable. Effective decentralization would also empower them to cover the recurring costs of their investments.

3. **Enable greater mobility of your people between lagging and leading areas.** Major gains in living standards can be reaped from greater domestic labor mobility. Research for this report shows that living standards of people moving internally to major cities can increase by 37 percent on average across the Middle East and North Africa region. Women are more likely to move and find jobs in urban areas, but they need support to do so. One of the key constraints on greater mobility is the credentialist education system prevalent across the region. It needs to be more oriented toward marketable skills.

4. **Build dense and connected cities.** Well-functioning cities offer a wide variety of jobs for women and men. Making land markets in cities more efficient is critical for agglomeration and specialization—two dynamics that enhance job creation and economic prosperity. Whether in larger or in smaller (secondary) cities, agglomeration and specialization require the benefits from high economic density,

which concentrates economic activity geographically. For this, the fabric of cities needs to be spatially connected, dense with people, and transit oriented—not sprawling, which perpetuates the dispersion of people and jobs. Planners and regulators can attract firms to invest in cities by reducing frictions such as zoning regulations; impediments to property acquisition and new construction (costs, height limits, and density limits); challenges to local business registration and licensing; limits on news and information; and obstacles to developing local business networks.

5. **Enhance market access for lagging areas, nationally and regionally.** Historically, the region's cities were part of economically central global trade networks. Many of these cities persisted into modern times as large, often vastly populated urban areas. Yet with today's thick national borders, their economic reach has been limited. Countries across the region need to enhance links across national borders—reducing tariffs and nontariff barriers (such as logistics and trade facilitation) and easing movements of goods and people. They may also need to enact policies to strengthen domestic markets. Such efforts will expand the size of urban economies, providing much-needed tax resources to redistribute in areas left behind.

The extent and sequence for implementing each transitional step will depend on your assessment of your country's readiness—political, technical, and administrative—to implement these recommendations.

These steps will allow you to promote the building blocks of a convergence machine for spatial inclusion by pursuing economic growth and inclusion rather than spatially targeted mandates. The only spatial requirements are that people across your country have access to high-quality basic services—and that economic development interventions harness the spatial and economic dynamics of agglomeration, migration, and specialization.

All levels of your government have roles: the national, the provincial, and the local. By requiring that all interventions be responsive to the basic needs of all, you can put far more of your nation's forgotten people into jobs than ever before. How? Not by trying solely to bring jobs where people are but by also focusing on where the jobs are most likely to be and enabling people to move there, while complementing every investment with institutional measures that make the desired jobs more likely to appear.

These steps may appear daunting, even painful. But evidence from two centuries of experience from around the world has shown that the potential gains are worth the pain.

The World Bank Group can help as you decide on a way forward.

# About the Authors

**Somik V. Lall** is the World Bank's global lead on territorial development solutions, a lead economist for urban development, and the team leader of this report. He is a recognized expert on development policy related to urban and territorial competitiveness, agglomeration and clusters, and infrastructure, with over 20 years' global experience, most notably in Africa, Asia, and Latin America. He has been a core team member of the *World Development Report 2009: Reshaping Economic Geography* and developed the policy framework for development of lagging areas within countries. He is the lead author of the World Bank's flagship report on urbanization, *Planning, Connecting & Financing Cities—Now*, as well as the recent *Africa's Cities: Opening Doors to the World*. Somik heads a World Bank global research program on urbanization and spatial development and previously founded the Urbanization Reviews program. His research and policy advisory interests focus on place-shaping policies around cities, clusters, and corridors and the functioning of factor and product markets, with more than 40 publications featured in peer-reviewed journals including the *Journal of Development Economics* and *Journal of Urban Economics*; edited volumes, including the *Handbook of Regional and Urban Economics;* and working papers. He holds a bachelor's degree in engineering, a master's degree in city planning, and a doctorate in economics and public policy.

**Paolo Avner** has been working as an urban economist at the World Bank for the past five years. His current work focuses on the links between urban form, land uses, transport systems, labor markets, and vulnerability to natural hazards in the cities of low- and middle-income countries. He has worked on a number of analytical products, including the World Bank's Urbanization Reviews (Ethiopia, Guinea, Haiti, Kenya, and Mali) and flagship reports, and is the author of several policy-oriented research papers. Prior to joining the World Bank, he worked as a researcher at Laboratoire d'Economie de la Production et de l'Intégration Internationale in Grenoble before joining the International Research Center on Environment and Development in Paris, where he collaborated on the development of an applied land use and transport interaction model (NEDUM-2D). His work specifically focused on the ability of public policies and investments to curb greenhouse gas emissions from urban transport while limiting the costs of these policies for urban residents.

**Julie Biau** works with the World Bank office in Brussels, overseeing the lending and technical assistance portfolio in European Union countries and serving as a focal point with the European Commission on structural reform projects. She previously worked in the World Bank's Middle East and North Africa region, based in Washington, DC, where she provided analytical work and operational support in the urban sector. Between 2011 and 2013, she was a junior professional associate, supporting project design and supervision in urban and water teams, particularly in Central America and Haiti. Her experience outside of the World Bank includes work at the Inter-American Development Bank's (IDB) Office of Evaluation and Oversight, where she led the evaluation of IDB country portfolios in various sectors. She also spent a year as a research analyst at the Brookings Institution, working on the sustainable development agenda and statistical analysis of topics such as global poverty trends and aid effectiveness in fragile states. She holds a master's degree in public policy from Georgetown University.

**Alex Chunet** is an urban economist, focusing on topics linked to urban fragmentation, transportation, and access to services in Africa, Latin America, and the Middle East and North Africa. In the past year, he has worked as a consultant for the World Bank and participated in several Urbanization Reviews and one flagship report. Alex completed his undergraduate and graduate studies in public policy at Sciences Po in Paris before specializing in local economic development, earning a master's degree at the London School of Economics, which gave him the opportunity to do World Bank–sponsored field research on cities' competitiveness in Cameroon. Previously, he worked in several other international organizations, including the Organisation for Economic Co-operation and Development and the United Nations, as well as in a consulting firm specializing in sustainable development in Bogotá, Colombia.

**Olivia D'Aoust** is an urban economist with the World Bank's Urban and Disaster Risk Management team for Africa, based in Washington, DC. Her work cuts across issues of the economics of urbanization, territorial development, and conflict and fragility. She has worked on several analytical products focusing on the drivers of and impediments to cities' productivity and livability, including the flagship report, *Africa's Cities: Opening Doors to the World*. As a core member of the Global Solutions Group on Territorial Development, her work expanded to inform spatial development strategies, identify priorities for action in lagging regions, and explore avenues for operations to leverage spatial synergies and address missing complements. Olivia holds a doctorate in economics from the European Center for Advanced Research in Economics and Statistics at the Solvay Brussels School of Economics and Management and a master's degree in demography from the Center for Demographic Research at UCLouvain.

**Uwe Deichmann** is an independent consultant based in Berlin. Previously, he spent almost 20 years in the Development Research Group at the World Bank, where his main research interests included the role of infrastructure in promoting regional growth, urbanization, and the impacts of natural hazards and global change on economic development. He was a principal author of *World Development Report 2009: Reshaping Economic Geography* and codirector of *World Development Report 2016: Digital Dividends*. Before joining the World Bank, he worked for the United Nations Environment Programme and the UN Statistics Division. He holds a doctorate in economic geography and regional science from the University of California, Santa Barbara.

**Mathilde Lebrand** is an economist in the World Bank's Transport Global Practice. Her current work focuses on the economic impacts of transport investments, such as corridors in China's Belt and Road Initiative or urban transport systems, the role of labor and firm mobility, and the spatial impacts of trade opening in low- and middle-income countries. She holds a doctorate in economics from the European University Institute in Italy. Her research focuses on economic geography, international trade, networks, and political economy. Mathilde previously taught at the University of Montreal and has worked at the World Trade Organization in Geneva. She is also a research fellow of the Ifo Institute for Economic Research, Munich.

**Ayah Mahgoub,** a senior urban development specialist at the World Bank, is the co-team leader of the *Convergence* report. She leads urban and territorial development lending and analytical projects in North Africa and leads the World Bank knowledge groups on competitive cities and results-based financing. Her focus areas currently are urban and territorial development, city competitiveness, intergovernmental fiscal systems, municipal finance, smart cities, and results-based financing. Ayah completed her undergraduate and graduate studies in economics and international development at Harvard University. Before joining the World Bank, she worked for the Center for Global Development, the United States Agency for International Development's Development Innovation Ventures program, the Crown Prince Court of Abu Dhabi, and Phipps Community Development Corporation. She has also worked on urban development in New York City, economic integration of minorities in France, and peace-building initiatives in Sudan.

**Sally Murray** is a consultant for the World Bank's Global Solutions Group on Territorial Development, where her work focuses on regional development and urbanization. Before joining the World Bank in April 2018, she was senior country economist for the International Growth Centre (IGC) in Rwanda (previously South Sudan), where she coauthored several IGC policy papers on urbanization, taxation, state effectiveness and fragility, and technology for

development. She completed her master's degree in development studies (research) at the London School of Economics and her bachelor's degree in philosophy, politics, and economics at the University of Oxford.

**Emiko Naomasa** is an economist in the Development Economics Vice Presidency of the World Bank. Her specialization includes agricultural economics, natural resource management, and rural sector development. Her current research focus is on the adaptation of climate-smart agricultural management. She also has extensive experience in macroeconomic monitoring and sovereign risk assessment. Before joining the World Bank, Emiko was an economist at the Japan Bank for International Cooperation, where she was responsible for analyzing fiscal policies and sovereign credit risks in European and North African countries. She holds a doctorate in economics from the University of Hawaii.

**Diana Tello** is an urban economist working as a consultant at the World Bank. Her work focuses on territorial development, local economic development, urban resilience, competitive cities, and the spatial dimension of government expenditures. Most recently, her work has focused on building the evidence base for identifying instruments of territorial development that have the potential to boost economic activity in a place and reduce gaps in the quality of life between places, spanning Africa, Latin America and the Caribbean, and the Middle East and North Africa. She also has experience in Malaysia, where she worked on an economic assessment at the subnational level to propose policies that could trigger development in Melaka state. Before joining the World Bank, Diana worked in the financial markets of New York City and Monterrey, Mexico, advising on fintech solutions and credit risk management. She completed her undergraduate studies in economics at Tecnológico de Monterrey, Mexico, and holds a master's degree in local economic development from the London School of Economics.

**Yuan Xiao** is an urban development specialist in the World Bank's Beijing office, where she plays a key role in the lending portfolio and advisory services as well as analytical work in the urban field in China. Before this assignment, she worked in the World Bank's Middle East and North Africa Region. Before joining the World Bank, Yuan was an assistant professor of urban planning at Columbia University. She holds a doctorate from the Massachusetts Institute of Technology, a master's degree from University of Toronto, and bachelor's degrees from Peking University.

# Abbreviations

| | |
|---|---|
| AGOA | African Growth and Opportunity Act |
| CDD | Civil Defense Department |
| CEPGL | Economic Community of the Great Lakes Countries (Communauté Économique des Pays des Grand Lacs) |
| COFOG | Classification of Functions of Government |
| COMESA | Common Market for Eastern and Southern Africa |
| CPER | State-Region Plan Contract (contrat de plan État-région) |
| DAI | Digital Adoption Index |
| EBA | enterprise bargaining agreement |
| EPCI | Établissement Public de Coopération Intercommunale (Public Establishment for Intercommunal Cooperation) |
| EU | European Union |
| FDI | foreign direct investment |
| GAM | Greater Amman Municipality |
| GCC | Gulf Cooperation Council |
| GCI | Global Competitiveness Index (WEF) |
| GDP | gross domestic product |
| GFS | Government Finance Statistics (IMF) |
| GHSL | Global Human Settlement Layers (dataset) |
| GUF | Global Urban Footprint (dataset) |
| HIP | Hawassa Industrial Park |
| ICT | information and communication technology |
| IDA | Industrial Development Authority (Egypt) |
| IDP | internally displaced person |

| | |
|---|---|
| IMF | International Monetary Fund |
| ISIL | Islamic State of Iraq and the Levant |
| LEI | Landscape Expansion Index |
| LGPA | Local Government Performance Assessment |
| LGU | local government unit |
| LPI | Logistics Performance Index (World Bank) |
| MNAPOV | Middle East and North Africa Poverty database |
| NASA | National Aeronautics and Space Administration |
| OECD | Organisation for Economic Co-operation and Development |
| OSM | OpenStreetMap |
| PAFTA | Pan-Arab Free Trade Area |
| PARAS | Project to Restructure Local Government and Services |
| PIRLS | Progress in International Reading Literacy |
| PISA | Programme for International Student Assessment |
| PVH | Phillips-van Heusen |
| SEDAC | Socioeconomic Data and Applications Center |
| SEZ | special economic zone |
| TEN-T | Trans-European Transport Network |
| TFP | total factor productivity |
| TIMSS | Trends in International Mathematics and Science Study |
| TMSA | Tanger Med Special Agency |
| TTN | Tunisia TradeNet |
| TVA | Tennessee Valley Authority |
| UDLGP | Urban Development and Local Government Program |
| UN-Habitat | United Nations Human Settlements Programme |
| VAT | value added tax |
| WEF | World Economic Forum |
| WGI | World Governance Indicators |
| WTO | World Trade Organization |
| WVS | World Values Survey |

# Overview

The Middle East and North Africa is suffering from spatially divergent development. The uprisings of the Arab Spring in part reflected grievances of citizens who were (or were perceived to have been) left behind, particularly by accidents of where they were born. Although the trajectory of every nation in the region varies, one stated objective is clear for them all: improve outcomes for people in areas that have been left behind.

Policy makers across the region have long been trying to integrate their people spatially and economically. Wishing to bring communities together and narrow economic gaps, governments have made large capital investments in transport corridors and "new cities." Wishing to provide jobs in places with little economic activity, governments have designated new industrial zones supported by spatially targeted business incentives and subsidized land and energy.

Yet the results of these place-based initiatives in these countries are mostly disappointing (box O.1). The disparities between capital cities and lagging areas, and between richer and poorer quarters of cities, remain stark. Across much of the region, a fortunate few are connected to opportunity, while many more

people are marginal to the formal economy—or live outside it, seemingly forgotten.

## Why do so many place-based interventions fail?

Why have place-based spatial initiatives largely failed in the region's countries? Why have they not yielded more sustainable jobs and growth? Although the challenges are many and vary across the region, recent work in economic geography shows that most of these place-based policies get one thing wrong: they attempt to treat inequity's spatial and physical symptoms, not its causes. Thus, to add jobs in a country's poorer areas, policy makers try to push new production facilities into these areas. And to meet the need for decent homes and amenities in poor urban neighborhoods, funds support mass housing projects. Neither effort has succeeded widely—because the causes of spatial exclusion are not themselves spatial and physical; they are economic and institutional.

First, a *lack of economic density* in rural areas, and even in many smaller municipalities, makes them inherently less competitive than large cities because they are less suitable

BOX O.1 **Place-based policies have not led to spatial convergence**

Insufficient attention to the economic causes of spatial exclusion has led governments in the Middle East and North Africa to pursue spatially targeted interventions—yet most countries have little to show for these place-based policies for several reasons:

- *New cities have not yielded the hoped-for returns.* Governments are building new cities as a respite from the chaos of today's large and bustling metropoles—but the main result is that residents are marooned far from jobs. In the Arab Republic of Egypt in 2012, 30 percent of the national built environment budget was allocated to new cities, which host just 2 percent of the nation's people. Today, the people who moved to those new cities must rely on their own cars or fleets of buses to shuttle daily to the older urban centers where they work (especially the Cairo agglomeration) (Sims 2015).
- *New industrial zones and newly designated growth centers lack promise.* Governments have undertaken large-scale investments and offered generous subsidies to create jobs in socially and economically excluded areas. But the proposed new industrial zones and growth centers often lack the agglomeration benefits that larger cites already have. Supplying infrastructure and amenities to

such remote locations can be far more expensive than supplying them in a city (where the cost can be spread across a larger number of customers). And firms that locate far from large urban areas cite constraints in their business environment—the main challenges being political instability, low access to finance, and low access to electricity.

- *New transport corridors have not facilitated regional trade.* Most middle-income Middle East and North Africa countries have invested heavily in national transport infrastructure, yet firms encounter high nonphysical barriers to trade within the region. Outside the Gulf Cooperation Council (GCC),[a] the region's countries score poorly on such trade facilitation measures as the quality of customs and logistics procedures. As a result, less than 7 percent of global intraregional merchandise trade occurs within the Middle East and North Africa, compared with 40 percent within East Asia and more than 50 percent within Europe.[b]

a. The Gulf Cooperation Council (GCC) includes Bahrain, Kuwait, Oman, Qatar, Saudi Arabia, and the United Arab Emirates.
b. Global intraregional trade data are derived from the World Trade Flows database, Bilateral Data files, of the Center for International Data, University of California, Davis, HYPERLINK https://cid.econ.ucdavis.edu/Html/WTF_bilateral.html.

for large-scale investment. Large urban areas have well-understood advantages in today's global economy. Dense agglomerations favor specialized, scaled-up production for international markets (box O.2). So, an industrial zone set up far from a country's main cities is, most likely, set up to fail.

Second, not only rural but also urban economies in the Middle East and North Africa are constrained by widespread *institutional inefficiencies.* Five main types will be considered here:

- *Barriers to market entry and lopsided business environments, which vary within countries.* Several of the region's countries significantly underperform relative to comparator countries on indexes

of competitiveness, business environment, and governance. Subnationally, firms report in surveys a range of impediments to doing business, and the challenges vary from city to city within countries. One major challenge is the limited coordination of complementary investments and policies needed to make cities and regions attractive for entrepreneurs to establish and grow businesses. Sectorally siloed interventions make cities and regions inadequate homes for businesses that need complementary factors such as good market access, well-serviced land, and a relevant talent pool.

- *Centralized control over local public services.* Outside the capital city in the region's countries, smaller cities and

---

BOX O.2 **Economic density and agglomeration effects: The urban advantage**

For firms participating in today's regional and global value chains, *economic density*—the geographic concentration of economic activity—gives large cities an edge over smaller cities and rural areas. Such density boosts efficiency by making workers and firms more productive. Economic density can make public service provision less costly. And as production becomes more complex and diversified, the physical proximity of firms becomes more critical. Thanks to these agglomeration effects, firms that specialize in producing tradables can operate more efficiently at scale and can thus compete more effectively. (Scale economies and specialization are two key drivers of firm and sectoral productivity. Scale allows a firm to reduce unit costs, increasing productivity. Specialization allows it to narrow its focus to a few products, making the most of its key advantages.)

The higher productivity of efficient urban agglomerations can promote a virtuous circle of economic growth. As a rule, if firms and workers are mobile, both will pursue productive opportunities across space, preferring to settle near existing agglomerations. Large cities become even larger and denser.

Agglomeration effects imply that an efficient economic landscape is not smooth—with equal economic density everywhere—but is instead lumpy, with large cities driving growth. However, *economic distance* (the difficulty of access from lagging to leading areas) may limit economic actors' mobility and location choices by making migration costlier or less beneficial. Friction can also result from less obvious economic factors, such as *divisions*—ethnic, political, religious, or linguistic barriers to interaction.

*Source:* World Bank 2009.

---

other localities lack the authority to raise their own revenues and to manage local service provision. These functions can, however, generally be conducted more efficiently by localities—and local government officials can be more easily held accountable.

- *Urban regulatory frictions.* Especially in urban areas, rigid and outdated regulations distort land markets and stymie development. For example, Tunisia prohibits residential buildings higher than three stories, and Jordanian regulations impose a minimum lot size of 100 square meters—restrictions that effectively limit the supply of affordable formal housing. In addition, land transfer fees and building permit fees tend to be high in the region's countries.
- *Credentialist education systems.* In the Middle East and North Africa, education is widely seen as providing a credential—and the credential is valued mainly as a ticket to public sector employment. As a result, even the most educated workers

often lack the tradable skills demanded by the private sector. So, the region's cities are less attractive than they could be to firms and investors, and citizens are constrained in their ability to leverage their skills for employment across places. The emphasis on credentials, rather than on portable skills, also reduces the chances for young women and men to move to cities where they can access better job opportunities.

- *Barriers to the spatial mobility of goods and people.* Input and output flows are impeded within the Middle East and North Africa by barriers, sometimes called "thick borders." Among the main barriers are limits on news and information and practical constraints on travel and trade (such as visa difficulties, weak infrastructure, and logistical hurdles). Thick borders discourage firms in the region's cities from creating jobs and expanding their economic reach—and also inhibit the growth of smaller specialized cities. In addition, within countries, migration controls can distort labor markets by reducing mobility from rural to urban areas.

Based on the research for *Convergence*, this overview outlines the roots of spatial institutional inefficiencies across the Middle East and North Africa—within cities, within countries, and across national borders—and it proposes institutional remedies and investment priorities informed by economic geography. The proposed reforms are ambitious. They will require strong leadership from city and national governments. However, getting the region on a path to spatial convergence is worth being ambitious and taking on a challenging agenda.

## How can the region's countries approach convergence?

The overview identifies five transitional steps that Middle East and North Africa countries can take starting now, with the urgent aim of getting the region to a path toward convergent development.

*Step 1: Enact new, evidence-based criteria to guide future spatial interventions.* To move on from decades of failed place-based policy, require that the next generation of spatial interventions ensure efficient access to a large urban market either within the country or across national boundaries. Also focus on identifying major bottlenecks that spatial initiatives could clear—whether in land markets, skill markets, service provision, or trade and labor mobility. And thoroughly consult all stakeholders in an area, including local firms, authorities, and residents as well as potential investors. The key issues here are spatial coordination across complementary sectoral investments and measures to reduce subsidies to large firms that distort the price of labor relative to capital and discourage labor-intensive economic activities.

*Step 2: Devolve greater functional authority over local revenue generation and service provision to local governments.* To empower lagging areas, make localities more responsible, equipped, and accountable for both revenue and services. With greater functional authority, they can better tailor their service delivery models to the characteristics of their territories and varied needs of their citizens, including better leveraging digital technologies for service provision. Decentralization of functions and finance is urgent in lagging areas that have been targeted for place-based investments, where local governments need to be empowered to cover the recurring costs of these investments. The speed and design of decentralization may vary based on current and historical institutional architecture, economic geography, and other strategic decisions. But regardless of the specific design choices, decentralization is likely to deliver better results when shifts in functional assignment are accompanied by commensurate shifts in resources and capacity.

*Step 3: Step away from credentialist education and toward schooling that cultivates globally tradable skills.* Decentralizing school systems could help. But also needed is a shift in public sentiment: citizens who now see the government as chiefly a job creator must come to recognize that marketable skills will attract investment and growth. Such skills will also make workers more mobile between lagging and leading regions, and such mobility is economically productive and desirable.

*Step 4: Renew the focus on nurturing urban agglomerations by streamlining land transfer procedures and relaxing zoning regulations in existing cities, lowering the regulatory barriers to their redevelopment.* Spatial inclusion is less likely to happen in new cities, since they are often disconnected from contiguous urban fabric. Instead, inclusion follows economic growth, which will most likely occur in existing urban areas. To promote the agglomeration and specialization that drive growth, policies should make cities more economically dense. A first step is to make existing urban land markets more efficient.

*Step 5: Expand market access for cities by thinning the "thick borders" that inhibit mobility across the Middle East and North Africa, for both regional trade and migration.*

For regional trade, add transit links and other critical infrastructure and reduce nontariff barriers. For migration, streamline customs and reduce internal migration controls. Focus on areas near major cities—but also on any lagging areas that have already been targeted for place-based investment. Expanding cities' access to markets will help to expand the fiscal base that can support greater redistribution to lagging areas.

As Step 1 suggests, policy makers are urged to enhance the design and implementation of place-based policies such that they enable markets to take full advantage of three growth drivers associated with economic geography: agglomeration, migration, and specialization. Rather than solely focusing on attracting capital to places where it is scarce, a refined approach should focus on developing the broader ecosystem that can make places attractive for investment while providing the opportunities for people to seek opportunities *wherever* their talents provide the highest returns.

In the long term, making the most of these growth drivers will require reforming core institutions and, in particular, working toward regional integration in the Middle East and North Africa. But in the short to medium term, the five transitional steps should speed economic growth and thus add to the momentum and demand for further spatial convergence. All levels of government—national, provincial, and local—have roles to play.

## Fragmented cities, stuck people, walled-off countries: The symptoms of institutional constraints on growth

Today, Middle East and North Africa countries are not notably benefiting from the three spatial dimensions of market-driven economic growth: agglomeration, migration, and specialization. Instead, their economic development is characterized by three striking symptoms of institutional inefficiency, all of which appear widely (though not universally)

across the Mashreq, the Maghreb, and the Gulf Cooperation Council (GCC) subregions:[1]

- *Cities are physically and economically fragmented, precluding the economic benefits of agglomeration.* In the large cities of the Middle East and North Africa, planners and policy makers have tended to start anew rather than work within the existing urban fabric. The resulting new cities and modernist neighborhoods do not support the amount of interaction seen in historic districts or in newer informal settlements. A comparison of 20 neighborhoods across 8 of the region's cities shows that intersection density—a proxy for interaction potential—is almost three times higher in historic city centers and informal neighborhoods than in modernist neighborhoods. Planners who put physical form before economic and social function have thus inhibited agglomeration effects.

- *People are spatially and economically stuck in place, lacking tradable skills and therefore limited in mobility.* Around the world, migration from places not doing well to those doing well has been key for economic integration and the reduction of spatial inequalities. And although disparities between subnational regions in the Middle East and North Africa contribute to a 63 percent larger share of total inequality in consumption than elsewhere (see chapter 2), people are stuck in place. In contrast with other parts of the world where higher education generally increases spatial mobility, earning a university degree in the Middle East and North Africa does not make a person more likely to migrate. One reason is that higher education confers credentials for coveted local public sector jobs, not tradable skills that are in demand by the private sector. Other reasons analyzed in this report include weak private sector dynamism limiting the economic "pull" of cities and frictions in trade and use of land.[2]

• *Economies are **walled off** from others, regionally and globally, by many barriers that governments in the Middle East and North Africa have created—or failed to remove.* Compared with Europe or East Asia, few countries in the Middle East and North Africa benefit from growth spillovers from their neighbors. Indeed, most export facilities in the region ship raw materials directly to global markets. The automobile production chains that include Morocco are based in Europe, not in the Middle East and North Africa.

## Excess centralization, the nature of place-based investments, and weak institutions have created less competitive economic environments than elsewhere in the world

Why are the Middle East and North Africa's urban areas fragmented, its people still stuck in place, and its economies walled off from each other and from the world? These symptoms have historical roots in a legacy of centralized administration and inattention to lagging areas, first under the Ottomans, then under the Western colonial powers (Brixi, Lust, and Woolcock 2015; World Bank 2011). Since independence, most of the region's countries have ineffectively sought to address this imbalance with interventionist social contracts that focus on state planning and redistribution over market outcomes. While keeping government central and hierarchical, such social contracts make the state responsible not only for service provision but also for other aspects of welfare—including much employment (Yousef 2004). Yet because natural resource rents and foreign aid have limited the need to collect tax revenues, citizen participation in governance is low across the region (Mills and Alhashemi 2018). In short, institutions remain weak even as the public sector dominates markets.

National governments in the Middle East and North Africa have long used public funds and subsidies to bet heavily on sectors and industrial locations—and these development bets shape markets. More than elsewhere, governments in the region tend to assume an activist role in shaping markets, whether at the national or the neighborhood scale. The preference for place-based investments inspires various interventions, from industrial location regulations to growth poles and new cities. The bets have high stakes: they consume an outsize share of public expenditures. Yet these countries appear to have worse outcomes than their global peers, with isolated exceptions.

Policies that distort markets, spatially or otherwise, usually fall short of their stated goals. Many place-based interventions fail to achieve even their redistribution objectives—and few are well designed and managed for economic growth. Today, the economic environment across the Middle East and North Africa is less efficient and less competitive than those of comparator countries and benchmark regions. On the World Economic Forum's Global Competitiveness Index, most of the region's countries underperform for their income level (Schwab 2017), as further discussed in chapter 4.[3]

Most countries in the Middle East and North Africa have national strategies that aim to balance growth spatially, bringing economic activity to lagging areas—but at what cost? Even assuming that a given place-based policy can meet its spatial equity and redistribution goals, do those gains justify the associated compromises in economic efficiency? Such trade-offs presuppose careful calibration. However, in the Middle East and North Africa, the pursuit of spatial equity through central planning has skewed spending toward risky supply-driven interventions that do not yield compensating benefits for growth or inclusion. Celebrated successes—such as Dubai and Tangier—are isolated exceptions that prove the rule: all have inherent geographic advantages, and all receive unusually well-coordinated support.

The weakness of national institutions across the region's countries—combined with the state's activist economic role and compounded by high political risk—is deterring outside investment and thus hobbling economic growth and job growth. On the

World Bank's World Governance Indicators, Middle East and North Africa countries score lower across the board than other middle-income and high-income regions.[4] Executives in the region perceive corruption and inefficient government interventions as the most significant barriers to doing business there. And in the eyes of the world, despite high financial openness, the Middle East and North Africa is economically a pariah region: its countries receive the lowest inflows globally of foreign direct investment (FDI) relative to gross domestic product (GDP).[5]

Across many of the region's countries, a thriving informal sector attests to the economic potential of the poor. The poor have few roles in the formal economy and no real stake in the formal sector, which is largely overseen by the state. The vast importance of informal employment to the poor points to failed policies and to the urgent necessity of institutional reforms. Without new policies that enable formal markets to function more efficiently, the energies of the poor will not be turned to more economically productive uses, and the Middle East and North Africa will not achieve shared prosperity.[6]

When will the region's countries begin to see faster progress on economic growth and spatial inclusion? Not until governments see and harness the economic potential of all and enable factor markets while expanding them through regional integration. Otherwise, the following will occur:

- As long as the region's cities and city systems remain *fragmented*—with masses of potential workers constrained from accessing opportunities and unable to enter the formal economy—they cannot form the economically dense, efficient agglomerations that equip them to create productive jobs and produce goods and services for regional and global markets.
- As long as the region's education systems keep producing *stuck* people—locally credentialed workers with limited tradable, portable skills—the regional labor force will remain small relative to the population, predominantly local, and lacking in economic mobility.
- As long as the region's countries are *walled off*—disconnected from their regional neighbors and from the world—their cities cannot fulfill their potential: cities need large markets.

Whereas people throughout the Middle East and North Africa still look to the public sector for social services and for jobs, the region would benefit far more from institutional reforms to integrate markets—creating incentives for private investment, skill acquisition, and urban specialization in tradable goods and services. Short of this set of ideal reforms, the region's economies can realize some benefits by better aligning government interventions with policies for efficiency and competitiveness (see chapter 6). This report presents findings on many specific aspects of the region's economic geography (box O.3). For regional policy makers, the challenge is to confront the picture thus revealed and to give due weight to this evidence in their deliberations.

The moment is critical. Choices today can set the next generation on a course either toward more spatially convergent economic growth—or toward further spatial interventions that, in many cases, are likely to fail.

## Fragmented cities

To document the institutional constraints on economic growth and inclusion, this report looks at the Middle East and North Africa across three spatial scales: within cities, within countries, and across national boundaries. Why start with cities? Not just because cities drive economic growth globally but also because the region's urban population share is among the highest in the world (box O.4).

In the Middle East and North Africa's cities, the built-up area is on average quite spatially dispersed—a fact likely to increase future development costs and thus limit productivity and welfare. The cost of this fragmentation is borne by all city residents, but it is especially costly to low-income households. Take the Abdallah family, forced to move from the home they built in Ìzbit Khayrallah (a well-located and dynamic informal neighborhood in Cairo's center) to the new government development Masākin Ùthmān on the outskirts of Cairo (TADAMUN 2015).[7] The move proved hugely expensive for the Abdallahs. It involved transport costs to access current jobs; service costs for

---

BOX O.3 **Many signs point to one problem: The Middle East and North Africa's economies are moving insufficiently**

Many recent economic findings, reviewed in this report, raise pointed questions about the Middle East and North Africa's slow economic and job growth—and the relation of these indicators to national policies. For example, why do the region's countries receive the world's lowest net inflows of FDI relative to GDP?[a] And why are people with university degrees in the Middle East and North Africa no more likely to be hired away from their places of origin than people with only a primary education?[b]

Underlying these and many other symptoms is a basic problem that the region's governments have yet to face: for generations, national institutions and

policies have distorted factor markets. Specifically, *place-based policies* have shaped inefficient land markets and discouraged labor-intensive job creation, while *spatial equity policies* and *a reliance on public jobs* have reinforced a local orientation in the labor market and reduced the regional demand for tradable skills. For the region to achieve faster economic growth—and more convergent growth, with economic mobility and shared prosperity—national governments will need to reduce these distortions.

a. The question of low FDI inflows is examined in chapter 3.
b. For discussion of the returns on education, see chapter 2.

---

BOX O.4 **Drivers and results of high urbanization in the Middle East and North Africa**

Urbanization in the Middle East and North Africa has been rapid, driven by economic development as well as by environmental and political crisis. The region's urban population increased fourfold from 1970 to 2010, and forecasts predict that it will double again between 2015 and 2050 (UN-Habitat 2012). The pace of urbanization partly reflects economic development, geography, and migration to oil-rich countries, especially the GCC countries. But it also reflects drought and conflict: in 2018, the Middle East and North Africa contained an estimated 7.2 million refugees, 10.5 million internally displaced persons, and about 15 million economic migrants.[a]

The region's countries nevertheless display varying urbanization shares and urban growth rates resulting from varying confluences of factors. Today's urban population share ranges from

43 percent in Egypt to around 80 percent in the most urbanized countries of the GCC and about 87 percent in Lebanon.[b] Among three major Middle East and North Africa subregions—the Mashreq, the Maghreb, and the GCC—the Maghreb now has the lowest national urban growth rates (less than 2 percent a year on average).

The Mashreq is seeing faster urban growth, driven in part by refugees. Economic migration to the cities of the Mashreq and the Maghreb has been chiefly internal and partly climate-driven as migrants are pushed out of rural areas where agriculture is suffering from higher temperatures (UN-Habitat 2012). By contrast, migration to the GCC "city-states" (such as Bahrain, Kuwait, and Qatar) has come mostly from abroad, especially during the oil price boom of 2003–13.

*box continues next page*

BOX O.4    **Drivers and results of high urbanization in the Middle East and North Africa** *(continued)*

FIGURE BO.4.1    **The Middle East and North Africa is a highly urbanized region**

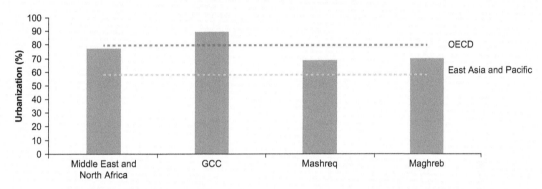

*Source:* World Development Indicators Database 2016.
*Note:* "Urbanization" is measured as the percentage of total population living in urban areas. The orange dashed line designates the Organisation for Economic Co-operation and Development (OECD) average. The yellow dashed line designates the East Asia and Pacific average. Maghreb refers to Algeria, Libya, Morocco, and Tunisia; Mashreq to the Arab Republic of Egypt, Iraq, Jordan, Lebanon, the Syrian Arab Republic, and West Bank and Gaza; and the Gulf Cooperation Council (GCC) to Bahrain, Kuwait, Oman, Qatar, Saudi Arabia, and the United Arab Emirates.

a. Refugee data from the UN Refugee Agency (UNHCR) 2018 database: http://reporting.unhcr.org/node/36.
b. In some countries, the definition of what constitutes "urban" contributes to significant disparities in reporting of urbanization versus agglomeration index levels—the latter being a metric of urbanization that classifies *economic density* using standardized criteria for population density, the population of a "large" urban center, and travel time to that urban center.

amenities that were limited and thus more expensive in the new city; and the cost of losing the family's social network. Significant hardships resulted.

Although cities in the Middle East and North Africa are not equally fragmented (box O.5), many are quite fragmented in population density and the layout of physical structures, especially when controlling for population.[8]

Within a city, spatial dispersion and fragmentation make networked infrastructure and service provision costlier. They also make job matching less efficient and formal housing more difficult to provide. In a highly fragmented city, firms are less likely to quickly find people with the right skills. And low-density neighborhoods may indicate lost opportunities for infill development, contributing to dysfunction in the formal housing market. For example, most Egyptians cannot

afford formal housing, in part because planning and building standards are rigid and outdated. In Cairo, formal housing units are reported to be 20–30 percent vacant—even as 70 percent of the city's population occupies informal housing (World Bank 2012).

The spatial fragmentation of many cities in the Middle East and North Africa reflects both long-term and short-term growth patterns. Thus, Amman's layout has become more linear with the expansion of Zarqa, a nearby industrial town. But low-density informal settlements have also increased spatial fragmentation in Amman as well as in other refugee destinations, such as Baghdad.

In the long term, modernist urban planning in the Middle East and North Africa has increased spatial dispersion, fragmentation, and infrastructure costs—a pattern that continues today. The low-density urban plans of the modernist era assumed horizontal

**In the Middle East and North Africa, some cities are more spatially fragmented than others**

In the Middle East and North Africa, Casablanca and Baghdad have a fairly high potential for interaction among residents: people are more spatially concentrated than fragmented (figure BO.5.1, panels a and b). In contrast, Amman and Tripoli have linear layouts and less concentrated populations (figure BO.5.1, panels c and d).

FIGURE BO.5.1 **Fragmentation varies significantly across urban areas of several capital cities in the Middle East and North Africa**

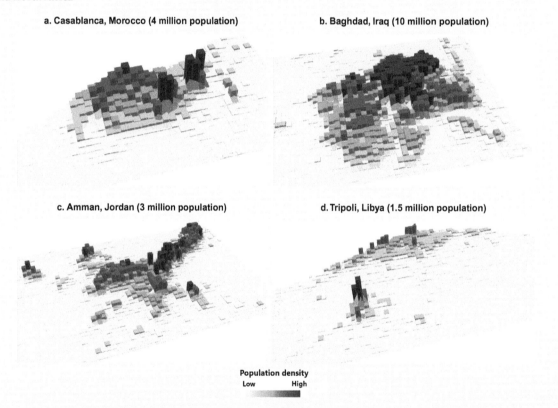

**a. Casablanca, Morocco (4 million population)**

**b. Baghdad, Iraq (10 million population)**

**c. Amman, Jordan (3 million population)**

**d. Tripoli, Libya (1.5 million population)**

**Population density**
Low          High

*Source:* Developed from LandScan Global 2012 dataset, Oak Ridge National Laboratory, https://landscan.ornl.gov/.
*Note:* Fragmentation is represented by the distribution of population within urban areas. (Each square represents population density per square kilometer.) For a detailed analysis, see chapter 1.

expansion and private car travel. Globally, many cities now reject such plans and promote density through vertical and infill development. Yet most of the region's cities have not adopted policies for density.

In the GCC subregion, city centers are being replaced with business and commercial districts. And urban expansion in the GCC is nearly as likely to occur through leapfrog development as through infill—while in the Maghreb subregion, infill development is also rare, and extension development is the norm (figure O.1). Leapfrog and extension development both tend to increase a city's infrastructure costs—leapfrog development more so.

In the short term, the wars and turmoil that have shaken the region since 2010 are transforming many cities, with consequences for their spatial forms and patterns of service delivery. As with past conflicts, such as the Lebanese civil war (box O.6), recent waves of war and unrest have altered urban footprints. Cities in the Mashreq subregion have seen large informal settlements come into being as people flee conflict—in Iraq, Fallujah and Ramadi are two of the country's fastest-growing urban centers—or as people spill over from refugee camps, such as the 58 established by the United Nations Relief and Works Agency for Palestine Refugees in the Near East (UNRWA) for more than 1.5 million such refugees in Jordan, Lebanon, the Syrian Arab Republic, and the West Bank and Gaza (Serageldin, Vigier, and Larsen 2015). In recent years, Jordan's population growth rate has more than doubled with the refugee influx. Satellite photos show how the city lights of Amman have visibly spread and brightened (see chapter 1, box 1.1).

Across the Middle East and North Africa, informal settlements are spontaneously stitching together the gaps in the urban fabric created by modernist city plans—offering a possible model for formal, planned densification. All but invisible to their governments, the poor build economies of their own. Take the informal areas of Greater Cairo, where about 12 million people lived in 2010: these areas spatially resemble the city's oldest neighborhoods (photo O.1). Often viewed as relics of medieval squalor, such compact neighborhood structures may in fact represent an approach to reduce future urban spatial fragmentation and limit negative externalities such as air pollution (UN-Habitat 2012).

## Stuck people

While fragmented cities limit efficiency and thus reduce workers' economic prospects, the Middle East and North Africa's high inequality may also reflect low

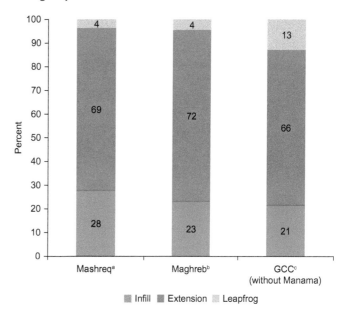

FIGURE O.1 **Aggregated 1990–2004 urban expansion trends of capital cities in the Mashreq, Maghreb, and GCC subregions show divergent patterns**

*Sources:* Datasets from the European Commission Joint Research Centre's Global Human Settlement Layers. See Annex 1D for sensitivity analysis.
*Note:* The analysis uses the Landscape Expansion Index developed by Liu et al. (2010), in which extension and leapfrog expansion increase infrastructure costs, with leapfrog having a higher cost impact.
a. Mashreq comprises the Arab Republic of Egypt, Iraq, Jordan, Lebanon, and the Syrian Arab Republic.
b. Maghreb comprises Algeria, Libya, Morocco, and Tunisia. For Morocco, Casablanca was analyzed instead of the capital city, Rabat.
c. GCC = Gulf Cooperation Council, comprising Bahrain, Kuwait, Oman, Qatar, Saudi Arabia, and the United Arab Emirates. Manama, the capital of Bahrain, was excluded because of the bias created by its geographical constraints and resulting in an exceptionally high share of infill urban expansion.

geographic mobility: its people are stuck in place, both spatially and economically. Socioeconomic inequality between areas of most of the region's countries far exceeds that seen in countries with comparable GDP around the world (figure O.2). This exceptionally high spatial inequality can be related to low spatial mobility. Being located far from a large city also increases business development constraints in the region's countries (figure O.3).

In most parts of the world, people vote with their feet and move toward opportunity, but this happens less in the Middle East and North Africa (figure O.4).

Similarly, around the world, higher education generally increases spatial mobility—but not in the Middle East and North Africa, where earning a university degree

BOX O.6    **Urban fragmentation as a legacy of conflict: Today's polycentric Beirut**

In 1975, civil war splintered Beirut into sectarian neighborhoods. The city center, once vibrant, became a no-man's-land. Economic activity relocated to new areas that were defined by firm owners' religion and ethnicity. The result today is a polycentric city with a Christian sector, a Muslim sector, and the now reoccupied historical center (figure BO.6.1).

FIGURE BO.6.1    **After decades of conflict, Beirut became a polycentric city**

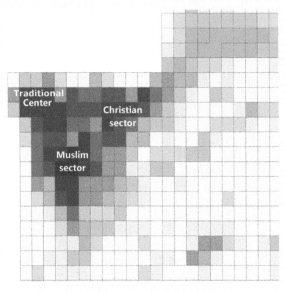

Source: Hanna 2016.
Note: The darker the square, the higher the population density.

PHOTO O.1    **In Greater Cairo, recent informal settlements share a basic spatial structure with medieval neighborhoods**

**a. Aerial view of Bab el Wazir (established 800 years ago)**

**b. Aerial view of Fostat Plateau (established informally in the 1980s)**

Sources: UN-Habitat 2012, from Sims 2010; Google Earth satellite images.

**FIGURE O.2 Inequality within most Middle East and North Africa countries exceeds that of global peers**
*Level of inequality in relation to GDP per capita*

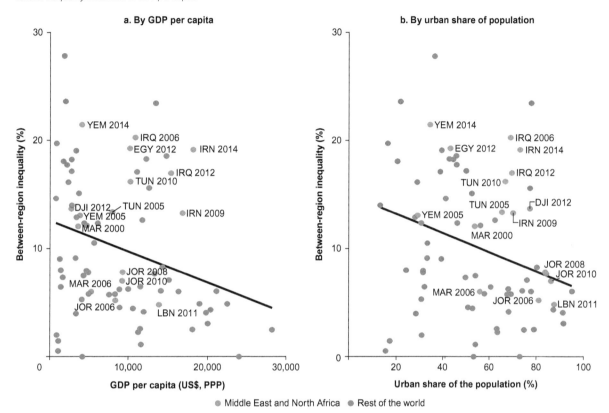

Source: Middle East and North Africa Poverty (MNAPOV) database, Team for Statistical Development, World Bank.
Note: Each point corresponds to a country's data for a particular year. (Countries represent all income levels. For a list of countries and survey years, see chapter 2, annex 2A.)
Inequality between subnational regions was calculated based on a country's first administrative level (for example, governorates, provinces, and so on).
PPP = purchasing power parity.

does not make a person more likely to migrate (figure O.5). One explanation is that, in this region, higher education confers credentials for coveted public sector jobs, not the tradable skills in demand by the private sector (box O.7). Notably, women are more likely than men to migrate in Algeria, Egypt, Jordan, Lebanon, Morocco, and Tunisia, which shows that female migrants in those countries are on average more likely to be employed at their destinations (as further discussed in chapter 2).

Across the Middle East and North Africa, rural residents face substantial barriers to migration or have preferences against it—or else they would have migrated already, given the returns to welfare from doing so.

**FIGURE O.3 In the Middle East and North Africa, companies located on the periphery face harsher constraints on business development than those in the capital city**
*Percentage-point change in probability of factor being a major constraint to company on the periphery instead of in the capital*

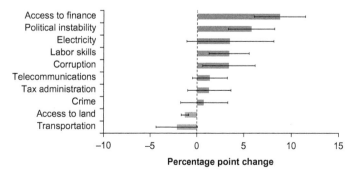

Source: World Bank Enterprise Surveys, 2011–18.
Note: T-bars indicate 90 percent confidence levels.

**FIGURE O.4**   **Within-country migration is lower in Middle East and North Africa countries (averaging 14 percent) than in the rest of the world (28 percent)**

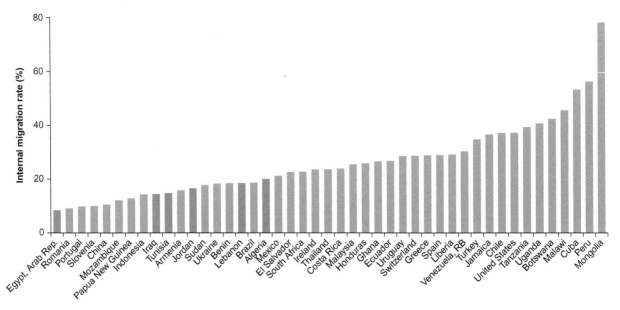

*Sources:* Arab Barometer Wave IV (2016–17) data; University of Minnesota's Integrated Public Use Microdata Series (IPUMS) International database.
*Note:* The internal migration rate is the number of lifetime within-country migrants per 100 population. Lifetime migration compares the place of current residence with the place of birth (within the same country). The data are from various years; see chapter 2, annex 2A, table 2A.1. The migration rates in Algeria, the Arab Republic of Egypt, Jordan, Lebanon, Morocco, and Tunisia are computed on the basis of the Arab Barometer Wave IV (2016–17) data; rates for other countries are from latest censuses available on IPUMS in which place of birth was available.

**FIGURE O.5**   **Globally, the probability of migration tends to rise with education—but not in the Middle East and North Africa**

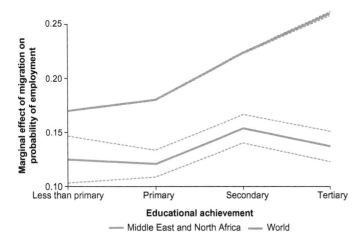

*Sources:* Arab Barometer Wave IV (2016–17) data; University of Minnesota's Integrated Public Use Microdata Series (IPUMS) International database.
*Note:* Estimations employ a Probit model with controls for gender, age, marital status, employment status, urban or rural residence, education level, and country fixed effects at 90 percent confidence intervals (dashed lines). Migration refers to lifetime internal migration, which compares the place of current residence with the place of birth (within the same country). In this figure, "Middle East and North Africa" comprises Algeria, the Arab Republic of Egypt, Jordan, Lebanon, Morocco, and Tunisia.

An analysis performed for this work of several countries across subregions, using 2006–14 data, shows that living in a metropolitan area brought welfare benefits independent of individual characteristics.[9] The analysis studies individual characteristics and the returns to these characteristics from living in metropolitan areas of Djibouti (2012), Egypt (2012), the Islamic Republic of Iran (2014), Iraq (2012), Jordan (2010), Morocco (2006), Tunisia (2010), and the Republic of Yemen (2014). The results show that people outside the metropolis were less well-off not simply because of their age, gender, education, marital status, labor force status, water access, electricity access, or possession of a computer. Rather, a substantial part of the welfare gap reflected higher returns to these individual characteristics in metropolitan areas. Similarly, another analysis suggests that across the entire region, if all people were living in capitals—where the returns on their characteristics would be the

**BOX 0.7** **Low spatial mobility—and high public employment—among university graduates suggest that the Middle East and North Africa's higher education systems do not impart tradable skills**

A university education in Middle East and North Africa countries confers locally valuable credentials—but does it provide marketable skills? Not according to international evidence. Globally, spatial mobility among the educated is a sign of human capital: people with tradable skills are likely to move to places where those skills are in demand (figure BO.7.1). Conversely, the low spatial mobility of the region's university graduates suggests that their human capital remains low.

This suspicion is strengthened by employment data. In the Middle East and North Africa, a tertiary degree increases the probability of getting a public sector job far more than the probability of working in the private sector (figure BO.7.2). If private sector jobs are lacking for graduates, one reason is that firms require complementarity between human and physical capital investments; they will not invest in a place that lacks a trained, skilled labor force.

**FIGURE BO.7.1** **Human capital in the form of tradable skills increases spatial mobility**

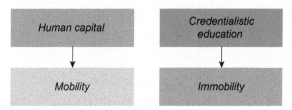

**FIGURE BO.7.2** **In the Middle East and North Africa, tertiary education diplomas are highly valued in the public sector**

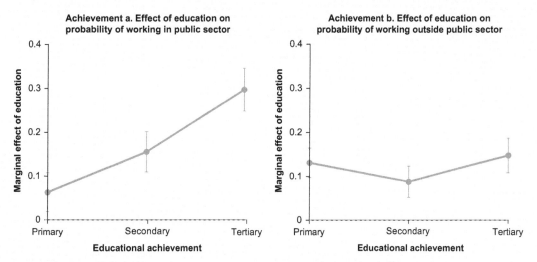

*Source:* Arab Barometer Wave IV 2016–17 data.
*Note:* Marginal effects use Probit regressions controlling for urban or rural residence, gender, age, number of children, marital status, and country fixed effects. T-bars indicate 95 percent confidence levels. The regressions were calculated for six countries in the Arab Barometer data: Algeria, the Arab Republic of Egypt, Jordan, Lebanon, Morocco, and Tunisia.

highest—per capita consumption would increase by 37 percent (D'Aoust and Lall, forthcoming).

People in remote areas of Middle East and North Africa countries—especially in the Mashreq and GCC subregions—are stuck partly because their countries lack secondary cities and dynamic private sectors: they live in the long shadow of the capital. Outside the Maghreb subregion, the Middle East and North Africa is dominated by its metropoles. People far from cities lack not only tradable

skills (because of the distorted incentives shaping education systems) but also the nearby markets or infrastructural links to markets that they would need to succeed in business. If not for barriers to migration, many more of these people would have moved to capitals already.

So why do many of the region's countries lack secondary, midsize cities? One reason is another sort of barrier: the "thick borders" that wall off countries, blocking trade and investment.

**FIGURE O.6    Urban populations in the Mashreq and GCC subregions are highly concentrated in the largest city and even more so in large cities (of more than 1 million people)**

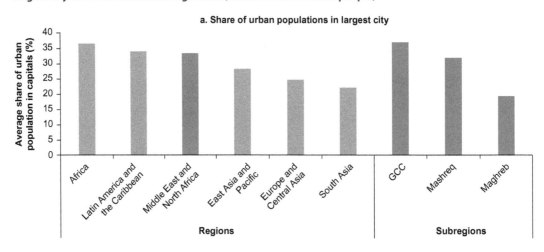

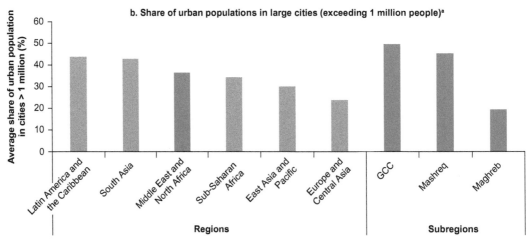

*Sources:* 2015 data from United Nations Department of Economic and Social Affairs (UN DESA) World Population Prospects database: https://population.un.org/wpp/.
*Note:* For subregional figures, the estimates of a few countries were modified, considering the population of the whole agglomerations (which was not always the case in the World Development Indicators dataset). Maghreb refers to Algeria, Libya, Morocco, and Tunisia; Mashreq to the Arab Republic of Egypt, Iraq, Jordan, Lebanon, the Syrian Arab Republic, and West Bank and Gaza; and the Gulf Cooperation Council (GCC) to Bahrain, Kuwait, Oman, Qatar, Saudi Arabia, and the United Arab Emirates.
a. The country-level figures were computed using either (a) cities of 1 million inhabitants or more, or (b) the share represented by the capital city in countries that had no cities exceeding 1 million inhabitants.

## Walled-off countries

Trade with nearby countries confers economic advantages. But Middle East and North Africa countries are encircled by thick borders that constrain regional trade: onerous customs regimes and visa difficulties, high tariffs and nontariff barriers, regional infrastructure bottlenecks, and customs and logistics inefficiencies. Lacking deep trade agreements, the region's countries are walled off from one another.

Accordingly, firms in these countries trade far less than the region's development levels might imply—and trade among countries within the region is strikingly low. These trade constraints are all the more striking given that the Middle East and North Africa is dominated by its largest cities, which economically should benefit from higher trade volumes. Across the Mashreq and GCC subregions, the share of a country's urban population concentrated in its largest city—termed urban primacy—is among the highest in the world (figure O.6, panel a). And in these subregions, cities of more than 1 million people contain even higher urban population shares (figure O.6, panel b). Yet because the region's large cities lack access to regional or global markets, they fall short of their economic potential.

As a rule, large cities need large markets to be productive and drive economic growth. That is because agglomeration effects presuppose scale. So, the specialized production tasks that make up links in global value chains tend to be concentrated in large urban agglomerations. In the Middle East and North Africa, though, the economic reach of large cities appears to be confined to domestic markets.

Although trade levels averaged across the Middle East and North Africa seem roughly in line with the region's share of global GDP, this statistic is deceptive: the region's trade consists disproportionally of fuel exports. Trade in electricity, by contrast, is less widespread in this region's countries than throughout much of the world (figure O.7).

**FIGURE O.7  Few Middle East and North Africa countries trade electricity**

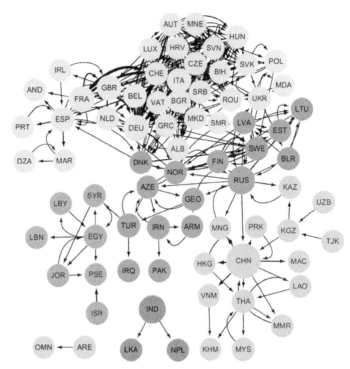

*Source:* Ji et al. 2016, based on the United Nations International Trade Statistics Database (UN Comtrade) electricity trade statistics (http://comtrade.un.org).
*Note:* Figure illustrates the Eurasian electricity trade network in 2010. Arrows indicate an electricity trading relationship between two countries. Full country names correspond to ISO 3 country codes. Colors indicate seven "communities" as defined by Ji et al. (2016): "A community in the electricity trade network consists of a group of nations tightly connected by electricity trade. Changes in one nation have more effects on nations within the same community than on nations outside the community." The Middle East and North Africa countries are spread over four of these communities.

In addition, when firms in the Middle East and North Africa trade across borders, the returns are lower than expected: firm-level data show that the region's exporting firms are no more productive than the firms that do not export. And when its manufacturing firms import critical intermediate inputs, they pay a large and statistically significant productivity premium (Francis and Schweiger 2017). These patterns hint at an economic environment where access is privileged; where firms face barriers to entry, even if their operations may be more efficient; and where countries impose high barriers to buying goods from abroad.

Logistics inefficiencies appear especially challenging—more so, for example, than infrastructure (as discussed further in chapter 6). In 2018, most Middle East and

North Africa countries fell in the middle or lower range of the World Bank's Logistics Performance Index of 160 countries. Among them, three Maghreb states (Tunisia, Morocco, and Algeria) scored between 105 and 117. Exceptions included the GCC countries and Israel, which ranked fairly high across logistics indicators, followed by Egypt and the Islamic Republic of Iran.[10]

A country whose major cities are cut off from regional markets loses the opportunity to reap positive spillovers from neighboring countries. Ideally, a favorably endowed and fast-growing country with good policies should add to regional demand for workers, capital, and knowledge. Nearby countries should accelerate their growth—creating a virtuous cycle of spillovers—and expanding regional markets should enable firms in connected countries to benefit from scale economies.[11] Because Middle East and North Africa countries lack deep trade agreements with their neighbors and trade facilitation is limited, the region's large cities are missing out on these spillover benefits (box O.8).

Other regions—notably Europe and East Asia—have made regional trade a key driver of economic growth, while Middle East and North Africa continues to suffer from high restrictions on movements of

---

**BOX O.8   Large cities in the Middle East and North Africa show few spillover benefits from regional trade**

The spatial economic analysis in chapter 3 shows that the positive spillovers to the Middle East and North Africa's large urban areas from regional trade are negligible (figure BO.8.1). In contrast, such spillovers are positive across all countries globally—and strongly positive in East Asia and Pacific countries with regional integration.

Given lower economic spillovers for neighbors in the Middle East and North Africa than elsewhere in the world, what would happen to economic output in a city from another region with greater spillovers if it were instead in the Middle East and North Africa? A counterfactual for Bangkok is revealing. If Bangkok were in the Middle East and North Africa, its per capita GDP is estimated to drop from approximately US$12,000 to US$9,000 (figure BO.8.2).

FIGURE BO.8.1   **Spatial economic spillovers to large city economies based on deep trade agreements with neighbors, by region**

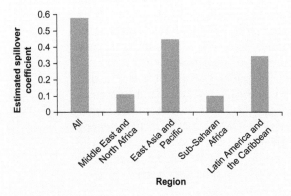

*Source:* Lebrand 2019.
*Note:* The dependent variable is city GDP. Figure excludes Europe and Central Asia because the analysis of that region is less relevant to the Middle East and North Africa given the economic differences between the two zones. Also excluded is South Asia because of the small number of observations for the region, rendering the results insignificant.

FIGURE BO.8.2   **Bangkok's per capita GDP would have shrunk had it experienced the regional economic spillovers of the Middle East and North Africa**
*GDP simulation for Bangkok without regional economic spillovers, 2000–15*

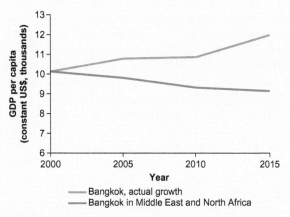

*Source:* Lebrand 2019.

goods and people. With increased market access, nonfuel exports could grow. Given the size of many national economies in the region, the regional service trade could be much higher. Countries could buy and sell much more electricity. Unfortunately, conflict and vested interests in many of the region's countries make comprehensive regional integration unlikely in the short term.

Because of thick national borders, Middle East and North Africa cities generally lack access to the large markets they need. To gain such access, the region's countries that border the European Union (EU)—a large world market—can enter its supply chain through trade agreements. So far, Morocco and Tunisia have benefited from this (although trade volumes are still low). The need for such agreements arises from the absence of a large regional anchor economy, as Western Europe was for Eastern Europe after 1990 or as Japan (succeeded later by the Republic of Korea) was for China and other East Asian neighbors. In the long term, regional integration should be a goal of Middle East and North Africa policy makers. Right now, more trade with Europe does not imply less trade within the Middle East and North Africa; the two are complementary.

## Place-based and centralized: How national policies and institutions in the Middle East and North Africa perpetuate economic inefficiency and spatial inequity

How does the Middle East and North Africa's fractured economic geography today reflect the impact of state interventions in factor markets, combined with the regional legacies of centralized administration and service provision? How have central governments shaped the region's land, labor, and skill markets economically and spatially at the city, country, and regional levels? What does the persistence of highly centralized government contribute to these spatially and economically distortive dynamics? This section looks at national preferences for place-based investments

and centralized public goods management, assessing their implications for prosperity and welfare.

## Place-based interventions in the Middle East and North Africa are distortive while yielding low returns

Public interventions in the economy may be *institution-based, people-based,* or *place-based.* Those that are *institution-based* support governance, trade, and functioning markets. Those that are *people-based* support human capital, from health and nutrition to higher education and skill development. In contrast to both these types, *place-based* interventions are often designed to improve development outcomes in particular locations—whether directly through infrastructure investments or indirectly through incentives, subsidies, and regulations.

Place-based interventions, while often well-intentioned to overcome market and coordination failures, typically distort factor markets, limiting economic efficiency by reducing the power of demand to drive specialization and agglomeration. Land markets are hobbled by heavy regulations on land use, which bottle up demand for both residential and industrial structures. Labor markets shrink with disincentives to migrate and to acquire tradable skills: Why specialize and migrate for a relatively high-productivity job in a distant city when you can hope that the state will one day lavish its largesse on your rural province? And private capital follows the lead of policy makers rather than seeking and meeting demand from domestic consumers and international business partners.

In the Middle East and North Africa's cities, many neighborhoods and livelihoods are strongly shaped by place-based policies—and not for the better. Favored policies include heavy zoning and location regulations as well as the construction of modernist neighborhoods and cities from scratch—often deterring formal redevelopment. In response, poor urban residents and migrants develop residential neighborhoods informally. The result is the spatially and socially fragmented city, a symptom of market and coordination failures (figure O.8).

Within Middle East and North Africa's countries, place-based investments typically loom large in the national budget—not the usual pattern for middle-income countries. The place-based, or spatially targeted, interventions often used in the region include

- Physical infrastructure investments;
- Capital subsidies and other fiscal incentives;
- Subsidies to places such as growth poles and industrial districts;
- Regulation of where industries may locate production; and
- Public sector industrialization, with central planning of investment locations.

Compared with institution-based and people-based policies, these place-based policies consume an outsize share of country investment expenditures in the region (box O.9). When resources flow so freely to place-based interventions, vital investments in institutions and people must be neglected or deferred. In effect, governments place large bets on specific locations and hope for a stroke of luck. Yet place-based interventions have a poor track record in the region's countries (box O.10).

From a regional perspective, place-based investments discourage the formation of

secondary cities that can specialize and trade with neighboring markets—as well as that of efficient agglomerations, which large cities need if they are to serve large international markets. Rather than fostering specialized production centers and economically dense agglomerations to meet market demands, the supply-driven initiatives used by the region's governments to attract private sector investment have done the opposite. Take Tunisia, which used incentives to attract domestic and foreign firms such as Benetton to lagging interior areas: as soon as the incentives expired, many firms closed their operations (World Bank 2018a). Generally, place-based firm location initiatives in the Middle East and North Africa have delivered few jobs, and many apparent success stories have proven elusive.

Since the 1950s, as the region's national governments have persisted in shaping markets directly through place-based policies, lagging areas have stubbornly remained behind. Governments initially adopted activist territorial development policies to answer the needs and grievances of neglected areas. Strongly spatial in their focus, such policies had two main aims: to direct compensatory support to the areas left behind and to create new geographic centers for economic activity. But lasting successes—such as Dubai and Tangier (box O.11)—are few and far between.

In cities, within countries, and throughout the region, place-based policies have yielded low economic returns—yet in spite of lessons like Tunisia's, Middle East and North Africa countries continue to rely on such policies. Indeed, several of the region's governments are increasing incentives and transfers for investments in lagging areas, new cities, and industrial development zones without rethinking their approach.

Why bet so much on policies with such unpromising track records? Four reasons stand out:

- *Vested interests.* Despite a spatial intervention's limited returns to the local and national economy, some groups may stand to gain considerably from it.

FIGURE O.8   **Place-based interventions distort urban markets— which then fail**

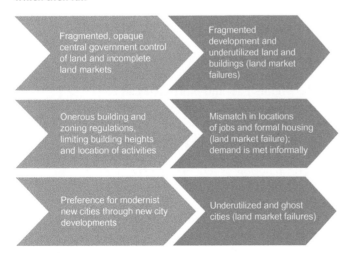

---

BOX O.9 **Middle East and North Africa countries stand out in directing a large share of investment expenditures toward place-based interventions**

Across the Middle East and North Africa, a larger share of public expenditures—including initial investments and recurrent expenditures—are channeled toward place-based interventions than toward institution-based or people-based interventions. In contrast, states outside the Middle East and North Africa spend less on spatially distortive interventions and more on investments in institutions and people. This pattern is illustrated in analyzing expenditure distributions for one year for several Middle East and North Africa and comparator countries for illustrative purposes.

**FIGURE BO.9.1** **Government expenditure distribution in selected Middle East and North Africa countries, by spatial category, differs greatly from international comparators**

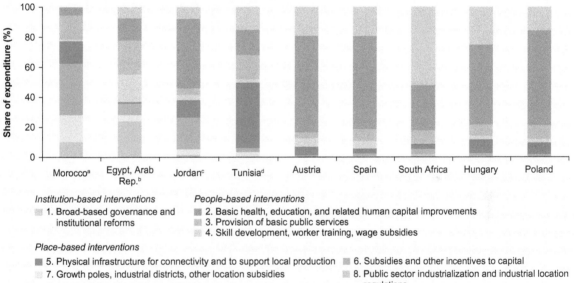

Institution-based interventions
1. Broad-based governance and institutional reforms

People-based interventions
2. Basic health, education, and related human capital improvements
3. Provision of basic public services
4. Skill development, worker training, wage subsidies

Place-based interventions
5. Physical infrastructure for connectivity and to support local production
6. Subsidies and other incentives to capital
7. Growth poles, industrial districts, other location subsidies
8. Public sector industrialization and industrial location regulations

Source: Government Finance Statistics (GFS) database, International Monetary Fund; government data for Middle East and North Africa countries (as described in notes below).
Note: The GFS database does not include data for Middle East and North Africa countries except for partial data for the United Arab Emirates. For Middle East and North Africa countries, report team analysis was based on national data as described in notes a–d:
a. Morocco information came from the 2017 Finance Law, specifically the "General Budget" and the "Public Establishments and Enterprises" segments.
b. Egypt on-budget data came from the Financial Statement 2018–19, and the total expenses of the 48 economic authorities were retrieved from their 2016–17 financial statements from the Ministry of Finance website.
c. Jordan information came from "Capital and Current Expenses (2018)," classified by all line ministries, reported by the General Budget Department of the Ministry of Finance.
d. The Tunisia analysis considers the most recent five-year plan, the Development Plan 2016–20, and in chapter 4, further analysis is provided drawn from the 2017 Finance Law.

- *Path of least resistance.* Investments in vacant land may present policy makers with a course of least resistance, sparking less opposition than reforms affecting developed areas.
- *Lack of credible evidence.* Little concrete information may be readily available on the failures (and the rare successes) of

territorial development policies in the Middle East and North Africa.
- *Extrapolating from rare success stories.* Successes such as Dubai and Tangier may inspire hope for replication. Yet the success may not be clearly replicable. Or even more likely, policies may not be carefully designed to account for challenges and complementary factors.

---

**Place-based investments amount to risky development bets—and the stakes are high**

Most place-based investments in Middle East and North Africa countries have been supply-driven rather than demand-driven. As a result, they have led to inefficiencies. Consider the poor track record of Egypt's 20th-century new cities. In the 23 new cities created from 1979 to 2000, the total population today is less than 800,000—a fraction of the targeted 20 million—and some cities are still unoccupied (Sims 2015). Similarly, Saudi Arabia's established "desert cities" remain unoccupied or house a fraction of their target populations.

Even so, the region's governments keep betting on new cities and vast capital investments. Egypt allocated 30 percent of its 2015–16 national built environment budget to new cities and zones that hosted only 2 percent of the country's population. In contrast, just 29 percent of that budget went toward existing cities and towns hosting 98 percent of the population (Sims 2015). And Saudi Arabia, with its balanced territorial development policy, allocated about 30 percent of its 2017 budget to developing eight planned new cities (see chapter 4, table 4.2).

---

**How to make successful spatial bets? Build on natural advantage**

Dubai and Tangier stand out as rare successes among the many spatial development bets made by Middle East and North Africa countries. What made these two spatially targeted policies succeed? And what lessons can the region's policy makers take from them to improve their own spatial bets? The answer, broadly, is that both Dubai and Tangier have been blessed with geographic advantages—and their governments introduced institutional reforms, and public investments, that enabled these cities to leverage those advantages.

Dubai benefited from its strategic location at the crossroads between continents. In the early 1900s—even before the 1950s oil discovery in the United Arab Emirates—Dubai was declared a free port, and Dubai Creek served as a trading post for deep-sea merchants. As demand for port services increased, the government of Dubai embarked on an expansion of port facilities that led to the establishment of Port Rashid and later Jebel Ali Port at the end of the 1970s.

In parallel, the government launched Dubai's first free zone at Jebel Ali Port in the early 1980s. The zone was governed by a legal framework that addressed a range of issues raised by investors and allowed local as well as foreign investments to be made in a business environment comparable to any in the world for private sector development. This helped demand for port services to skyrocket at Jebel Ali Port as

well as Port Rashid (jointly managed by Dubai Ports Authority until Port Rashid was closed). Today it is the biggest port between Rotterdam and Singapore and dominates the Arabian Gulf. Based on its success, the government launched many other free zones, each with institutional reforms oriented toward the specific industries Dubai sought to attract to its city.

Likewise, the Moroccan government recognized substantial unrealized potential in Tangier, driven by its strategic geographic location at a historical crossroads of the Middle East, Africa, and Europe. In 2002, the government of Morocco recognized that it could better leverage this locational advantage. It established Tangier-Med Port Authority and invested €1 billion to develop and expand the port and develop the surrounding city and region. The project was developed as part of an integrated framework, supporting the development of four critical sectors:

- Transport infrastructure in roads and rail
- Industrial and logistics free-trade zones
- Training and education of the local workforce
- Collaboration across levels of government agencies and private sector stakeholders to spur international investment.

The Tangier area was also governed by an alternative legal framework that addressed core institutional

*box continues next page*

BOX O.11    **How to make successful spatial bets? Build on natural advantage** (continued)

and business environment challenges elsewhere in the country. The development and expansion of the port boosted manufacturing, resulting in 28 percent employment growth over 2002–04 and an annual increase of investment of 13.2 percent (Kulenovic et al. 2015). Improvements in supply chain links, diversification of the local and regional economy, and production increases in manufacturing-intensive sectors such as the automotive industry all benefited from port growth. As a result, the region evolved from being one of Morocco's most lagging in 2000 to one of the most leading today.

Because the advantages of market access cannot be spread equally across a territory, spatial initiatives must be sensitive to a place's distinct advantages and potential. Most important is to ask whether a place is suitable to agglomerations. Efficient economies are not evenly distributed in space; rather, they are lumpy, with economic activity clustered in economically dense places—cities, leading areas, and regional economic hubs—and places naturally situated at a crossroads between continents, such as Dubai and Tangier.

Seen in a broader historical perspective, the region's governments have used place-based policies to offer visible responses to subnational grievances and citizens' expectation that the state will provide jobs. In a region with some of the world's worst rates of unemployment and labor force participation, and with episodes of violent conflict and terrorism, governments have identified jobs and stability as central policy goals. Surveys show that citizens across various Middle East and North Africa countries have come to regard the state's main function as providing jobs—not as providing services and not as providing a voice to citizens (figure O.9).

In practice, public policies that distort factor markets tend to undermine social stability by inhibiting private sector and job development. Policies to shape factor markets are likely to foster a vicious cycle of worse job and inclusion environments. Other distortions are less intentional—reflecting decisions that are centralized, yet uncoordinated, and insufficiently guided by a holistic view of needs across areas. Unless territorial development policy is guided by a strong territorial planning framework (World Bank 2018b), lagging areas are unlikely to get the specific help they need to develop their economies through specialization and agglomeration.

## Public investment decisions and service provision in Middle East and North Africa countries are still overly centralized—making spatial convergence through place-based policy even more unlikely

Centralized decision making and budgeting can limit the efficiency of place-based efforts to increase spatial equity. Spatial convergence policies are likely to fail wherever public investment allocation is centralized—especially if budgeting is also opaque, politicized, or unpredictable. In some Middle East and North Africa countries, sectoral and subnational investment expenditures flow to areas with the greatest bargaining power, as in Egypt (World Bank 2012). Thus, grants and transfers are too often directed to leading rather than lagging areas. Even budget allocation formulas risk being biased toward wealthier areas, such as those with natural resources (World Bank 2016).

Centralized service provision, too, can limit spatial convergence—both within cities and within countries. Top-down arrangements typically cause service delivery to be less efficient in places that are less connected to the center, especially poor urban neighborhoods (including informal settlements) or

**FIGURE O.9  Respondents in surveyed Middle East and North Africa economies identified jobs enablement—not public service provision or citizen representation—as the most essential function of a democratic state**

*Percentage of respondents selecting answers in multiple-choice format*

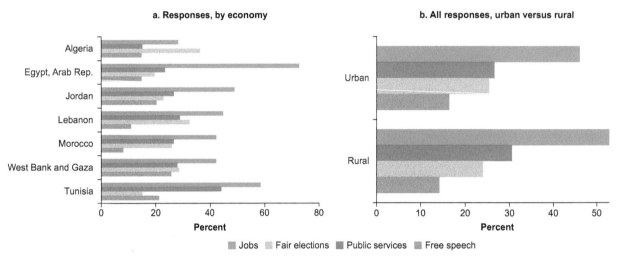

a. Responses, by economy

b. All responses, urban versus rural

■ Jobs  ■ Fair elections  ■ Public services  ■ Free speech

*Source:* Arab Barometer Wave IV (2016) data.

*Note:* Percentages add up to more than 100 because they reflect respondents' selection of one statement from each of four sets of answers to the question (Wave IV, no. 515): "If you have to choose only one from each of the four sets of statements that I am going to read, which one would you choose as the most essential characteristics of a democracy?" Categories shown summarize each choice described.

lagging areas of countries. In the Middle East and North Africa, most public services remain overly centralized, including health and education (though the United Arab Emirates is a rare exception in education [World Bank 2018d]).

When different neighborhoods or areas contain citizens with heterogeneous preferences, these differences make centralized administration even more inefficient. Whether within cities or within countries, residents of different areas may differ greatly in their preferences. If so, efficient service delivery will require local involvement, as emphasized in *World Development Report 2004: Making Services Work for Poor People* (World Bank 2003). The same is true for subnational areas.

Further, decentralized service provision can allow for experimentation and for leveraging a variety of service delivery models that allow, through the use of digital technologies and alternative institutional arrangements, more efficient service provision to marginalized populations. For low-density areas, providing mobile services—for example, mobile health units and mobile

schools—can reduce costs and improve access (Boex et al. 2016; Chambers, Wild, and Foresti 2013). For such areas, policy makers need to expand the connectedness of providers and clients: for instance, they could improve accessibility to services through distance learning with radio and cellphones. Other options include having nonstate service providers fill service gaps and training community members to deliver services themselves. For water and electricity provisions, off-grid or off-network solutions, such as local independent water providers or local generators for power provision may be more feasible because of the different levels of scale sensitivity of different types of infrastructure.

Although Middle East and North Africa countries are rightly concerned about spatial disparities in service provision, the prevailing response—territorial development policy directed from the capital—may be perpetuating poor outcomes and distrust of the state. Empirical studies link citizens' trust in government to their perceptions of government performance (Brixi, Lust, and Woolcock 2015).

Recently, countries including Lebanon and Tunisia have embraced initiatives to decentralize local services—a welcome challenge to the Ottoman and colonial legacy of centralized administration. Still, the bulk of service provision in the Middle East and North Africa that could be managed subnationally is not yet decentralized and remains, at best, deconcentrated, with local decisions assigned to remote arms of the central government.

## Five transitional steps to reduce institutional inefficiency, speed the Middle East and North Africa's economic development, and enable convergent growth

Can Middle East and North Africa governments steer from today's spatial symptoms and distortions—rooted in institutional inefficiencies—toward a more productive economic landscape, with faster growth and a prospect of spatial convergence? Yes, if policy makers end their overemphasis on traditional place-based development, supply-driven investments, and centralized investment decisions and service provision.

But that is not likely to happen all at once. The following five transitional steps can help policy makers chart a gradual path from territorial development policies that are predominantly place-based and focused on addressing the spatial symptoms of weak economies to ones that address the causes of depressed growth. This would entail a shift away from single-sector, supply-driven, place-based policies to an approach of first mapping a place's inherent economic advantages, then identifying suitable interventions.

### Step 1: Adopt new, evidence-based criteria to guide future spatial interventions

Ideally, broad institutional and people-based reforms would make cities more efficient, people more mobile, and countries more connected. But in practice, Middle East and North Africa governments may remain tied for the short term to spatially targeted initiatives—that is, to place-based policies. To contain the economic damage from these policies, the region's decision makers can, through a new framework, impose criteria on place-based interventions that will make them more efficient (though all are likely to be distortive).

This begins with market size: picking the right policies for each place requires understanding its existing and potential access to markets, which may be domestic or international. Not all places have equal access to domestic markets (including for labor and skills), which are concentrated in economically dense urban agglomerations. And not all places are equally connected to external markets: some have natural advantages such as coasts or borders, while others have better connective infrastructure. Because of varying density and market access, policies that yield high returns in one place may have no impact—or even a harmful impact—in another.

Where place-based policies have already been adopted, this framework would guide decision makers toward supporting it with complements—whether for markets and connectivity or for basic service provision. And those complements should be prioritized based on expressed demand from citizens and firms on what is needed to make those territories effective enabling environments. Yet wherever possible, the approach should also involve transitional steps to reform institutions (such as the other four transitional steps outlined below). And it should focus on enabling agglomeration, migration, and specialization based on a place's natural advantage (as discussed in box O.11). Thus, to enhance market access, locate industrial parks near large cities. Or identify a location's most constrictive trade bottlenecks and then clear them with new connective infrastructure, institutional reforms. Or both.

When considering whether to retain traditional supply-driven, place-based policies or to shift toward this approach, countries

---

BOX O.12    **Remembering the forgotten: Institution-based policies for the urban poor**

The poor of the Middle East and North Africa are, all too often, the region's forgotten people. They lack formal housing and the credentials or connections needed for a formal job. So, they live wherever they must—and work however they can.

The economic dynamism of the poor appears in the informal sector, especially among urban migrants. Their restless economic activity attests to their energy, effort, and ingenuity—but it is not economically efficient. Informal markets are unlikely to generate the specialized scale economies that spur faster, wider growth through trade in goods and services.

To bring poor urban residents and migrants into the formal sector and give them opportunity, countries would first need to reform factor markets. One reason that the region's cities create few opportunities for the poor in the formal sector is that these cities have only weak links to regional and global markets. So, governments should observe informal urban economies for hidden signs of demand and

productive potential within a city's fragmented economic landscape—and should enable formal investment in these hot spots, raising densities and loosening restrictive regulations. Informal settlements point to where labor is in demand and where potential formal sector productivity lies untapped. Policy makers can encourage formal investment in such neighborhoods with institution-based reforms: revising urban plans, relaxing zoning regulations, and allowing higher population densities.

If the urban poor often seem invisible to policy makers, the rural poor are even further from realizing their potential productivity—especially those who live far from cities. In the Mashreq and GCC subregions, the scarcity of secondary cities means that many rural residents cannot access urban markets. More and more of them migrate to the metropolitan capital, not simply because of conflict or climate change but because the investments needed at home are lacking. Once settled in cities, these internal migrants join the informal economy.

---

should keep one principle firmly in mind: spatial equity arises not from investments in a place but from the economic growth that creates jobs for a country's forgotten people—wherever those jobs may be—paired with policies focused on improving access to basic services for people regardless of their location. Only faster economic growth, with transitional but positive steps toward more efficient institutions, will allow the Middle East and North Africa to harness the economic energies of the poor (box O.12).

## Step 2: Devolve greater functional authority and resources for local revenue generation and service provision to local governments

Place-based policies to reduce spatial equity are often undermined by a lack of local authority and resources—whether to

raise revenues, to make investment decisions and allocate expenditures, or to deliver local services. Lagging areas are often the least able to mobilize and manage local revenues, because the central government wields more fiscal control over smaller municipalities than over larger ones. Further, transfers to these localities are often insufficient and lack objective standards, transparency, and predictability. This lack of budget authority, together with the lack of local control over service provision, can undermine the local execution and maintenance of place-based investments—the very investments that are supposed to reduce spatial disparities. In Morocco, for example, a lack of local capacity has caused many municipalities to execute less than 50 percent of their investment plans (World Bank 2018c).

Further, centralized service delivery models make it difficult to offer services tailored to heterogeneous preferences of citizens through the use of alternative delivery models and digital solutions. The way that functional authority and resources are devolved can and should vary based on economic geography, the current authorizing environment, and the current institutional architecture and historical trajectory. Such reforms, even if gradual and experimental, have proven most likely to succeed when they have ensured that the devolution of functional authority is accompanied by the critical complements of greater resources and capacity support.

### Step 3: Step away from credentialist education and toward schooling that cultivates globally tradable skills

Helping stuck people become more spatially and economically mobile could make the region's countries more prosperous—and more stable. Generally, people in underperforming areas around the world migrate to jobs and opportunities. Their choices help to manage excessive population densities in the lagging areas, and it can benefit their relatives in their places of origin.

But in the Middle East and North Africa, fewer people migrate than would be predicted from the welfare gains accruing to migrants. As noted earlier, this immobility results in part from credentialist education that does not impart tradable skills. It also reflects the many frictions that inhibit labor mobility—from land transfer fees to active controls. And it is compounded by strong local identities and identity-related divisions.

### Step 4: Renew the focus on nurturing urban agglomerations by streamlining land transfer procedures and relaxing zoning regulations in existing cities, lowering the regulatory barriers to their redevelopment

Making fragmented cities' land markets more efficient will be critical for agglomeration and specialization—two dynamics that amplify factors of production and drive economic growth and jobs. Whether in larger or in smaller (secondary) cities, agglomeration and specialization require the efficiencies arising from high economic density, or the geographic concentration of economic activity (as discussed earlier in box O.2). Urban economic density and efficiency generally are high if development is spatially compact, dense with people, and transit-oriented—but low if development is sprawling, as with leapfrog development and widely dispersed structures.

One way to make cities more efficient is to reduce local frictions—boosting demand and increasing economic density while also taking care to monitor the externalities (side effects) of economic and population density. Planners and regulators can attract firms to invest in cities by reducing frictions such as

- Impediments to property acquisition and new construction (costs, height limits, and density limits);
- Challenges in local business registration and licensing;
- Limits on news and information; and
- Obstacles to developing local business networks.

All these frictions are pervasive in the Middle East and North Africa and call for policy remedies.

Planners can also address friction affecting households, especially formal housing costs. And they can seek ways to internalize the negative externalities, or social costs, of urban density—for example, by levying congestion charges, repealing fuel subsidies, and improving traffic management.

Efficient city plans must be able to reflect changing demand: if they cannot, frictions, negative externalities, and market failures will result. Governments must, for example, enable zoning and building regulations to evolve with changing social and economic needs. Consider Jordan, where rigid zoning and building regulations impose standards that make housing unaffordable for all but the top 30 percent of the income distribution. More than 70 percent of new housing developed in Jordan is done without a building permit (CAPSUS 2018).

A city's density creates positive externalities in public service delivery, which tends to be more efficient with density—and less so with sprawl. Providing one cubic meter of piped water costs US$0.70–US$0.80 in Tunisia's dense urban areas, but it costs US$2 in sparsely populated areas. Similar differences appear in education and health care costs (World Bank 2014). And in Amman, Jordan, with its rapidly rising population, a World Bank study finds that the cost of new infrastructure through 2030 will depend on whether urban growth is sprawling (low density) or compact (high density). The study concludes that sprawling growth—the pattern of the recent past—will cost 14 times as much as compact growth (World Bank 2018b). Nevertheless, urban plans cannot simply pursue density but must also attend to service quality: where density is too high, service quality can decline (a negative externality from congestion).

### Step 5: Expand market access for cities by thinning the "thick borders" that inhibit mobility across the Middle East and North Africa, both for regional trade and for migration

Historically, Middle East and North Africa cities were part of economically central global trade networks. Many of these cities persist in modern times as large, often vastly populated urban areas. Yet with today's thick borders, their economic reach has been limited. Countries across the region today need to enhance links across national borders—reducing tariffs and nontariff barriers, easing movements of goods and people—though at the same time they may also enact policies to strengthen domestic markets.

Expanding the market regionally would help firms in small countries benefit from scale economies in production, including better access to inputs. It is also likely to support secondary cities that can be interlocutors with cross-border economies. Consider what can happen if Jordan and Egypt start trading more with each other following a decrease in border restrictions. As further discussed in chapter 6, a simulation exercise based on a quantitative economic geography model examined the implications of reducing border crossing times from 50 hours to 20 hours. There are major welfare benefits in South Sinai (Egypt) and around Aqaba (Jordan) from increases in market access. Greater market access can also introduce greater competition by promoting technology upgrading and greater productivity, often facilitated by cross-border investment. And it could trigger the emergence of regional production networks, leading to greater intraindustry trade within the region and allowing growth in one country to spill over to its neighbors.

Increasing the spatial mobility of people makes especially good sense for the Middle East and North Africa, not just because of how migration benefits migrants and their families but also because the alternative—growing productive jobs in lagging areas through place-based policy—is not broadly feasible. Policies to increase both spatial and economic mobility in the region's countries could adopt three central priorities: building skills and human capital, reducing frictions in spatial movement, and finding ways to manage social divisions.

The most urgent priority for making people more mobile is, arguably, to reorient education toward tradable skills (assuming first that health care, water and sanitation, and basic education are present). Next is to reduce the frictions that hinder spatial and economic mobility, including

- Low job market information, with high job search costs;
- High fees for land or property transfers;
- High permit fees for construction;
- Restrictive building regulations; and
- Government controls that limit internal migration.

Finally, social divisions related to identity—in some cases a strong local identity—can pose the greatest challenge to policy makers. Where intractable social divisions prevent labor mobility, place-based policies could in some cases be justified.

Some may see labor mobility as undesirable, given the challenge the region's cities face in absorbing migrants (including refugees). But leaving people stuck is not a pragmatic alternative. Efforts to induce growth in lagging areas face an even more unyielding challenge: lumpy economic landscapes are persistent. For poverty to be rapidly and sustainably reduced, people must be able to move where the jobs are.

## The prospects for regional integration: Distant yet vital to the Middle East and North Africa

This overview has recommended five transitional steps toward more efficient spatial investments and initiatives to promote faster growth and eventual spatial convergence. In the longer term, the Middle East and North Africa should envision regional integration that will break down walls between countries; connect firms to larger markets; and foster ever-larger scale and agglomeration economies that are specialized for tradable goods and services. All of the region's countries would gain from such integration— just as some are already gaining from trade agreements with large markets elsewhere.

Although the prospects for the Middle East and North Africa's regional integration may seem remote today, the subject bears discussing because of the high stakes of regional trade. Cooperation among the region's countries today is strikingly weak, but not for any known structural reason. A more apparent cause lies in political tensions and violent conflict. The upshot of today's scant cooperation is clear: the Middle East and North Africa's economies produce less than they could by trading more—and more freely— with each other.

Closer regional integration has been a long-stated objective of the region's countries, and there have been a number of initiatives.

But the economic impacts of those efforts have been minor, especially when compared with those in other world regions. Apart from natural resource exports, trade and integration with the rest of the world have also remained below potential, with such notable exceptions as Morocco's automobile sector.

Regional integration and global trade are complementary, so both should be pursued. Both expand product markets: regional integration also increases supply capacity in large part by enlarging input (factor) markets, and global integration facilitates investment and access to technology and know-how. Deeper trade agreements that the EU is negotiating with Morocco and Tunisia could perhaps become templates for similar cooperation between neighbors.

Ultimately, effective steps to closer regional integration will always require giving up some sovereignty to regional institutions that set and enforce certain rules. So far, governments of the Middle East and North Africa have not been willing to transfer regulatory powers to regional institutions that would govern intraregional trade. But steps can be taken today that do not require giving up sovereignty or giving it up only in limited areas. Such steps would help to build the trust and experience to promote more comprehensive integration later. Initial examples involving different types of policy instruments could initially involve just two or a few neighboring countries, as follows:

• Tariffs have mostly been removed within the Pan-Arab Free Trade Area, but trade costs remain relatively high because of nontariff measures and transport prices. Information about nontariff measures is scarce, but they mostly represent red tape and cause major complaints. They contribute to the Middle East and North Africa's low scores on logistics performance. Transport prices would fall if more competition were allowed in logistics and restrictions to operations in neighboring countries were reduced.

- Institutions could be established in limited areas where contributions and benefits can be more clearly defined and a transfer of some sovereignty is therefore more acceptable. For example, regional electricity pools, a regional transport authority, or, where willingness of countries is greater, even a competition authority or dispute settlement mechanism would be possible.
- Cross-border integration of physical infrastructure is generally quite acceptable, but there is often little coordination in upgrading transport links on different sides of a border. A clear, long-term vision for regional transport integration could guide future investments including, in the longer term, reestablishing or newly constructing rail links in the region and consolidating port operations where several smaller ports currently operate.

Although prospects for formal integration may remain uncertain, spatially sensitive physical infrastructure investments that connect neighbors can create conditions for later growth to spread. Again, places with access to large markets—whether in existing urban agglomerations or potentially through regional and global trade—are the most favorable to scale economies and specialization.

Regional integration for the Middle East and North Africa can be broadly envisioned as a six-point plan.

- *Make the business climate more favorable and state functions more efficient.* Institution-based reforms to speed government processes—and to make doing business easier across the region—would be a prerequisite for integration.
- *Reduce tariffs and nontariff barriers.* Tariff reductions would be accompanied by the removal of inefficient subsidies (such as energy subsidies) with care to address regressive impacts of removal.
- *Liberalize the logistics sector.* Private sector logistics firms would replace today's inefficient state monopolies. Morocco offers a model with its logistics zones,

elimination of regulatory barriers, and introduction of new customs regimes suitable for logistics activities (Rouis and Tabor 2013).
- *Reform customs regimes.* Customs procedures would be streamlined and customs regulations harmonized across borders with private sector participation (as in logistics), and border control information would be shared internationally.
- *Fill infrastructure gaps.* Connective infrastructure—perhaps on the emerging model of a development corridor anchored by transport links (roads, rail, and ports)—would involve not just paving roads and laying rail but also ensuring an environment that benefits the wider economy, with incentives for development.
- *Ensure compensation for relative losers.* Gains from integration should more than suffice to compensate those who may end up worse off as a result of trade.

## Notes

1. The Maghreb subregion includes Algeria, Libya, Morocco, and Tunisia. The Mashreq subregion includes Egypt, Iraq, Jordan, Lebanon, the Syrian Arab Republic, and West Bank and Gaza.
2. These and other reasons are being further analyzed in forthcoming World Bank Middle East and North Africa reports.
3. The GCC countries are no exception: most score below their income peers.
4. Data from the World Governance Indicators Database, https://info.worldbank.org/governance/wgi/.
5. Data from the World Development Indicators Database: https://databank.worldbank.org/source/world-development-indicators.
6. Even middle-income citizens in Middle East and North Africa countries participate extensively in the informal economy. Their resources, too, could be used more productively if factor markets in the formal sector were more efficient.
7. Actual names of the interviewees in the TADAMUN (2015) report, "The Hidden Cost of Displacement," have been withheld.

8. The potential-of-interaction method (De la Roca and Puga 2017) measures the average number of people within a given distance from any spot in the city. To capture the practical likelihood of interpersonal interaction, one can control for city population, and one can also control for GDP—an inverse proxy for the cost burden of commuting. Controlling for both, cities in the Mashreq and GCC subregions have some of the world's highest potentials for interaction, making the average across all Middle East and North Africa cities still quite high. But controlling for population alone (that is, disregarding the commuting advantage conferred by higher GDP), the average city in the region appears more fragmented.

9. The welfare aggregate (in most countries comprising total food and nonfood expenditures) was temporally and spatially deflated to account for price differences over time and between areas.

10. See the World Bank Logistics Performance Index (LPI) 2018: https://lpi.worldbank.org/.

11. Close proximity remains advantageous in buyer-supplier networks despite the rapid decline in global transport costs.

## References

Boex, Jamie, Ammar Malik, Devanne Brookins, and Ben Edwards. 2016. "Dynamic Cities? The Role of Urban Service Delivery Performance in Africa and Asia." Working paper, International Growth Centre, London.

Brixi, Hana, Ellen Lust, and Michael Woolcock. 2015. *Trust, Voice and Incentives: Learning from Local Success Stories in Service Delivery in the Middle East and North Africa.* Washington, DC: World Bank.

CAPSUS (CAPSUS Sustainable Capital). 2018. "Urban Growth Scenarios. Hashemite Kingdom of Jordan." Project brief for the World Bank, Washington, DC.

Chambers, Victoria, Leni Wild, and Marta Foresti. 2013. "Innovations in Service Delivery: International Experience in Low-Density Countries." Research report, Overseas Development Institute (ODI), London.

D'Aoust, Olivia, and Somik V. Lall. Forthcoming. "Unequal Places and Stuck People." Unpublished manuscript, World Bank, Washington, DC.

De la Roca, Jorge, and Diego Puga. 2017. "Learning by Working in Big Cities." *Review of Economic Studies* 84 (1): 106–42. doi:10.1093/restud/rdw031.

Francis, D. C., and H. Schweiger. 2017. "Not So Different from Non-Traders: Trade Premia in the Middle East and North Africa." *Economics of Transition* 25 (2): 185–238.

Hanna, J. 2016. "Changing Realities: Traumatic Urbanism as a Mode of Resilience in Intra-War Beirut." *International Planning History Society Proceedings* 17 (3): 383–88.

Ji, L., X. Jia, A. S. F. Chiu, and M. Xu. 2016. "Global Electricity Trade Network: Structures and Implications." *PLoS ONE* 11 (8): e0160869.

Kulenovic, Z. Joe, Alexandra Cech, Drilon Gashi, Luke Jordan, Austin Kilroy, Megha Mukim, and Juni Tingting Zhu. 2015. "Six Case Studies of Economically Successful Cities: What Have We Learned?" Companion Paper 3 for "Competitive Cities for Jobs and Growth: What, Who, and How," World Bank, Washington, DC.

Lebrand, Mathilde. 2019. "International Growth Spillovers from Deep Agreements for Countries and Cities." Unpublished manuscript, World Bank, Washington, DC.

Liu, X., X. Li, Y. Chen, Z. Tan, S. Li, and S. Ai. 2010. "A New Landscape Index for Quantifying Urban Expansion Using Multi-Temporal Remotely Sensed Data." *Landscape Ecology* 25 (5): 671–82.

Mills, R., and F. Alhashemi. 2018. "Resource Regionalism in the Middle East and North Africa: Rich Lands, Neglected People." Brookings Doha Center Analysis Paper No. 20, Brookings Institution, Washington, DC.

Rouis, Mustapha, and Steven R. Tabor. 2013. *Regional Economic Integration in the Middle East and North Africa: Beyond Trade Reform.* Directions in Development Series. Washington, DC: World Bank.

Schwab, Klaus, ed. 2017. *The Global Competitiveness Report 2017–2018.* Geneva: World Economic Forum.

Serageldin, Mona, François Vigier, and Maren Larsen. 2014. "World Migration Report 2015: Urban Migration Trends in the Middle East and North Africa Region and the Challenge of Conflict-Induced Displacement." Background paper, International Organization for Migration (IOM), Geneva.

Sims, David. 2010. *Understanding Cairo: The Logic of a City Out of Control.* New York: American University in Cairo Press.

———. 2015. *Egypt's Desert Dreams: Development or Disaster?* Oxford: Oxford University Press.

TADAMUN. 2015. "The Hidden Cost of Displacement: The Move from Ìzbit Khayrallah to Masākin Ùthmān." Report of the TADAMUN Initiative, American University, Washington, DC.

UN-Habitat (United Nations Human Settlement Programme). 2012. *The State of Arab Cities 2012: Challenges of Urban Transition.* Nairobi, Kenya: UN-Habitat.

World Bank. 2003. *World Development Report 2004: Making Services Work for Poor People.* Washington, DC: World Bank.

———. 2009. *World Development Report 2009: Reshaping Economic Geography.* Washington, DC: World Bank.

———. 2011. *Poor Places, Thriving People: How the Middle East and North Africa Can Rise Above Spatial Disparities.* MENA Development Report Series. Washington, DC: World Bank.

———. 2012. "Arab Republic of Egypt: Reshaping Egypt's Economic Geography: Domestic Integration as a Development Platform." Report No. 71289-EG, World Bank, Washington, DC.

———. 2014. "Tunisia Urbanization Review: Reclaiming the Glory of Carthage." Report, World Bank, Washington, DC.

———. 2016. "Syrians in the Middle East: The Lives and Livelihoods of Refugees and Their Hosts." Unpublished manuscript, World Bank, Washington, DC.

———. 2018a. "From Disfavored to Unique: Tunisia's Territorial Variety as an Asset. Policy Note on How Tunisia Can Leverage Its Regions in a Differentiated Manner for Shared Prosperity." Report No. 130184, Project No. 159072, World Bank, Washington, DC.

———. 2018b. "Jordan—Urban and Municipal Program for Balanced and Inclusive Growth: Concept State Program Information Document (PID)." Concept Note, Report No. PIDC151796, World Bank, Washington, DC.

———. 2018c. "Maroc: Tirer avantage de l'urbanisation pour promouvoir un nouveau modèle de croissance et réduire les disparités territoriales." [Morocco : Take advantage of urbanization to promote a new growth model and reduce territorial disputes]. Policy Note, World Bank, Washington, DC.

———. 2018d. "Unleashing the Potential of Education in the Middle East and North Africa." MENA Education Flagship Draft for Decision Meeting, World Bank, Washington, DC.

Yousef, Tarik M. 2004. "Development, Growth and Policy Reform in the Middle East and North Africa since 1950." *Journal of Economic Perspectives* 18 (3): 91–116.

# Fragmented Cities, Constrained Growth | 1

Urbanization is strongly and positively linked to economic growth. This is because cities, by reducing the distance between people, allow ideas to spread easily, improve matching between employers and employees, enable firm specialization and the emergence of value chains, allow for cost sharing of expensive but growth-enabling infrastructure, and, finally, create consumer markets large enough to sustain scale economies.

Although urbanization levels in the Middle East and North Africa are among the highest in the world, economic performance has on average been disappointing and below average for countries with comparable urbanization rates. In particular, the share of urban jobs in the tradable sector is surprisingly low compared with South Asia, East Asia and the Pacific, and Europe and Central Asia, while it is on par with the Sub-Saharan Africa region. By largely limiting themselves to local markets, firms in the Middle East and North Africa impede returns to scale, economic growth, and job creation.

This chapter uncovers a complementary, and possibly more important, explanation for the poor economic performance in urban areas of the Middle East and North Africa region: the spatial fragmentation of its cities. The underutilization of land in the region's cities—through either low-density or leapfrog development—increases the costs of providing infrastructure and services to firms and populations. Low-density, noncontiguous urban spatial development affects the costs of networked infrastructure (such as electricity, sewerage, roads, and water) because it increases the distances that need to be covered by the infrastructure per capita. In capital-constrained economies, this can result in lower coverage or maintenance of these services. It is also likely to hinder the functioning of urban labor markets by limiting matching between employers and employees.

However, spatial fragmentation displays high variations across subregions of the Middle East and North Africa. While the Maghreb displays high fragmentation, the Mashreq on the whole has dense built-up areas in part stitched together by recent informal neighborhoods that authorities have over recent decades sought to eliminate, following the (somewhat unrealistic) dream cities of some urban planners.[1] In the Gulf Cooperation Council (GCC) countries, state-of-the-art transport infrastructure—geared toward personal vehicles and financed through natural resource revenues—currently overcomes urban fragmentation through speedy transport.

But none of these coping strategies encourages the densification of urban areas. They rely on fiscally intensive workarounds to mitigate (in some cases) the nascent costs of urban land-use fragmentation. This is both costly and unlikely to foster the economies of agglomeration needed for firms of the Middle East and North Africa to make urbanization work for all.

## Rapid urbanization has not brought commensurate economic benefits to the Middle East and North Africa

### Urbanization is high across the region

The Middle East and North Africa region has become one of the most urbanized regions in the world, with 65 percent of its population living in cities in 2018.[2] Although only 34 percent of these economies' populations were living in cities back in 1960, the region has been progressively closing the gap with Europe and following the urbanization rhythm of Latin America (figure 1.1).

Over 1970–2010, the region's urban population almost quadrupled. Forecasts predict that, compared to 2015, it will double by 2050, with the urbanization level reaching 71 percent (UN DESA 2019).[3] This rapid urban growth has been driven by economic development, migration to oil-rich countries, drought, and conflict. In 2018, the Middle East alone hosted an estimated 7.2 million refugees, 10.5 million internally displaced persons (IDPs), and 15 million economic migrants.[4]

Urbanization varies across subregions, reflecting different drivers, as follows:[5]

- *The Mashreq* is moderately to highly urbanized (from 43 percent in the Arab Republic of Egypt to 87 percent in Lebanon). As a result of wars and ongoing conflicts, it shelters half the world's registered refugees, adding to the pressure on large cities (box 1.1). With limited options for expansion in the larger cities, governments are emphasizing development of secondary cities and satellite locations.

**FIGURE 1.1** **Urbanization in the Middle East and North Africa is catching up with Europe and Latin America, 1960–2015**

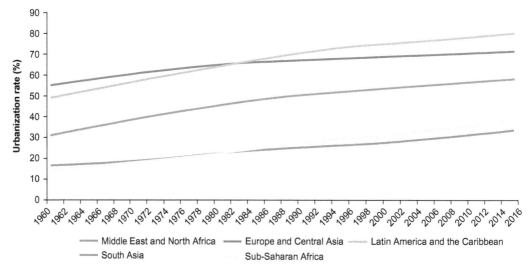

*Source:* World Development Indicators database.
*Note:* The "urbanization rate" is the percentage of total population living in urban areas.

**The impact of conflicts on urbanization in the Middle East and North Africa**

The wars and turmoil that have shaken the Middle East and North Africa since 2010 have also shaped patterns of urbanization. They created an estimated 2 million refugees and over 6 million internally displaced persons (IDPs), most of whom have settled in large urban areas (Serageldin, Vigier, and Larsen 2014). The number and location of displaced populations shift regularly in response to the changing levels of violence in Iraq, Libya, Sudan, the Syrian Arab Republic, and the Republic of Yemen (UNHCR 2014).

A comparison of urban footprints (proxied by nighttime lights) in the Mashreq subregion reveals a clearly visible change between 2012 and 2015 as luminosity increased in urban areas in Jordan and Lebanon and decreased in Syria (map B1.1.1). Jordan's population growth rate, which averaged 3.2 percent over 2000–16, rose to 7 percent a year from 2011 onward as a consequence of the large influx of refugees (World Bank 2017).

Similarly, the ongoing crisis in the West Bank and Gaza from conflict with Israel has led to uncontrolled urban expansion in neighboring countries, while the Iraq war led to large waves of internal displacement (Serageldin, Vigier, and Larsen 2014).

More than 60 percent of the West Bank and Gaza population has migrated, and most of the migrants have settled in neighboring Arab countries.[a] An estimated 1.5 million people from the West Bank and Gaza are living in the 58 recognized United Nations Refugee Agency (UNHCR)-run camps for this population in Jordan, Lebanon, Syria, and the West Bank and Gaza.[b] Over the years, the population has overflowed the camp boundaries and contributed to the formation of large informal settlements in the urban centers of the region, especially in Jordan and Lebanon.

Internal displacements since 2003 from the war in Iraq (more than 1.8 million people) have also affected urbanization patterns, leading to the expansion of a few cities. Baghdad, one of the cities closest to the conflict-affected areas, has been the major recipient of IDPs. Many other cities in the country attract large numbers, contributing to unplanned urbanization (Serageldin, Vigier, and Larsen 2014). In the Anbar region, 66 percent of IDPs have remained in the province, making Fallujah and Ramadiyah the two fastest-growing urban centers of the country.

MAP B1.1.1 **Massive migration patterns to urban areas in the Mashreq region are visible through nighttime light changes**

a. 2012                    b. 2015

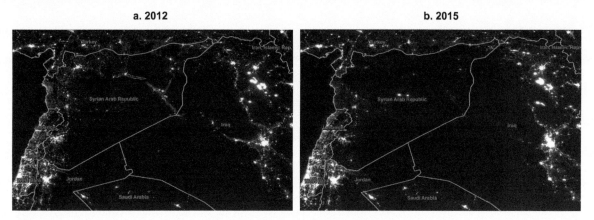

*Source:* Images from the Visible Infrared Imaging Radiometer Suite (VIIRS) instrument of the National Aeronautics and Space Administration (NASA) Applied Sciences Program, 2015.
*Note:* Map shows the intensity of light in urban areas of the region surrounding the war-torn Syrian Arab Republic (Damascus), including in the countries of Lebanon (Beirut) and Jordan (Amman), to which many war refugees have fled.

a. West Bank and Gaza migration data from "Estimated number of Palestinians in the world by country of residence, end year 2010," Palestine Central Bureau of Statistics website: http://www.pcbs.gov.ps/Portals/_Rainbow/Documents/PalDis-POPUL-2010E.htm.

b. West Bank and Gaza refugee data from "Palestine Refugees" web page of the United Nations Relief and Works Agency for Palestine Refugees in the Near East (UNRWA): https://www.unrwa.org/palestine-refugees.

- *The Maghreb* has an urbanization rate typically above 50 percent, but current urban growth rates are low (below 2 percent a year on average over 2000–16, as shown in figure 1.2).
- *The GCC countries* are among the richest and most urbanized in the world, in part owing to environmental factors. Several (Bahrain, Kuwait, and Qatar) are like city-states, with an urbanization rate of around 80 percent and a foreign-born population of around 40 percent.

The main drivers of urbanization vary considerably by subregion, leading to different urbanization patterns. Urbanization in the GCC "city-states" is driven predominantly by external and internal migration to cities, whose development is fueled by the wealth accumulated from oil exports. This pattern resulted in spectacularly high urban growth rates over 2003–13 (5–8.5 percent a year on average), when international oil prices were high (figure 1.2). The GCC cities have thus become major nodes in the flow of people, global capital, and services.

In the Mashreq and Maghreb subregions, urbanization has resulted largely from the internal migration of rural people seeking better opportunities as rising temperatures reduced agricultural productivity by 10–40 percent (UN-Habitat 2012). Improved public services, better education, and a high concentration of jobs in urban areas have attracted rural populations into the main cities of these countries. The Mashreq area has also received large waves of war refugees who moved within and between countries and settled in major cities, contributing to consistently higher urban growth rates than in Maghreb countries over the past 20 years (box 1.1).

The Middle East and North Africa region overall displays a spectacular urbanization rate. When measured with the agglomeration index—a metric of urbanization that uses consistent criteria for all countries (Uchida and Nelson 2008, see Annex 1A)—the Middle East and North Africa is by far the world's most urbanized region, with an index of 68; followed by Europe and Central Asia, whose high agglomeration index seems to be driven by high-quality transport

**FIGURE 1.2**   **Urban population growth rates in the Middle East and North Africa vary by subregion, 1990–2016**

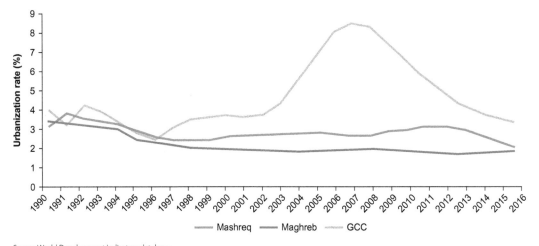

*Source:* World Development Indicators database.
*Note:* Maghreb refers to Algeria, Libya, Morocco, and Tunisia; Mashreq to the Arab Republic of Egypt, Iraq, Jordan, Lebanon, and the Syrian Arab Republic; and the Gulf Cooperation Council (GCC) to Bahrain, Kuwait, Oman, Qatar, Saudi Arabia, and the United Arab Emirates.

FIGURE 1.3    **The Middle East and North Africa displays the world's highest urban concentration as measured by the agglomeration index**

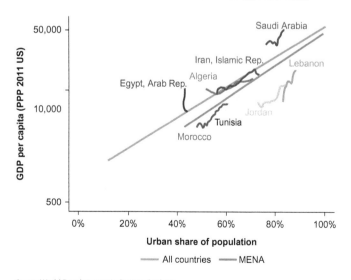

*Source:* World Bank 2009b.
*Note:* The agglomeration index is a metric of urbanization that classifies the economic density of economies using standardized criteria for population density, the population of a "large" urban center, and travel time to that urban center.
a. Maghreb refers to Algeria, Libya, Morocco, and Tunisia; Mashreq to the Arab Republic of Egypt, Iraq, Jordan, Lebanon, and the Syrian Arab Republic; and the Gulf Cooperation Council (GCC) to Bahrain, Kuwait, Oman, Qatar, Saudi Arabia, and the United Arab Emirates.

infrastructure; and Latin America and the Caribbean, where it is driven by high urban primacy (figure 1.3).[6] The GCC and Mashreq subregions display even higher scores, driving the high regional agglomeration index.

## Yet the region's economies have not reaped the full benefits of urbanization

Urbanization in the Middle East and North Africa has not been accompanied by commensurate economic growth. The relationship between urbanization and economic growth per capita in the region is below the trend observed in the rest of the world (figure 1.4).

Cities allow workers to be closer to jobs, increasing opportunities and fueling productivity. They bring people together physically, facilitating the exchange of ideas and bringing about innovations. So, urbanization has usually gone hand in hand with sustained economic growth, as measured by gross domestic

FIGURE 1.4    **Economic growth per capita has not kept pace with urbanization in the Middle East and North Africa, 1990–2016**

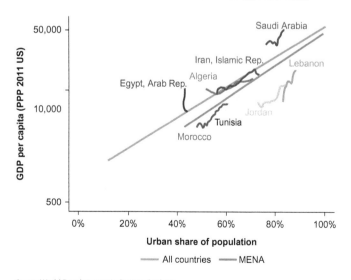

*Source:* World Development Indicators database.
*Note:* Country curves represent the evolution of the urbanization-to-gross domestic product (GDP) per capita ratio in selected countries from 1990 to 2016. MENA = Middle East and North Africa; PPP = purchasing power parity.

FIGURE 1.5   **Cities in the Middle East and North Africa display a lower share of urban tradable employment than in other regions of the world**

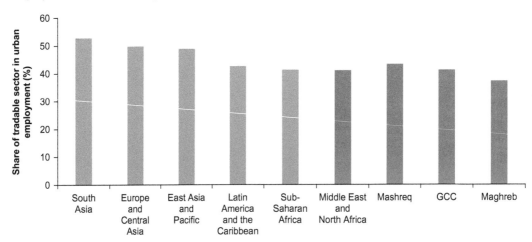

*Source:* Oxford Economics data 2015.
*Note:* The nontradable sector is defined as "consumer services + public services" and the tradable sector as "agriculture + financial and business services + industry + transport." Maghreb refers to Algeria, Libya, Morocco, and Tunisia; Mashreq to the Arab Republic of Egypt, Iraq, Jordan, Lebanon, and the Syrian Arab Republic; and the Gulf Cooperation Council (GCC) to Bahrain, Kuwait, Oman, Qatar, Saudi Arabia, and the United Arab Emirates.

product (GDP) per capita. However, when compared with international standards, GDP in the Middle East and North Africa is below its potential. Although urbanization is indeed associated with economic growth, GDP per capita remains, on average, below what could be expected for any given urbanization level based on the world average.

Notably, however, the patterns vary widely by country. Egypt, for example, displays astonishing economic growth with a near constant urbanization rate, whereas Algeria is associated with rapid urbanization but slower growth of GDP per capita.

Among the possible factors in the lower GDP per capita is the domination of the nontradables (services) sector in the region's urban employment, which limits returns to scale, economic growth, and job creation. The share of the tradable sector (such as manufacturing) in urban employment is only around 41 percent (figure 1.5), in line with Sub-Saharan Africa (42 percent) but well below South Asia (53 percent), Europe and Central Asia (50 percent), and East Asia and Pacific (49 percent).

Specializing in nontradable goods means that the demand for the region's urban output is local and necessarily limited in volume.

Faced with limited demand, urban firms in the Middle East and North Africa benefit from limited scale economies and, all else equal, create fewer jobs (Lall, Henderson, and Venables 2017). Conversely, specialization in tradable goods such as manufactured products allows for a larger and elastic potential demand that goes well beyond local markets. Catering to such international needs implies making the most of firm-level scale economies and beyond, often boosting agglomeration economies through a buoyant ecosystem of local suppliers. In the Middle East and North Africa, cities and their firms risk being unable to reverse the current trend and break into tradables because cities are too costly. Expensive cities typically require wages that would compensate workers for high urban costs and so would entail production costs above the international price for any given good (Venables 2017).

## Modernist planning and informality play crucial roles in the fragmented urban fabric

Urban compactness drives economic growth by increasing the efficiency of matching jobs and workers. From a pure economic standpoint, the ideal city can be viewed as an efficient labor market, matching employers and job seekers through connections (Bertaud 2014). When the matching is efficient, cities benefit because by increasing the size and diversity of their labor force, employers and job seekers are more likely to find appropriate matches that make the best of workers' skills and aspirations. As such, compact cities have the potential to reduce the separation between people and jobs by reducing commuting time and cost (Burton 2000a).

Fragmentation—understood as either low-density development or spatial development broken up by areas of underdeveloped land use—implies higher costs to ensure access to public networked infrastructure. To service fragmented urban areas with networked infrastructure (such as roads, sewerage, and water) is typically costlier per capita for a given service quality because it requires longer and more intricate networks. For example, in the context of U.S. cities, Burchell et al. (2005) found that urban sprawl increases local road lane-miles by 10 percent and public services and housing costs by 8 percent.

Besides, in financially constrained urban areas, these high costs may be difficult to match with resources, decreasing service quality. Libertun de Duren and Guerrero Compeán (2016) examined the relationship between municipal spending on services and population density in 8,600 municipalities in Brazil, Chile, Ecuador, and Mexico. They find that optimal expenditures for a given quality of services are obtained for high population densities (around 9,000 persons per square kilometer). The authors also find that coverage is strongly and positively associated with population density. Urban planning for higher density and lower land consumption can also decrease infrastructure costs, as further described below.

Urban fragmentation typically impedes public transport and other public services, because minimum densities are needed for those infrastructures to be viable. In a compact city, households are not only close to facilities (such as hospitals) but also likely to enjoy more facilities per capita. Localized

public services (again, such as hospitals) require a minimum density to be economically viable (Burton 2000a). So compact cities present some advantages, especially for low-income households, many of whom lack access to a car and would find public transport to be more efficient in nonfragmented urban areas.

Newman (1992) has provided strong evidence that higher-density cities are associated with higher use of public transportation. Such impact also inherently promotes social equity, because the disadvantaged rely primarily on public transportation. And although the investment needed to build public transport is high, the usage costs, provided sufficient ridership, are low compared with large road infrastructure. Rode et al. (2017) show that although the up-front costs of collective transportation infrastructure are on the same order of magnitude as—or even higher than—the costs of high-capacity highways, collective transportation has the edge when cost estimates take carrying capacity into account. Capital costs divided per capita (after dividing by capacity) would be in the range of US\$300–US\$500 for a bus rapid transit system, compared with US\$5,000–US\$10,000 for a dual-lane highway.

Finally, it is widely argued that compact cities offer more opportunities for social interaction and reduce segregation. Compactness encourages interaction between urban dwellers from different economic strata and origins (locals and migrants). Sprawling development, characterized by scattered gated communities or informal development in the peri-urban region, tends to increase residential segregation (Zhao 2013). This sometimes gets reinforced by unevenly distributed public services and unbalanced investments.

## Do the region's cities truly function as cities?

Can cities in the Middle East and North Africa qualify as well functioning? Arguably, a primary raison d'être of cities is to reduce the economic distance between people and economic opportunities and to reduce the costs of providing networked basic services.

Cities thrive, in particular, because they enable matchmaking—between people, between firms, and between people and job opportunities (Avner and Lall 2016). With this framework in mind, we ask whether cities in the Middle East and North Africa enable matching and provide networked infrastructure at reduced costs. In other words, are cities in the Middle East and North Africa functioning as efficient cities?

Cities' urban footprints and fragmentation vary considerably. Using satellite imagery, this section examines the growth patterns of the region's urban areas and their degree of spatial fragmentation. Fragmentation is approached here through two different metrics: (a) the interaction potential index (hereafter called the Puga index), which measures fragmentation in the spatial distribution of the urban population; and (b) the noncontiguity index, which measures spatial fragmentation in the urban built environment.

The Puga index was calculated for the capital cities of the Middle East and North Africa using a methodology that measures the number of people an average person can interact with in a specific city within a given travel distance (De la Roca and Puga 2017).[7] The results show important gaps in many cases. For example, while Casablanca and Baghdad display fairly concentrated population patterns with high interaction potential, Amman and Tripoli rank much lower in terms of interaction potential because of their more linear layout with higher fragmentation (figure 1.6). In Amman and Baghdad, although low-density informal settlements have contributed to urban expansion, the urban footprint of each city largely results from long-term urban patterns. Amman's linear layout reflects

**FIGURE 1.6** **Fragmentation varies significantly across urban areas in several capital cities in the Middle East and North Africa**

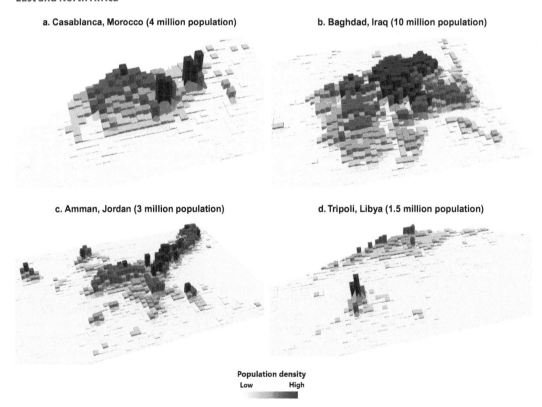

a. Casablanca, Morocco (4 million population)

b. Baghdad, Iraq (10 million population)

c. Amman, Jordan (3 million population)

d. Tripoli, Libya (1.5 million population)

Population density

Low          High

*Source:* Developed from LandScan Global 2012 dataset, Oak Ridge National Laboratory, https://landscan.ornl.gov/.
*Note:* Fragmentation is represented here by the distribution of population within urban areas. (Each square represents population density per square kilometer.)

largely the growth of Zarqa, the industrial town on the northeast side of the city.

Although Middle East and North Africa cities display average potential for interaction compared with other regions, its subregions have high variations (figure 1.7).[8] On average, controlling only for population, an individual living in a city of 2 million inhabitants in the Middle East and North Africa is exposed to around 1.13 million people—which, taking confidence intervals into account, is below South Asia's potential for interaction and not significantly different from East Asia's or Sub-Saharan Africa's.

However, the interaction potential is significantly lower in Organisation for Economic Co-operation and Development (OECD) countries and in Latin America and the Caribbean. Among the subregions, the Mashreq displays a relatively high potential for interaction (exceeding 1.5 million), while the GCC and Maghreb subregions lag behind.

The Maghreb subregion's high intraurban fragmentation—with lower interaction potential than in the comparator subregions—increases the costs of providing networked infrastructure. This high urban fragmentation (as measured by the Puga

**FIGURE 1.7   The Middle East and North Africa as a whole displays average interaction potential compared with other regions but varies widely by subregion**

*Interaction potential, controlling for population, by region and subregion*

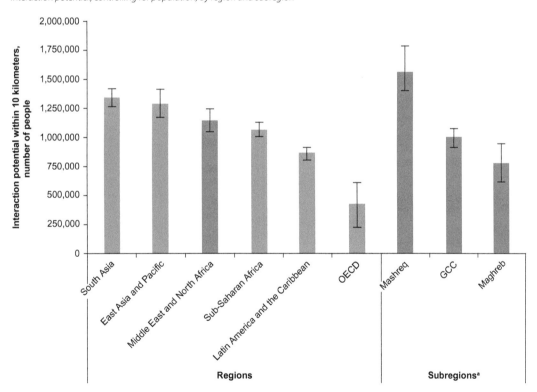

*Sources:* World Bank calculations using the European Commission Joint Research Centre's Global Human Settlement Layers 2014; Henderson and Nigmatulina 2016.
*Note:* OECD = Organisation for Economic Co-operation and Development. "Interaction potential" is measured here as the number of people an average person can interact with in a specific city within 10 kilometers. (The selected cities include the primary [largest] city of each country and, depending on data availability, all cities above 500,000.) As the Puga index equation illustrates (annex 1B), an increase in a city's population mechanically increases the index of interaction potential. Therefore, to compare several cities, it was necessary to control for at least the city population (the T-bars indicating the confidence intervals controlling for population). As such, the method used to produce the graph consisted of predictions from the statistical model based on the Henderson and Nigmatulina (2016) methodology, setting city population at 2.019 million and controlling for city population.
a. Maghreb refers to Algeria, Libya, Morocco, and Tunisia; Mashreq to the Arab Republic of Egypt, Iraq, Jordan, Lebanon, and the Syrian Arab Republic; and the Gulf Cooperation Council (GCC) to Bahrain, Kuwait, Oman, Qatar, Saudi Arabia, and the United Arab Emirates.

index, controlling for population) indicates low-density or leapfrogged urban fabrics. To service such urban areas with networked infrastructure (roads, electricity, sewerage, and water) is typically costlier per capita, for a given service quality, because it requires longer and more intricate networks.

In financially constrained urban areas, these high costs may be difficult to match with resources and can lead to a decrease in service quality. Prospective scenario modeling exercises in Jordan, for example, find that future urban growth patterns significantly affect the costs of providing infrastructure. Comparing a business-as-usual urban growth scenario with one that implements Amman's master plan and results in lower

land consumption, CAPSUS (2018) finds that implementing the master plan would decrease new infrastructure costs by 42 percent (from JD 231.67 million to JD 135.23 million).[9] The Jordan study is a partial costing exercise of urban development trajectories—partial because it does not account for the barriers to accessing jobs, for example.

Urban fragmentation can also hinder accessibility to labor market opportunities (by lengthening trips and travel times), but higher investments in transportation seem to compensate for this effect in the Middle East and North Africa. When controlling for both GDP and population, the Puga index results tell a different story than when controlling for population alone (figure 1.8).

**FIGURE 1.8** **Gulf Cooperation Council countries seem to compensate for their urban fragmentation with lower commuting costs**

*Interaction potential, controlling for population and GDP per capita, by region and subregion*

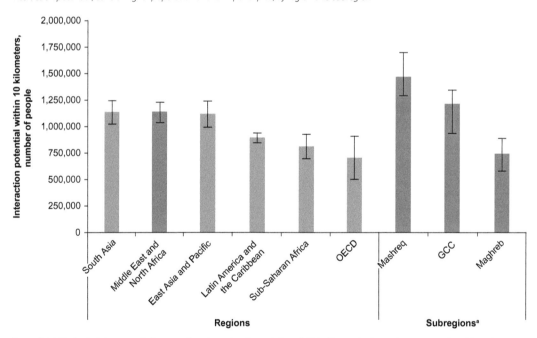

*Sources:* World Bank calculations using the European Commission Joint Research Centre's Global Human Settlement Layers 2014 and World Development Indicators database; Henderson and Nigmatulina 2016.
*Note:* OECD = Organisation for Economic Co-operation and Development. "Interaction potential" is measured here as the number of people an average person can interact with in a specific city within 10 kilometers. (The selected cities include the primary [largest] city of each country and, depending on data availability, all cities above 500,000.) As the Puga index equation illustrates (annex 1B), an increase in a city's population mechanically increases the index of interaction potential. Therefore, to compare several cities, it was necessary to control for both city population and gross domestic product (GDP) (the T-bars indicating the confidence intervals controlling for population and GDP per capita). Predictions for representative cities—from the statistical model based on the Henderson and Nigmatulina (2016) methodology—set the city population at 2.019 million inhabitants and GDP per capita at US$4,280 as a proxy for commuting costs (averages of the sample cities in the Middle East and North Africa).
a. Maghreb refers to Algeria, Libya, Morocco, and Tunisia; Mashreq to the Arab Republic of Egypt, Iraq, Jordan, Lebanon, and the Syrian Arab Republic; and the Gulf Cooperation Council (GCC) to Bahrain, Kuwait, Oman, Qatar, Saudi Arabia, and the United Arab Emirates.

Although the difference between the Middle East and North Africa and most regions remains or becomes insignificant (apart from Latin America and the Caribbean, Sub-Saharan Africa, and the OECD countries), the subregional picture changes: the interaction potential decreases in the Maghreb and Mashreq countries, but it strongly increases in the GCC countries—from about 1 million potential interactions (figure 1.7) to about 1.2 million (figure 1.8). As such, the difference in potential interactions between the GCC and Mashreq subregions becomes less significant, and the gap between GCC and the Maghreb subregion increases significantly.

This change occurs because countries with higher GDP tend to display high urban fragmentation, as their populations can afford higher commuting costs than those in lower-income countries. Therefore, the richest countries compensate for urban dispersion with faster transport within cities. Adding GDP as a control (in addition to population) is a proxy for increased motorized mode shares (that is, higher shares of people driving instead of walking) and accounts for the compensation of faster transport for more fragmented urban fabrics.

Similarly, an urban footprint analysis shows that the Mashreq subregion has the lowest noncontiguity, which is a measure of built-up spatial fragmentation. (See annex 1B for methodology.) When controlling for city size, the urban footprint noncontiguity of cities of around 2 million inhabitants in the GCC is twice as high as in the Mashreq subregion and 30 percent higher than in the Maghreb subregion. However, when controlling for both city population size and GDP per capita, the difference between subregions disappears. This reinforces the conclusion that the Mashreq subregion displays the lowest fragmentation and that the GCC subregion compensates for its fragmentation through lower commuting costs.

## Subregional differences reflect tension between modernist urban planning theory and the traditional "compact city"

The subregional differences embody a much larger tension between two paradigms: the modernist approach to urban planning and the return of the "compact city" pattern. Many historians point to the medieval Arab cities (such as Fes in Morocco and Aleppo in Syria) as supreme representations of dense, compact, and livable urban centers. In the past century, those urban systems progressively became representations of underdeveloped urban systems as modernist planning theory prevailed, focusing on urban functional segregation, private car orientation, and low-density spatial layouts—the international norm. However, many unforeseen impacts of the modernist city such as depopulated centers, traffic congestion, urban air pollution, or fragmentation have led Western planners and urban theorists to rediscover the viability of compact cities.

The compact city concept, however, is still not one of the drivers of most of today's planners in the Middle East and North Africa, and many countries have taken the modernist planning theory to its extreme. Gulf cities are among the greatest examples. Abu Dhabi, United Arab Emirates, for example, displays a very fragmented urban fabric (photo 1.1, panel a) of modern low-density neighborhoods, such as the Mohammed Bin Zayed City neighborhood (photo 1.1, panel b). Even downtown areas of GCC countries created in the 1950s and 1960s are being pulled down and replaced with large business buildings surrounded by parking garages and vacant lots.

Similarly, in Egypt, a strategy was implemented in the 1970s based on the construction of functionally segregated and isolated new towns (photo 1.1, panel c), which ended up attracting few people. New Cairo, built on the southeastern edge of Cairo Governorate, is a good example (photo 1.1, panel d). In Morocco, the state developer Omrane has been proceeding to construct satellite dormitory towns miles away from

PHOTO 1.1 **Developments in or near the capitals of United Arab Emirates and Egypt represent modernist urban planning theory**

**a. Aerial image of fragmented urban fabric in Abu Dhabi**

**b. Aerial image of Abu Dhabi's Mohammed Bin Zayed City neighborhood**

**c. Aerial image showing New Cairo's isolation from Cairo metropolitan area**

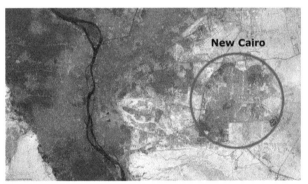

**d. Aerial image of detail of New Cairo's layout**

*Source:* Google Earth 2018.

existing cities. Although wealthy countries compensate for fragmentation with lower commuting costs, the trend creates many problematic aspects, as discussed earlier, such as providing urban public services.

## Informality stitches gaps in the urban fabric

Nonetheless, in some Middle East and North Africa countries, informal settlements have been constituting a new path to emerging compact neighborhoods. Although informal settlements are considered as overcrowded and illegal, in many cities, they are dense, inclusive, energy-efficient, and multifunctional urban neighborhoods, displaying spatial patterns similar to medieval historic

centers (photo 1.2). In Cairo, for example, although the informal neighborhood of Fostat Plateau was established in the 1980s (photo 1.2, panel a.2), its structure is very similar to the neighborhood of Bab el Wazir, established more than 800 years ago (photo 1.2, panel a.1).

In 2010, in Greater Cairo alone, 12 million inhabitants lived in informal areas, and 75 percent of the demographic increase found homes in informal areas. Informal neighborhoods in other cities have been stitching gaps in the urban fabric as well, filling vacant or abandoned spaces. Still, this does not mean that urban informality is the desired future of the Arab city, but rather that urban dwellers are rejecting the modernist city and that urban planners must consider

PHOTO 1.2    **Aerial views show that, in density and spatial patterns, recent informal settlements highly resemble historic districts across several cities of the Middle East and North Africa**

### a. Cairo, Egypt

a.1 Bab el Wazir (established 800 years ago)

a.2 Fostat Plateau (established informally in the 1980s)

### b. Beirut, Lebanon

b.1 Beirut historic center

b.2 Jnah slum

### c. Rabat, Morocco

c.1 Rabat historic center

c.2 Douar el Garaa slum

*photo continues next page*

**PHOTO 1.2**   **Aerial views show that, in density and spatial patterns, recent informal settlements highly resemble historic districts across several cities of the Middle East and North Africa** *(continued)*

**d. Tyre, Lebanon**

d.1 Tyre historic center

d.2 Borj el Chmali (West Bank and Gaza settlement)

*Sources:* UN-Habitat 2012; Google Earth 2018.

---

**BOX 1.2**   **The impact of Lebanon's civil war on Beirut's urban form**

In 1975, violence erupted in the streets of Beirut, and in a matter of days, the city became a battlefield, with clashes among different Lebanese factions and global political players. The urban warfare continued almost uninterrupted for the next 15 years and resulted in massive destruction and widespread displacement of people. The city eventually became divided between Christians and Muslims—and the city center, once cosmopolitan and vibrant, became an uninhabited green buffer between the rivals.

Each community started gathering in its respective sector of the city, and economic activity progressively shifted from the center to the community sectors (Hanna 2016). This resulted a few decades later in a polycentric city with three centers: the traditional center, the Christian sector, and the Muslim sector (figure B1.2.1).

**FIGURE B1.2.1**   **After decades of conflict, Beirut became a polycentric city**

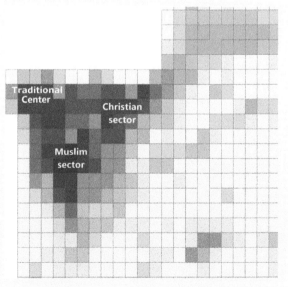

*Source:* Hanna 2016.
*Note:* The darker the square, the higher the population density.

readapting their framework for higher efficiency and welfare (UN-Habitat 2012).

Informal neighborhoods, being similar in structure to the medieval historic centers of Middle East and North Africa cities, display much denser road lengths and intersections, characterizing higher compactness. In a subset of 20 historic centers and informal neighborhoods in the region, the road density is on average higher than 40 kilometers per square kilometer, and intersection density is higher than 300 per square kilometer. In contrast, modernist neighborhoods (such as New Cairo) have an average road density of 27 kilometers per square kilometer and intersection density of 131 per square kilometer (figure 1.9). (For the methodology used to compute road intersection density, see annex 1C.)

## Urban spatial expansion is trending toward compactness in the Mashreq, less so in other subregions

The trend of compactness has been especially strong in the Mashreq subregion. Between 1990 and 2014, the urban population increased four times quicker than the built-up areas in Mashreq capitals, which highlights a strong densification. By comparison, the urban population has increased on average only 1.3 times quicker than built-up expansion in the Maghreb subregion, which implies that Maghreb cities have been densifying more slowly.[10] The Mashreq's faster densification can be linked to its higher urban population growth and strong migratory flows to the cities generated by conflict and lack of economic opportunities.

Based on the methodology developed by Liu et al. (2010) and used in Baruah, Henderson, and Peng (2017), we classified the 1990–2014 urban expansion in the capital cities of each subregion (with the exception of Casablanca, which we used for Morocco instead of Rabat) in the three following categories: infill, extension, and leapfrog. As expected, the Mashreq countries showed the largest share of infill expansion (28 percent) and the lowest share of leapfrogging (3.7 percent) compared with the two other regions (figure 1.10).[11]

FIGURE 1.9 **In the Middle East and North Africa, historic centers and informal neighborhoods display higher road and intersection density than modernist neighborhoods**

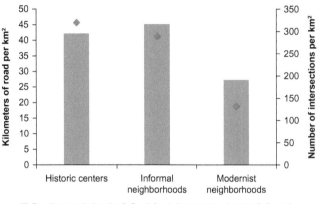

Legend: ■ Road network density (left axis)  ◆ Intersection density (left axis)

*Source:* World Bank calculations based on OpenStreetMap data 2018, available under the Open Data Commons Open Database License (ODbL) by the *OpenStreetMap* Foundation.
*Note:* km² = square kilometer.

FIGURE 1.10 **Aggregated urban expansion trends in capital cities in the Mashreq, Maghreb, and GCC subregions show divergent patterns, 1990–2014**

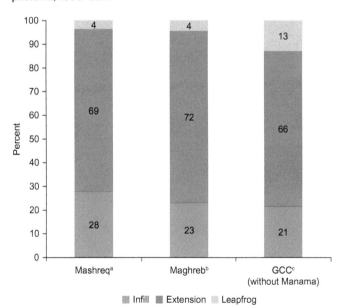

Legend: ■ Infill  ■ Extension  ▨ Leapfrog

*Sources:* Datasets from the European Commission Joint Research Centre's Global Human Settlement Layers. See Annex 1D for sensitivity analysis.
*Note:* The analysis uses the Landscape Expansion Index developed by Liu et al. (2010), in which extension and leapfrog expansion increase infrastructure costs, with leapfrog having a higher cost impact.
a. Mashreq comprises the Arab Republic of Egypt, Iraq, Jordan, Lebanon, and the Syrian Arab Republic.
b. Maghreb comprises Algeria, Libya, Morocco, and Tunisia. For Morocco, Casablanca was analyzed instead of the capital city, Rabat.
c. GCC = Gulf Cooperation Council, comprising Bahrain, Kuwait, Oman, Qatar, Saudi Arabia, and the United Arab Emirates. Manama, the capital of Bahrain, was excluded because of the bias created by its geographical constraints and resulting in an exceptionally high share of infill urban expansion.

The divergence between the Mashreq and GCC subregions corresponds to the consequences of extensive modernist urban planning policies in GCC cities and trends of compactness in the Mashreq subregion. The larger shares of extension in the Maghreb and leapfrogging in the GCC subregion reflect the trends previously highlighted in our analysis of noncontiguity and interaction potential.

However, the cities of the same subregion vary in their development patterns. Although each subregion, on average, displays different trends, some countries display distributions similar to the averages from other subregions (figure 1.11). For example, in the GCC subregion, the cities of Riyadh and Manama display relatively high shares of infill and low shares of leapfrog expansion. In the case of Manama, this is the consequence of high geographical constraints considering that the

city growth is constrained and contained because of its location on the peninsula of the island. Similarly, Tunis and Casablanca in the Maghreb subregion have higher shares of infill expansion than Cairo, Damascus, and Amman in the Mashreq subregion.

These variations within subregions and city-specific scenarios often reflect discrete place-based policy interventions (map 1.1). For example, in Cairo, a large share of extension can be attributed to a government policy: the construction of New Cairo, a settlement on the east side of the city created to unclog downtown Cairo. In Dubai, the leapfrog and extension patches at the south and southwest of the city can also be attributed to the government's industrial policy through which the Dubai Investments Park was created in 1997, which in turn incentivized the placement of industries around the urban area.

**FIGURE 1.11  The urban expansion of Middle East and North Africa capital cities varies within subregions, 1990–2014**

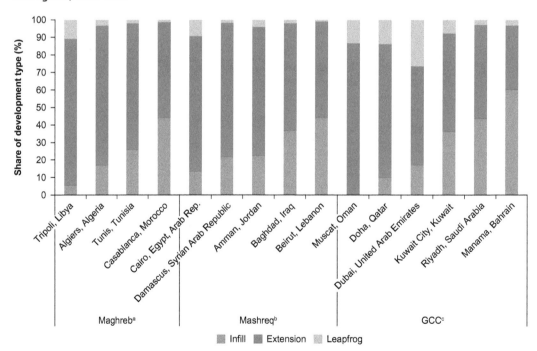

*Source:* Datasets from the European Commission Joint Research Centre's Global Human Settlement Layers.
*Note:* Uses the Landscape Expansion Index developed by Liu et al. (2010), in which extension and leapfrog expansion increase infrastructure costs, with leapfrog having a higher cost impact.
a. Maghreb comprises Algeria, Libya, Morocco, and Tunisia. For Morocco, Casablanca was analyzed instead of the capital city, Rabat.
b. Mashreq comprises the Arab Republic of Egypt, Iraq, Jordan, Lebanon, and the Syrian Arab Republic.
c. GCC = Gulf Cooperation Council, comprising Bahrain, Kuwait, Oman, Qatar, Saudi Arabia, and the United Arab Emirates. Manama, the capital of Bahrain, was excluded because of the bias created by its geographical constraints and resulting in an exceptionally high share of infill urban expansion.

MAP 1.1    **Visual representations of urban expansion show the extent of development, by type, in selected Middle East and North Africa capitals, 1990–2014**

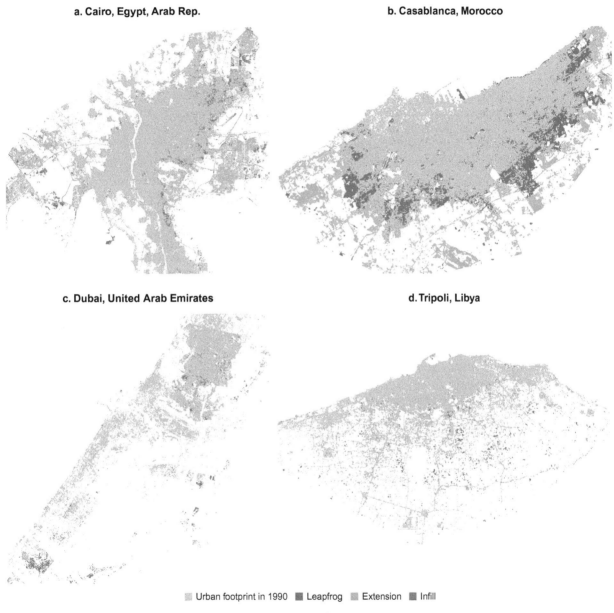

**a. Cairo, Egypt, Arab Rep.**

**b. Casablanca, Morocco**

**c. Dubai, United Arab Emirates**

**d. Tripoli, Libya**

Urban footprint in 1990    Leapfrog    Extension    Infill

*Source:* Datasets from the European Commission Joint Research Centre's Global Human Settlement Layers.

## Urban fragmentation and sprawl foster socioeconomic segregation, with broad consequences

Urban sprawl and spatial fragmentation are linked to social segregation, while urban compactness is found to reduce this phenomenon.[12]

The positive impact of urban compactness on social interaction and the reduction of segregation has been documented in several studies. As Burton (2000b) stated, "Lower levels of social segregation are more strongly associated with higher housing density than with any intervening variable." As such, social segregation can decrease with a dense urban form, where the communities are more mixed and not spatially segregated (Burton 2001).[13] However, the link between urban form and the extent of segregation has mostly been demonstrated in high-income countries.

Spatial fragmentation is intertwined with social and economic dimensions that foster segregation. Space is a critical factor when seeking to make cities more inclusive because it is a core determinant of either segregation or inclusion. Usually, socially and economically marginalized groups inhabit physically deprived spaces, where basic infrastructure is lacking and economic opportunities are distant (World Bank 2009a). Often these populations live in informal settlements.

Urban land underpins the spatial dimension of segregation. Informal land development occurs because formal land options are unaffordable or inconveniently situated and public housing is too isolated (Serageldin 2016). This situation exacerbates a lack of access to basic services and amenities as well as difficulties in accessing economic opportunities.

The broader consequences of exclusion for urban areas or even at the national level raise a wide set of concerns for democracy, crime, and economic growth (Shah et al. 2015). The social and economic exclusion of low-income populations may render governments unable to act in the interest of all, including segregated people, because of the social distance between those populations and decision makers. The policies implemented will probably not favor those populations, consequently increasing inequality and undermining democratic and participatory processes. Besides, the feeling of being left out, polarization, and spatial segregation are root causes of violence and crime in urban areas. In Honduras, where 54 percent of the urban population is poor, social exclusion and a lack of public services and economic opportunities underlie violence. Such conditions affect social interactions and economic growth, directly influencing the investment climate and business opportunities (Shah et al. 2015).

For individuals, the lack of opportunities and the spatial and skills mismatch limit members of the marginalized population to low-paying or informal jobs with unstable income streams (World Bank 2009a). Lack of a formal address or identity may preclude access to formal jobs, while lack of education and poor health can also restrict access to higher-paying jobs. Additionally, unaffordable transit fares and lack of connection to the public transportation network further suppress access to economic opportunities. Low incomes and multiple necessary expenditures leave individuals and households with a very limited capacity to save or invest and little ability to withstand shocks (Shah et al. 2015).

Within cities, the proliferation of informal settlements has resulted in more pressure on urban infrastructure and less access to health, sanitation, and public services for newcomers. Except in the GCC "city-states" (Bahrain, Kuwait, and Qatar), cities in the Middle East and North Africa have fragile urban administrations, with urban services often overwhelmed by the needs of growing populations. Slums and informal settlements have proliferated in almost all cities except the urban centers of the GCC city-states.

Given the region's instability, many cities have been receiving increasing numbers of refugees and IDPs and are becoming increasingly "campified" (box 1.3) The Manshiet Nasser neighborhood in Cairo, for example, is home to 1 million inhabitants living in poverty under precarious conditions. Similarly, large parts of the Beirut suburbs have become informal settlements predominantly housing refugees, IDPs, and lower-economic-strata nationals. People living in these settlements suffer systemically from poor access to health care and poor housing quality, according to research from the American University of Beirut (Yassin 2016).

In Tunisia, most migrants from the interior to the coast, particularly to the Greater Tunis area, settle in peripheral urban neighborhoods, with associated higher commuting costs and often poorer access to services. Migrants to the coastal area have longer

## BOX 1.3 Refugee self-sorting and fragmentation in migration to urban areas

Migrants living outside camps tend to self-sort spatially into low-income neighborhoods with high access to services, creating a spatial and social divide between migrants and host communities. Refugees and internally displaced persons (IDPs) settle according to their economic and social preferences, which often differ from those of the host communities. These displaced populations usually sort into areas with high population density, high service availability, easy access to aid, high potential for employment in the informal sector, and high availability of informal housing. Thus, they tend to concentrate in low-income neighborhoods within cities and informal settlements close to the city center, where they can find informal jobs while enjoying lower rents than in the city center (World Bank 2017).

In Lebanon, however, refugees and IDPs living in standard housing have better access than the refugees living in informal neighborhoods (World Bank 2016), as found by sorting results in spatial segregation between refugee-majority neighborhoods and host communities. In Tripoli (Lebanon), the different

waves of refugees have been concentrating in the same neighborhoods. As such, Palestinian refugees from Syria and Syrian refugees have been concentrating in the same neighborhoods that were already inhabited by Palestinian refugees from Lebanon, who arrived before 2011 (see map B1.3.1).

Displaced populations are often forced to settle in parts of the city that were previously uninhabited. This is the consequence of several constraints such as high rents and housing shortages. The presence of refugees in urban areas has reportedly caused rent prices to increase so much, particularly in Amman, that some Jordanians cannot afford the higher rents (CAPSUS 2018; World Bank 2016). Refugees will therefore settle in informal settlements on the edges of urban areas in hazard-prone locations such as low-lying areas or landfill sites with substandard or unsanitary housing. This puts additional stress on urban services; increases the risk of conflict, exclusion, and competition; and worsens the potential for urban fragility (Zetter 2015; Zetter and Deikun 2010).

MAP B1.3.1 **Refugees are concentrating in three main neighborhoods in Tripoli, Lebanon, 2015**

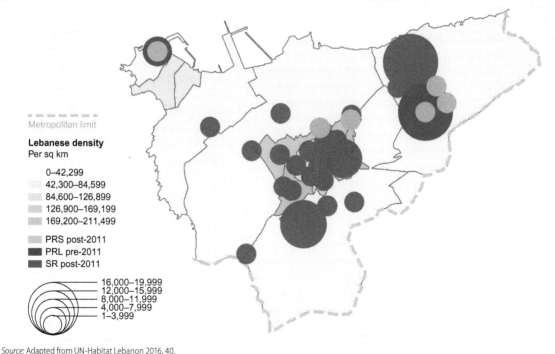

*Source:* Adapted from UN-Habitat Lebanon 2016, 40.
*Note:* PRS = Palestinian refugees from Syria. PRL = Palestinian refugees from Lebanon. SR = Syrian refugees. Syrian refugees are presented by location as registered with the United Nations Refugee Agency (UNHCR) as of May 31, 2015.

commutes than workers who remain in the interior. They also have longer commutes, on average, than longer-term residents on the coast. Migrants often live in areas with less access to basic services than the areas serving longer-term residents (but comparable access to that of inhabitants in the interior of the country). The widespread perception that migrants to the coast are disadvantaged compared with longer-term residents may restrain migration from the country's lagging regions to its leading ones (World Bank 2013).

As this discussion suggests, spatial segregation is a vicious circle, since lack of access to basic services impedes future prospects for earnings and upward mobility. Although documentation of this dynamic is scarce in the Middle East and North Africa region, extensive studies in the United States show that to partially overcome the handicaps posed by racial segregation,[14] one of the most powerful tools is access to good schools, which are usually located in wealthier parts of urban areas (Fryer and Katz 2013).

## Concluding remarks

As this chapter has established, urban areas in the Middle East and North Africa region display high potential for interaction when population and wealth are controlled for. This means that they are acting as cities, enabling people to meet and exchange and allowing labor markets to function adequately. However, when only population is accounted for, they show high fragmentation, implying larger costs to provide infrastructure, which could lead to low coverage rates in fiscally constrained settings.

There are also large differences across the region, with cities in the Maghreb subregion comparing unfavorably in terms of interaction potential and built-up contiguity to other subregions of the Middle East and North Africa and even of Sub-Saharan Africa when only demographics are accounted for. Cities in the Mashreq and, to a lesser extent, the GCC countries show lower noncontiguity and leapfrog development patterns than in the Maghreb, limiting the costs of providing

infrastructure and reducing the risk that urban areas will be underserved.

Two contrary forces seem to be at play in the Mashreq urban areas: First, informal settlements *limit* urban noncontiguity by being located in central areas. Second, however, urban policies aiming to decongest the large urban areas *increase* noncontiguity by choosing to develop areas far from current urban footprints, increasing infrastructure provision costs. The fragmentation of urban space segregates marginalized populations, reducing welfare outcomes and contributing to a vicious circle that traps households in poverty.

## Annex 1A Methodology for calculating the agglomeration index

The agglomeration index is the first measure allowing comparisons of urban concentration across countries using a common definition. It is based on a uniform definition of what constitutes an "urban" or agglomerated area, using the technique elaborated in Uchida and Nelson (2008). The United Nations maintains the World Urbanization Prospects database, a treasure trove of information on urban areas that provides urban shares and population data for 229 countries back to 1950.[15] But these data are based on country definitions, which can differ greatly. The agglomeration index adjusts these data to make them comparable.

The agglomeration index is calculated using the following steps:

- *Specify thresholds.* To be classified as "urban," an area must satisfy three criteria: (a) minimum population size used to define a sizable settlement, (b) minimum population density, and (c) maximum travel time, by road, to the sizable settlement.
- *Locate the centers of sizable settlements.* This mapping is done for cities that meet the minimum population size criterion, using data from the Global Rural-Urban Mapping Project (GRUMP)

human settlements database produced by the National Aeronautics and Space Administration's (NASA) Socioeconomic Data and Applications Center (SEDAC).

- *Determine the sizable settlement's border.* The border surrounding a sizable settlement center is calculated based on the maximum travel time to the center.
- *Create population density grids.* These are created at a 1 kilometer spatial resolution using two global grid-based population data sources: GRUMP and LandScan (of the Oak Ridge National Laboratory).
- *Identify the areas.* Identify the grid cells that satisfy thresholds for all three criteria.
- *Aggregate grid cell populations.* The result is analogous to urban population. The ratio of this number to that country's total population is the agglomeration index, a summary measure of the proportion of the population living in areas of high density.

This report uses the results presented in *the World Development Report 2009* (World Bank 2009b). To calculate the index for the *World Development Report 2009*, a base set of thresholds was used: 50,000 for minimum population size of a settlement, 150 people per square kilometer for population density, and 60 minutes for travel time to the nearest large city. The density and travel time thresholds are those employed in Chomitz, Buys, and Thomas (2005). The density threshold is the same as the one used by the OECD.

## Annex 1B Methodology for developing indicators of urban form

### Measuring the interaction potential

The interaction potential between people is measured through an indicator, the Puga index, developed by De la Roca and Puga (2017). The number of people within a given radius (here, 10 kilometers) is calculated for each pixel of built-up area. The Puga index over the city is a sum of these pixel-level indexes, weighted by the fraction of the total population living in each pixel area, as follows:

$$Puga_{10} = \sum_i \frac{n_i}{N} \sum_j n_j \left( d_{ij} < 10km \right), \quad (1B.1)$$

where $n$ represents the population of a pixel area; $N$ represents the total population in the urban area; $i$ represents the pixel area for which the population residing within a 10 kilometer radius is calculated; $j$ represents the other pixels; and $d_{ij}$ represents the distance between pixels $i$ and $j$. The condition $d_{ij} < 10km$ returns a binary value of 0 or 1 to enable accounting for or eliminating people living within or outside of the 10 kilometer radius of a given pixel.

### Measuring the contiguity or leapfrogging of urban development

The contiguity of urban development—or more precisely its opposite, noncontiguity—aims to quantify the phenomenon of leapfrogging, a measure of the fragmentation of built-up area proposed by Amindarbari and Sevtsuk (2013). The measure accounts for (a) the number of isolated built-up patches, and (b) their relative size. The higher the number of isolated built-up patches, the higher the noncontiguity (or fragmentation). The size of the isolated patches is also important: the larger the isolated patches, the higher the fragmentation. An urban area with four isolated patches of the same size would be more fragmented than one with a single large isolated patch and three much smaller ones.

The noncontiguity of urban development is calculated as follows:

$$DI = \sum_{n=1}^{N} \left( \frac{\sum_{i=n+1}^{N} A_i}{A_n} \right) \left( \frac{\sum_{i=n}^{N} A_i}{A_{total}} \right), \quad (1B.2)$$

where $DI$ is the discontinuity index; $N$ is the number of isolated patches; $A_n$ is the area of urban patch $n$; and $A_{total}$ is the total surface of the built-up area.

Urban isolated patches are sorted by their surface areas in decreasing order. Therefore $A_1$ is the surface area of the largest urban patch so that the first right-hand term in the equation measures, for example, the ratio between surface areas of the second and the first patches (ordered by size).

## Annex 1C Methodology for analyzing road and intersection densities

The analysis was executed using the OSMnx library, which enables downloading of OpenStreetMap (OSM) data and calculation of a set of statistics.

The neighborhoods were selected based on existing literature and qualitative observation of satellite imagery (table 1C.1).

## Annex 1D Comparison of Global Human Settlement Layers and Global Urban Footprint datasets

The analysis of urban built-up area was based on the European Commission's Global Human Settlement Layers (GHSL) dataset, which uses optical sensors technology. This dataset was chosen because data are available for multiple years (1975, 1990, 2000, and 2014), which enables comparing built-up areas over time.

However, some anomalies appeared in the identification of urban built-up areas when specific surfaces were analyzed. To identify those anomalies, the data were compared with another dataset, the German Aerospace Center's Global Urban Footprint (GUF), which is only available for 2011. The GUF dataset uses radar technology, which enables more precise and accurate detection of urban built-up areas.

Comparing both datasets reveals that some cities suffer from much larger anomalies than others (map 1D.1). For example, although the GHSL and GUF layers align in Casablanca, there are wide disparities in Cairo. The following recurrent anomalies were detected:

- The GHSL layer tends to overestimate built-up areas, identifying wider areas than the GUF dataset and sometimes specific open areas within the city (such as the airport in Cairo).
- In many cases, rivers crossing through cities are incorrectly identified as built-up areas in the GHSL dataset (such as the Nile River in Cairo).

When possible, those anomalies were corrected manually. For example, built-up area associated with the Nile River in Cairo was erased before running the analysis. However, it is important to highlight that any anomalies that could not be corrected (such as the overestimation of random built-up areas) might result in moderate margins of error in the analysis.

TABLE 1C.1 **Selected neighborhoods for analysis of road and intersection densities in the Middle East and North Africa**

| City | Historic center | Informal neighborhood | Modernist neighborhood |
|------|-----------------|----------------------|------------------------|
| Cairo, Egypt, Arab Rep. | Bab el Wazir | Fostat | New Cairo |
| Abu Dhabi, United Arab Emirates | n.a. | n.a. | Mohammed Bin Zayed |
| Dubai, United Arab Emirates | n.a. | n.a. | Al Warqa 2 |
| Beirut, Lebanon | Bourj Abi Haydar | Borj-el Barajneh | Jnah |
| Rabat, Morocco | Medina | Kariat | Secteur 10 |
| Tripoli, Libya | Old City | Al Hadba Al Khadra | Asahabah |
| Tunis, Tunisia | Ez-Zitouna | Cité Khalid Ibn al-Walid | El Mourouj 5 |
| Amman, Jordan | Ras al-Ain | Awajan | Al Zohour |

*Source:* Compilation based on Google Earth.
*Note:* n.a. = not applicable.

**MAP 1D.1** **Comparison of Global Human Settlement Layers and Global Urban Footprint datasets for Cairo and Casablanca, 2016**

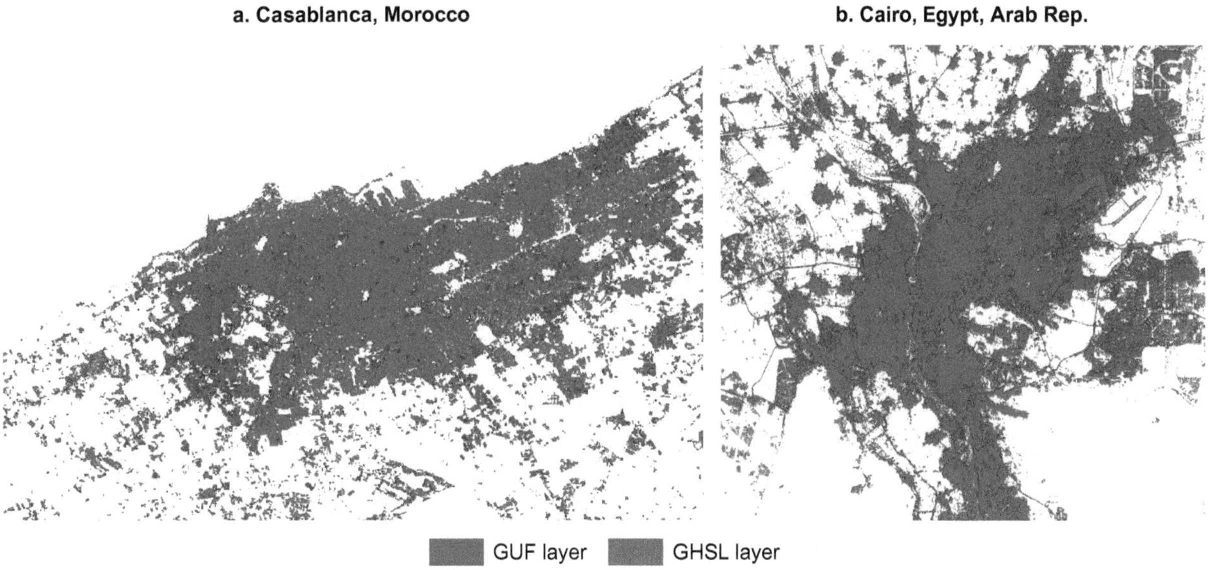

a. Casablanca, Morocco                          b. Cairo, Egypt, Arab Rep.

GUF layer          GHSL layer

*Sources:* European Commission Joint Research Centre's Global Human Settlement Layers 2015 and German Aerospace Center's Global Urban Footprint 2016 datasets.
*Note:* GHSL = Global Human Settlement Layers. GUF = Global Urban Footprint.

## Notes

1. In this report, the Maghreb refers to Algeria, Libya, Morocco, and Tunisia; the Mashreq to the Arab Republic of Egypt, Iraq, Jordan, Lebanon, the Syrian Arab Republic, and West Bank and Gaza; and the Gulf Cooperation Council (GCC) to Bahrain, Kuwait, Oman, Qatar, Saudi Arabia, and the United Arab Emirates. Middle East and North Africa regional aggregates typically include all of these countries as well as Djibouti and the Republic of Yemen, with some notable exceptions.
2. Population data from the World Development Indicators database.
3. Urbanization here refers to the percentage of total population living in urban areas.
4. Refugee estimates from the United Nations High Commissioner for Refugees (UNHCR) 2018 data portal: http://reporting.unhcr.org /node/36.
5. Urbanization rates are from the World Development Indicators database: https:// data.worldbank.org/.
6. Urban primacy indicates the ratio of the primate city to the next largest (that is, the

second largest) in a country or region. In other words, urban primacy can be defined as the central place in an *urban* or city network that has acquired or obtained a great level of dominance.
7. The urban form indicators used in this chapter are discussed in annex 1B.
8. By replicating the methodology established by Henderson and Nigmatulina (2016), we analyze the difference in fragmentation controlling first for city size (population) and then for both city size and national GDP per capita (which is used as a proxy for commuting costs).
9. For the findings of the CAPSUS (2018) study, see the "Urban Growth Scenarios: Hashemite Kingdom of Jordan" website: http://jordan .capitalsustentable.com.mx/.
10. Densification figures were calculated using the European Commission Joint Research Centre's Global Human Settlement Layers datasets.
11. The LEI (Landscape Expansion Index)—a spatial metric developed by Liu et al. (2010)— enabled us to capture the information of the formation processes of a landscape pattern. Classification: 0 = Leapfrog, 0–50 = Extension, 50–100 = Infill.

12. "Segregation" in this chapter is interpreted as the opposite of inclusion (loosely based on Shah et al. [2015]): the marginalization of groups and individuals on the basis of socio-economic status, gender, age, caste, ethnicity, and other categories and where space acts as catalyst for such exclusion.

13. Compactness is also associated with negative effects, such as an increase in criminality (Burton 2001), which can produce contradictory effects. For example, in Mexico City, growing criminality and violence have deeply influenced social interactions. Privileged classes have abandoned public spaces, defected from public schools and health services, and are using the car for transport, which has resulted in a drastic reduction in interaction opportunities with strangers. All this has rendered multiclass interactions virtually nonexistent (Bayón, Saraví, and Breña 2013).

14. But *only* partially, as Chetty et al. (2018) show that, for black males in the United States, differences in upward mobility cannot be entirely explained by socioeconomic or spatial dimensions.

15. For the UN World Urbanization Prospects database, see https://population.un.org/wup/.

## References

Amindarbari, Reza, and Andres Sevtsuk. 2016. "Measuring Growth and Change in Metropolitan Form." Unpublished. Working Paper, City Form Lab, Massachusetts Institute of Technology, Cambridge, MA.

Avner, Paolo, and Somik V. Lall. 2016. "Matchmaking in Nairobi: The Role of Land Use." Policy Research Working Paper 7904, World Bank, Washington, DC.

Baruah, N., J. V. Henderson, and C. Peng. 2017. "Colonial Legacies: Shaping African Cities." Discussion Paper 226, Spatial Economics Research Centre, London School of Economics, London.

Bayón, M., G. Saraví, and M. Breña. 2013. "The Cultural Dimensions of Urban Fragmentation: Segregation, Sociability, and Inequality in Mexico City." *Latin American Perspectives* 40 (2): 35–52.

Bertaud, Alain. 2014. "Cities as Labor Markets." Working Paper 2, Marron Institute on Cities and the Urban Environment, New York University, New York.

Burchell, R. W., A. Downs, B. McCann, and S. Mukherji. 2005. *Sprawl Costs: Economic Impacts of Unchecked Development.* Washington, DC: Island Press.

Burton, E. 2000a. "The Compact City: Just or Just Compact? A Preliminary Analysis." *Urban Studies* 37 (11): 1969–2001.

———. 2000b. "The Potential of the Compact City for Promoting Social Equity." In *Achieving Sustainable Urban Form*, edited by K. Williams, E. Burton, and M. Jenks. Abingdon, U.K.: Routledge.

———. 2001. "The Compact City and Social Justice." Housing Studies Association Spring Conference, "Housing, Environment and Sustainability," University of York, April 18–19.

CAPSUS (CAPSUS Sustainable Capital). 2018. "Urban Growth Scenarios, Hashemite Kingdom of Jordan." Project brief for the World Bank, Washington, DC. http://jordan.capitalsustentable.com.mx/index.php/brief.

Chetty, Raj, Nathaniel Hendren, Maggie Jones, and Sonya Porter. 2018. "Race and Economic Opportunity in the United States: An Intergenerational Perspective." NBER Working Paper 24441, National Bureau of Economic Research, Cambridge, MA.

Chomitz, Kenneth M., Piet Buys, and Timothy S. Thomas. 2005. "Quantifying the Rural–Urban Gradient in Latin America and the Caribbean." Policy Research Working Paper 3634, World Bank, Washington, DC.

De la Roca, Jorge, and Diego Puga. 2017. "Learning by Working in Big Cities." *Review of Economic Studies* 84 (1): 106–42. doi:10.1093/restud/rdw031.

Fryer, Roland G., and Lawrence F. Katz. 2013. "Achieving Escape Velocity: Neighborhood and School Interventions to Reduce Persistent Inequality." *American Economic Review* 103 (3): 232–37. doi:10.1257/aer.103.3.232.

Hanna, J. 2016. "Changing Realities: Traumatic Urbanism as a Mode of Resilience in Intra-War Beirut." *International Planning History Society Proceedings* 17 (3): 383–88.

Henderson, V., and D. Nigmatulina. 2016. "The Fabric of African Cities: How to Think about Density and Land Use." Draft manuscript, London School of Economics.

Lall, Somik V., J. Vernon Henderson, and Anthony J. Venables. 2017. *Africa's Cities: Opening Doors to the World.* Washington, DC: World Bank. doi:10.1596/978-1-4648-1044-2.

Libertun de Duren, N., and R. Guerrero Compeán. 2016. "Growing Resources for Growing Cities: Density and the Cost of Municipal Public Services in Latin America." *Urban Studies* 53 (14): 3082–107. doi:10.1177/0042098015601579.

Liu, X., X. Li, Y. Chen, Z. Tan, S. Li, and S. Ai. 2010. "A New Landscape Index for Quantifying Urban Expansion Using Multi-Temporal Remotely Sensed Data." *Landscape Ecology* 25 (5): 671–82.

Newman, P. 1992. "The Compact City: An Australian Perspective." *Built Environment* 18 (4): 285–300.

Rode, Philipp, Graham Floater, Nikolas Thomopoulos, James Docherty, Peter Schwinger, Anjali Mahendra, and Wanli Fang. 2017. "Accessibility in Cities: Transport and Urban Form." In *Disrupting Mobility: Impacts of Sharing Economy and Innovative Transportation on Cities*, edited by Gereon Meyer and Susan Shaheen, 239–73. Cham, Switzerland: Springer International Publishing. doi:10.1007/978-3-319-51602-8_15.

Serageldin, Mona. 2016. "Inclusive Cities and Access to Land, Housing, and Services in Developing Countries." Urban Development Series Knowledge Papers 22, World Bank, Washington, DC.

Serageldin, Mona, François Vigier, and Maren Larsen. 2014. "World Migration Report 2015: Urban Migration Trends in the Middle East and North Africa Region and the Challenge of Conflict-Induced Displacement." Background paper, International Organization for Migration (IOM), Geneva.

Shah, Phoram, Ellen Hamilton, Fernando Armendaris, and Heejoo Lee. 2015. "World: Inclusive Cities Approach Paper." Report No. AUS8539, World Bank, Washington, DC.

Uchida, H., and A. Nelson. 2008. "Agglomeration Index: Towards a New Measure of Urban Concentration." Background paper for *World Development Report 2009: Reshaping Economic Geography*. Washington, DC: World Bank.

UN DESA (United Nations Department of Economic and Social Affairs). 2019. *UN Urbanization Prospects: The 2018 Revision.* New York: UN DESA.

UN-Habitat (United Nations Human Settlements Programme). 2012. *The State of Arab Cities 2012: Challenges of Urban Transition.* Nairobi, Kenya: UN-Habitat.

UNHCR (United Nations High Commissioner for Refugees). 2014. "2014 Syria Regional Response Plan: Strategic Overview." Sixth Syria Regional Response Plan, UNHCR, Geneva.

Venables, Anthony J. 2017. "Breaking into Tradables: Urban Form and Urban Function in a Developing City." *Journal of Urban Economics* 98 (March): 88–97. doi:10.1016/j.jue.2017.01.002.

World Bank. 2009a. "Systems of Cities: Harnessing Urbanization for Growth and Poverty Alleviation." Working Paper No. 51860, World Bank, Washington, DC.

———. 2009b. *World Development Report 2009: Reshaping Economic Geography*. Washington, DC: World Bank.

———. 2013. "Bridging the Spatial Divide: Labor Market Outcomes in Urban Tunisia." Survey report for the Republic of Tunisia, Report No. 89132, World Bank, Washington, DC.

———. 2016. "Syrians in the Middle East: The Lives and Livelihoods of Refugees and Their Hosts." Unpublished manuscript, World Bank, Washington, DC.

———. 2017. "Cities of Refuge in the Middle East: Bringing an Urban Lens to the Forced Displacement Challenge." Policy Note, Report No. 121515, World Bank, Washington, DC.

Yassin, N. 2016. "Urbanization in the Arab World: Between 'Dubaification' and 'Campification.'" *Human & Health* 35 (Spring 2016).

Zetter, R. 2015. "Protection in Crisis: Forced Migration and Protection in a Global Era." Report, TransAtlantic Council on Migration, Migration Policy Institute, Washington, DC.

Zetter, R., and G. Deikun. 2010. "Meeting Humanitarian Challenges in Urban Areas." *Forced Migration Review* 34 (February 2010): 5–7.

Zhao, P. 2013. "The Impact of Urban Sprawl on Social Segregation in Beijing and a Limited Role for Spatial Planning." *Journal of Economic and Social Geography* 104 (5): 571–87.

# Unequal Spaces and Stuck People | 2

While variation across space is a feature of development the world over, the Middle East and North Africa displays greater spatial disparity than expected. Cities and regions in a country will vary in their productivity and the average income produced within their boundaries, but as countries' per capita gross domestic product (GDP) increases, spatial disparities tend to decline. The countries of the Middle East and North Africa are outliers to this trend, displaying some of the world's highest between-region spatial inequality relative to comparator countries of similar per capita GDP. And although the region' countries exhibit spatial disparities across varying dimensions, virtually all of them stand to benefit from greater convergence across *all* dimensions (consumption expenditure, access to basic services and infrastructure, and so on).

Across the world, many individuals and households move from their birthplaces to seek opportunities for improving their lives. But the Middle East and North Africa shows anomalies here, too. Internal migration rates within these countries are considerably lower than in comparator countries. In the region, on average, 14 percent of adults have moved from their places of birth, compared with 28 percent elsewhere (D'Aoust and Lall, forthcoming). And although higher educational attainment is associated with greater likelihood of migration across most of the world, that does not hold true in the Middle East and North Africa, where completing tertiary education is not associated with a greater likelihood of migration (D'Aoust and Lall, forthcoming).

Greater internal migration in the region could increase consumption expenditures among migrants. Estimates vary across countries in the region, but for the broader region, migration from lagging areas to leading areas could enable a 37 percent increase in migrants' consumption expenditures (D'Aoust and Lall, forthcoming). Given this substantial potential, low internal migration rates present a further puzzle.

One possible explanation is the credential-focused education system prevalent throughout the Middle East and North Africa. The region's education systems have been oriented toward offering credentials that are key for accessing public sector jobs, which are often local. Relative to countries of comparable income in other regions, students in the Middle East and North Africa underperform in international exams that measure skill acquisition. That education systems focus on offering these credentials but not necessarily on the quality and caliber of skills needed to compete for private sector jobs across the country could be limiting individuals' abilities to acquire jobs outside of their home region.

## High disparities and low migration hinder economic mobility

### Regional inequality is high in the Middle East and North Africa

Despite relatively low within-country inequality, the Middle East and North Africa is among the most spatially unequal regions in the world. Although most of its countries are middle income, their spatial inequality is high and rising compared with countries elsewhere in the world, where inequality generally decreases with rising income and urbanization (figure 2.1).[1]

Spatial variables consistently account for at least half of all the reported variation in economic opportunities in most Middle East and North Africa countries (World Bank 2011). Disparities between subnational regions account for a larger share (63 percent or 6 percentage points) of inequality in household

consumption in the Middle East and North Africa than in the rest of the world. Djibouti, the Arab Republic of Egypt, the Islamic Republic of Iran, and the Republic of Yemen show the starkest regional inequalities.

Most of the region's 444 million people live near coasts, where they are closer to international markets and where economic activity is concentrated. People and economic activity have naturally concentrated in places that are better endowed: closer to coasts and markets and farther from remote deserts (map 2.1).

These natural endowments—land suitability, resources, or coastal access—mattered to the concentration of people and activity. Natural geography in the Middle East and North Africa explains 42 percent of the variation in economic activity, as measured by nighttime lights (table 2.1). This is higher than in Latin America and Sub-Saharan Africa but quite a bit lower than in Europe and Asia, suggesting that the

**FIGURE 2.1**    **Inequalities within most Middle East and North Africa countries exceed those of global peers**

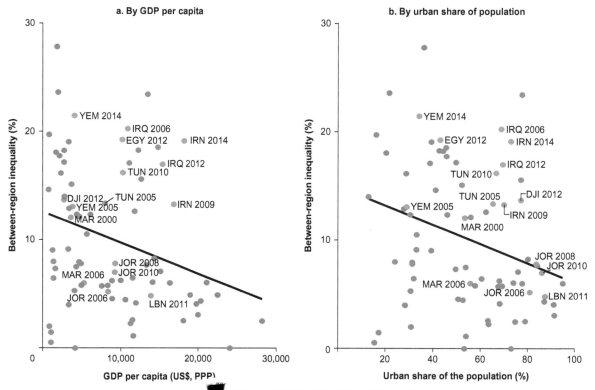

*Source:* Middle East and North Africa Poverty database (MNAPOV ~eam for Statistical Development, World Bank.
*Note:* Each point corresponds to a country's data for a particular y r. (For a list of countries and survey years, see annex 2A.) Inequality between subnational regions was calculated based on a country's first administrative level (for example, governorates, provinces, and so on). PPP = purchasing power parity.

**MAP 2.1   Middle East and North Africa populations are concentrated in the areas closest to international markets**

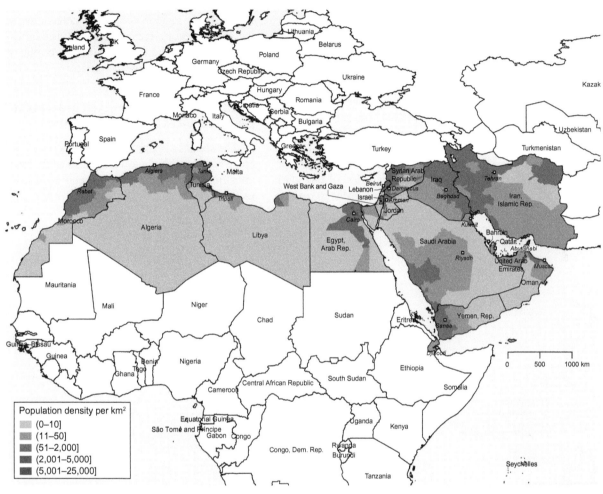

Population density per km²
- (0–10]
- (11–50]
- (51–2,000]
- (2,001–5,000]
- (5,001–25,000]

*Source:* Center for International Earth Science Information Network (CIESIN) of Columbia University, "Gridded Population of the World, Version 4 (GPWv4): Administrative Unit Center Points with Population Estimates, Revision 11." doi:10.7927/H4BC3WMT.

**TABLE 2.1   Economic activity benefits more from natural geography in the Middle East and North Africa than in Sub-Saharan Africa and Latin America but less so than in other regions**

*percent*

| Region | Share of economic activity explained by natural geography (%) |
| --- | --- |
| East Asia and Pacific | 56 |
| Europe and Central Asia | 65 |
| Latin America and the Caribbean | 33 |
| Middle East and North Africa | 42 |
| North America | 59 |
| South Asia | 58 |
| Sub-Saharan Africa | 31 |
| World | 53 |

*Source:* World Bank calculation based on Henderson et al. 2017.
*Note:* Lights at night are used as the measure of economic activity because such data are measured consistently worldwide at the same spatial scale. Henderson et al. (2017) applied a set of 24 physical geography characteristics—including those primarily important for agriculture and those primarily important for trade—in the analytical model.

region defies the global association of coastal proximity with better and cheaper access to global markets (Malik and Awadallah 2013).

Even so, those who could most benefit from concentrated economic activity in the Middle East and North Africa tend not to live in those areas. Within countries, the bottom of the welfare distribution is concentrated in particular areas—often lagging areas. For example, almost 85 percent of Egypt's bottom 40 percent lives in rural Upper and Lower Egypt. In Iraq, most of the bottom 40 percent lives outside the capital city region of Baghdad and the relatively prosperous Kurdistan region.

Only 14 percent of Tunisia's bottom 40 percent live in the largest urban metropolitan area of Grand Tunis; in Morocco, only 6 percent live in its effective economic capital, the Casablanca-Settat region;[2] and in the Islamic Republic of Iran, only 4 percent live in Tehran.

## Spatial disparities also exist in access to public services and infrastructure

The spatial disparities extend to service coverage rates, which are lower in areas with lower consumption expenditures as well as in low-income countries in general (figures 2.2 and 2.3).

**FIGURE 2.2**   **Access to electricity has converged except in low-income economies of the Middle East and North Africa, where the poorest regions remain underserved**

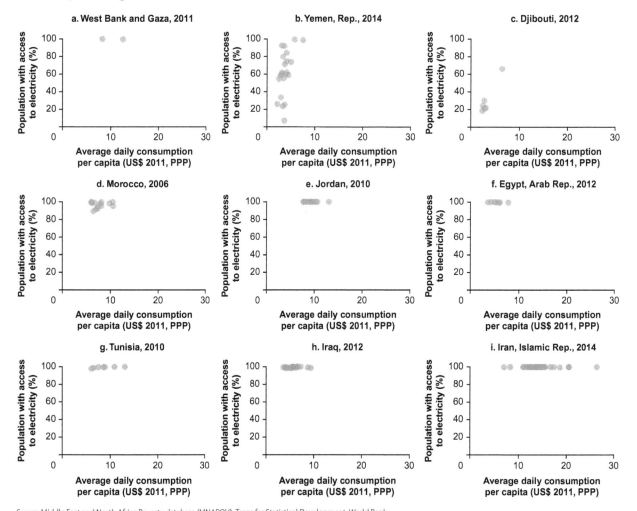

*Source:* Middle East and North Africa Poverty database (MNAPOV), Team for Statistical Development, World Bank.
*Note:* Each point corresponds to a subnational region. Of the economies shown, only the Republic of Yemen is a low-income economy (US$1,025 or less in gross national income [GNI] per capita) according to World Bank classifications. Djibouti, the Arab Republic of Egypt, Morocco, Tunisia, and West Bank and Gaza are lower-middle-income economies (US$1,026–US$3,995). Jordan, the Islamic Republic of Iran, and Iraq are upper-middle-income economies (US$3,996–US$12,375). PPP = purchasing power parity.

FIGURE 2.3   **Primary school completion remains lower in the poorest regions of the Middle East and North Africa, except in the Islamic Republic of Iran**

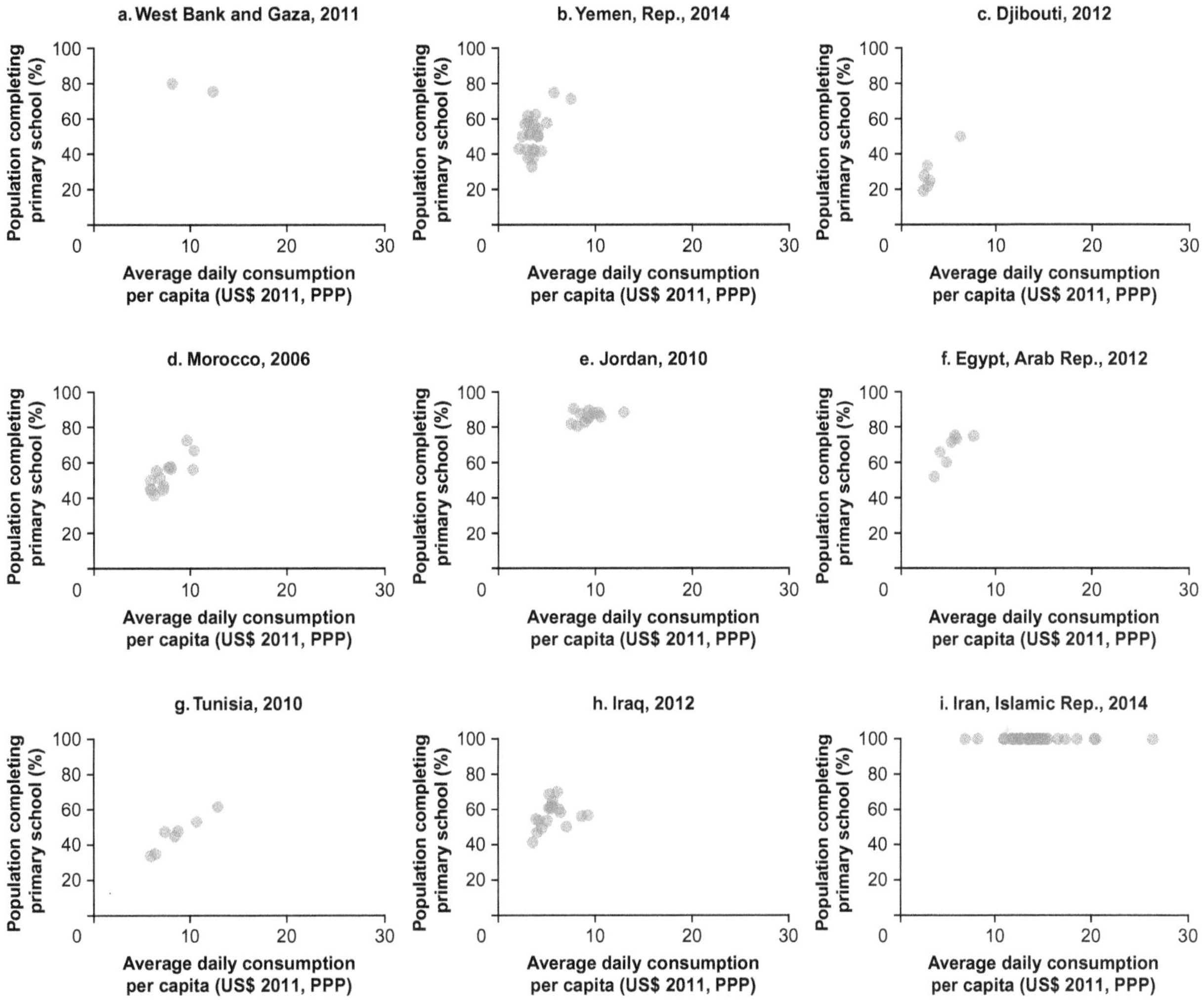

*Source:* Middle East and North Africa Poverty database (MNAPOV), Team for Statistical Development, World Bank.
*Note:* Each point corresponds to a subnational region. Of the economies shown, only the Republic of Yemen is a low-income economy (US$1,025 or less in gross national income [GNI] per capita) according to World Bank classifications. Djibouti, the Arab Republic of Egypt, Morocco, Tunisia, and West Bank and Gaza are lower-middle-income economies (US$1,026–US$3,995). Jordan, the Islamic Republic of Iran, and Iraq are upper-middle-income economies (US$3,996–US$12,375). PPP = purchasing power parity.

This lagging coverage—in electricity, education, road networks, health services, and even adequate water and sanitation—potentially exacerbates inequality of opportunity and creates poverty traps that can have lifetime and intergenerational repercussions. For example, in rural areas of the Middle East and North Africa, an estimated 28 million people lack access to electricity (Krishnan et al. 2016).

In addition, people living in poor regions of the Middle East and North Africa (often rural areas) have limited access to road networks and therefore lower access to markets, schools, clinics, and other public services. Only 22 percent of the region's rural population live within 2 kilometers of an all-weather road (World Bank 2010). These areas with limited connections to the centers of economic activity are left out from the world of opportunity and growth, and this could potentially end in political discontent.

In regions with unrealized economic potential, these connectivity constraints also reduce the chance of developing local agglomeration economies. In Egypt, for instance, shipping goods for short distances within the nation's most lagging region is *more* expensive than shipping to more-distant urban centers. Shipping general cargo from Aswan to Qena or Fayoum, for instance, can be more expensive than shipping to Cairo or Alexandria, both farther away. In addition, even where transport networks are relatively extensive, their poor quality and limited capacity hinder the impact of economic growth (World Bank 2010).

Even where access to basic services is converging, quality remains a major challenge. To be sure, the Middle East and North Africa has made marked progress in building physical infrastructure for service delivery and in expanding basic access to health and education. The Gulf Cooperation Council (GCC) countries and other oil exporters will be able to meet their national infrastructure needs if they maintain investment spending at the rates prevailing in the 2000s, although oil importers—such as Egypt, Morocco, and Tunisia—will fall short (figure 2.4).[3]

However, the region has been unable to ensure *quality* in the delivery of these services.

There are therefore large spatial disparities and deficiencies in the quality of infrastructure services, with lagging regions suffering particularly from insufficient investment and low quality. And dissatisfaction with the quality of delivery is pervasive across all services.

Overloaded electricity networks, traffic congestion, and port overcrowding are just a few examples of overwhelmed infrastructure networks (Devarajan 2016; World Bank 2019a). In Iraq, for instance, electricity provision varies greatly. In 2012, although 99 percent of households were connected to the public electricity grid, less than 10 percent of households in Baghdad and the central and southern governorates received more than 12 hours of power a day (World Bank 2014a). As for the local or site-specific infrastructure, the quality of water and sanitation services is poor, and localities face gas and other energy shortages (World Bank 2014a). Needs vary across the region.

Access to safe water is an example where large spatial disparities remain despite some convergence in the share of people with access to an improved water source (figure 2.5). The water and sanitation sector is critical for survival and growth, and the water crisis is one of the greatest threats to the region (WEF 2015). In Middle East and North Africa countries, 61 percent of their populations live in areas with high or very high levels of surface water stress—exceeding the global average of about 35 percent (World Bank 2017a).[4] And more than 71 percent of the regional GDP is generated in areas with high or very high levels of surface water stress, more than triple the world average of 22 percent (figure 2.6). Economic losses from inadequate water supply and sanitation in the region's countries are stark (figure 2.7).

Water quality matters. If not managed properly, improved infrastructure can become an efficient distributor of disease. Systematic contamination of improved sources, which includes all protected sources,[5] is common because of inadequate maintenance of infrastructure, interrupted supply, and improper disinfection. But contamination also occurs during transport to and unsafe storage within households (Bain et al. 2014; World Bank 2017d).

**FIGURE 2.4**  **Projected infrastructure needs and financing in the Middle East and North Africa**

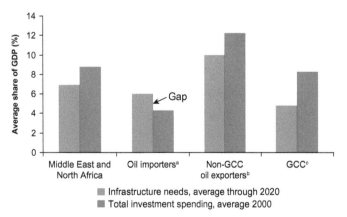

*Source:* Estache et al. 2013.
*Note:* "Total investment spending" refers to public expenditures. More recent data for the region project similar needs in terms of GDP per capita but slightly lower spending.
a. The oil importing economies include Djibouti, the Arab Republic of Egypt, Jordan, Lebanon, Morocco, Tunisia, and West Bank and Gaza.
b. The non-GCC oil exporting economies include Algeria, the Islamic Republic of Iran, Iraq, Libya, the Syrian Arab Republic, and the Republic of Yemen.
c. GCC = Gulf Cooperation Council countries, comprising Bahrain, Kuwait, Oman, Qatar, Saudi Arabia, and the United Arab Emirates.

**FIGURE 2.5** **Access to a safe water source lags behind in the poorest regions of the Middle East and North Africa**

**a. West Bank and Gaza, 2011**

**b. Yemen, Rep., 2014**

**c. Djibouti, 2012**

**d. Morocco, 2006**

**e. Jordan, 2010**

**f. Egypt, Arab Rep., 2012**

**g. Tunisia, 2010**

**h. Iraq, 2012**

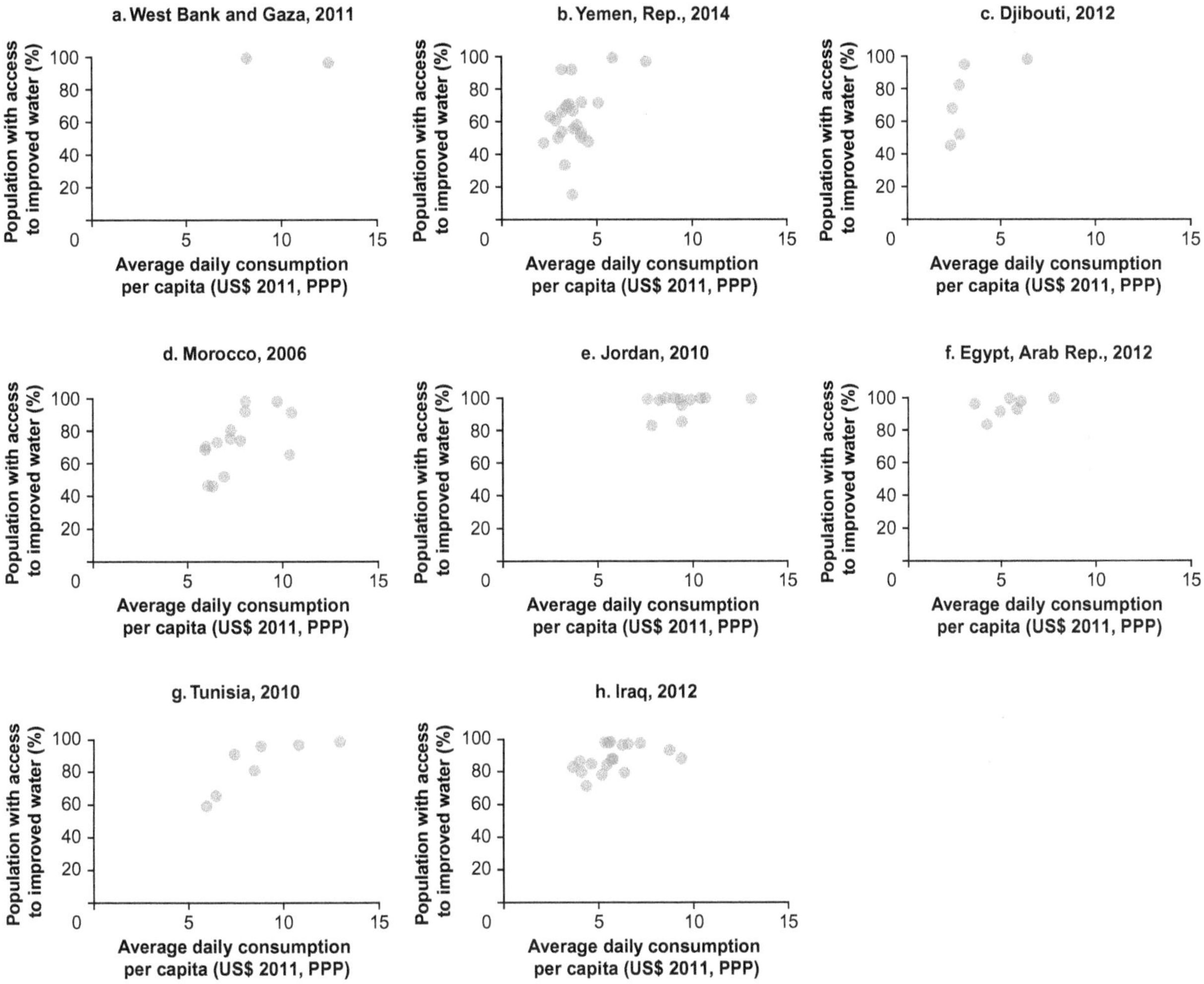

*Source:* Middle East and North Africa Poverty database (MNAPOV), Team for Statistical Development, World Bank.
*Note:* Each point corresponds to a subnational region. An "improved" drinking-water source is defined as one that, by nature of its construction or through active intervention, is protected from outside contamination, in particular from contamination with fecal matter (World Bank 2017a). Of the economies shown, only the Republic of Yemen is a low-income economy (US$1,025 or less in gross national income [GNI] per capita) according to World Bank classifications. Djibouti, the Arab Republic of Egypt, Morocco, Tunisia, and West Bank and Gaza are lower-middle-income economies (US$1,026–US$3,995). Jordan and Iraq are upper-middle-income economies (US$3,996–US$12,375). PPP = purchasing power parity.

**FIGURE 2.6** **Far higher shares of population and economic activity are exposed to high or very high water stress in the Middle East and North Africa than in world averages**

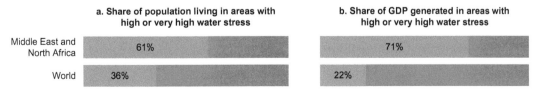

**a. Share of population living in areas with high or very high water stress**

**b. Share of GDP generated in areas with high or very high water stress**

| | a. | b. |
|---|---|---|
| Middle East and North Africa | 61% | 71% |
| World | 36% | 22% |

*Source:* World Bank 2017a.
*Note:* Water stress arises when water withdrawals for human, agricultural, and industrial uses are relatively high compared with the level of renewable water resources—in other words, when the ratio of water withdrawal to water availability is high. Estimates of surface water stress do not account for withdrawals from groundwater and nonconventional water supplies.

FIGURE 2.7   **Economic losses from inadequate water supply and sanitation in the Middle East and North Africa vary by economy**

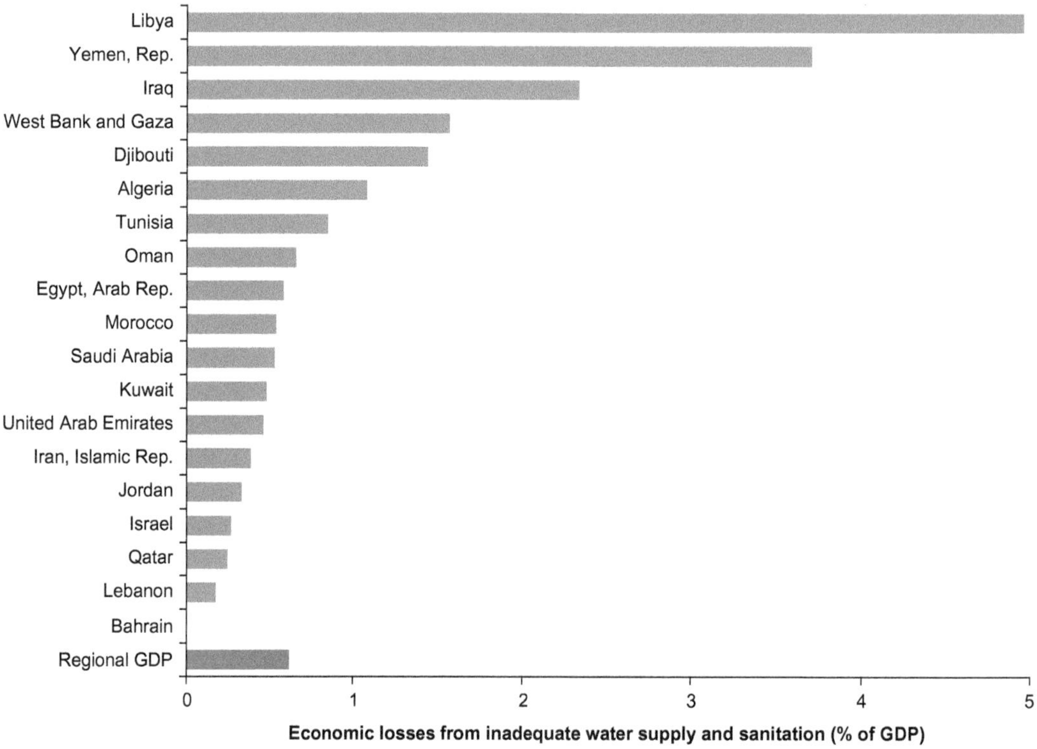

Economic losses from inadequate water supply and sanitation (% of GDP)

*Sources:* Hutton 2013; Sadoff et al. 2015.
*Note:* Data are from 2010.

Insufficient water provision impedes the growth of lagging regions through two channels: First, it reduces quality of life and directly affects human resources and capacities. People cannot effectively participate in economic production when they have insufficient or unsafe water to drink. Second, lack of safe water impedes already limited economic activity in lagging regions. When factories face limited or unreliable water supply (similar to the effect of unreliable energy supply), it greatly hinders productivities and makes it economically unviable for companies to operate in lagging regions. These lagging regions with limited local infrastructure usually have difficulty in attracting and retaining private investment.

In this regard, policies followed by governments in the region tend to benefit wealthier households more than the poor. Despite water scarcity, water service fees in the Middle East and North Africa are very low, and its water subsidies are the highest in the world (Berglöf and Devarajan 2015). These policies not only promote resource degradation and aggravate fiscal deficits but also compound vulnerabilities and further disadvantage the poor and marginalized. Water subsidies typically benefit wealthier households more than poor households, and wealthier areas benefit more than poorer neighborhoods from subsidized water (Berglöf and Devarajan 2015).

As such, poor households may be located in areas unserved by utilities, requiring residents to buy water of dubious quality from vendors in the informal sector at prices much higher than those paid by the rich. Even when the poor have access to piped water, they capture a smaller share of the benefits from subsidies because they use less water (Whittington et al.

2015). Social inclusion protection of the poor and marginalized populations must be central to the delivery of water services and protection from water-related risks.

More important, water scarcity could lead to political instability and conflict if not dealt with properly. In addition to the existing challenges, sudden population spikes due to a large refugee influx have further strained the infrastructure in many of the region's cities. Additional demand for basic services by refugees puts heavy pressure on public spending, further stresses infrastructure services, and may create potential resentment between the host communities and the refugees. For example, in the northern border towns of Jordan, water supply used to be available three times a week, each time for two hours. Since the refugee influx, service has been reduced to once a week for only one hour.[6]

If refugees and internally displaced persons (IDPs) flow into *leading* subnational regions,

the shortage in infrastructure services may slow down economic growth. If they continue to come to *lagging or poor* regions, the existing problems of limited infrastructure investment and public services could be exacerbated and regional gaps in income and economic performance further widened.

## Spatial inequality sits at the heart of conflict and climate fragility

Violence and climate risks are associated with higher spatial inequalities (figure 2.8). Instability and turmoil in the Middle East and North Africa have reached new levels in the past decade (box 2.1). Because flood and drought risks are also increasing, challenges surrounding economic and regional integration are piling up. Compounded violence and climate shocks result in instability, undermining existing institutions and affecting service delivery. The demand for services cannot

**FIGURE 2.8**  **Violent events and water risk are associated with higher spatial inequalities in the Middle East and North Africa**

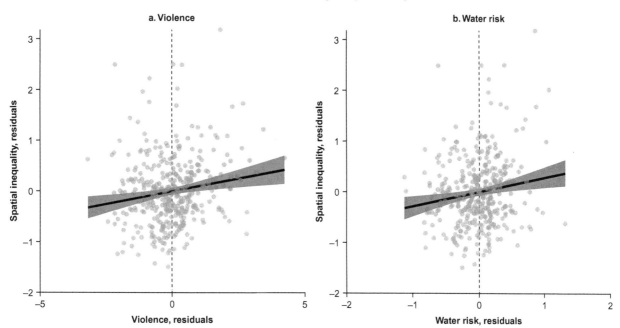

*Sources:* Middle East and North Africa Poverty database (MNAPOV), Team for Statistical Development, World Bank; Armed Conflict Location & Event Data (ACLED) database, https://www.acleddata.com/; and World Resources Institute's Aqueduct Water Risk Atlas, https://www.wri.org/resources/maps/aqueduct-water-risk-atlas.
*Note:* The figures show residual-on-residual plots with 95 percent confidence intervals. The x-axis depicts the residuals from an ordinary least squares (OLS) regression on the log number of violent events from the ACLED database and water risk from Aqueduct data controlling for population, area, time to access nearest city, economic density, and country fixed effects. The y-axis corresponds to mean log deviation of poverty rate (as an indicator of inequality [Haughton and Khandker 2009]) on the same controls. Each point is an administrative region corresponding to the lowest administrative area with poverty rates available. Most correspond to the first administrative level; Morocco and Lebanon are the second administrative level, province and district respectively; and Jordan is the third administrative level (subdistrict). No data were available for the Gulf Cooperation Council (GCC) countries, Libya, and the Syrian Arab Republic.

BOX 2.1   **The ongoing effects of conflict on people of the Middle East and North Africa**

The region is suffering from different types of conflict, ranging from terrorism, the rise of the Islamic State of Iraq and the Levant (ISIL),[a] and open civil war and violence—causing large-scale displacement of populations—to sporadic violence stemming from political instability that is largely contained within countries.

In the wake of the 2011 Arab Spring revolts, some countries experienced gains while others encountered increased conflict and instability. Several countries are experiencing open civil war, such as Libya, the Syrian Arab Republic, and the Republic of Yemen. In Iraq, Syria, and the Republic of Yemen, civil war is further aggravated by the presence of terrorist groups such as ISIL and al-Qaeda. Other countries such as Tunisia and Egypt have more-contained political unrest with sporadic violence. Finally, in Jordan and Lebanon, social tensions are growing because of the influx of refugees and increasing strains on service delivery.

The recent conflicts in Libya, Syria, and the Republic of Yemen caused large numbers of casualties, severe destruction of public infrastructure, and catastrophic humanitarian emergencies (table B2.1.1). In modern conflict, violence is a minor cause of mortality. The burden of losses in modern conflict has shifted from combatants to civilian populations, now the main target of hostilities. Civilian casualties have doubled between 2010 and 2016 alone, with many more deaths caused by unmet medical needs, inadequate shelter, and famine because of conflict (World Bank 2017b).

Civil conflict also leads to breakdowns in food systems, in health and water infrastructure, and in access to these services. These breakdowns often increase the death toll. The frequent outbreaks of measles and cholera in refugee camps and among internally displaced persons (IDP) populations is another important cause of death. In the Republic of Yemen, food insecurity and the threat of famine placed 17 million people at risk (UNOCHA 2017). From April 2017 to July 2017, more than 2,300 people have died in the Republic of Yemen from cholera (WHO 2018).

TABLE B2.1.1   **Violence in four current major crises has affected between one-third and two-thirds of the population**

| Country | Total population (millions) | Within 2 kilometers from event (2016–18) | | Displaced | |
|---|---|---|---|---|---|
| | | Total (millions) | Share (%) | Total | Share (%) |
| Libya | 6 | 2 | 32.2 | 197,000 | 3.2 |
| Iraq | 36 | 13 | 35.4 | 2,648,000 | 7.3 |
| Yemen, Rep. | 27 | 13 | 49.4 | 2,014,000 | 7.5 |
| Syrian Arab Republic | 19 | 13 | 69.1 | 6,784,000 | 36.7 |

*Source:* Center for International Earth Science Information Network (CIESIN) of Columbia University, "Gridded Population of the World, Version 4 (GPWv4): Administrative Unit Center Points with Population Estimates, Revision 11"; Armed Conflict Location & Event Data (ACLED) database, https://www.acleddata.com/; and UN Refugee Agency (UNHCR) population statistics, http://popstats.unhcr.org/.
*Note:* An "event" refers to battles, explosions, and violence against civilians. Events are georeferenced, and a radius of 2 kilometers was taken around each event to count the population within 2 kilometers.
a. ISIL is alternatively referred to as the Islamic State in Iraq and al-Sham (ISIS) or as the Islamic State group (IS).

be met when infrastructure or the provision of water, education, electricity, and transportation are disrupted by war or flooding (Brixi, Lust, and Woolcock 2015).

In Iraq, for example, the failure to preserve water resources in the marshes in the south is not only driving displacement but also reinforcing local perceptions of marginalization and exclusion and perpetuating fragility (Mahdi and Fawzi 2014). Iraqi marshes have a long history of upstream diversions, dam building, and uncoordinated and fragmented planning in the Tigris and Euphrates basins.

Given the strains placed on host communities through protracted displacement, refugees can potentially catalyze social conflict that diminishes trust in public institutions. There can be a perception that displaced persons compete with the poorest hosts and push them deeper into poverty. Yet the reality is more nuanced. In many areas, the challenges for host communities already existed before the influx of forcibly displaced persons. Refugees and IDPs may provide convenient scapegoats for deep-rooted issues, but they are often not the main cause of all the difficulties facing host countries (World Bank 2017c). The presence of refugees and IDPs typically increases demand and creates jobs, but it also adds newcomers to the labor force. The impact on prices is also unevenly distributed, with prices of land and housing typically going up and owners benefiting to the detriment of renters.

Water scarcity is a key source of tension in the Mashreq subregion. Displaced people living in camps or among host communities can struggle to access basic water supply and sanitation services, and they place significant burdens on both service delivery systems and underlying water resources in host communities. The most impoverished and disenfranchised northern region of Jordan is now faced with the influx of refugees from the Syrian war. Forced displacement has accelerated an unsustainable exploitation of groundwater and pollution of aquifers. Water prices are rising, and supply systems are straining to meet increased demand (World Bank 2017a).

Most refugees live among the host communities instead of in refugee camps, placing an unplanned burden on water resources and services. Jordan's average annual population growth rate, which was 3.2 percent between 2000 and 2010, has increased to 7 percent since the start of the Syrian Civil War in 2011 (as seen in nighttime images since 2011)—more than half of which (3.8 percent) is estimated to be from the influx of forcibly displaced persons (World Bank 2017b). In Lebanon, the population has increased by an estimated 30 percent since the start of the Syrian Civil War, in turn increasing water demand and the volume of sewage requiring treatment (Farajallah 2016). Domestic water demand in Lebanon has increased by an estimated 43 million cubic meters (to 70 million cubic meters a year), which corresponds to an 8–12 percent increase in national water demand. Similarly, an influx of refugees has led to an 8–14 percent increase in wastewater volume, placing an unplanned burden on limited wastewater treatment facilities (World Bank 2017a).

## Low migration suppresses labor mobility in the Middle East and North Africa

Labor mobility is key for economic integration and the reduction of spatial inequalities. Globally, inequalities in regional economic activity tend to persist. There is a lag in the convergence process, which is not fast enough to offset initially faster change in leading areas. Spatial inequalities are likely to increase if there are barriers to labor flows between regions and benefits do not spill over to less fortunate regions.[7]

Compared with the rest of the world, however, few people in the Middle East and North Africa have moved from their birthplaces. Unlike international migration, labor mobility *within* countries is largely free of legal constraints. Yet, internal migration rates in the region are lower than in the rest of the world. Lifetime migration compares place of birth (within the country) with the place of current residence. On average, 14 percent of the region's people have moved from their places of birth, compared with an average of 28 percent elsewhere (figure 2.9).[8] People seem to be staying in the region where they were born, reducing the potential gains for migrants and their families.

The differences between countries are partly driven by the presence of a primate city. The Maghreb countries (as well as Syria [Khawaja 2002]) have regional capitals that could lead people to migrate to a city without going too far (see chapter 3), which explains those countries' high shares of population living in urban areas. Countries in the Middle East and North Africa are "urbanizing but not metropolitanizing" (World Bank 2011)—that is, their urbanization is more fragmented and less agglomerated than in other regions, as further discussed in chapter 1. Among the Mashreq countries, Jordan's and Lebanon's systems of cities—dominated by Amman and Beirut, respectively—push internal migrants to cross regional borders. Hence, interregional migration is higher in these countries.

FIGURE 2.9 **Within-country migration is lower in the Middle East and North Africa than in the rest of the world**

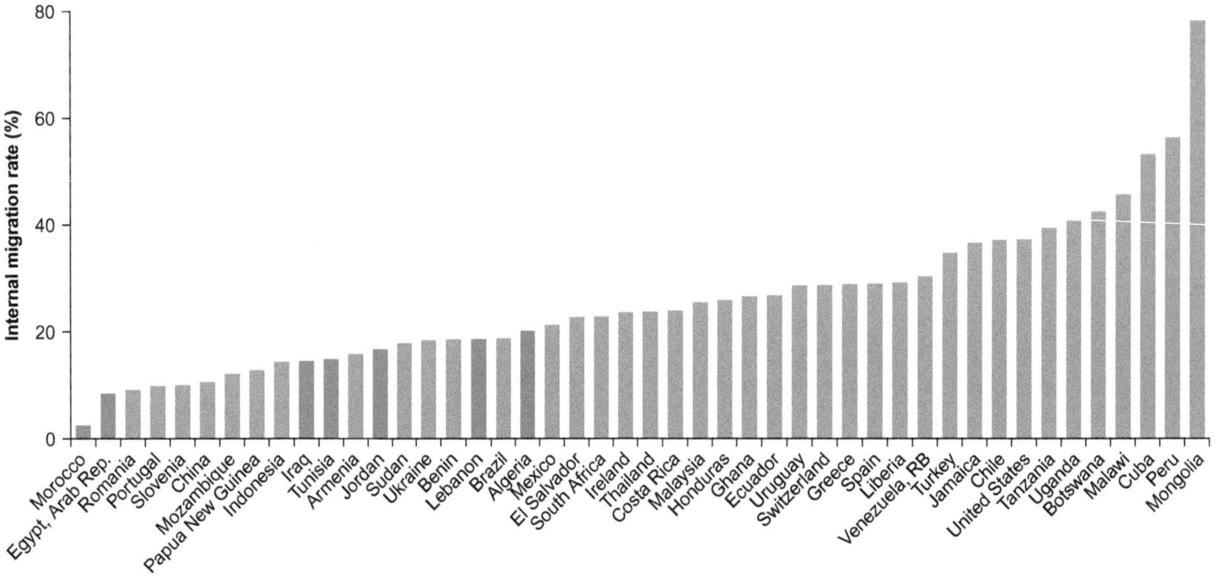

*Sources:* Arab Barometer Wave IV (2016–17) data; University of Minnesota's Integrated Public Use Microdata Series (IPUMS) International database.
*Note:* The internal migration rate is the number of lifetime within-country migrants per 100 adults. Lifetime internal migration compares the place of current residence with the place of birth (within the same country). The data are from various years (see annex 2A, table 2A.1). The migration rates in Algeria, the Arab Republic of Egypt, Jordan, Lebanon, Morocco, and Tunisia are computed on the basis of the Arab Barometer Wave IV (2016–17) data; rates for other countries are from latest censuses available on IPUMS in which place of birth was available.

FIGURE 2.10 **Net migration flows in Tunisia reflect the movement of people from high-poverty to low-poverty regions**

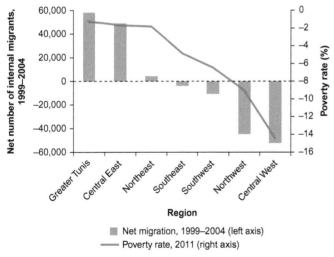

Net migration, 1999–2004 (left axis)
Poverty rate, 2011 (right axis)

*Source:* World Bank 2014c.

## The returns to migration are high

Given high regional inequality, citizens may be expected to migrate across regions in pursuit of better opportunities. Globally, migration within countries constitutes a fundamental process of socioeconomic change.

The United Nations estimates that approximately 760 million people are internal migrants—almost four times as many as those who have moved internationally (Skeldon 2013).

Human mobility is beneficial for households' welfare, health, and education prospects. Globally, workers move in search of welfare-improving opportunities. Domestic migration can offer a way for people in areas with limited opportunities to significantly improve the use of their human capital and the quality of both their lives and the lives of the families and communities they leave behind. International evidence shows that the more workers can move across regions to take advantage of economic opportunities, the better the skill matches and the higher welfare gains from trade, employment, and wages. Migrants also continue to interact with their places of origin, increasing trade and transferring capital, ideas, and institutions (Hollweg et al. 2014; Testaverde et al. 2017). In Tunisia, for example, internal migration flows indicate that people are moving from high-poverty to low-poverty regions in search of opportunity (figure 2.10).

We can estimate the cost of barriers to migration in the Middle East and North Africa in terms of the large benefits that increased migration would bring: consumption per capita could increase by 37 percent on average if migration to leading regions were to increase.[9] (For the methodology of calculating the costs of barriers to migration, see box 2.2.) The higher returns to residents' endowments in the leading regions explains

---

### BOX 2.2 Methodology for calculating the cost of barriers to migration

Decomposing the sources of welfare gaps between individual endowments and returns to these endowments demonstrates the difference between observed welfare and its counterfactual *if migration had occurred*.

In a world where migration is unrestricted and free, nobody would move if standards of living were determined only by households' nongeographic, portable attributes. If living in another location would improve a worker's welfare, given his or her profile, the worker would move to that location.[a] Spatial disparities in living standards can be explained by the sorting of people by endowment levels (for example, education levels) or by differences in the returns to such endowments. If large differences in the welfare gap are attributable to the returns of household endowments in a particular location, it suggests that there are labor mobility barriers across regions (Ravallion and Wodon 1999).

Based on a geographic analog of Blinder-Oaxaca decomposition across locations,[b] spatial disparities in living standards can be measured and decomposed between endowments and returns to endowments, controlling for gender, age, education level, marital status, status in the labor force, access to electricity and water, and possession of a computer.

Figures 2.11 and 2.12 show the gap of consumption expenditures between the metropolitan leading regions and other regions and its decomposition into endowments and returns from endowments. The consumption gap is based on a welfare ratio that deflates expenditures per capita by a spatially differentiated price index to account for price differences between regions.[c] The share of the gaps explained by returns to endowments indicates that returns to one's endowments would be higher in the metropolis.

The decomposition is obtained by estimating equation (B2.2.1) for both the country's metropolitan leading region and all other regions:

$$y_i = X_i\beta_i + \varepsilon_i, \qquad (B2.2.1)$$

where $y_i$ is the log of consumption per capita in region $i$—denoted as either leading ($M$, for metropolis) or as nonleading ($O$, for other regions)—and $X_i$ is a set of endowments mentioned above.

The average consumption gap can be expressed as equation (B2.2.2):

$$\bar{y}_M - \bar{y}_O = \bar{X}_M\beta_M - \bar{X}_O\beta_O, \qquad (B2.2.2)$$

which can be rewritten as equation (B2.2.3):

$$\bar{y}_M - \bar{y}_O = \left(\bar{X}_M - \bar{X}_O\right)\beta_M + \bar{X}_M\left(\beta_M - \beta_O\right) \\ + \left(\bar{X}_M - \bar{X}_O\right)\left(\beta_M - \beta_O\right). \qquad (B2.2.3)$$

If residents outside the metropolis are the worse off and we consider the normal returns to be $\beta_M$, the last term of equation (B2.2.3) can be dropped (see Blinder 1973; Oaxaca 1973; Cotton 1988; Jann and Zurich 2008), and we have

$$\bar{y}_M - \bar{y}_O = \left(\bar{X}_M - \bar{X}_O\right)\beta_M + \bar{X}_M\left(\beta_M - \beta_O\right). \quad (B2.2.4)$$

The first part $\left(\bar{X}_M - \bar{X}_O\right)\beta_M$ measures the effect of the differential in endowments, while the second $\bar{X}_M\left(\beta_M - \beta_O\right)$ captures the differential in returns to endowments.

Graphically, figure B2.2.1 shows that for a set of endowments $\bar{X}_M$, the consumption of the residents in the leading area is estimated to be $\bar{Y}_M$. The same applies to residents elsewhere, denoted by the subscripts O. There are two drivers of the gap: the endowments themselves (on the x-axis) and their returns, captured by the slope of the income curves, which is steeper for residents who live in the leading region.

In figure B2.2.2, the endowments of residents in other regions are shifted to reach the ones of leading regions, and the resulting consumption increases are

*box continues next page*

FIGURE B2.2.1    **Consumption gap between leading and other regions**

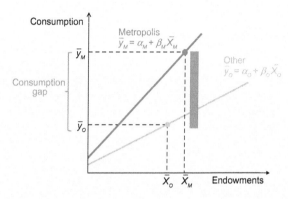

FIGURE B2.2.2    **Share of the consumption gap explained by endowments**

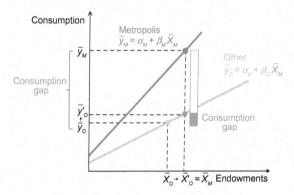

FIGURE B2.2.3    **Share of the consumption gap explained by returns to endowments**

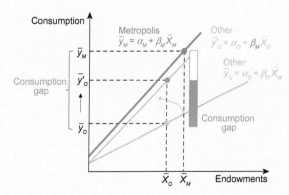

shown along their income curve (from $\bar{Y}_O$ to $\overline{Y'}_O$). Closing the income gap in these regions will require closing the gaps in endowments between residents in all regions, which requires investing in education and health as well as promoting gender equality in access, for example.

In figure B2.2.3, the slope of the curve increases to offer the same returns to all regions, showing a consumption increase from $\bar{Y}_O$ to $\overline{Y'}_O$ if people were to move.

The estimation of welfare gaps based on the ordinary least squares (OLS) version of the Blinder-Oaxaca decomposition focuses on mean effects. The effect of the covariates is limited to an average effect that remains constant across the welfare distribution. However, the effect of each covariate might in fact vary across the welfare distribution. Using quantile regression allows for the estimation of the welfare gap and extends the decomposition of endowments and returns effects across the welfare distribution. We apply the method proposed in Chernozhukov, Fernández-Val, and Melly (2013) to estimate the welfare decomposition for each quantile.

a. The welfare aggregate (total expenditures, which includes food and nonfood expenditures such as clothing, services, furniture, vehicles, medicines, transportation services, and education) was deflated spatially to account for the difference in costs of living across space.
b. The source of inequalities is typically analyzed using the Blinder-Oaxaca decomposition method. See, for example, Fortin, Lemieux, and Firpo (2011) for a review of studies decomposing the sources of gender or race inequality and a more recent stocktaking of the explanations advanced in the literature for the gender wage gap. In the Middle East and North Africa, Bouassida and El Lahga (2018) explore the sources of the wage distribution between the public and the private sectors in Tunisia. The geographic analog of the Blinder-Oaxaca decomposition decomposes average wage or consumption across space and has been pioneered by Ravallion and Wodon (1999) to highlight geographic differences in living standards in Bangladesh. Given the limitations of estimating differences only at the mean, Machado and Mata (2005), Melly (2005), and Chernozhukov, Fernández-Val, and Melly (2013) developed an estimation procedure transforming each observation into a counterfactual based on quantile regression, enabling the analysis of inequalities across the welfare distribution. Applications in the Middle East and North Africa include analyses of the sources of spatial disparities in consumption in Egypt (World Bank 2012) and Tunisia (World Bank 2014c) as well as regional wage differentials in Colombia, Portugal, and Spain (Herrera-Idárraga, López-Bazo, and Motellón 2016; Motellón, López-Bazo, and El-Attar 2011; Pereira and Galego 2014).
c. Except in Djibouti, where the poverty line is national. In the Islamic Republic of Iran, the welfare aggregate excludes expenditures on health and durables for technical reasons and is intertemporally and spatially deflated to account for changes in prices during the survey period and spatial variation in prices. A detailed explanation of methodology to construct the welfare aggregate is available from Atamanov et al. (2016).

two-thirds of the consumption gap between those regions and others. The other third is explained by lower endowments in the non-leading regions. Improving the endowments of residents in nonleading regions to reach the levels of residents in leading areas would increase consumption by 17 percent—half of the consumption benefit from migrating.

Figure 2.11, panel a, shows the estimated welfare gap between the leading regions and the others for each decile of the welfare distribution.[10] The gap increases with consumption expenditures. In other words, relative to their consumption group, richer people are worse off from living in the nonleading regions than poor people. A decomposition of the difference between endowments and returns to endowments (figure 2.11, panel b) confirms the previous conclusion: income differences across the consumption distribution are more strongly driven by returns than endowments—suggesting the existing

cost of barriers to migration as well as the gains from migration. The gains from (and hence implied costs of barriers to) migration are highest for the richest (most productive) people—varying between a 32 percent and a 52 percent increase in consumption—suggesting heterogeneity in the gap across the distribution, which is increasing with wealth.

Comparing the bottom 40 percent living in leading regions against those who do not, a different picture emerges. First, the consumption gaps between leading and nonleading areas are much lower for the bottom 40 percent than for the entire distribution, and they are higher for the poor than for the less poor (for example, urban informal employment is more of a better choice than farming for the poorest than for the not-so-poor), as shown in figure 2.12, panel a. Second, endowments matter more only for the bottom of the bottom 40 percent

**FIGURE 2.11** Migration to leading regions could increase consumption potential significantly in the Middle East and North Africa

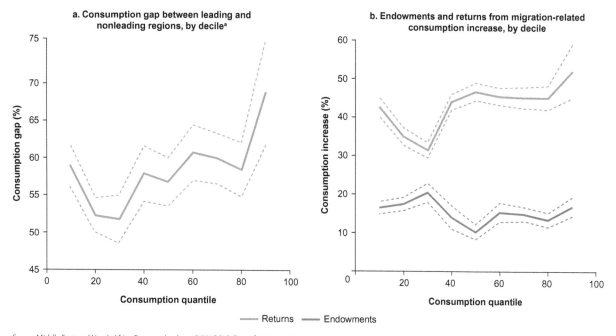

a. Consumption gap between leading and nonleading regions, by decile[a]

b. Endowments and returns from migration-related consumption increase, by decile

——— Returns ——— Endowments

Source: Middle East and North Africa Poverty database (MNAPOV), Team for Statistical Development, World Bank.
Note: Consumption expenditures are per capita, spatially deflated and converted in terms of US$ (2011) purchasing power parity. Solid lines designate point estimates; dashed lines designate 95 percent confidence intervals. "Leading regions" are Great Tunis in Tunisia; Amman in Jordan; Cairo, Alexandria, Suez, and Port-Said in the Arab Republic of Egypt; the Kurdistan governorates (Duhouk, Erbil, and Suleimaniya) in Iraq; Djibouti City in Djibouti; Tehran in the Islamic Republic of Iran; the Casablanca-Settat area in Morocco; and Sana'a in the Republic of Yemen.
a. The total consumption gap is the sum of consumption effects from endowments and returns.

FIGURE 2.12   **Among the bottom 40 percent who migrate to leading regions, the migration benefits are restricted to the top**

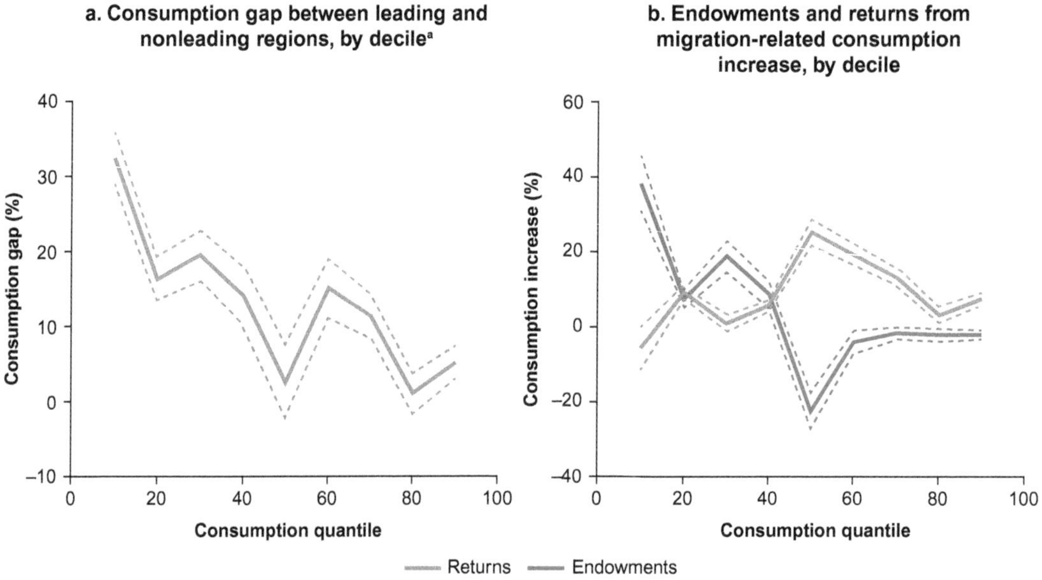

**a. Consumption gap between leading and nonleading regions, by decile**[a]

**b. Endowments and returns from migration-related consumption increase, by decile**

Returns — Endowments

*Source:* Middle East and North Africa Poverty database (MNAPOV), Team for Statistical Development, World Bank.
*Note:* Consumption expenditures are per capita, spatially deflated and converted in terms of US$ (2011) purchasing power parity. Solid lines designate point estimates; dashed lines designate 95 percent confidence intervals. "Leading regions" are Greater Tunis in Tunisia; Amman in Jordan; Cairo, Alexandria, Suez, and Port-Said in the Arab Republic of Egypt; the Kurdistan governorates (Duhouk, Erbil, and Suleimaniya) in Iraq; Djibouti City in Djibouti; Tehran in the Islamic Republic of Iran; the Casablanca-Settat area in Morocco; and Sana'a in the Republic of Yemen.
a. The total consumption gap is the sum of consumption effects from endowments and returns.

(figure 2.12, panel b). The top of the bottom 40 percent is actually better endowed outside of the metropolitan area (think about being unemployed in metropolitan areas relative to being employed elsewhere), but they could gain from moving, particularly if they are unemployed.

Overall patterns hide differences across consumption groups in different regions. Welfare gaps vary across and within countries (figure 2.13).

In Djibouti, for example, 26 percent of the gap in welfare between regions is explained by barriers to migration, the elimination of which which would translate to a 51 percent increase in consumption on average. Djibouti shows one of the highest gaps between metropolitan areas and other regions. It is a low-income country that has yet to improve convergence in access to basic services (as discussed in the previous section). As such, differences in endowments (education, health, and so on) are

substantial, and they matter significantly in explaining regional differences, explaining on average 74 percent of the gap—the highest among all Middle East and North Africa countries.

In Egypt, living standards are highest in urban Lower Egypt governates, which are in the fertile Nile Delta and closest to the urban agglomerations of Alexandria, Cairo, Port-Said, and Suez.[11] In the poor region of Upper Egypt, urban residents are expected to consume on average 25 percent more if they relocate to major urban agglomerations, and rural residents are expected to consume 36 percent more. The potentially high return to endowments for people from Upper Egypt who move to major cities elsewhere suggests that barriers to mobility are the highest in Upper Egypt.

In the Islamic Republic of Iran, people's consumption in southernmost provinces[12] would increase by 75 percent if they moved to Tehran (map 2.2). In general, the farther

**FIGURE 2.13**   **Consumption gaps between the metropolitan region and others vary across countries and are largely explained by differences in returns to endowments**

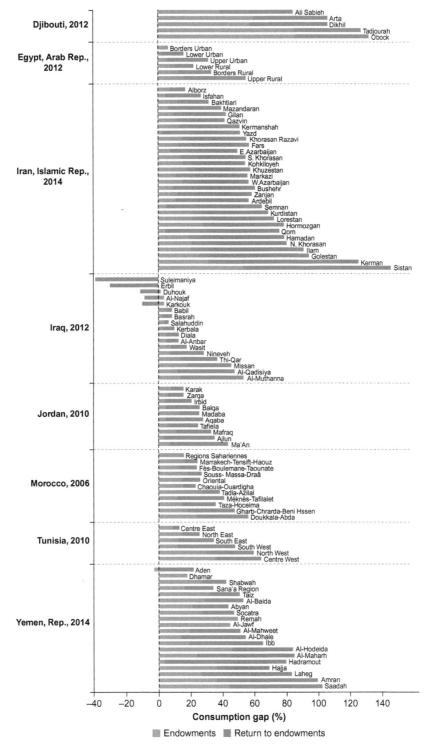

Consumption gap (%)

▨ Endowments    ▉ Return to endowments

*Source:* Middle East and North Africa Poverty database (MNAPOV), Team for Statistical Development, World Bank.
*Note:* Consumption expenditures are per capita, spatially deflated and converted in terms of US$ (2011) purchasing power parity. The consumption gap is the difference in expenditures between each region and the leading region, disaggregated to distinguish the share explained by endowments versus returns to endowments.

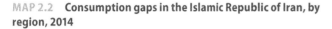

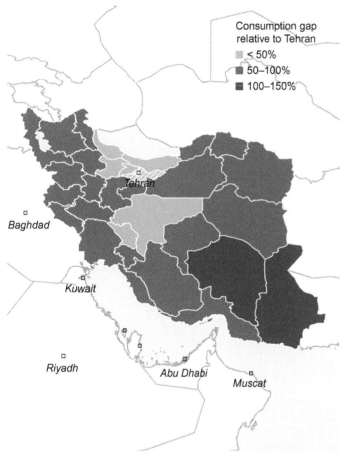

*Source:* Iran Household Income and Expenditure Survey 2014 via the Global Monitoring Database (GMD), World Bank Team for Statistical Development, using the Datalibweb Stata Package, including the correction detailed in Atamanov et al. 2016.
*Note:* Consumption expenditures are per capita, spatially deflated and converted in terms of US$ (2011) purchasing power parity. The consumption gap is the difference in expenditures between each region and the leading region.

from Tehran, the starker the drop in consumption, meaning that in the south of the country, the average consumption is less than half consumption in the capital. Apart from the two southern provinces of Kerman and Sistan, endowments explain a minimal share of the consumption difference.

In Iraq, consumption levels and returns to endowments are better than in Baghdad in several governorates (map 2.3). Endowments are similar. Located at the border of Kuwait, Basra Governorate consumption levels are lower than in Baghdad but higher than its

northern neighbors. These are governorates where consumption is 35–50 percent what it is in Baghdad, largely explained by low returns to endowments. Kirkuk likely benefits from links with Kurdistan, and Najaf is well connected to Baghdad.

In Jordan, barriers to migration explain a large share of the welfare difference across regions. Outcomes are best in the capital, Amman, and the top-performing regions are those along the connected desert highway—Amman, Karak, and Jerash. Only Jerash offers returns to endowments similar to Amman. People in other regions would gain from moving toward Amman, especially those in governorates far from the desert highway corridor. Residents of Ma'an, in southeast Jordan, could increase household consumption by more than 30 percent if they were to move to Amman. Ma'an is the furthest from Amman on the consumption distribution and is one of Jordan's disconnected and sparsely populated lagging regions. Migrants from Aljoun, in north Jordan, would realize similar potential gains, although Aljoun is much closer and better connected to Amman.

In Morocco, convergence is slowly happening. The country's living standards have shown convergence between 2001 and 2014, but the pace of convergence in consumption remains slow (figure 2.14). In 2006, there was no difference in consumption expenditures between Grand Casablanca (Morocco's largest region)[13] and the regions of Rabat-Salé-Zemmour-Zaër (hosting the Moroccan administration) and Tanger-Tétouan (hosting the Tanger-Med port, Morocco's logistics gateway on the Strait of Gibraltar). The government estimated that, at current conditions, it would take 24 years for the process of convergence to reduce the disparity in regional consumption by half (HCP and World Bank 2017). The large share of the gaps explained by the returns that people would have had in Casablanca signals barriers to mobility in locations where the starker gaps exist. Where the gaps are lower,

MAP 2.3    **Consumption gaps in Iraq, by governorate, 2012**

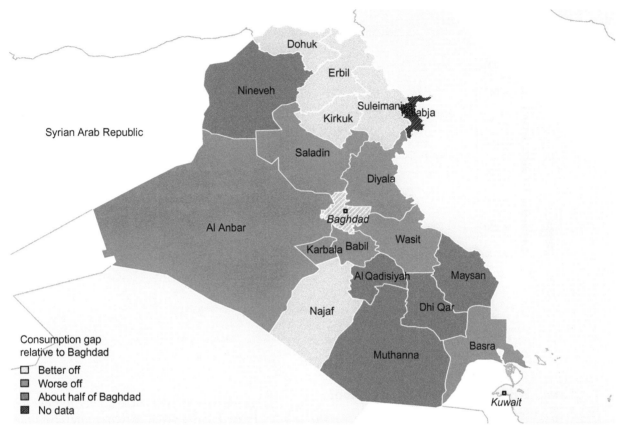

Consumption gap
relative to Baghdad

- ☐ Better off
- ▨ Worse off
- ▨ About half of Baghdad
- ▨ No data

*Source:* Iraq Household Socio-Economic Survey 2012 via the Global Monitoring Database (GMD), World Bank Team for Statistical Development, using the Datalibweb Stata Package.
*Note:* Consumption expenditures are per capita, spatially deflated and converted in terms of US$ (2011) purchasing power parity. The consumption gap is the difference in expenditures between each region and the leading region.

improving endowments should be enough to accelerate convergence.

In Tunisia, the leading East region contrasts with the West region, which lags behind. The Center-East subregion—grouping the Mahdia, Monastir, Sfax, and Sousse governorates—has standards of living similar to Greater Tunis. The gap is a bit larger in the country's North-East region, largely explained by endowments. (Improving education, which is lower there than in the Center-East and Greater Tunis, would translate to an increase of consumption by 11 percent and bridge 43 percent of the gap.) Migrating from the North-East subregion to Greater Tunis would lead to a 10 percent increase in consumption. In the West and North-West regions, the largest share of the consumption gap is explained by households' endowments, contrasting with the South-East and South-West subregions, where returns explain the largest share of the divergence in living standards (above 60 percent). On average, migrating in Tunisia would translate to an increase of 22 percent in consumption.

In the Republic of Yemen, households in Aden (where the port and international airport are located) have slightly better endowments but greater differences in returns than in Sana'a. In the rest of the country, lower endowments explain a large share of the difference.

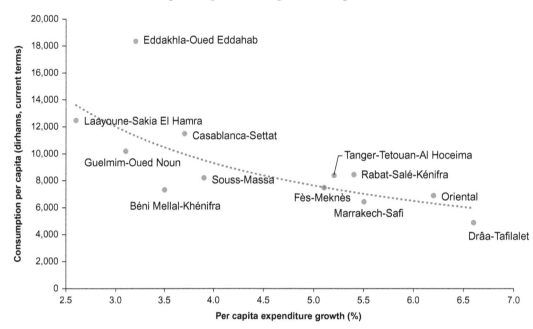

FIGURE 2.14    **Morocco shows signs of regional convergence in living standards**

*Source:* HCP and World Bank 2017.
*Note:.* Consumption expenditures are annual, per capita, spatially deflated and in annual dirhams in current terms.

## What causes such low migration?

From an economic perspective, the low internal migration rate is surprising given the high disparities between regions and the potential returns to migration. Why do so few people in the Middle East and North Africa migrate to pursue better standards of living?

Social, regulatory, and economic barriers can prevent people from migrating despite economic gains. Structural community factors, social capital, and cultural attachment to a particular region affect people's likelihood of migrating (Zelinsky 1973). Government policy (such as land-use management and valuation information systems) or migration costs (whether driven by transport, risk, or relocation costs) can also impede migration (Ravallion and Wodon 1999; World Bank 2014b). Overcoming these barriers should therefore promote mobility.

Better educational achievement, incomes, access to information, and transport and communication infrastructure have been shown to give people the ability to migrate. These factors often increase migration not only directly but also through accompanying processes of social and cultural change. Most people tend to migrate domestically first, and in later stages, they cross borders (Sabadie et al. 2010).

Social networks also play a role in facilitating moves. Migration networks can be a source of information, thus increasing the certainty about returns in potential destinations. Globally, internal migration is higher in countries where more people have access to a mobile phone, because it facilitates information flows and connections (Bell et al. 2015).

As observed in the rest of the world, migrants in Algeria, Egypt, Jordan, Lebanon, Morocco, and Tunisia are significantly richer than the nonmigrants living in their destinations after they move, and they are most likely to have moved to urban areas, while married residents are less likely to migrate.[14] Migrants typically originate from regions

**FIGURE 2.15**   **Poverty rates at origin and destination influence migration in the Middle East and North Africa**

**a. Probability of migration, by origin and destination poverty rate**

**b. Probability of migration, by difference in poverty between origin and destination**

Origin   Destination

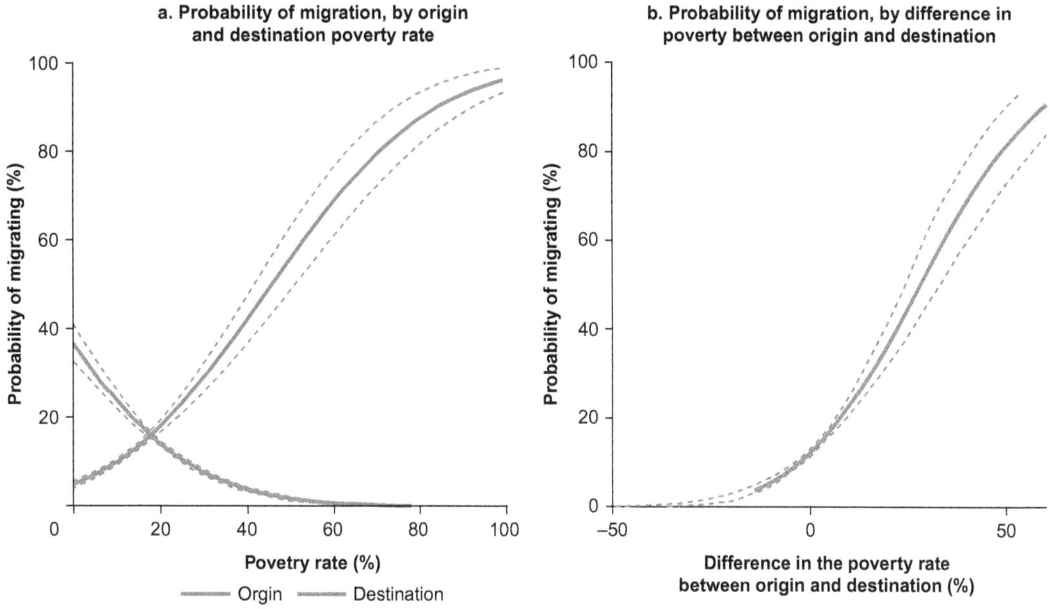

*Source:* Arab Barometer Wave IV (2016–17) data; and Middle East and North Africa Poverty database (MNAPOV), Team for Statistical Development, World Bank.
*Note:* Predictions are based on a Probit model with the dependent variable being whether the person is a migrant and covariates including gender, age, marital status, educational attainment, number of children, poverty rate at destination and origin and the log of population density at origin, and country fixed effects at 90 percent confidence intervals (dashed lines). Average poverty rates from World Bank staff at the first administrative level were matched to place of residence and place of birth. Population density was estimated based on Center for International Earth Science Information Network (CIESIN) of Columbia University, "Gridded Population of the World, Version 4 (GPWv4): Administrative Unit Center Points with Population Estimates, Revision 11."

with higher poverty rates and move to regions where poverty rates are lower (figure 2.15, panel a). The larger the difference in poverty headcount, the more likely migration is to occur (figure 2.15, panel b).

Poverty traps associated with the agriculture map dampen migration. In Egypt, those who do not migrate are predominantly from low-productivity regions and work in agriculture. The reliance on agricultural activities can push individuals into an agricultural poverty trap, in which a large share of total consumption comes from the food they produce, and little is left to finance and bear the risks of seeking new opportunities, such as through migration (Herrera and Badr 2012).

In Syria, migrants were less likely than nonmigrants to be engaged in agricultural work in 2002. Those who moved were clerks, salespeople, or worked in professional occupations (Khawaja 2002), as shown in figure 2.16.

**FIGURE 2.16**   **Distribution of occupations among internal migrants and stayers in the Syrian Arab Republic, 2002**

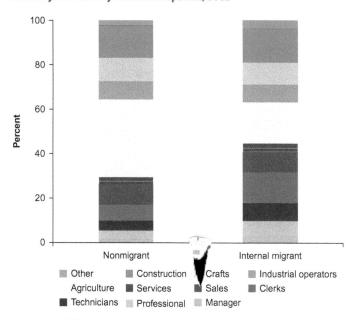

Other   Construction   Crafts   Industrial operators
Agriculture   Services   Sales   Clerks
Technicians   Professional   Manager

*Source:* Khawaja 2002.

**FIGURE 2.17** **Internal migration rates are higher among women than men in several Middle East and North Africa countries**

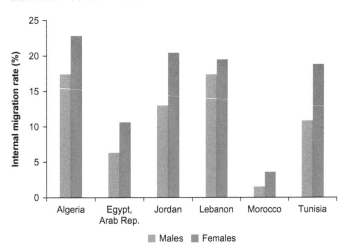

Source: Arab Barometer Wave IV (2016–17) data.
Note: The internal migration rate is the number of lifetime within-country migrants per 100 adults. Lifetime internal migration compares the place of current residence with the place of birth (within the same country). For the Probit model estimating probability, see figure 2.15.

**FIGURE 2.18** **Unemployment rates are higher in the Middle East and North Africa than in upper-middle-income countries of other regions, particularly for educated women**

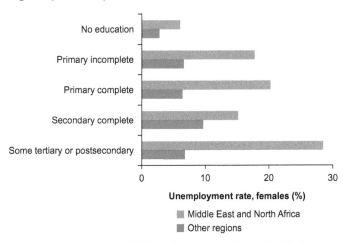

Source: Global Monitoring Database (GMD), Team for Statistical Development, World Bank.
Note: In this figure, "Middle East and North Africa" comprises Djibouti (2012), the Arab Republic of Egypt (2012), the Islamic Republic of Iran (2014), Iraq (2012), Jordan (2010), Lebanon (2011), Morocco (2006), Tunisia (2010), and the Republic of Yemen (2014).

In Egypt, individuals who move usually only do so once in a lifetime, and those who do so tend to move at the time of marriage (Herrera and Badr 2012). In Tunisia, families frequently identify one member to move, and only those with strong networks will move (Zuccotti et al. 2018). In Syria, individuals who move are more likely to receive help from relatives (Khawaja 2002).

In Algeria, Egypt, Jordan, Lebanon, Morocco, and Tunisia, women are on average 5 percent likelier than men to migrate (figure 2.17).[15] Among the reasons could be marriage or job-seeking opportunities, given the high unemployment rate among educated women, which is particularly high in the Middle East and North Africa compared with middle-income countries in other regions (figure 2.18). Although information is not available about the reasons for migration, it is worth noting that at any level of education, female migrants are on average more likely than male migrants to be employed at their destinations in Algeria, Egypt, Jordan, Lebanon, Morocco, and Tunisia (figure 2.19).

## Credential-oriented education systems offer one explanation for low internal mobility

International evidence shows a strong positive relationship between human capital and migration. Economic, geographic, or policy-imposed barriers make it harder for low-skilled people to move and succeed in new locations (UNDP 2009). Census data suggest a strong relationship between educational attainment and the probability to migrate when demographics and employment status are controlled for. For instance, the probability of moving is much higher for university graduates than for adults with less than primary education. This migration effect is one of the major channels through which education supports growth, and education of the poor ensures equitable growth and poverty reduction.

In the Middle East and North Africa, however, having no education is no different from having a university degree in terms of the probability of migrating (figure 2.20).

Elsewhere in the world, the probability of migrating increases with every additional year of schooling. In the Middle East and North Africa, the likelihood remains the same regardless of highest degree acquired. This is true at all levels of income.

One explanation for this anomaly is the credential orientation of most educational systems in the Middle East and North Africa. Despite the region's high educational completion rates relative to comparator countries, the extent of learning is relatively low. Not a single Middle East and North Africa country's students performed near the international median on the recent Trends in International Mathematics and Science Study (TIMSS) and Progress in International Reading Literacy (PIRLS) assessments (World Bank 2019b). Learning-adjusted schooling years in the region reflect, on average, approximately three fewer years of educational completion than the world average (World Bank 2019b).

Postsecondary education in the region's households is not reflected in higher daily expenditure. Consumption expenditure usually rises with educational attainment, but not in the Middle East and North Africa (figure 2.21). Nevertheless, demand remains strong for credentials to access public sector jobs in the region, but the demand for skills remains relatively weak, partly because of weak signals for the need for skills from the region's private sector (World Bank 2019b).

The effect of education on the likelihood of getting a public sector job is significantly higher than the likelihood of simply being employed in the region. In the 1990s, the central government's wages equated to 10 percent of GDP in the Middle East and North Africa—almost double the world average (Makdisi, Fattah, and Limam 2006). As governments rapidly raised requirements for employment, the desired terminal degree that was once a high school diploma became a university education (Salehi-Isfahani 2009). A diploma in hand

**FIGURE 2.19** **In the Middle East and North Africa, female migrants are more likely than male migrants to be employed**

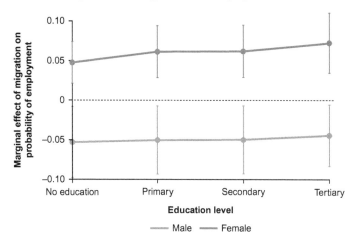

*Source:* Arab Barometer Wave IV (2016–17) data; Middle East and North Africa Poverty database (MNAPOV), Team for Statistical Development, World Bank.
*Note:* In this figure, "Middle East and North Africa" comprises six countries covered in the Arab Barometer Wave IV: Algeria, the Arab Republic of Egypt, Jordan, Lebanon, Morocco, and Tunisia. Predictions are based on a Probit model with the dependent variable being whether the person is employed and covariates include being a migrant interacted with gender, age, marital status, educational attainment, number of children, poverty rate at destination and origin, the log of population density at origin, and country fixed effects at 90 percent confidence intervals. Average poverty rates from World Bank staff at the first administrative level were matched to place of residence and place of birth. Population density was estimated based on Center for International Earth Science Information Network (CIESIN) of Columbia University, "Gridded Population of the World, Version 4 (GPWv4): Administrative Unit Center Points with Population Estimates, Revision 11."

**FIGURE 2.20** **Education has virtually no effect on migration in the Middle East and North Africa, in contrast with the rest of the world**

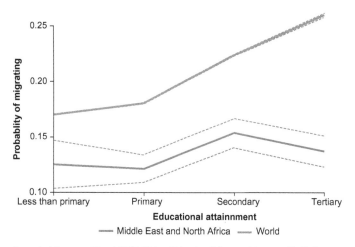

*Source:* Arab Barometer Wave IV (2016-17) data; University of Minnesota's Integrated Public Use Microdata Series (IPUMS) International database.
*Note:* Both estimations are based on a Probit model (as in figure 2.15), restricting controls to gender, age, marital status, educational attainment, and country fixed effects for comparability perspective at 90 percent confidence intervals. In this figure, "Middle East and North Africa" comprises six countries covered in the Arab Barometer Wave IV: Algeria, the Arab Republic of Egypt, Jordan, Lebanon, Morocco, and Tunisia. "World" comprises all countries listed in annex 2A, table 2A.1.

increases the chances of working in the public sector (figure 2.22).

By the mid-1990s, the region's governments faced fiscal contractions, limiting their ability to serve as the employer of

choice. Nevertheless, the wage bill has not changed much since then and remains the highest in the world at 9 percent of GDP, or 30 percent of expenditures (Baddock, Lang, and Srivastava 2016). As such, credentials have historically been viewed as critical to access local public sector jobs, but those credentials have not necessarily endowed individuals with portable skills and may play a part in limiting internal migration.

## Concluding remarks

In the Middle East and North Africa, countries exhibit within-country spatial disparities that are generally higher than those in countries of comparable income in other regions. In some cases, such as Tunisia, spatial disparities have increased across certain dimensions over time instead of declining, as is the pattern elsewhere in the world as incomes rise.

Internal migration rates within many of the region's countries are significantly lower than in comparator countries—and all while the potential gains from moving to relatively

**FIGURE 2.21**   **Higher education in Middle East and North Africa households is not reflected in daily expenditure as much as in other regions**

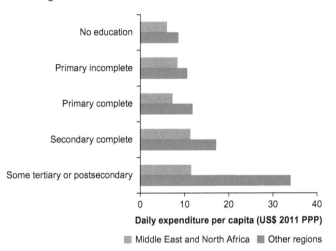

**Daily expenditure per capita (US$ 2011 PPP)**

Middle East and North Africa    Other regions

*Source:* Middle East and North Africa Poverty database (MNAPOV), Team for Statistical Development, World Bank.
*Note:* PPP = purchasing power parity.

**FIGURE 2.22**   **In the Middle East and North Africa, tertiary education diplomas are highly valued in the public sector**

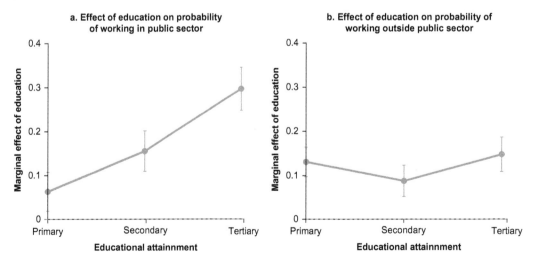

*Source:* Arab Barometer Wave IV (2016–17) data.
*Note:* The marginal effects are based on Probit regressions controlling for area of residence (urban or rural), gender, age, number of children, marital status, and country fixed effects at 90 percent confidence intervals.

leading regions could be significant with respect to consumption expenditures. Unlike elsewhere in the world, the likelihood of migration does not increase with attainment of tertiary education. One explanation for lower internal migration is the credential-orientation of most of the region's education systems, whereby higher diplomas historically enabled greater access to local public sector jobs but did not necessarily confer skills needed to compete for private sector jobs outside of home regions.

## Annex 2A Data sources and coverage

This chapter relies on various sources of data. Socioeconomic surveys cover nine countries and 69 percent of the Middle East and North Africa population. Consumption expenditure and access to services and related spatial inequality measures are calculated based on these surveys. Poverty rates were also made available for Lebanon and Algeria, which increases coverage from 69 percent to 80 percent of the region's population.

Wave IV (2016–17) of the Arab Barometer includes six countries, covering 45 percent of the region's population: Algeria, Egypt, Jordan, Lebanon, Morocco, and Tunisia. Empirical analyses on the links between credentialistic education and mobility undertaken in this chapter are based on this dataset and complemented by existing literature. No data were available for the GCC countries, Syria, and Libya.

## Measuring inequalities in consumption expenditures within countries

The Theil T index can be used to assess the major contributors to inequality by different subgroups of the population, such as between regions. Average expenditures vary not only between regions but also inside each region, adding a "within-group" component to total inequality. The generalized entropy class of indicators, including the Theil

indexes, can be decomposed across these partitions in an additive way (while the Gini index cannot).

The Theil T Index can be written as

$$T = \frac{1}{N} \sum_{i=1}^{N} \frac{y_i}{\overline{y}} \ln\left(\frac{y_i}{\overline{y}}\right), \qquad (2A.1)$$

with $y_i$ denoting the expenditure of individual $i$ in a country, $\overline{y}$ the average expenditure of the population, and $N$ the total population. The country is divided into M regions $j = 1...M$. We can rewrite as

$$T = \frac{1}{N} \sum_{j=1}^{M} \sum_{i=1}^{N_j} \frac{y_{ij}}{\overline{y}} \ln\left(\frac{y_{ij}}{\overline{y}}\right). \qquad (2A.2)$$

Following Sali-i-Martin (2002), equation 2A.2 can be rewritten as

$$T = \sum_{j=1}^{M} s_j \ln\left(\frac{y_j}{\overline{y}}\right) + \sum_{j=1}^{M} s_j \ln\left(\frac{y_{ji}}{y_j}\right), \qquad (2A.3)$$

where the first term represents the between-group inequality, and the second term represents the within-group inequality. Typically, at least three-quarters of inequality in a country is due to within-region inequality, and the remaining quarter to between-group differences.

## Census data

The author wishes to acknowledge the statistical offices that provided the underlying census data making this research possible (table 2A.1).

## Survey data

The household survey data were gathered using the Global Monitoring Database (GMD) and Middle East and North Africa Poverty database (MNAPOV) ex post harmonization of the World Bank's Team for Statistical Development (2018) via the Datalibweb Stata Package for the countries listed in table 2A.2.

TABLE 2A.1  **Sources and years of global census data, by country**

| Country | Year | Source |
|---|---|---|
| Armenia | 2011 | National Statistical Service |
| Benin | 2013 | National Institute for Statistics and Economic Analysis |
| Botswana | 2011 | Central Statistics Office |
| Burkina Faso | 2006 | National Institute of Statistics and Demography |
| Brazil | 2010 | Institute of Geography and Statistics |
| Cameroon | 2005 | Central Bureau of Census and Population Studies |
| Cambodia | 2008 | National Institute of Statistics |
| Chile | 2002 | National Institute of Statistics |
| China | 2000 | National Bureau of Statistics |
| Colombia | 2005 | National Administrative Department of Statistics |
| Costa Rica | 2011 | National Institute of Statistics and Censuses |
| Cuba | 2002 | Office of National Statistics |
| Dominican Republic | 2010 | National Statistics Office |
| Ecuador | 2010 | National Institute of Statistics and Censuses |
| Egypt, Arab Rep. | 2006 | Central Agency for Public Mobilization and Statistics |
| El Salvador | 2007 | Department of Statistics and Censuses |
| Ghana | 2010 | Ghana Statistical Services |
| Greece | 2011 | National Statistical Office |
| Haiti | 2003 | Institute of Statistics and Informatics |
| Honduras | 2001 | National Institute of Statistics |
| Indonesia | 2010 | BPS Statistics Indonesia |
| Iraq | 1997 | Central Organization for Statistics and Information Technology |
| Ireland | 2011 | Central Statistics Office |
| Jamaica | 2001 | Statistical Institute |
| Kenya | 2009 | National Bureau of Statistics |
| Kyrgyz Republic | 2009 | National Statistical Committee |
| Liberia | 2008 | Institute of Statistics and Geo-Information Systems |
| Malawi | 2008 | National Statistical Office |
| Malaysia | 2000 | Department of Statistics |
| Mali | 2009 | National Directorate of Statistics and Informatics |
| Mexico | 2015 | National Institute of Statistics, Geography, and Informatics |
| Mongolia | 2000 | National Statistical Office |
| Mozambique | 2007 | National Institute of Statistics |
| Papua New Guinea | 2000 | National Statistical Office |
| Paraguay | 2002 | General Directorate of Statistics, Surveys, and Censuses |
| Peru | 2007 | National Institute of Statistics and Informatics |
| Portugal | 2011 | National Institute of Statistics |
| Romania | 2011 | National Institute of Statistics |
| Rwanda | 2012 | National Institute of Statistics |
| Senegal | 2002 | National Agency of Statistics and Demography |
| Sierra Leone | 2004 | Statistics Sierra Leone |
| Slovenia | 2002 | Statistical Office of the Republic of Slovenia |
| South Africa | 2011 | Statistics South Africa |
| Spain | 2011 | National Institute of Statistics |
| Sudan | 2008 | Central Bureau of Statistics |
| Switzerland | 2000 | Federal Statistical Office |
| Tanzania | 2012 | Bureau of Statistics |
| Thailand | 2000 | National Statistical Office |
| Turkey | 2000 | Turkish Statistical Institute |
| Uganda | 2002 | Bureau of Statistics |
| Ukraine | 2001 | State Committee of Statistics |
| United States | 2015 | Bureau of the Census |
| Uruguay | 2011 | National Institute of Statistics |
| Venezuela, RB | 2001 | National Institute of Statistics |
| Zambia | 2010 | Central Statistics Office |

TABLE 2A.2 **Countries and years of survey data**

| Country | Survey year(s) |
|---|---|
| Argentina | 2012, 2014 |
| Benin | 2015 |
| Brazil | 2009, 2014 |
| Burkina Faso | 2009 |
| Cameroon | 2007 |
| Chile | 2011, 2013 |
| Colombia | 2014, 2016 |
| Congo, Dem. Rep. | 2012 |
| Costa Rica | 2012, 2014, 2016 |
| Djibouti | 2012 |
| Ecuador | 2014, 2016 |
| Egypt, Arab Rep. | 2012 |
| Ethiopia | 2010 |
| Ghana | 2012 |
| Haiti | 2012 |
| Honduras | 2012, 2013, 2016 |
| India | 2009, 2011 |
| Indonesia | 2005, 2011, 2014, 2016 |
| Iran, Islamic Rep. | 2009, 2014[a] |
| Iraq | 2006, 2012 |
| Jordan | 2006, 2008, 2010 |
| Kenya | 2005 |
| Lao PDR | 2007, 2012 |
| Lebanon | 2011 |
| Madagascar | 2010 |
| Malawi | 2010 |
| Malaysia | 2016 |
| Mali | 2010 |
| Mexico | 2014 |
| Mongolia | 2010, 2011, 2012, 2014 |
| Morocco | 2000, 2006 |
| Mozambique | 2008 |
| Niger | 2011 |
| Nicaragua | 2014 |
| Papua New Guinea | 2009 |
| Paraguay | 2014 |
| Peru | 2014, 2016 |
| Senegal | 2011 |
| Sierra Leone | 2011 |
| South Africa | 2010 |
| Sudan | 2009 |
| Tanzania | 2011 |
| Thailand | 2006, 2009, 2012 |
| Tunisia | 2005, 2010 |
| Turkey | 2014 |
| Uganda | 2012 |
| Ukraine | 2016 |
| Uruguay | 2012, 2014 |
| Vietnam | 2006, 2010, 2012, 2014 |
| Yemen, Rep. | 2005, 2014 |
| Zambia | 2010 |

a. For the Islamic Republic of Iran in 2014, the international poverty rate is slightly different from the poverty rate reported by the World Bank in World Development Indicators and PovcalNet. The difference comes from the way welfare aggregate is created. This welfare aggregate excludes expenditure on health and durables for technical reasons and is inter-temporally and spatially deflated to account for changes in prices during the survey period and spatial variation in prices. Detailed explanation of methodology to construct welfare aggregate is available in Atamanov et al. (2016).

## Notes

1. Inequality in consumption is calculated based on the Theil index (see annex 2A for data and methodology). Expenditures have been spatially deflated to account for price differences across regions. The regional comparison controls for income, population, the share of urban population, and the share of population in the largest city.
2. The Casablanca-Settat region of Morocco was so named in 2015 after the region formerly referred to as Greater Casablanca or Grand Casablanca annexed several provinces.
3. More recent data are available for the entire region and portray a similar picture. Unfortunately, there is no disaggregation by country. In 2014, estimated infrastructure spending in the Middle East and North Africa was 6.9 percent of GDP (Fay et al. 2019). Needs were also assessed in various scenarios. In the preferred scenario, the Middle East and North Africa needs to spend 7.1 percent of GDP to develop infrastructure between 2015 and 2030 to reach ambitious goals. This scenario assumes high spending efficiency, which depends on the quality of complementary policies and on measures to reduce unit costs (like better procurement, planning, or execution) (Rozenberg and Fay 2019).
4. Water stress arises when water withdrawals for human, agricultural, and industrial uses are relatively high compared with the level of renewable water resources—in other words, when the ratio of water withdrawal to water availability is high. It is quantified as the ratio of annual water withdrawals to average annual surface water availability, driven by either climate change under a high emission scenario or socioeconomic change under a business-as-usual scenario for population growth and the economy. Estimates of surface water stress do not account for withdrawals from groundwater and nonconventional water supplies.
5. An "improved" drinking-water source is defined as one that, by nature of its construction or through active intervention, is protected from outside contamination, in particular from contamination with fecal matter (World Bank 2017a).
6. Task team interviews with local residents.
7. Chapters 1 and 3 explore other key contributors to convergence, such as agglomeration, specialization, and interregional links.

8. Internal migration rates are based on census data from 38 countries outside the Middle East and North Africa, whose censuses include birthplace at the first administrative level for comparability purposes. The only Middle East and North Africa countries with a census were Egypt and Iraq. Random respondents ages 18 and above were selected from available censuses (see annex 2A, table 2A.1), with half men and half women to be comparable with the Arab Barometer data—which are available for Algeria, Jordan, Lebanon, Morocco, Tunisia, and West Bank and Gaza. The latter was excluded given the peculiarity of that economy. For Egypt, the Arab Barometer was used *instead* of that country's census because that survey was more recent (2016 versus 2006). In Egypt, the Arab Barometer did not survey the Sinai Peninsula, Matruh, New Valley, and Red Sea governorates where collectively less than 2 percent of the population lives.

9. Leading regions are Djibouti City in Djibouti; Cairo, Alexandria, Suez, and Port-Said in Egypt; Tehran in the Islamic Republic of Iran; the Kurdistan governorates (Duhouk, Erbil, and Suleimaniya) in Iraq; Amman in Jordan; the Casablanca-Settat area in Morocco; Great Tunis in Tunisia; and Sana'a in the Republic of Yemen.

10. The sum of endowments and returns effects gives the total welfare gap.

11. These governorates include Sharkiya, Behira, Dakahliya, Domiyat, Gharbiya Ismailia, Kafr-elsheikh, Menofiya, and Kaliobiya.

12. The southernmost provinces exclude Kerman and Sistan.

13. The survey was conducted before the regions were redrawn, after which the region's name changed to Casablanca-Settat.

14. All data here from the Arab Barometer unless otherwise stated. This is the only dataset with comparable information on lifetime internal migration in six countries in the region. Although the data and sample are limited in terms of representation and of sector of employment and social network information, the dataset contains the main migration drivers such as age, income, and education.

15. Figure 2.17 is a simple bar graph, while the estimated probability is based on the Probit model estimated in figure 2.15.

## References

Atamanov, A., M. Mostafavi, D. Salehi-Isfahani, and T. Vishwanath. 2016. "Constructing Robust Poverty Trends in the Islamic Republic of Iran: 2008–2014." Policy Research Working Paper 7836, World Bank, Washington, DC.

Baddock, Emily, Peter Lang, and Vivek Srivastava. 2016. "Size of the Public Sector: Government Wage Bill and Employment." Summary Note, World Bank, Washington, DC.

Bain, R., R. Cronk, J. Wright, H. Yang, T. Slaymaker, and J. Bartram. 2014. "Fecal Contamination of Drinking Water in Low- and Middle-Income Countries: A Systematic Review and Meta-Analysis." *PLOS Medicine* 11 (5): e1001644.

Bell, M., E. Charles-Edwards, P. Ueffing, J. Stillwell, M. Kupiszewski, and D. Kupiszewska. 2015. "Internal Migration and Development: Comparing Migration Intensities Around the World." *Population and Development Review* 41 (1): 33–58.

Berglöf, E., and S. Devarajan. 2015. "Water for Development: Fulfilling the Promise." In *Water for Development: Charting a Water Wise Path*, edited by Anders Jägerskog, Torkil Jønch Clausen, Torgny Holmgren, and Karin Lexén, 23–27. Stockholm: Stockholm International Water Institute (SIWI).

Blinder, A. S. 1973. "Wage Discrimination: Reduced Form and Structural Estimates." *Journal of Human Resources* 8 (4): 436–55.

Bouassida, I., and A.-R. El Lahga. 2018. "Public-Private Wage Disparities, Employment, and Labor Market Segmentation in Tunisia." In *The Tunisian Labor Market in an Era of Transition*, edited by R. Assaad and M. Boughazala, 86–112. London: Oxford University Press.

Brixi, H., E. Lust, and M. Woolcock. 2015. *Trust, Voice, and Incentives: Learning from Local Success Stories in Service Delivery in the Middle East and North Africa*. Washington, DC: World Bank.

Chernozhukov, V., I. Fernández-Val, and B. Melly. 2013. "Inference on Counterfactual Distributions." *Econometrica* 81 (6): 2205–68.

Cotton, J. 1988. "On the Decomposition of Wage Differentials." *Review of Economics and Statistics* 70 (2): 236–43.

D'Aoust, O., and V. S. Lall. nd. "Unequal Spaces and Stuck People." Unpublished manuscript. World Bank, Washington DC.

Devarajan, Shantayanan. 2016. "An Exposition of the New Strategy, 'Promoting Peace and Stability in the Middle East and North Africa.'" Working paper, Report No. 102936, World Bank, Washington, DC.

Estache, A., E. Ianchovichina, R. Bacon, and I. Salamon. 2013. *Infrastructure and Employment Creation in the Middle East and North Africa*. Washington, DC: World Bank.

Farajalla, N. 2016. "Water Resources and Conflict in Lebanon." In *Losing Paradise: The Water Crisis in the Mediterranean*, edited by Gail Holst-Warhaft and Tammo Steenhus, 125–40. Abingdon, U.K.: Routledge.

Fay, M., S. Han, Y. Lee, M. Mastruzzi, and M. Cho. 2019. "Hitting the Trillion Mark–A Look at How Much Countries Are Spending on Infrastructure." Policy Research Working Paper 8730, World Bank, Washington, DC.

Fortin, N., T. Lemieux, and S. Firpo. 2011. "Decomposition Methods in Economics." In *Handbook of Labor Economics,* Vol. 4A: 1–102. Amsterdam: Elsevier.

Haughton, Jonathan, and Shahidur R. Khandker. 2009. *Handbook on Poverty and Inequality.* Washington, DC: World Bank.

HCP and World Bank (Haut-Commissariat au Plan and World Bank). 2017. «Pauvreté et prospérité partagée au Maroc du troisième millénaire, 2001–2014.» (In French.) Report, HCP and World Bank, Washington, DC.

Henderson, J. V., T. Squires, A. Storeygard, and D. Weil. 2017. "The Global Distribution of Economic Activity: Nature, History, and the Role of Trade." *Quarterly Journal of Economics* 133 (1): 1–50.

Herrera, S., and K. Badr. 2012. "Internal Migration in Egypt: Levels, Determinants, Wages, and Likelihood of Employment." Policy Research Working Paper 6166, World Bank, Washington, DC.

Herrera-Idárraga, P., E. López-Bazo, and E. Motellón. 2016. "Regional Wage Gaps, Education and Informality in an Emerging Country: The Case of Colombia." *Spatial Economic Analysis* 11 (4): 432–56.

Hollweg, C., D. Lederman, D. Rojas, and E. Ruppert Bulmer. 2014. *Sticky Feet: How Labor Market Frictions Shape the Impact of International Trade on Jobs and Wages.* Washington, DC: World Bank.

Hutton, G. 2013. "Global Costs and Benefits of Reaching Universal Coverage of Sanitation and Drinking-Water Supply." *Journal of Water and Health* 11 (1): 1–12.

Jann, B., and E. Zurich. 2008. "A Stata Implementation of the Blinder-Oaxaca Decomposition." *Stata Journal* 8 (4): 453–79.

Khawaja, M. 2002. "Internal Migration in Syria: Findings from a National Survey." Report 375, Fafo Research Foundation, Oslo, Norway.

Krishnan, N., G. L. Ibarra, A. Narayan, S. Tiwari, and T. Vishwanata. 2017. *Uneven Odds, Unequal Outcomes. Inequality of Opportunity in the Middle East and North Africa*. Directions in Development Series. Washington, DC: World Bank.

Machado, J. A., and J. Mata. 2005. "Counterfactual Decomposition of Changes in Wage Distributions Using Quantile Regression." *Journal of Applied Econometrics* 20 (4): 445–65.

Mahdi, B. A., and N. A. M. Fawzi. 2014. "Iraq's Inland Water Quality and Their Impact on the North-Western Arabian Gulf." *Marsh Bulletin* 9 (1): 1–22.

Makdisi, S., Z. Fattah, and I. Limam. 2006. "Determinants of Growth in the MENA Countries." In *Explaining Growth in the Middle East,* edited by Jeffrey Nugent and Hashem Pesaran, 32–60. Bingley, U.K.: Emerald Group Publishing Limited.

Malik, A., and B. Awadallah. 2013. "The Economics of the Arab Spring." *World Development* 45: 296–313.

Melly, B. 2005. "Decomposition of Differences in Distribution Using Quantile Regression." *Labour Economics* 12 (4): 577–90.

Motellón, E., E. López-Bazo, and M. El-Attar. 2011. "Regional Heterogeneity in Wage Distributions: Evidence from Spain." *Journal of Regional Science* 51 (3): 558–84.

Oaxaca, R. 1973. "Male–Female Wage Differentials in Urban Labor Markets." *International Economic Review* 14 (3): 693–709.

Pereira, J., and A. Galego. 2014. "Interregional Wage Differentials in Portugal: An Analysis across the Wage Distribution." *Regional Studies* 48 (9): 1529–46.

Ravallion, M., and Q. Wodon. 1999. "Poor Areas, or Only Poor People?" *Journal of Regional Science* 39 (4): 689–711.

Rozenberg, J., and M. Fay. 2019. "Beyond the Gap: How Countries Can Afford the Infrastructure They Need while Protecting the Planet." World Bank, Washington, DC.

Sabadie, Jesus Alquezar, Johanna Avato, Ummuhan Bardak, Francesco Panzica, and Natalia Popova. 2010. *Migration and Skills: The Experience of Migrant Workers from Albania, Egypt, Moldova, and Tunisia*. Directions in Development Series. Washington, DC: World Bank.

Sadoff, C. W., J. W. Hall, D. Grey, J. C. J. H. Aerts, M. Ait-Kadi, C. Brown, A. Cox, et al. 2015. *Securing Water, Sustaining Growth: Report of the GWP/OECD Task Force on Water Security and Sustainable Growth*. Oxford: University of Oxford.

Sala-i-Martin, X. 2002. *The Disturbing Rise of Global Income Inequality*. NBER Working Paper No. 8904, National Bureau of Economic Research, Cambridge, MA.

Salehi-Isfahani, D. 2009. "Education and Earnings in the Middle East: A Comparative Study of Returns to Schooling in Egypt, Iran, and Turkey." Working Paper Series 504, Economic Research Forum, Giza, Egypt.

Skeldon, R. 2013. "Global Migration: Demographic Aspects and Its Relevance for Development." Technical Paper 2013/6, Population Division, United Nations Department of Economic and Social Affairs (UN DESA), New York.

Testaverde, M., H. Moroz, C. Hollweg, and A. Schmillen. 2017. *Migrating to Opportunity: Overcoming Barriers to Labor Mobility in Southeast Asia*. Washington, DC: World Bank.

UNDP (United Nations Development Programme). 2009. *Human Development Report 2009: Overcoming Barriers: Human Mobility and Development*. New York: UNDP.

UNOCHA (United Nations Office for the Coordination of Humanitarian Affairs). 2017. "Yemen: 2018 Humanitarian Needs Overview." Report, UNOCHA, New York and Geneva.

WEF (World Economic Forum). 2015. "Global Risks 2015, 10th Edition." Insight Report, WEF, Geneva.

Whittington, D., C. Nauges, D. Fuente, and X. Wu. 2015. "A Diagnostic Tool for Estimating the Incidence of Subsidies Delivered by Water Utilities in Low- and Medium-Income Countries, with Illustrative Simulations." *Utilities Policy* 34: 70–81.

WHO (World Health Organization). 2018. "Epidemic and pandemic-prone diseases. Outbreak update: Cholera in Yemen, 19 July 2018." Release, WHO Regional Office for the Eastern Mediterranean (EMRO), Cairo.

World Bank. 2010. "Transport. Sectoral Notes, Middle East and North Africa-Regional Transport Annual Meetings." Internal document, World Bank, Washington, DC.

———. 2011. *Poor Places, Thriving People: How the Middle East and North Africa Can Rise Above Spatial Disparities*. MENA Development Report Series. Washington, DC: World Bank.

———. 2012. "Arab Republic of Egypt: Reshaping Egypt's Economic Geography: Domestic Integration as a Development Platform." Report No. 71289-EG, World Bank, Washington, DC.

———. 2014a. "Iraq: The Unfulfilled Promise of Oil and Growth: Poverty, Inclusion and Welfare in Iraq, 2007–2012." Report No. 92681-IQ, World Bank, Washington, DC.

———. 2014b. "Tunisia Urbanization Review: Reclaiming the Glory of Carthage." World Bank, Washington, DC. https://bit .ly/2WqQKaT.

———. 2014c. "The Unfinished Revolution: Bringing Opportunity, Good Jobs and Greater Wealth to All Tunisians." Development Policy Review, Report No. 86179-TN, World Bank, Washington, DC.

———. 2017a. *Beyond Scarcity: Water Security in the Middle East and North Africa*. MENA Development Report Series. Washington, DC: World Bank.

———. 2017b. "Cities of Refuge in the Middle East. Bringing an Urban Lens to the Forced Displacement Challenge." Policy Note, Report No. 121515, World Bank, Washington, DC.

———. 2017c. *Forcibly Displaced: Toward a Development Approach Supporting Refugees, the Internally Displaced, and Their Hosts*. Washington, DC: World Bank.

———. 2017d. "Reducing Inequalities in Water Supply, Sanitation, and Hygiene in the Era of the Sustainable Development Goals: Synthesis Report of the WASH Poverty Diagnostic Initiative." Report No. 127135, World Bank, Washington, DC.

———. 2019a. "Economic and Social Inclusion for Peace and Stability in the Middle East and

North Africa: A New Strategy for the World Bank Group." PowerPoint presentation, World Bank, Washington, DC. http://pubdocs .worldbank.org/en/335571450333797609 /121815-middle-east-and-north-africa-seminar .pdf.

———. 2019b. *Expectations and Aspirations: A New Framework for Education in the Middle East and North Africa.* Washington, DC: World Bank.

Zelinsky, W. 1973. *The Cultural Geography of the United States.* Englewood Cliffs, NJ: Prentice-Hall.

Zuccotti, C. V., A. Geddes, A. Bacchi, M. Nori, and R. Stojanov. 2018. *Drivers and Patterns of Rural Youth Migration and its Impact on Food Security and Rural Livelihoods in Tunisia.* Rome: Food and Agriculture Organization of the United Nations (FAO).

# Walled Urban Economies | 3

Economies are walled off from others, regionally and globally, by many barriers that Middle East and North Africa governments have created—or failed to remove. These walls limit regional market access and dampen the potential for economies of scale and specialization for the region's cities. To improve local business ecosystems, the large cities need large markets, and secondary cities need complementary policy and investment.

Many of the Middle East and North Africa's largest cities appear too large for their domestic markets. Especially in the Mashreq and Gulf Cooperation Council (GCC) countries, urban primacy—the share of the urban population in the largest city—is higher than in any other world region.[1] This may be due to region-specific differences in urban management or policy as well as public investment bias toward politically important large cities, where a better business environment and supply of urban services might attract more firms and people. Alternatively, these large cities may reflect a long history of agglomeration economies that continue to serve as attractive areas for colocation. The largest cities thus become magnets for migrants. There is evidence for both explanations, but another aspect must also be considered.

The region's largest cities may be too large for their local markets but may be rightsized if they could more easily serve much larger regional markets. The largest cities in well-integrated regions attract human and financial capital from their neighbors and produce goods and services for the entire region. London, Paris, or Vienna are large relative to their countries' populations but not relative to the markets they can serve. In the Middle East and North Africa, in contrast, most cities that could play a much greater regional role are prevented from doing so by numerous barriers to regional economic integration.

The region's secondary cities suffer from a variety of complementary policy and investment constraints. Unlike in other regions of the world, firm productivity appears to be most influenced by location rather than firm size. While not problematic per se, such a finding raises the possibility that the lack of an enabling environment in the periphery[2]—either through limited fiscal decentralization, suboptimal spatial distribution of infrastructure, or cronyism—might be skewing the distribution of economic activity toward the capital.

It is important here that secondary cities and large cities not be viewed as substitutes; they should perform as complements.

Three decades of research worldwide highlight that businesses and people can exploit economies of scale and agglomeration if their cities perform their intended functions. Policy makers should start by treating their cities as a portfolio of assets, each asset differentiated by characteristics that include size, location, and population density.

This chapter documents the unbalanced urban size distribution in most Middle East and North Africa countries and its implications for regional integration. On average in this region, the country's largest city is home to about a quarter of the national urban population, while most secondary cities are small. Historically, the region's largest cities were closely connected and served as centers for production, innovation, and learning for the entire region. But, as this chapter shows, Middle East and North Africa countries today are poorly integrated, with lower interaction between countries than in economically more dynamic world regions.

The chapter provides evidence that the flows of goods, services, capital, and labor—what the European Union (EU) calls the "four freedoms"—face high barriers, as do the flows of ideas, for instance, through media or personal exchanges. The status of regional integration agreements also reflects these barriers. Although such agreements are relatively strong among the Gulf countries, the rest of the region is linked internally by shallow regional integration agreements that have not promoted the emergence of regional production networks supported by strong urban agglomeration economies. This chapter discusses the state of regional integration, chapter 4 discusses some of the main reasons explaining limited regional integration, and chapter 6 suggests some of the steps toward greater integration in the face of existing barriers.

## Large cities will remain important in the Middle East and North Africa landscape

Urban primacy—the share of the urban population residing in a country's largest urban area—is a defining characteristic of the Middle East and North Africa's urban system. In the region, on average, around 25 percent of the urban population is concentrated in a country's largest city (figure 3.1). Sub-Saharan Africa is the only region with a higher urban primacy, at 28 percent. Urban primacy—the share of the urban population residing in a country's largest urban area—is a defining

**FIGURE 3.1** **Urban primacy rates are high in the Middle East and North Africa, driven mainly by population distributions in the GCC and Mashreq subregions**

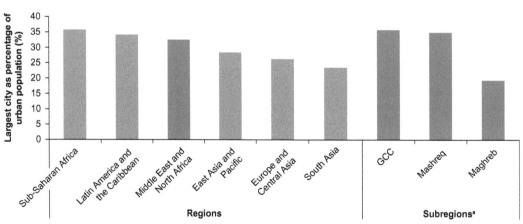

*Source:* UN DESA database: https://population.un.org/wup/
a. States composed of a single urban settlement and with a primacy equal to 1 (100% of urban population in the largest city) were excluded from the analysis. Maghreb refers to Algeria, Libya, Morocco, and Tunisia; Mashreq to the Arab Republic of Egypt, Iraq, Israel, Jordan, Lebanon, and the Syrian Arab Republic; and the Gulf Cooperation Council (GCC) to Bahrain, Kuwait, Oman, Qatar, Saudi Arabia, and the United Arab Emirates.

characteristic of the Middle East and North Africa and its subregions' urban system. On average, around 32 percent of the urban population is concentrated in a country's largest city in the region, which places it slightly below Latin America and the Caribbean (34 percent) and Sub-Saharan Africa (36 percent) (figure 3.1). Urban primacy is significantly lower on average in other regions such as East Asia and Pacific (28 percent), Europe and Central Asia (26 percent), and it is especially low in South Asia (only 23 percent).

## The region's urban population is heavily skewed toward its largest cities

The Middle East and North Africa region's high average urban primacy is largely due to the high concentration of urban population in the largest cities in the Mashreq and GCC subregions—36 percent and 35 percent, respectively. It is far lower in the Maghreb subregion, with the largest cities only accounting for an average of about 19 percent of the urban population.

Across countries within subregions, urban primacy varies significantly. In the GCC subregion, the concentration of the urban population in the largest city ranges from 24 percent in Saudi Arabia to 65 percent in Kuwait. In the Maghreb subregion, all countries are included in an interval between 9 percent (Algeria) and 23 percent (Libya), and in the Mashreq subregion, in an interval between 22 percent (Jordan) and 64 percent (Israel).

The primate city in each of the region's countries is the main area of wealth production as well as population. In most countries, gross domestic product (GDP) concentration is higher than population concentration because agglomeration economies tend to raise residents' productivity.

More general measures of urban concentration—the share of population living in cities larger than 1 million—are also higher in the GCC and Mashreq than in the Maghreb (figure 3.2). While the Middle East and North Africa as a whole is close to the overall average urban concentration (around 40 percent), the Mashreq and GCC subregions display very high concentration patterns (43 percent and 46 percent, respectively). Conversely, the Maghreb subregion displays low urban concentration, with only 20 percent.

The evolution of urban population distribution in the past 35 years shows the

**FIGURE 3.2** **Urban population distribution is skewed toward large cities in the GCC and the Mashreq, but concentrations are much lower in the Maghreb**

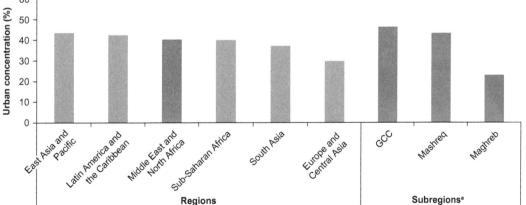

*Source:* UN DESA database, https://population.un.org/wup.
*Note:* "Urban concentration" is the share of population living in large cities. The country-level figures were computed using either (a) cities of 1 million inhabitants or more, or (b) the share represented by the capital city in countries that had no cities exceeding 1 million inhabitants.
a. Maghreb refers to Algeria, Libya, Morocco, and Tunisia; Mashreq to the Arab Republic of Egypt, Iraq, Israel, Jordan, Lebanon, and the Syrian Arab Republic; and the Gulf Cooperation Council (GCC) to Bahrain, Kuwait, Oman, Qatar, Saudi Arabia, and the United Arab Emirates.

increasing divergence between subregions of the Middle East and North Africa. As in Europe and Central Asia and in Sub-Saharan Africa, about 40 percent of the urban population growth in the Middle East and North Africa has been in cities with more than 1 million inhabitants. Although this points to a significant increase in the share of urban population living in secondary cities, the speed of this expansion is rather slow (UN DESA 2019). And the dynamics vary significantly from one subregion to another: more than 60 percent of the GCC countries' urban expansion has occurred in cities above

1 million, as has around 45 percent in the Mashreq subregion and less than 20 percent in the Maghreb subregion.

This urban hierarchy is skewed more toward the largest cities in the Middle East and North Africa than it is in other regions of the world (figure 3.3). In the Maghreb subregion, cities above 1 million concentrate only about 20 percent of the urban population, which fits a rather low urbanization growth rate in the past decade (figure 3.3, panel b). This pattern is similar to the one observed in European countries, where urbanization has happened gradually over time and the urban

**FIGURE 3.3**  **Distribution of the urban population skews toward the largest cities in the Middle East and North Africa**

*Share of urban population, by city population class, 2015*

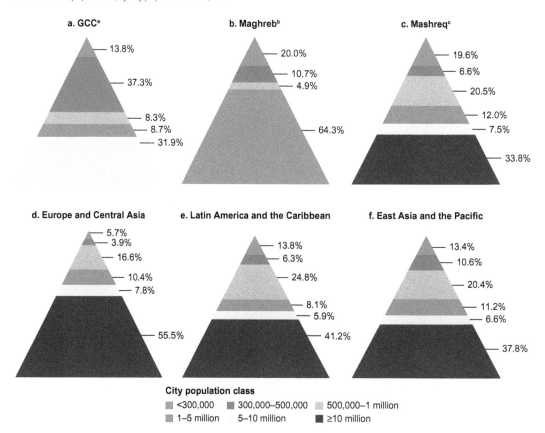

*Source:* UN DESA database, https://population.un.org/wup.

a. The Gulf Cooperation Council (GCC) comprises Bahrain, Kuwait, Oman, Qatar, Saudi Arabia, and the United Arab Emirates.

b. The Maghreb subregion comprises Algeria, Libya, Morocco, and Tunisia.

c. The Mashreq subregion comprises the Arab Republic of Egypt, Iraq, Israel, Jordan, Lebanon and the Syrian Arab Republic.

system is fairly well balanced. The urban systems of the Mashreq and GCC regions, in contrast, present imbalances, with cities above 1 million representing a disproportionate share of the urban system pyramid (figure 3.3, panels a and c).

Medium-size and small cities represent significantly lower shares of the urban system. In this sense, the urban systems of the GCC and Mashreq countries look much like the urban systems of the Latin America and Caribbean region (figure 3.3, panel e), which is known for its imbalances and relatively high primacy. While in Europe and Central Asia, the ratio between cities above 1 million and cities below 1 million is around 0.74 (figure 3.3, panel d), in the Mashreq it is about 1.84.

## Why do the region's urban systems so favor primate cities?

There are several possible explanations why urban systems in the Middle East and North Africa could be fragmented and skewed toward larger cities:

- *Resource-rich countries tend to have less diversified economies* because private sector initiatives get crowded out. Major cities become consumer cities rather than producer cities, attracting large shares of the population.
- *Exceptional urban management attracts a disproportionate share of firms and people.* If city leaders of the largest urban areas can reduce congestion costs and foster urban agglomeration economies, their cities will continue to grow.
- *Political choices and biases benefit the main urban areas* relative to the rest of the urban system through investments and incentives. Populations living in secondary cities are left behind and have a greater reason to migrate.

The high primacy and imbalanced urban systems observed in many countries of the region could be expected in the case of small, oil-dependent economies. When comparing

urban concentration with the share that fuel exports represent in each country's total merchandise exports, we observe that oil economies tend to display higher urban concentration. High fuel exports tend to crowd out the private sector and foster the emergence of consumption cities. The resource-poor Maghreb countries are concentrated in the lower part of figure 3.4 given their low urban concentration. All countries of the Mashreq subregion but Iraq, in contrast, display high urban concentration but low fuel exports. The correlation between resource richness and urban concentration is thus weak, which means that such concentration is not the consequence of oil exports but of other causes.

In the Mashreq subregion, the excessive urban primacy and underdevelopment of secondary cities seem to be predominantly the consequence of a political bias favoring the primate cities. High population growth, migration-driven rapid urbanization, nondemocratic and centralized political government, and colonial history have all been identified as factors driving further urban concentration (Faraji 2016). Politically centralized regimes in low- and middle-income countries tend to provide better services and safety in the capital city and give more attention to the local population. As such, there is evidence that migrants settling in the primate city come not only from rural areas but also from small towns and medium-size cities (El-Din Haseeb 2012).

Primate cities that are also political capitals are on average 25 percent bigger than primate cities that do not concentrate political power (Henderson 2002). Besides, as Bosker, Buringh, and Van Zanden (2013) highlight, the larger size of cities in the Arab world can be linked to several centuries of predatory state rule and low trade openness, which also contributed to making them consumer cities instead of producer cities.[3] These political biases seem to have deeply affected the development of urban systems in the Mashreq subregion, resulting in high urban concentration and the underdevelopment of secondary cities.

**FIGURE 3.4**   **High urban concentration in the Middle East and North Africa cannot be explained solely by fuel-export-driven consumption cities**

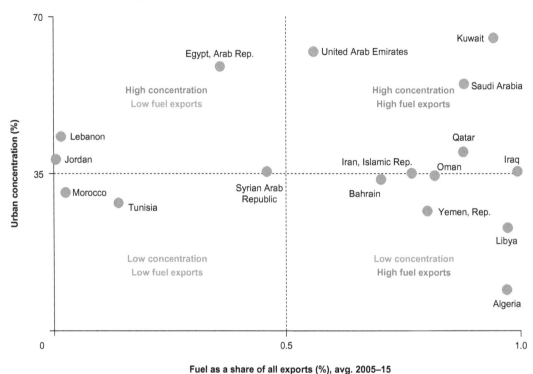

Fuel as a share of all exports (%), avg. 2005–15

*Source:* World Development Indicators and United Nations Department of Economic and Social Affairs (UN DESA) databases.
*Note:* As earlier, "urban concentration" here is calculated as the share of the population concentrated in cities above 1 million. However, for smaller countries with no cities above 1 million, the measure consisted in the share represented by the largest city.

## Policy and investment constraints are limiting the productivity and development of secondary cities

Compared with other regions of the world, the Middle East and North Africa is where geographical location has the highest impact on firms' productivity, systematically giving an advantage to companies in the capital city. To analyze the determinants of firms' productivity across regions, we established a model controlling for firm size, sector of activity, location (either periphery or capital city), and country effects. (For this methodology, see annex 3A.) In other regions of the world (excluding the Middle East and North Africa), firms' size is the highest predictor of productivity. For example, in the East Asia and Pacific region, large companies systematically enjoy a productivity 14 percent higher than small firms. On the contrary, the Middle East and North Africa

is the only region where location has a strong and significant effect on firms' productivity, with companies in the capital city having a productivity 6 percent higher than firms located in the periphery (figure 3.5).

This gap can be explained by higher constraints on many dimensions affecting firms' activity in geographically peripheral areas in the Middle East and North Africa. With a similar model controlling for location, firm size, and sector of activity, we estimated the increase or decrease in the probability of facing a major constraint for a firm located in the periphery compared with a firm located in the capital city. As such, firms in the periphery systematically experience a higher probability of facing major constraints in terms of access to finance (+9 percent), political instability (+6 percent), skills (+3 percent), and corruption (+3 percent), as shown in figure 3.6.

FIGURE 3.5    **In the Middle East and North Africa, firms in the capital city have 6 percent higher productivity than firms on the periphery—the highest location-related effect of any region in the world**

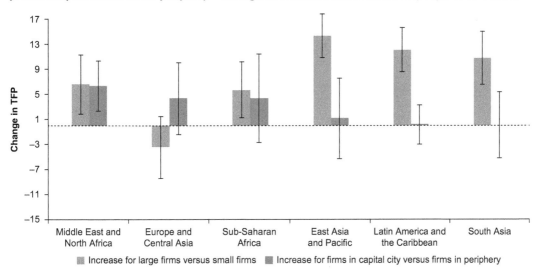

Increase for large firms versus small firms    Increase for firms in capital city versus firms in periphery

*Source:* World Bank Enterprise Surveys 2017.
*Note:* TFP = total factor productivity. T-bars indicate 90 percent confidence levels. "Large firms" = above 100 employees. "Small firms" = fewer than 20 employees. "Periphery" refers to the peripheral areas outside of the capital city. For the methodology, see annex 3A.

These higher constraints could be explained by two underlying factors: the unequal spatial pattern of access to basic services and low fiscal decentralization. The unequal spatial pattern of access to basic services—when considered either as a bundle or when quality is factored in—supports the idea that spatially biased public policies might be leading to imbalanced systems of cities throughout the Middle East and North Africa (figure 3.7). At first view, access to services seems to be relatively equally distributed through space with only relatively small differences between access levels when each service (electricity, water, and education) is considered individually. But if basic services are considered as complements, these small differences add up to large gaps.

Equally, if the *quality* of services is considered—such as number of daily hours that electricity is available rather than the simpler metric of the proportion of households connected—then the spatial inequity also appears even larger. As a 2016 World Bank report on access to opportunities in the region concludes, "Opportunities are far from universal in access to basic

FIGURE 3.6    **In the Middle East and North Africa, companies on the periphery are likelier than those in the capital city to face major constraints**

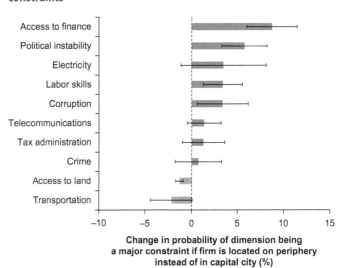

**Change in probability of dimension being a major constraint if firm is located on periphery instead of in capital city (%)**

*Source:* World Bank Enterprise Surveys 2011.
*Note:* "Periphery" refers to the peripheral areas outside of the capital city. T-bars indicate 90 percent confidence levels.

infrastructure, when opportunity is defined as access to a *bundle* of basic services, or when the *quality* of services is taken into account. Coverage of infrastructure services such as improved sources of drinking water

**FIGURE 3.7   Selected countries, including Tunisia (the most centralized Maghreb state), show large gaps in access to public services between the primary city and the other urban areas**

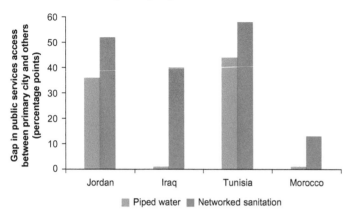

*Source:* Demographic and Health Surveys (DHS) since 2005.

**FIGURE 3.8   Fiscal transfers to local governments in the Middle East and North Africa are among the lowest in the world, only slightly above Sub-Saharan Africa**

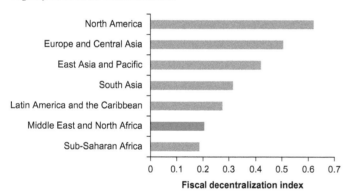

*Source:* Ivanyna and Shah 2012.
*Note:* The fiscal decentralization index considers numerous variables: local government autonomy in rate and base setting for local revenues, self-financing of local expenditures, local responsibility for and control over municipal and social services, and many others. "North America" here comprises Canada and the United States.

and (especially) adequate sanitation is markedly lower, with significant disparities in how they are distributed. Location of residence explains more than half the variation, with spatial advantages accruing to capital cities and large metropolitan areas that coincide with poles of economic activity" (Krishnan et al. 2016, 49).

The extent of fiscal decentralization is another influential factor. Based on the fiscal decentralization index elaborated by Ivanyna and Shah (2012), the Middle East and North Africa is the second least fiscally decentralized region in the world (slightly above Sub-Saharan Africa), which implies that secondary cities have a lower margin of maneuver there than in other regions of the world (figure 3.8).

Across countries, the Mashreq subregion is significantly less decentralized than the other two subregions, which could explain its higher urban primacy and concentration (figure 3.9, panel a). This could support the argument that the Mashreq subregion is more concentrated because of its historical lack of margin for maneuvering for secondary cities given the concentration of resources in the capital city.

At the country level, we can argue that in most of the Mashreq countries—Egypt, Iraq, and eventually Syria and Jordan—the level of fiscal centralization explains urban concentration at the national level. However, Lebanon displays a relatively high score on the decentralization index (figure 3.9, panel b). Therefore, it is possible that, in Lebanon, high urban concentration results partly from factors other than political biases.

However, the productivity premium could also be linked to cronyism for firms in the capital city. Cronyism is the practice of partiality in awarding jobs and other advantages to friends, family relatives, or trusted colleagues, especially in politics and between politicians and supportive organizations. For example, firms that were politically connected to the Ben Ali family in Tunisia enjoyed an important profit and market share premia (Rijkers, Freund, and Nucifora 2014). Similarly, Diwan and Chekir (2015) estimate the market valuation of political connections to be 20–23 percent of the value of connected firms. Those firms are naturally more likely to be in the capital city to be closer to the political power, which could explain a certain share of the productivity premium observed.

FIGURE 3.9  **Fiscal decentralization in the Middle East and North Africa reflects larger transfers of fiscal autonomy in the Maghreb than in the GCC and Mashreq subregions**

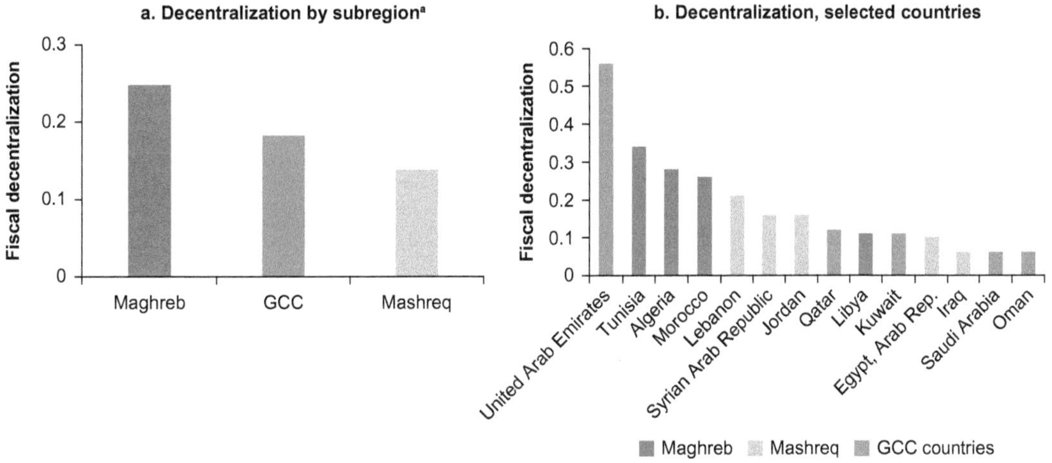

**a. Decentralization by subregion[a]**

**b. Decentralization, selected countries**

■ Maghreb  ▨ Mashreq  ■ GCC countries

*Source:* Ivanyna and Shah 2012.
*Note:* The fiscal decentralization index considers numerous variables: local government autonomy in rate and base setting for local revenues, self-financing of local expenditures, local responsibility for and control over municipal and social services, and many others.
a. Maghreb refers to Algeria, Libya, Morocco, and Tunisia; Mashreq to the Arab Republic of Egypt, Iraq, Jordan, Lebanon, and the Syrian Arab Republic; and the Gulf Cooperation Council (GCC) to Bahrain, Kuwait, Oman, Qatar, Saudi Arabia, and the United Arab Emirates.

## Regional integration can deliver large markets for the Middle East and North Africa's cities

Regional integration policies do not only guide trade and cross-border factor mobility; they also shape economic geography within countries by guiding the placement of infrastructure, the location of investments, and the movement of people. Regional integration therefore also influences national urban dynamics. Just as economic development has meant a sectoral reorientation of economies from agriculture to manufacturing and services, accelerating growth also requires a geographical reorganization of production within and between countries. Most important, regional integration raises cities' access to markets, unlocking the scale of demand needed to support the Middle East and North Africa's largest and most productive agglomerations, which appear oversized relative to their domestic markets.

Although agglomeration economies favor large cities, large cities may also need large markets to flourish. Frick and

Rodríguez-Pose (2018) find that larger cities tend to drive the fastest growth in larger countries, while smaller cities were associated with higher growth in smaller countries (table 3.1). In contrast, several Middle East and North Africa countries have small domestic markets relative to the size of their cities. Kuwait, Oman, and Qatar all have fewer than 4 million urban inhabitants while their primate city populations are larger than 500,000.

Economic history has shown that greater regional integration goes together with economic growth and regional stability. Deep integration entails the EU's four freedoms[4] (plus one): the movement across borders of goods, services, capital, people, and ideas. Regional integration efforts often only touch a subset of these, even though they are interdependent. Falling costs of transport, communication, and data transfer have allowed trade to become increasingly specialized. Trade in components and parts, for instance, has allowed firms to organize in international production networks, specialize in specific

TABLE 3.1   **City size relative to a country's total urban population is associated with positive or negative effects on economic growth**

| City population | Effect on growth, by total urban population | | | |
|---|---|---|---|---|
| | < 4 million | 4–12 million | 12–30 million | > 30 million |
| Small cities (< 0.5 million) | Positive | Positive | Negative | Negative |
| Medium-size cities (0.5–3 million) | Negative | Positive | Positive | Positive |
| Megacities (> 10 million) | Negative | Negative | Negative | Positive |

*Source:* Frick and Rodríguez-Pose 2018.

products or components as links in a value chain, and benefit from economies of scale. In fact, interindustry and intraindustry trade (as opposed to trade in final goods) has increased tremendously over the past half century, especially in East Asia, North America, and Western Europe.

A consequence of these trends has been the agglomeration of production in specialized clusters that benefit from shared, specialized labor markets; proximity to specific input or output markets; and learning across companies, which fosters innovation. Trade between nearby countries increased significantly as regional production networks developed. Final demand may be global, but there are still benefits in sourcing important inputs from nearby countries. An example is the consumer technology cluster in East Asia where China has done most of the assembly, but high-tech inputs come from Japan or the Republic of Korea and some lower-tech ones from Southeast Asia.

Manufacturing, but increasingly also services, has become more about "specialized tasks" than finished products. A precondition for such cross-national production networks has been countries' willingness to open their markets for inputs and outputs and to reduce barriers to trade in goods and services as well as to the flows of capital and labor. Not all countries that have actively pursued regional integration strategies have benefited equally from globalization—a convenient shorthand for the processes just described. But practically all have raised their economic fortunes. And where there has been the political willingness to compensate those who fell

behind, regional integration has generated the resources to do so.

The Middle East and North Africa has a long history of regional trade; a common culture and language in most countries; abundant labor, capital, and natural resources within the region; and few geographic barriers. Yet while other world regions have profited from pooling input and output markets across borders, the Middle East and North Africa lags on many aspects of integration. Compared with Europe or East Asia, few of the region's countries benefit from growth spillovers from their neighbors. The region has "thick borders" restricting the flow of critical inputs (labor, capital, and ideas) and outputs (goods and services). It also scores poorly on integrating output markets for goods and services and is the most restrictive region when it comes to the exchange of ideas—the foundations of the modern economy.

This section documents the low integration of the region's countries across these four-plus-one dimensions: trade in goods, trade in services, capital flows, flow of people, and the flow of ideas. All countries that have reached high-income status allow a high degree of openness to these flows.

## Trade in goods

*Tariffs*

International borders reduce trade by an estimated 20–50 percent and increase trade costs by an average of about 40 percent (Anderson and van Wincoop 2003; Arvis et al. 2016; Coughlin and Novy 2016). Tariffs are a significant share of these costs; others arise from currency exchange and language

BOX 3.1    **Economic growth can be contagious—but in the Middle East and North Africa, it is not**

When a country with favorable endowments and good policies grows faster, its neighbors benefit when there is a high degree of economic integration. Growth spills over to other countries as growing areas take advantage of regional pools of workers, capital, and knowledge. Larger regional markets increase demand and let firms benefit from scale economies.

### Quantifying the benefits of growth spillovers across countries

Trade integration has become deeper over time, often going beyond traditional trade policy to encompass areas such as investment, competition, and intellectual property rights protection. This makes implementation more demanding. But the "deeper" the agreement, the more a country will benefit from the growth spillovers from other members. Even with the rapid fall of global transport costs, close proximity in buyer-supplier networks is still an advantage. Analysis of regional growth trends over the past several decades shows that from 1990 to 2015, membership in trade agreements was associated with a growth spillover of about 36 percent (Lebrand 2019). Associated with this is a spatial multiplier of 1.56, with deep trade integration increasing the effectiveness of growth-promoting domestic policies by 56 percent.

However, analysis of regional growth trends over the past several decades shows that economic spillovers have been strong in Europe and in Organisation for Economic Co-operation and Development (OECD) countries but largely absent in the Middle East and North Africa. Among OECD countries, where deep trade integration has been the strongest, the benefits over the past few decades have been even larger. In the Middle East and North Africa, growth rates among countries tied by weak integration agreements have been uncorrelated (Lebrand 2019; see also Roberts and Deichmann 2011).

### Putting Sweden in the Middle East and North Africa would have cost it US$1.375 billion

If Sweden had been subject to the lack of regional spillovers experienced by Tunisia between 1990 and 2015, its GDP per capita in 2015 would have been 30 percent

FIGURE B3.1.1    **Sweden would be far poorer under Tunisia's low regional economic spillovers**

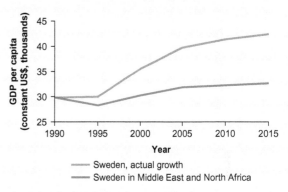

*Source:* Lebrand 2019.

lower (figure B3.1.1), with a cumulative GDP loss of US$1.375 billion (2010 constant U.S. dollars).

The analysis also suggests that openness by itself would not automatically raise growth significantly in the Middle East and North Africa. Simulation of economic growth trends assuming spillovers consistent with a deep regional integration agreement raises growth in some countries only moderately—and would even reduce growth in others where poor neighboring performance would impose a drag on the local economy.

Deeper integration will pull neighbors along only if domestic reforms create faster growth at least in some countries. But although deepening a regional integration agreement by itself will not raise a region's prospects, the reform pressure that builds through more open markets and the opportunities that come with greater integration can stimulate growth.

### Spillover benefits from countries to cities

Trade depth between countries allows cities to benefit directly from the growth of other cities. However, these spillovers between cities are absent in the Middle East and North Africa, while they are strong in the East Asia and Pacific as well as Latin America and the Caribbean (figure B3.1.2).

Most notably, East Asia and Pacific cities have experienced much larger spillovers from cities in countries with deep trade agreements than have cities in the

*box continues next page*

**Economic growth can be contagious—but in the Middle East and North Africa, it is not**
*(continued)*

**FIGURE B3.1.2** **Spatial spillovers based on deep trade agreements with neighbors, by region**

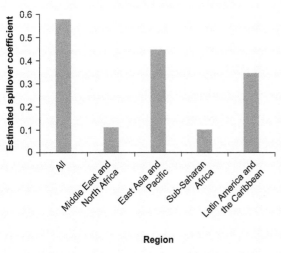

*Source:* Lebrand 2019.

**FIGURE B3.1.3** **Bangkok's per capita GDP would have shrunk had it experienced the Middle East and North Africa's regional economic spillovers**

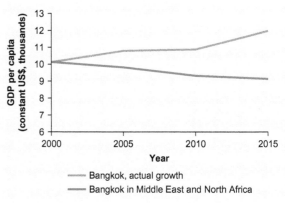

*Source:* Lebrand 2019.

Middle East and North Africa. Figure B3.1.3 shows the level of city GDP per capita if Bangkok had been in the Middle East and North Africa instead of in East Asia and Pacific. Over the 2000–15 period, Bangkok

was growing quickly in per capita terms, but its GDP per capita would have been shrunk significantly in the Middle East and North Africa for lack of growth spillovers.

*Note:* Two regions are excluded from the analysis. The results of the regional analysis were not significant for South Asia or not of interest for comparison for Europe and Central Asia.

**FIGURE 3.10** **Many Middle East and North Africa economies have higher average tariffs than their economic peers in other regions**
*Average tariff rates in relation to per capita income, 2015*

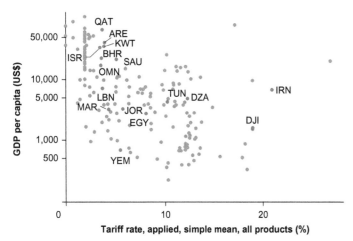

*Source:* World Development Indicators Database.
*Note:* Full country names correspond to ISO 3 country codes. No data were available for Iraq, Libya, the Syrian Arab Republic, and West Bank and Gaza.

and information barriers. In the Middle East and North Africa, countries' tariffs vary considerably. The region's high-income countries (that is, the GCC countries) have relatively low average tariffs, but these are still about twice those of their peers in other regions (figure 3.10). The middle- and low-income countries typically have higher tariffs as well—exceeding 10 percent in Algeria, Djibouti, the Islamic Republic of Iran, Syria, and Tunisia.

*Trade agreements*

As in other regions, Middle East and North Africa countries have specific agreements that allow some trading partners preferential market access, but those agreements are relatively weak. Three of these preferential trade agreements are registered with the World Trade Organization (WTO),

TABLE 3.2 **Trade agreements are fewer and shallower in the Middle East and North Africa than in other regions**
*Average number of provisions in intraregional trade agreements, 2015*

| Region | Total provisions | Total enforceable | Core enforceable[a] | Number of agreements |
|---|---|---|---|---|
| East Asia and Pacific | 18.3 | 14.4 | 11.4 | 32 |
| Europe and Central Asia | 14.4 | 12.2 | 8.8 | 85 |
| Latin America and the Caribbean | 21.7 | 15.3 | 12.7 | 30 |
| Middle East and North Africa | 16.0 | 9.7 | 6.3 | 3 |
| North America[b] | 22.0 | 21.0 | 17.0 | 1 |
| South Asia | 4.0 | 2.8 | 2.8 | 4 |
| Sub-Saharan Africa | 22.2 | 8.4 | 6.9 | 9 |

*Source:* World Bank calculations based on Hofmann, Osnago, and Ruta 2017.
a. "Core provisions" are those included under WTO+ as well as those concerning competition policy, investment, capital movement, and intellectual property rights. Under the World Trade Organization (WTO), WTO+ provisions include areas such as customs regulations, export taxes, antidumping, countervailing measures, technical barriers to trade, and sanitary and phytosanitary standards.
b. "North America" here comprises Canada and the United States.

binding the partners within the Middle East and North Africa:

- *The GCC*, which includes six high-income Gulf countries
- *The Pan-Arab Free Trade Area (PAFTA)*, which was initiated in 1997 under the umbrella of the Arab League and covers almost the entire Middle East and North Africa region
- *The Common Market for Eastern and Southern Africa (COMESA)*, which connects Egypt, Libya, and Djibouti as well as 16 Sub-Saharan African countries.

The strength or depth of an agreement is determined by its comprehensiveness and the extent to which its provisions are legally enforceable. On average, the Middle East and North Africa's intraregional agreements include 16 provisions—not too different from those in other world regions (table 3.2). They are shallower, however, as the lower number of total and core enforceable provisions shows.

"Core" provisions are those included under WTO+ as well as provisions concerning competition policy, investment, capital movement, and intellectual property rights.[5] Among the Middle East and North Africa's three intraregional agreements, COMESA is fairly comprehensive, with nine legally enforceable core provisions, but it covers only three Middle East and North Africa countries. The GCC is also comprehensive, with

TABLE 3.3 **The Middle East and North Africa has few agreements with important future markets**
*Number of agreements and average number of core legally enforceable provisions between Middle East and North Africa countries and those in other regions, 2015*

| Region | Number of agreements | Average number of provisions |
|---|---|---|
| East Asia and Pacific | 2 | 7.5 |
| Europe and Central Asia | 23 | 10.0 |
| Latin America and the Caribbean | 1 | 14.0 |
| North America[a] | 7 | 10.6 |
| South Asia | 0 | 0.0 |
| Sub-Saharan Africa | 2 | 5.5 |

*Source:* World Bank calculations based on Hofmann, Osnago, and Ruta 2017.
*Note:* "Core, legally enforceable" agreements are those included under WTO+ as well as those concerning competition policy, investment, capital movement, and intellectual property rights. Under the World Trade Organization (WTO), WTO+ provisions include areas such as customs regulations, export taxes, antidumping, countervailing measures, technical barriers to trade, and sanitary and phytosanitary standards.
a. "North America" here comprises Canada and the United States.

eight such provisions. However, PAFTA, which covers most of the region, is a "shallow" agreement, with only two legally enforceable core provisions, because it focuses mostly on tariff liberalization for industrial and agricultural goods only.

The largest number of Middle East and North Africa countries' interregional bilateral or multilateral agreements are with countries of the Europe and Central Asia region—mostly with Western European countries and the EU (table 3.3). Such agreements with countries of East Asia and the Pacific—the most important world market in the future—tend to be relatively shallow.

Europe and the Americas have more comprehensive agreements with that dynamic region.

### Exports and imports

At 4.1 percent each, the Middle East and North Africa's share of world exports and imports matches its share of global GDP almost exactly (table 3.4). The export share is largely due to a high share of raw materials exports—mostly oil and natural gas, which make up about a third of all exports.[6] The shares of other product types, especially capital goods exports, are relatively small.

TABLE 3.4    **Trade in the Middle East and North Africa is still dependent on natural resources**
*percent*

| Global share, type | Exports | Imports |
|---|---|---|
| *Trade* | | |
| Total | 4.1 | 4.1 |
| Raw materials | 10.5 | 3.3 |
| Intermediates | 3.0 | 4.7 |
| Consumer goods | 3.4 | 3.6 |
| Capital goods | 0.9 | 2.9 |
| *General* | | |
| GDP | | 4.1 |
| Population | | 5.9 |

*Source:* World Bank, World Integrated Trade Solution (WITS) database.

FIGURE 3.11    **Merchandise trade as a share of GDP in many Middle East and North Africa countries is quite low**

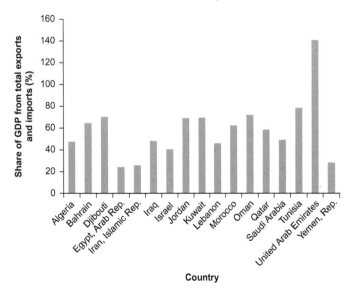

**Country**

*Source:* World Development Indicators Database.
*Note:* No data were available for Libya, the Syrian Arab Republic, and West Bank and Gaza.

The importance of trade is highest in the United Arab Emirates, where exports plus imports are about 140 percent of GDP, highlighting the importance of Dubai and Abu Dhabi as global trading hubs. Trade is important in fuel-exporting countries but also in Jordan, Morocco, and Tunisia, where trade is 60–80 percent of GDP (figure 3.11).

Although the region's overall trade levels roughly correspond to its share of the global economy, trade—especially nonfuel exports—could be significantly larger (Behar and Freund 2011; Bhattacharya and Wolde 2010; Bourdet and Persson 2014; Hoekman 2016). One study estimated that a typical Middle East and North Africa country could double to quadruple its exports given economic and geographic characteristics and assuming best-practice trade policies (Behar and Freund 2011). Imports, in contrast, are more in line with expectations.

Intraregional trade has been a key driver of trade and, in turn, of economic growth in other world regions, notably Europe and East Asia. The Middle East and North Africa's share of total intraregional trade had been gradually increasing from the 1980s through the mid-2000s before dropping during the 2008–09 world financial crisis and only recently recovering (figure 3.12).

## Trade in services

Trade in services has increased globally, commanding a substantial share of GDP, including in the Middle East and North Africa (Loungani et al. 2017). Services—such as financial and legal, telecom, and transport services—are critical intermediate inputs, and their trade can be an important mechanism to transfer know-how and innovations. Access to high-quality services consequently has a strong influence on manufacturing productivity, importantly through its effect on foreign direct investment (FDI) flows (Hoekman and Shepherd 2017).

In the Middle East and North Africa, the average share of GDP from services trade has fluctuated since 1990 between about 20 percent and 25 percent (figure 3.13).

**FIGURE 3.12    Only a small share of global intraregional merchandise trade occurs within the Middle East and North Africa**

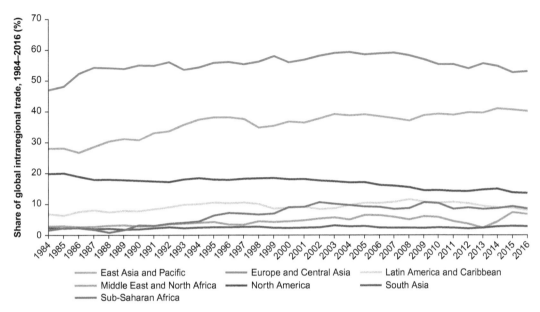

*Source:* Derived from the World Trade Flows database, Bilateral Data files, of the Center for International Data, University of California, Davis, https://cid.econ .ucdavis.edu/Html/WTF_bilateral.html.
*Note:* Regions include all countries regardless of income status. "North America" comprises Canada and the United States.

**FIGURE 3.13    As a share of GDP, the Middle East and North Africa's intraregional service trade is small relative to the size of its economies**

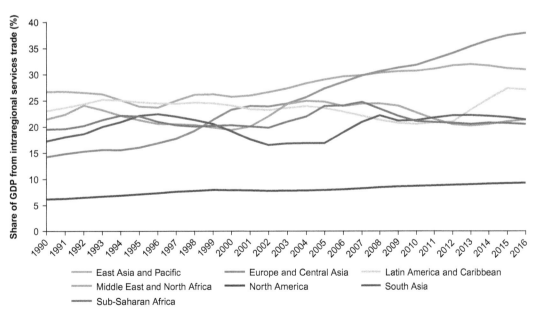

*Source:* World Development Indicators Database.
*Note:* The data shown are moving three-year averages of countries in each region for which numbers were reported, including high-income countries. "North America" here comprises Canada and the United States.

TABLE 3.5 **The Middle East and North Africa has higher service trade restrictions than any other region**
*Average service trade restriction index*

| Restriction category | East Asia & Pacific | Europe & Central Asia | Latin America & Caribbean | Middle East & North Africa | North America[a] | South Asia | Sub-Saharan Africa |
|---|---|---|---|---|---|---|---|
| Overall | 32.6 | 19.1 | 21.0 | 45.3 | 19.7 | 43.9 | 32.0 |
| Financial | 24.4 | 9.8 | 18.5 | 42.1 | 21.1 | 38.1 | 26.7 |
| Professional | 55.7 | 43.7 | 38.0 | 61.6 | 47.5 | 60.7 | 48.7 |
| Retail | 20.8 | 7.3 | 8.3 | 30.8 | 0.0 | 30.0 | 22.8 |
| Telecommunications | 34.4 | 8.1 | 20.8 | 44.2 | 25.0 | 45.0 | 38.6 |
| Transportation | 33.5 | 26.1 | 22.1 | 50.1 | 12.0 | 50.4 | 29.9 |

*Source:* Borchert, Gootiiz, and Mattoo 2013.
*Note:* The table displays the average index scores of countries in each region for which numbers were reported, including high-income countries.
a. "North America" here comprises Canada and the United States.

Shares are highest in Lebanon (where they represent more than 50 percent of GDP) and in Jordan, Kuwait, and Qatar.

Firm-level data most clearly show that restrictions to services trade affect productivity and export performance (Hoekman and Shepherd 2017).[7] When countries reduced their service sector restrictions, the performance of firms relying on such services improved. Given that such services inputs can be up to two-fifths of the gross value of manufactured exports, this is not surprising.[8]

Countries in the Middle East and North Africa for which data are available have, on average, larger restrictions than other world regions (table 3.5). Egypt, the Islamic Republic of Iran, and Qatar have the highest service restriction index scores, while Algeria, Morocco, and the Republic of Yemen have the lowest. The highest restrictions are in professional and transportation services. Retail sector restrictions are the lowest but still considerably higher than in Latin America and the Caribbean or in Europe and Central Asia. Thirteen Middle East and North Africa countries are in the dataset; in seven of those countries, professional services are the most restricted sector.

## Capital flows

Financial openness can generally be good for growth. It tends to reduce the cost of capital that can be invested for productive uses, encourages financial development, promotes portfolio diversification, and imposes greater discipline on monetary policy. Estimates of the economic benefits of capital liberalization range from a 1 percentage point increase in annual GDP to as much as a 14 percent permanent increase in consumption in the most capital-scarce countries (Hoxha, Kalemli-Ozcan, and Vollrath 2013; Kose et al. 2006).[9]

After North America[10] and Europe and Central Asia, the Middle East and North Africa region has the highest average level of financial openness, although it has retreated somewhat over the past 20 years (figure 3.14). Openness varies by country: several GCC countries as well as Israel, Jordan, and the Republic of Yemen have open capital markets, while eight other economies in the region maintain significant restrictions on capital flows.

The region's relatively high (average) capital openness does not seem to have led to corresponding FDI inflows. Among international capital flows, FDI is arguably the most important for development. It is usually aimed at new, productive investments and also often comes with know-how for technology transfer and innovation. Yet the average net inflows of FDI relative to GDP across Middle East and North Africa countries were lower than for any other region in 2016 (figure 3.15). After an increase in relative FDI flows in the mid-2000s, they reverted to levels last seen in 2000.

**FIGURE 3.14**  **Overall, the Middle East and North Africa has a high degree of capital openness**

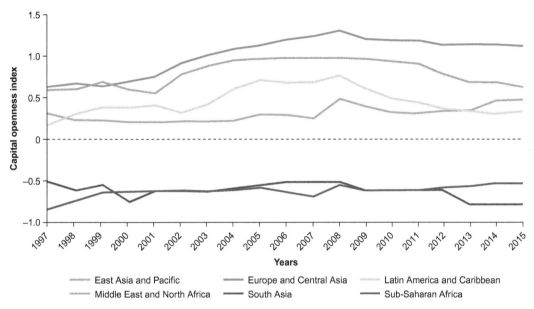

*Source:* World Bank calculations from the Chinn-Ito Financial Openness Index (KAOPEN) 2016: http://web.pdx.edu/~ito/Chinn-Ito_website.htm.
*Note:* North America (Canada and the United States), which has the maximum value, is not shown. KAOPEN draws on the International Monetary Fund's (IMF) *Annual Report on Exchange Arrangements and Exchange Restrictions* (AREAER). It is the first principal component of four binary variables: existence of multiple exchange rates, restrictions on current account, capital account transactions, and requirement of the surrender of export proceeds.

**FIGURE 3.15**  **FDI inflows to the Middle East and North Africa remain low despite the region's relatively high capital openness**

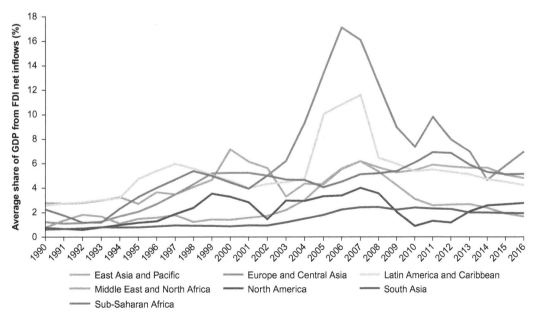

*Source:* World Development Indicators Database.
*Note:* FDI = foreign direct investment. "North America" comprises Canada and the United States.

Among the region's countries, Djibouti has received by far the largest relative FDI inflow. Large investments, notably from China, boosted Djibouti's relatively small economy, increasing strongly around 2003 and averaging about 9 percent of GDP between 2010 and 2015. Relative FDI inflows have also been large in Israel, Jordan, Lebanon, and Morocco, where they were 3 percent or higher during 2011–16. The lowest FDI shares (less than 1 percent of GDP) during this time were in Algeria, the Islamic Republic of Iran, Kuwait, Qatar, and the Republic of Yemen (which experienced net outflows).[11]

Institutional weakness may explain why capital openness has not translated into FDI in the Middle East and North Africa (Okada 2013). With higher-quality institutions, capital openness has a greater positive effect on international capital flows. A study of 17 of the region's economies from 1989 to 2009 shows that capital liberalization is effective only in an environment with good institutions and low political risk (Gammoudi and Cherif 2015).

## Flows of people

Moving from places with a low demand for labor and low wages to one where demand is higher is one of the best ways for people to improve their welfare. Open borders could more than double the wages of an average worker in a less-developed country (including nonmigrants) without significantly affecting real wage rates in high-income countries (Kennan 2013). Well-managed migration benefits both sending and receiving countries (EIU 2016; Pritchett 2006). Sending countries get remittances and investments from migrants and also benefit from the expertise and wealth brought back through circular migration. Receiving countries increase their labor supply in areas where there are shortages, which will be increasingly needed where demographic dynamics shrink the labor pool.

The gains from (and demands for) migration are likely to remain high given persistently large wage gaps between countries, continued slow growth in many poorer countries, and rising demand from high-income countries. When poorly managed, however, migration can encourage human trafficking and create social conflict as local workers compete with newcomers or as migrants become scapegoats for other social ills.

The Middle East and North Africa has high cross-country migration (table 3.6).[12] More than 40 million migrants live in the region, of whom about a third (14 million) are from within the region. So, the Middle East and North Africa, which has about 6 percent of the world's population, hosts 15 percent of the world's migrants. It is also a large source of migrants: about 28 million of its citizens live in other countries, about half of them in other Middle East and North Africa countries. For migration within the region, Egypt, Syria, and West Bank and Gaza are the largest source economies, accounting for three-quarters of all regional migration. Jordan, Lebanon, Saudi Arabia, and the United Arab Emirates combined host about two-thirds of all regional migrants.

**TABLE 3.6  Migration in the Middle East and North Africa has been driven by both job seekers and refugees**

*Largest intraregional bilateral migrant stocks, 2017 estimates*

| Origin | Destination | Migrants (thousands) |
|---|---|---|
| West Bank and Gaza | Jordan | 2,047 |
| Syrian Arab Republic | Lebanon | 1,209 |
| Egypt, Arab Rep. | Saudi Arabia | 872 |
| Egypt, Arab Rep. | United Arab Emirates | 858 |
| Syrian Arab Republic | Saudi Arabia | 746 |
| Syrian Arab Republic | Jordan | 725 |
| Yemen, Rep. | Saudi Arabia | 697 |
| West Bank and Gaza | Syrian Arab Republic | 630 |
| West Bank and Gaza | Lebanon | 507 |
| Egypt, Arab Rep. | Kuwait | 423 |

*Source:* World Bank Migration and Remittances Database 2017, Global Knowledge Partnership on Migration and Development (KNOMAD): https://www.knomad.org/data/migration/emigration.

The nature of migration varies greatly between countries by reasons for migration, dominant destination, and source of migrants, as these examples show:

- Several Maghreb countries (Algeria, Morocco, Tunisia) and the Islamic Republic of Iran have sent many migrants, but most seek employment in Europe or North America.
- Most migrants from Egypt and Jordan, in contrast, move to other countries in the region, mostly in the GCC.
- Among the largest migration flows are refugees from Iraq, Syria, and West Bank and Gaza, who have mostly moved to neighboring countries.
- The largest destination for economic migrants is the GCC, where migrant shares in the population are often well over 50 percent. Although the GCC is an important destination for migrants from some Middle East and North Africa countries, most of its migrants come from South Asia.

Remittances are second in magnitude only to FDI. Middle East and North Africa countries are the source of about 20 percent of global remittances and the destination of about 9 percent. Saudi Arabia and the United Arab Emirates are the world's second and third largest *origins* of remittances globally, behind only the United States. These two GCC countries account for two-thirds of all remittances from the Middle East and North Africa, most of which go to South Asian and East Asian countries.

For eight recipient economies in the Middle East and North Africa, remittances are equivalent to more than 3 percent of GDP—and are more than 10 percent of GDP in Lebanon, West Bank and Gaza, the Republic of Yemen, and Jordan (figure 3.16). Egypt, Lebanon, and Morocco are the largest recipients of such flows in the region (table 3.7).

Remittance flows in 2016 *between* Middle East and North Africa countries totaled about US$31.6 billion, or about 5 percent of global flows. About 77 percent of these come from GCC countries, particularly Saudi Arabia, Kuwait, and the United Arab Emirates, while Egypt, the Republic of Yemen, and Jordan are the largest recipients of intraregional remittances (table 3.8).

Remittances are an important social protection mechanism for the region's economies

FIGURE 3.16  **Remittances are significant contributors to several Middle East and North Africa economies**

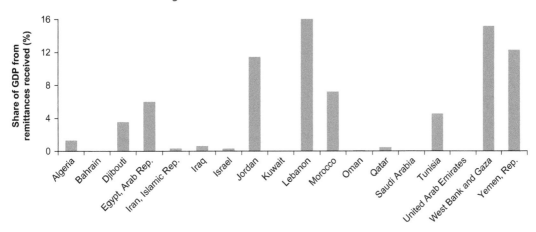

*Sources:* World Bank Migration and Remittances Database 2017 (Global Knowledge Partnership on Migration and Development [KNOMAD]: https://www.knomad.org/data/migration/emigration); World Development Indicators Database.
*Note:* No GDP data are available for Libya and the Syrian Arab Republic. Because remittances are negligible for Bahrain, Kuwait, Oman, Saudi Arabia, and the United Arab Emirates, their totals amount to 0 percent of GDP in the figure.

**TABLE 3.7** **Large migration flows have led to equally large remittance flows in the Middle East and North Africa**

*Estimated remittance flows and global rank, 2016*

| Sending countries | | | Receiving countries | | |
|---|---|---|---|---|---|
| Country | Remittances (US$, millions) | Global rank | Country | Remittances (US$, millions) | Global rank |
| Saudi Arabia | 46,725 | 2 | Egypt, Arab Rep. | 19,983 | 7 |
| United Arab Emirates | 32,978 | 3 | Lebanon | 7,955 | 18 |
| Kuwait | 11,733 | 13 | Morocco | 7,467 | 20 |
| Qatar | 10,677 | 14 | Jordan | 4,418 | 34 |
| Oman | 4,486 | 24 | Yemen, Rep. | 3,351 | 39 |
| Israel | 2,926 | 31 | Algeria | 2,093 | 56 |
| Jordan | 2,857 | 34 | West Bank and Gaza | 2,034 | 57 |
| Bahrain | 2,705 | 38 | Tunisia | 1,903 | 61 |
| Lebanon | 1,167 | 55 | Syrian Arab Republic | 1,623 | 66 |
| Libya | 1,004 | 61 | Iran, Islamic Rep. | 1,379 | 72 |
| West Bank and Gaza | 915 | 65 | Iraq | 1,035 | 84 |
| Syrian Arab Republic | 418 | 85 | Israel | 990 | 85 |
| Egypt, Arab Rep. | 400 | 88 | Qatar | 668 | 92 |
| Iran, Islamic Rep. | 296 | 96 | Saudi Arabia | 287 | 117 |
| Algeria | 200 | 118 | Djibouti | 62 | 147 |
| Iraq | 193 | 122 | Oman | 40 | 155 |
| Morocco | 102 | 142 | Kuwait | 4 | 177 |
| Tunisia | 71 | 158 | Bahrain | .. | 182 |
| Yemen, Rep. | 62 | 163 | Libya | .. | 182 |
| Djibouti | 7 | 200 | United Arab Emirates | .. | 182 |
| Total | 119,922 | n.a. | | 55,291 | n.a. |

*Source:* World Bank Migration and Remittances Database 2017, Global Knowledge Partnership on Migration and Development (KNOMAD): https://www.knomad.org/data/migration/emigration.
*Note:* .. = negligible. n.a. = not applicable.

**TABLE 3.8** **Largest intraregional estimated remittance flows in the Middle East and North Africa, 2016**

| Origin | Destination | Remittances (US$, millions) |
|---|---|---|
| Saudi Arabia | Egypt, Arab Rep. | 7,739 |
| Kuwait | Egypt, Arab Rep. | 3,156 |
| Saudi Arabia | Yemen, Rep. | 2,062 |
| United Arab Emirates | Egypt, Arab Rep. | 1,953 |
| Saudi Arabia | Jordan | 1,713 |
| Saudi Arabia | Lebanon | 1,624 |
| Jordan | Egypt, Arab Rep. | 1,293 |
| Qatar | Egypt, Arab Rep. | 1,070 |
| Jordan | West Bank and Gaza | 936 |
| United Arab Emirates | Jordan | 864 |

*Source:* World Bank Migration and Remittances Database 2017, Global Knowledge Partnership on Migration and Development (KNOMAD): https://www.knomad.org/data/migration/emigration.

with large shares of out-migrants (Devereux 2016). Their impact on labor markets and economic growth are somewhat more ambiguous (Chami et al. 2018). There is evidence that remittances reduce labor force participation in receiving countries and raise informality. But they also reduce unemployment in some sectors, such as construction and real estate, while reducing employment in manufacturing. These findings do not hold in fragile states, however, where remittances support wage growth and do not have the same negative effects on labor force participation. Countries can develop strategies to counter these potentially negative impacts to take full advantage of these external financial resources.

## Flow of ideas

The four freedoms—of the movement of goods, services, capital, and people—are core principles of regional integration. But they also reflect an economic structure that has been changing. In the traditional economy, manufacturing tends to be highly concentrated to exploit scale economies, services are delivered in person through local branch offices or traveling consultants, access to capital often requires face-to-face contacts, and people must move to where the jobs are. The largest share of the economy in most countries still follows this pattern.

However, digitization of almost every aspect of the economy is disrupting the way we trade and work (World Bank 2016). Automation will enable more decentralized production, even in higher-wage locations. Many services become tradable and can be delivered over the internet from anywhere. Capital flows freely around the world, a trend that could be boosted by digital currencies. And although most jobs are still place-specific, people can perform more and more tasks remotely.

With these trends, a "fifth freedom" is becoming more important: the free movement of ideas across borders. Growth will come from knowledge-intensive activities, and new ideas and data will become ever more important factors of production.

Countries do not generally block information that has a clear economic use, such as technical publications, patent documentation, or financial data. Many block other types of information that they see as inconvenient or challenging to existing power structures. Yet the most innovative and productive places allow all information to flow freely and promote discussion and exchange of ideas. By contrast, where information exchange is constrained, governments often try to induce innovation through planning, intervention, and subsidies—frequently with limited success.

Middle East and North Africa countries do poorly when it comes to the free flow of information.[13] In surveys of press freedom, almost all of the region's countries rank among the lower half of countries, with several near the bottom, indicating severe restrictions on the media. In Freedom House's 2017 index of press freedom for 199 countries and territories, the average rank of Middle East and North Africa countries was 155, with only one country in the top 100: Israel, ranking 64th (Freedom House 2017a). Such rankings persist in other press freedom indexes as well (RSF 2018a, 2018b). Similar restrictions also exist on communication via the internet. Of 11 Middle East and North Africa countries included among 65 worldwide in Freedom House's Freedom on the Net index, six ranked as "not free," six as "partially free," and none as "free" (Freedom House 2017b).

In the use of digital technology more generally, the region's countries do somewhat better (figure 3.17). The World Bank's Digital Adoption Index (DAI) is a summary measure of the availability and use of digital technology among businesses, people, and government.[14] The average rank of Middle East and North Africa economies among 183 economies globally was 82 in the 2016 DAI. Bahrain, Israel, and the United Arab Emirates ranked in the top 20, while Iraq, Djibouti, Syria, and the Republic of Yemen were near the bottom.

However, as the *World Development Report 2016: Digital Dividends* has argued, technology adoption is only one aspect of digital development (World Bank 2016). At least as important are the so-called analog complements that allow firms, workers, and officials to use these tools effectively: regulations that ensure that all firms can connect and compete; skills that complement technology so workers can be more productive; and a high degree of accountability among public officials so e-government is deployed to improve service delivery, not to increase government control.

A further channel for information exchange is face-to-face interaction, which suffers in the Middle East and North Africa because of visa restrictions. The number of

FIGURE 3.17   **Use of digital technologies correlates closely with economic wealth**
*Digital Adoption Index, 2016*

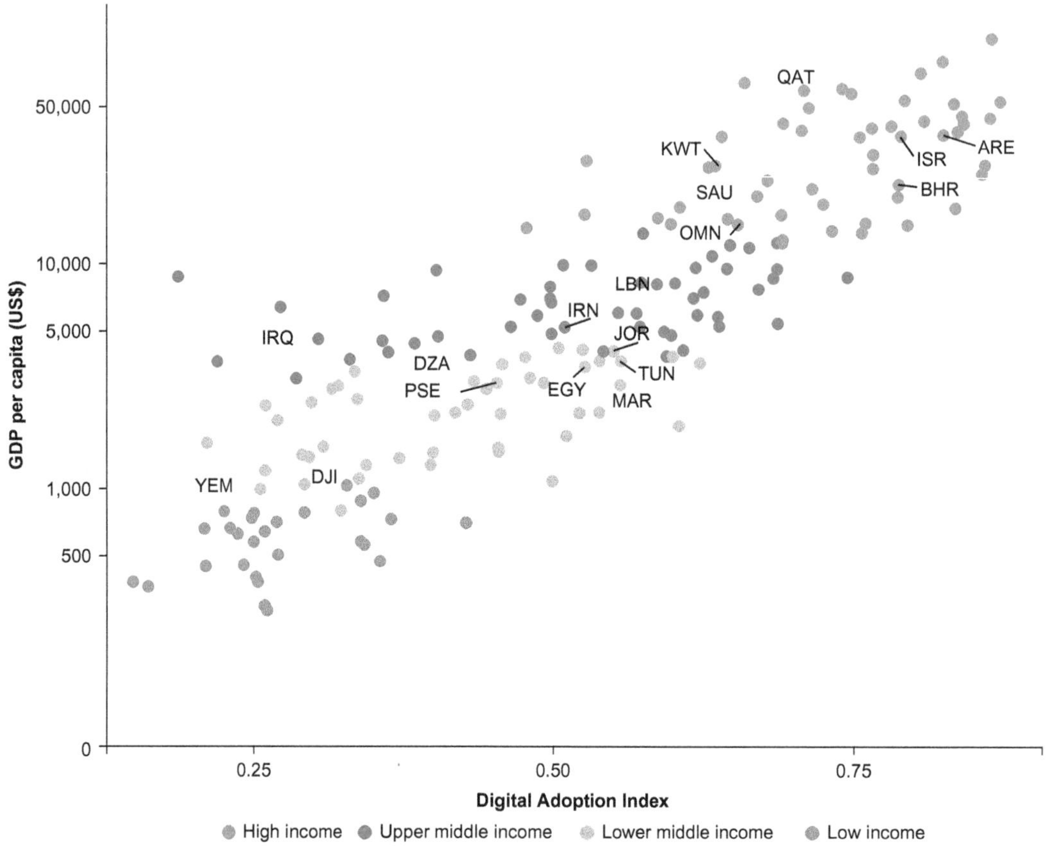

Source: World Bank 2016.
*Note:* Insufficient data were available for Libya and the Syrian Arab Republic. The World Bank's Digital Adoption Index (DAI) includes business, people, and government components, each comprising several subindexes. Full country names correspond to ISO 3 country codes.

other countries that require visas from the region's residents is high, even for wealthy GCC countries (figure 3.18).[15] A significant number of its economies also require visas from most other countries' nationals. In contrast to most other regions, Middle East and North Africa countries also require visas from residents of neighboring countries more often than one might expect. Within the region, visas are required in 60 percent of all country-pairs, as opposed to less than 20 percent in Latin America and the Caribbean, a region where most countries also share a similar culture and language.

## The region's port cities can amplify their role as regional hubs and gateways

Global and regional integration are complementary. Regional integration enlarges markets for outputs. Perhaps even more important, it also increases access to critical inputs including labor, capital, and components. This makes it easier for firms to break into global value chains such as those that stretch from Europe to East Asia.

The nonphysical barriers to closer integration in the Middle East and North Africa are formidable, as argued elsewhere in this report. But upgrading of transport infrastructure will still be important in much of the region. For regional integration, ports play a central role (Arvis et al. 2018).[16]

Transshipment ports are hubs where cargo (usually containers) is exchanged between large vessels serving global trunk trade routes and smaller ones serving regional ports. Smaller ports serve as gateways to a local or national hinterland and sometimes also serve neighboring countries. Ports compete for cargo. They can focus on transshipment business if they are in a favorable location. They can concentrate on so-called captive cargo, which is produced or consumed in and around the port location. Or they can serve a larger hinterland if it is well connected to the port.

Arvis et al. (2018) analyze port development in the Mediterranean, which borders eight Middle East and North Africa countries. Port development strategies need to consider three elements: (a) maritime connectivity (the ease of reaching other ports); (b) port efficiency (the time and money cost of processing cargo); and (c) hinterland connectivity (the size and proximity of economic and population centers). Connectivity within the Mediterranean has been declining; it dropped from 2,279 interport links in 2009 to 1,532 in 2016. Seventy percent of Mediterranean cargo traffic is between European ports, 15 percent between Europe and North Africa, and 10 percent between Europe and West Asia. Only 5 percent is between Middle East and North Africa countries. Port efficiency depends largely on size. There are large economies of scale in port operations and related services, so larger ports will attract larger ships and more cargo. Smaller ports will struggle if they cannot scale up traffic by developing local economic clusters or by expanding their hinterland.

Hinterland connectivity is not required for transshipment hubs, but such ports can exploit scale advantages when also serving as gateway ports. Port Said (Egypt) and Tanger Med (Morocco) are transshipment ports at the eastern and western end of the Mediterranean, respectively. Port Said had limited land connectivity to Egypt's population centers and has largely focused on

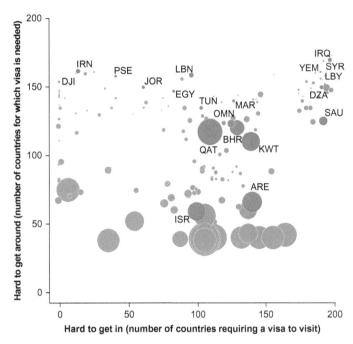

FIGURE 3.18    **Many Middle East and North Africa countries make it hard to visit, and their citizens also face difficulties traveling elsewhere**
*Visa requirements, 2017*

*Source:* Passport Index database, http://www.passportindex.org.
*Note:* For instance, citizens of Jordan require a visa when visiting about 150 countries ("hard to get around"), but citizens from only about 60 countries need a visa to visit Jordan ("hard to get in"). Circles are proportional to per capita GDP. Visa on arrival and eTA (electronic travel authority) are considered visa-free in this chart.

transshipment only, with few spillovers to local or hinterland development. Tanger Med, in contrast, was built as part of an overall development strategy for northern Morocco. It serves not just as a transshipment but also as a gateway port connecting a large and populous area with many European ports. Its hinterland is well connected by rail and road and has become a large center for automobile component manufacturing and assembly among other industries. In Port Said, after a change of governance structure in 2014, there is also now a development plan to better connect to Cairo and the rest of Egypt. However, the port will compete with several other Egyptian ports that aim to serve the same domestic markets.

For most Mediterranean ports in the Middle East and North Africa, becoming a transshipment hub is unrealistic, especially for those that are farther from the trunk trade route. But many ports can enhance their roles as national or even regional gateway ports. The best would benefit if Mediterranean economic regions become less fragmented and if further concentration of maritime networks occurs. This requires policies to strengthen both local economic potential and hinterland connectivity. Port development thus needs to be integrated with broader regional and trade strategies, including infrastructure investments, logistics development, and broader governance reforms that ease doing business. Although governments cannot directly influence maritime networks, they can make their ports more attractive through local development and by expanding their regional reach.

## Concluding remarks

Although urban primacy in Middle East and North Africa countries is higher than in any other world region, the region's major cities appear to be too large, in part because of the constraints on market access confronting them. They may be too large for their *local* markets but would be rightsized if they could more easily serve a much larger *regional* market.

The largest cities in well-integrated regions attract human and financial capital from their neighbors and produce goods and services for the entire region. London, Paris, or Vienna are large relative to their countries' populations but not relative to the markets they can serve. Historically, this was the case in the Middle East and North Africa, whereby the largest cities were once closely connected and served as centers of production, innovation, and learning both regionally and elsewhere in the world. Today, in contrast, most cities that could play much greater regional roles are prevented from doing so by numerous barriers to regional economic integration.

The chapter has provided evidence that the flows of goods, services, capital, and labor—what the EU calls the "four freedoms"—face high barriers, as do the flows of ideas, for instance, through media

or personal exchanges. Further, secondary cities can have a more significant role in their national economies if coordinated complementary policies and investments support improvements in the business ecosystem alongside providing critical services and infrastructure. Recommendations to reduce the barriers to these four freedoms and the flow of ideas will follow in chapter 6.

## Annex 3A Methodology for analyzing productivity across regions

Firm total factor productivity (TFP)—the ability to generate greater outputs with lower inputs—is one of the key elements of economic growth. Considerable scholarly analysis has been devoted to measuring productivity, especially since Robert Solow's groundbreaking work (Solow 1957). To estimate the productivity of firms in lower-income economies, researchers have turned to analysis using survey-based data, often in the absence of comparable census data. The World Bank's Enterprise Surveys, which provide detailed firm-level data collected by the Bank's Enterprise Analysis unit, is well suited for such an inquiry.

To estimate TFP, we begin with a Cobb-Douglas production function in the following form:

$$VA_i = A_i K_i^{a_k} L_i^{a_l}, \qquad (3A.1)$$

where $VA_i$ is firm-level value added, a function of inputs of capital $(K_i)$, and labor $(L_i)$.

Firms' efficiency of production is measured by the term $A_i$, which is the portion of output that cannot be directly attributed to the utilized inputs. We refer to the above model, or rather its version with natural logarithm applied on both sides, as VAKL. VA, K, and L are proxied using the questions available in the Enterprise Surveys. More precisely, VA is proxied by the difference between the total annual sales of the establishment (variable d2 in the data) and total annual cost of inputs (variable n2e); K is proxied by the replacement value of machinery, vehicles, and equipment (variable n7a); and L is proxied by the total annual cost of labor (variable n2a).

To analyze differences in productivity across regions, regression analysis was used, including controls for sector of activity, firm size, and location, as follows:

$$\log(TFP\_VAKL)_i = \alpha + \beta\, Loc_i + \gamma\, country_i$$
$$+ \alpha s + \sigma g + \varepsilon_i,$$

$$(3A.2)$$

where $TFP\_VAKL$ is the TFP estimate obtained from the VAKL model for each firm; $Loc_i$ is the firm location (either periphery or capital city); $country_i$ are country dummies; $\alpha s$ are sector dummies; $\sigma g$ are size dummies (small, medium, and large); and $\varepsilon_i$ is the discrepancy term.

This regression was run individually for each region to identify the effect of location and firm size on TFP, controlling for other factors.

Then, to explore the factors leading to the high importance of location in the Middle East and North Africa region, a second regression, consisting of a linear probability model was used to identify the increase in the probability for firms to face a constraint if they are located in the periphery instead of in the capital city. The equation was specified as follows:

$$Const_i = \alpha + \beta\, Loc_i + \gamma\, country_i$$
$$+ \alpha s + \sigma g + \varepsilon_{i\cdot}, \qquad (3A.3)$$

where $Const_i$ is a dummy qualifying the constraint as being either a major constraint or a minor constraint; $Loc_i$ is the firm location (either periphery or capital city); $country_i$ are country dummies; $\alpha s$ are sector dummies; $\sigma g$ are size dummies; and $\varepsilon_i$ is the discrepancy term.

It is important to note that, in the case of the constraint associated with access to electricity, the $Loc_i$ was not defined as a dummy differentiating periphery and capital city but a dummy differentiating cities above 1 million and cities below 1 million.

## Notes

1. The Gulf Cooperation Council (GCC) countries are Bahrain, Kuwait, Oman, Qatar, Saudi Arabia, and the United Arab Emirates. The Mashreq subregion comprises the Arab Republic of Egypt, Iraq, Jordan, Lebanon, and the Syrian Arab Republic. The Maghreb subregion comprises Algeria, Libya, Morocco, and Tunisia.
2. "Periphery" refers to the peripheral areas outside of the capital city.
3. This typology comes from Weber (1958).
4. One of the original core objectives of the European Economic Community (EEC), set out in the 1957 Treaty of Rome, was the development of a common market offering free movement of goods, service, people, and capital.
5. WTO+ provisions include areas such as customs regulations, export taxes, antidumping, countervailing measures, technical barriers to trade, or sanitary and phytosanitary standards.
6. Jaud and Freund (2015) estimate that nonpetroleum exports were as low as 64 percent below what would be expected given the region's characteristics, and imports were as high as 22 percent over what one would expect. In other words, the region seems to underexport and overimport.
7. Examples of service trade restrictions include limits or discrimination in licensing, constraints on foreign equity, or various requirements or limitations applied to foreign providers. Not all of these are explicitly designed to restrict foreign firms' access; some apply to domestic firms as well and may be designed to ensure safety and quality. But de facto these often favor domestic firms.
8. The nature of service trade restrictions has not been studied as extensively as those for goods trade, but a recent effort generated a first overview for 103 countries (Borchert, Gootiiz, and Mattoo 2013). OECD and other high-income countries maintain restrictions in sectors such as professional services and some types of transportation, while some low- to middle-income countries are surprisingly open.
9. Recent financial crises have challenged the prevailing notion that free capital flows support low- and middle-income countries (Rodrik 2018). But this is mostly an argument about

the benefits of *temporary* capital account restrictions as a "second best" instrument to avert severe financial or macroeconomic imbalances.

10. In this chapter, North America refers to Canada and the United States.

11. No FDI data were available for Libya and Syria.

12. Migration statistics are difficult to collect. These numbers are estimates from the World Bank Migration and Remittances Database 2017, which are largely based on data compiled by the United Nations Statistics Division.

13. Form of government strongly correlates with freedom of information access. Of the 20 Middle East and North Africa economies, 14 are considered authoritarian, 4 are hybrid regimes, and 2 are flawed democracies. None is a full democracy (EIU 2018).

14. Each component of the Digital Adoption Index comprises several subindexes (World Bank 2016): The business component includes the share of firms with a website, the number of secure servers, download speeds, and 3G coverage. The people component includes mobile access and internet access at home. The government component includes core administrative systems, online public services, and digital identification.

15. Visa requirement data are from the Passport Index database, http://www.passportindex.org.

16. This subsection is based largely on Arvis et al. (2018).

## References

Anderson, J., and E. van Wincoop. 2003. "Gravity with Gravitas: A Solution to the Border Puzzle." *American Economic Review* 93 (1): 170–92.

Arvis, J. F., Y. Duval, B. Shepherd, C. Utoktham, and A. Raj. 2016. "Trade Costs in the Developing World: 1996–2010." *World Trade Review* 15 (3): 451–74.

Arvis, J.-F., V. Vesin, R. C. Carruthers, C. Ducruet, and P. W. De Langen. 2018. *Maritime Networks, Port Efficiency, and Hinterland Connectivity in the Mediterranean.* Washington, DC: World Bank.

Behar, A., and C. Freund. 2011. "The Trade Performance of the Middle East and North Africa." Middle East and North Africa Working Paper Series 53, World Bank, Washington, DC.

Bhattacharya, M. R., and H. Wolde. 2010. "Constraints on Growth in the MENA Region." Working Paper 10-30, International Monetary Fund, Washington, DC.

Borchert, I., B. Gootiiz, and A. Mattoo. 2013. "Policy Barriers to International Trade in Services: Evidence from a New Database." *World Bank Economic Review* 28 (1): 162–88.

Bosker, M., E. Buringh, and J. L. Van Zanden. 2013. "From Baghdad to London: Unraveling Urban Development in Europe, the Middle East, and North Africa, 800–1800." *Review of Economics and Statistics* 95 (4): 1418–37.

Bourdet, Yves, and Maria Persson. 2014. "Expanding and Diversifying South Mediterranean Exports through Trade Facilitation." *Development Policy Review* 32 (6): 675–99.

Chami, Ralph, Ekkehard Ernst, Connel Fullenkamp, and Anne Oeking, 2018. "Are Remittances Good for Labor Markets in LICs, MICs and Fragile States?" IMF Working Papers 18/102, International Monetary Fund, Washington, DC.

Coughlin, C. C., and D. Novy. 2016. "Estimating Border Effects: The Impact of Spatial Aggregation." Working Paper 2016-006C, Federal Reserve Bank of St. Louis, St. Louis, MO.

Devereux, S. 2016. "Social Protection and Safety Nets in the Middle East and North Africa." World Food Program and Institute of Development Studies, Brighton, U.K.

Diwan, I., and H. Chekir. 2015. "Crony Capitalism in Egypt." *Journal of Globalization and Development* 5 (2): 177–211.

EIU (Economist Intelligence Unit). 2016. "Measuring Well-Governed Migration: The 2016 Migration Governance Index." Study, EIU, London.

———. 2018. "Democracy Index 2017: Free Speech under Attack." Study, Economist Intelligence Unit (EIU), London.

El-Din Haseeb, K. 2012. *The Future of the Arab Nation: Challenges and Options.* Abingdon, U.K.: Routledge.

Faraji, S. 2016. "Urban Primacy in Urban System of Developing Countries: Its Causes and Consequences." *Human Research in Rehabilitation* 6 (1): 34–45.

Freedom House. 2017a. "Freedom of the Press 2017: Press Freedom's Dark Horizon." Annual report on global media independence, Freedom House, Washington, DC.

———. 2017b. "Freedom on the Net 2017: Manipulating Social Media to Undermine Democracy." Booklet, Freedom House, Washington, DC.

Frick, Susanne A., and Andrés Rodríguez-Pose. 2018. "Big or Small Cities? On City Size and Economic Growth." *Growth and Change* 49 (1): 4–32.

Gammoudi, M., and M. Cherif. 2015. "Capital Account Openness, Political Institutions and FDI in the MENA Region: An Empirical Investigation." Economics Discussion Papers 2015-10, Kiel Institute for the World Economy, Kiel, Germany.

Henderson, V. 2002. "Urbanisation in Developing Countries." *World Bank Research Observer* 17 (1): 89–112.

Hoekman, B. 2016. "Intraregional Trade: Potential Catalyst for Growth in the Middle East." Policy Paper 2016-1, Middle East Institute, Washington, DC.

Hoekman, B., and B. Shepherd. 2017. "Services Productivity, Trade Policy and Manufacturing Exports." *The World Economy* 40 (3): 499–516.

Hofmann, C., A. Osnago, and M. Ruta. 2017. "Horizontal Depth: A New Database on the Content of Preferential Trade Agreements." Policy Research Working Paper 7981, World Bank, Washington, DC.

Hoxha, I., S. Kalemli-Ozcan, and D. Vollrath. 2013. "How Big Are the Gains from International Financial Integration?" *Journal of Development Economics* 103 (C): 90–98.

Ivanyna, M., and A. Shah. 2012. "How Close is Your Government to Its People? Worldwide Indicators on Localization and Decentralization." Policy Research Working Paper 6138, World Bank, Washington, DC.

Jaud, M., and C. Freund. 2015. *Champions Wanted: Promoting Exports in the Middle East and North Africa.* Washington, DC: World Bank.

Kennan, J. 2013. "Open Borders." *Review of Economic Dynamics* 16 (2): L1–L13.

Kose, M. Ayhan, Eswar Prasad, Kenneth Rogoff, and Shang-Jin Wei. 2006. "Financial Globalization: A Reappraisal." Working Paper 06/189, International Monetary Fund, Washington, DC.

Krishnan, Nandini, Gabriel Lara Ibarra, Ambar Narayan, Sailesh Tiwari, and Tara Vishwanath. 2016. *Uneven Odds, Unequal Outcomes: Inequality of Opportunity in the Middle East and North Africa.* Directions in Development Series. Washington, DC: World Bank.

Lebrand, Mathilde. 2019. "International Growth Spillovers from Deep Agreements for Countries and Cities." Unpublished manuscript, World Bank, Washington, DC.

Loungani, Prakash, Saurabh Mishra, Chris Papageorgiou, and Ke Wang. 2017. "World Trade in Services: Evidence from a New Database." Working Paper WP17/77, International Monetary Fund, Washington, DC.

Okada, K. 2013. "The Interaction Effects of Financial Openness and Institutions on International Capital Flows." *Journal of Macroeconomics* 35: 131–43.

Pritchett, L. 2006. *Let Their People Come: Breaking the Gridlock on International Labor Mobility.* Washington, DC: Center for Global Development.

Rijkers, B., C. Freund, and A. Nucifora. 2014. "All in the Family: State Capture in Tunisia." Policy Research Working Paper 6810, World Bank, Washington, DC.

Roberts, M., and U. Deichmann. 2011. "International Growth Spillovers, Geography and Infrastructure." *The World Economy* 34 (9): 1507–33.

Rodrik, D. 2018. "What Do Trade Agreements Really Do?" *Journal of Economic Perspectives* 32 (2): 73–90.

RSF (Reporters without Borders). 2018a. "RSF Index 2018: Journalism Sorely Tested in North Africa." Regional analysis, World Press Freedom Index 2018, RSF, Paris.

———. 2018b. "RSF Index 2018: Middle East Riven by Conflicts, Political Clashes." Regional analysis, World Press Freedom Index 2018, RSF, Paris.

Solow, Robert M. 1957. "Technical Change and the Aggregate Production Function." *The Review of Economics and Statistics* 39 (3): 312–20.

UN DESA (United Nations Department of Economic and Social Affairs). 2019. *UN Urbanization Prospects: The 2018 Revision.* New York: UN DESA.

Weber, Max. 1958. *The City.* English translation, edited by Don Martindale and Gertrud Neuwirth. New York: The Free Press.

World Bank. 2016. *World Development Report 2016: Digital Dividends.* Washington, DC: World Bank.

World Bank. 2017. Enterprise Surveys, Firm level TFP estimates and Factor Ratios Data, World Bank, Washington, DC.

# How States Shape Markets through Spatial and Private Sector Development Bets | 4

Jobs and stability: these have been two stated drivers of several governments' policy priorities in the Middle East and North Africa. As a region with some of the world's highest unemployment rates and lowest labor force participation rates, with a youth bulge and rising demand for housing, and with episodes of violent conflict and terrorism, these stated policy orientations are unquestionable. But several of the region's governments are making policy choices and adopting market orientations that are contributing to a vicious cycle of worse job and inclusion environments.

Distinct patterns in many of these governments' orientations toward private sector-led development and citizen welfare help explain the current economic geography of these countries. The patterns converge on an observation—that governments in the Middle East and North Africa are more inclined than many of their peers to take activist roles in physically shaping markets at every spatial scale. And for many, their outcomes appear worse than those of their peers, with some exceptions. This chapter analyzes how government orientations toward shaping markets through spatial and private sector development bets has limited the region's private sector and jobs development potential.

The chapter addresses five overarching questions:

1. How does government intervention in markets and competition in the Middle East and North Africa compare with other regions and why? We compare these countries' performance on competitiveness and governance indexes, and we offer a political economy analysis to help explain the current state of affairs.
2. How are Middle East and North Africa governments intervening to shape markets at each of the three spatial scales described in chapters 1 through 3— within cities, within countries, and across countries?
3. How does the extent of the governments' spatially distortive interventions in the Middle East and North Africa compare with those in benchmark countries? We analyze government intervention preferences by analyzing their expenditure patterns—both across different types of interventions and with respect to different territories. We compare these patterns with expenditure patterns in comparator countries.
4. What are the implications of these intervention choices?

5. Finally, given the limited impact of some of the main territorial development policy instruments in the region, why do countries continue to use them?

Recent research has found that most Middle East and North Africa countries have significant barriers to competition. Relative to most benchmark countries and regions, they have less competitive, less efficient environments. This outcome is likely linked to the development model many of the region's governments chose after independence and the evolution of those systems since then, as further discussed later in the chapter.

The interventionist approach is not limited to competition in product and service markets; it also dictates the spatial development of the region's countries at all three spatial scales:

- *Within cities,* several Middle East and North Africa countries have onerous land market and building development regulations that contribute to patchy and sometimes underdemanded formal development and to considerable informal development except in the Gulf Cooperation Council (GCC) subregion.[1]
- *Within countries,* most allocate considerable resources toward building new cities and zones and toward incentives to divert economic activities to those new places. With few exceptions, these efforts have had large costs with minimal returns, despite the stated intent of reducing congestion and spreading population and economic activities.
- *Across countries,* historical barriers to trade have stifled cross-country trade and contributed to the Middle East and North Africa's position as one of the least integrated regions in the world.

As for the governments' emphasis on different instruments for enhancing economic development with spatial implications, the Middle East and North Africa countries are outliers in their policy and intervention orientations. Relative to comparator countries,

many of the region's countries have reverse expenditure patterns: They allocate a larger share of expenditures (investment and recurrent expenditures) to spatially distortive targeted interventions such as public sector industrialization and industrial location regulations; growth poles, industrial districts, and other location subsidies; subsidies and other incentives to capital; and physical infrastructure for connectivity and to support local production. Conversely, they allocate a smaller share toward people-based and institution-based interventions. Among most comparator countries across the world, the expenditure emphasis is reversed: they allocate most of their expenditures toward people-based and institution-based interventions.

Place-based interventions are associated with relatively high expenditures, limited results, and physical and economic geographies that are falling short of stated national goals. In the Middle East and North Africa, the focus on directly shaping and controlling markets beginning in the 1950s contributed to an economic geography that left many areas behind. To respond to the needs and grievances of those regions, countries took on activist territorial development policies with a strong spatial focus. These policies, which directed compensatory support to lagging territories and created new geographic centers for economic development, saddled the region's governments with high expenditures and limited returns.

Why do most Middle East and North Africa governments pursue the same territorial development interventions despite the limited impact? First, even if the overall impact of these interventions is limited, some groups benefit considerably from them. Second, starting an initiative on new land may face less resistance than addressing ongoing challenges in an established area. Third, concrete information is scarce on the relative successes and failures of the region's territorial development policies. And fourth, the occasional successes inspire hope for replication, even if the recipe for success is not replicable.

## Competition regimes in the Middle East and North Africa: How do they differ from other regions, and why?

### The region stacks up poorly on world competitiveness and governance indexes

Global indexes of countries' competitiveness, ease of doing business, and governance indicate that the Middle East and North Africa as a region offers a less competitive and more constrained market environment than comparator regions. The latest scores in the World Economic Forum's (WEF) 2017–18 Global Competitiveness Index (GCI), the WEF Executive Opinion Survey on doing business, and the World Bank's Worldwide Governance Indicators (WGI) reveal some consistent patterns.

*Global Competitiveness Index*

According to the 2017–18 GCI, most Middle East and North Africa countries underperform relative to their development levels (figure 4.1). The region's countries have an average score of 4.28 out of 7 (Schwab 2017).[2] Half of the world's countries (out of 137 included in the GCI) score higher, including countries at earlier stages of development.[3] The Middle East and North Africa countries' rankings range from last (the Republic of Yemen) to 17th (the United Arab Emirates). Further, they face a challenging duo of the most significant barriers to doing business as perceived by executives in the region: inefficient government interventions and corruption.

The WEF attributes the region's weak performance on the GCI to several factors. First is the extent of the state's presence in several sectors, including manufacturing, construction, finance, transport, and infrastructure. Over 2010–12, the central government wage bill as a percentage of gross domestic product (GDP) for Middle East and North Africa countries averaged

**FIGURE 4.1   Middle East and North Africa countries are less competitive than most countries of comparable income**

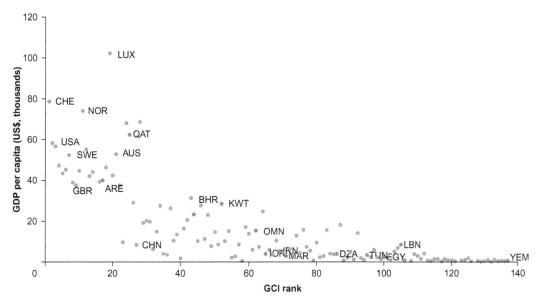

*Sources:* World Development Indicators Database; Schwab 2017.
*Note:* The World Economic Forum's 2017–18 Global Competitive Index (GCI) ranked 137 countries, including 15 in the Middle East and North Africa (Schwab 2017). GDP per capita uses latest available data from 2016 or 2017.

approximately 8.1 percent versus about 5.9 percent for Organisation for Economic Co-operation and Development (OECD) countries and 7.1 percent for Europe and Central Asia (WEF and World Bank 2018). The region's GCC countries average a 2-to-1 ratio of public to private sector employment, one of the highest in the world.

Second are several investment climate factors that constrain private investment: political instability, a complex regulatory environment, skills mismatches, and barriers to competition in critical factor markets. One of the only areas in which the region's countries have made significant progress relative to OECD countries over the past few decades is infrastructure, but the WEF report notes that this has not been associated with gains in competitiveness.

*Doing Business Index*

The Middle East and North Africa has also underperformed with respect to its business environment in the World Bank's Doing Business Index. In 2017, the region's countries ranked above South Asia in how the private sector functions but below Latin America and the Caribbean, Europe and Central Asia, and the OECD countries. For instance, to start a business in the Middle East and North Africa takes 7.8 procedures over 20.1 days, and costs 26.3 percent of income per capita, compared with South Asia at 8.1 procedures over 15.4 days and 13.4 percent of income per capita. The region's businesses also pay high and frequent taxes to operate—17.8 payments a year on average—whereas Europe and Central Asian countries incur 17.6 payments, and OECD countries, 10.9 payments. Again, South Asia ranks lower, at 31.8 payments a year on average (World Bank 2017a). Business regulations in the Middle East and North Africa are rated distant from good practice with respect to efficiency and quality, relative to other regions (figure 4.2).

**FIGURE 4.2    Business regulations in the Middle East and North Africa are rated distant from good practice with respect to efficiency and quality**

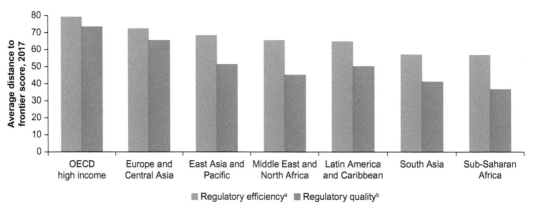

*Source:* World Bank 2017b.

*Note:* OECD = Organisation for Economic Co-operation and Development. The distance to frontier score in the World Bank's Doing Business Index measures the gap between an economy's performance and the "frontier," representing good practice across the entire sample of indicators (excluding labor market regulation indicators) across all economies since 2005 (World Bank 2017b).

a. The distance to frontier score for "regulatory efficiency" is the aggregate score for the procedures (where applicable) and time and cost indicators from the following indicator sets: starting a business (also including the minimum capital requirement indicator), dealing with construction permits, getting electricity, registering property, paying taxes (also including the postfiling index), trading across borders, enforcing contracts, and resolving insolvency.

b. The distance to frontier score for "regulatory quality" is the aggregate score for getting credit and protecting minority investors as well as the regulatory quality indexes from the indicator sets on dealing with construction permits, getting electricity, registering property, enforcing contracts, and resolving insolvency.

*Worldwide Governance Indicators*

Concerning five governance indicators that affect the local business environment, the Middle East and North Africa scores lower across the board than other middle- to high-income regions of the world: East Asia and Pacific, Europe and Central Asia, and Latin America and the Caribbean. The region's scores in the World Bank's Worldwide Governance Indicators (WGI) have been declining consistently since 2007, with the exception of brief positive upticks regarding regulatory quality and rule of law in 2012. In the WGI 2017,

- *On government effectiveness,* the Middle East and North Africa scores approximately 10–25 percentage points lower than the other regions (figure 4.3, panel a);
- *On regulatory quality,* the region scores about 10–15 percentage points lower (figure 4.3, panel b);
- *On rule of law,* the region scores about 10–20 percentage points lower (figure 4.3, panel c);
- *On political stability,* the region consistently scores about half the score of the other regions, and this score declined markedly from 2007 to 2017 (figure 4.3, panel d); and
- *On control of corruption,* the region scores about 10–20 percentage points lower (figure 4.3, panel e).

Adding to the evidence of governance-related effects on competitiveness, several recent studies have found that industrial policy and regulatory environments in Middle East and North Africa countries are highly correlated with firm connectedness (Rijkers, Freund, and Nucifora 2014; Schiffbauer et al. 2015). In the Arab Republic of Egypt, for example, a small number of politically connected firms have been permitted to operate in energy-intensive industries (Schiffbauer et al. 2015). Any firm seeking to operate in energy-intensive industries needs a

government license, and access to these licenses has been restricted to insider firms. Firms with licenses to operate in this field benefit from large energy subsidies. This state of affairs limits both competition in energy-intensive industries and the growth of labor-intensive industries.

In Tunisia, there is evidence that industrial policy was oriented toward rent creation for former President Ben Ali and his family (Rijkers, Freund, and Nucifora 2014). Differences in performance between firms connected to the former president and competitors are much larger in sectors with higher regulation. Further, the sectors in which connected firms are active are disproportionately more regulated than other sectors.

In both Egypt and Tunisia, there is evidence that barriers to entry in trade protect connected firms from foreign competition and orient them toward domestic markets (Schiffbauer et al. 2015). These barriers include privileged access to factors of production, inconsistent implementation of rules and regulations within a given sector, and exclusive operating licenses in profitable service sectors.

## Competitive constraints stem from the region's political economy

The Middle East and North Africa's underperformance in creating an environment that promotes competition and ease of doing business does not seem driven by an absence of efforts to reform the legal and regulatory environment. The region's governments have introduced about as many market-enhancing reforms as comparator regions, but the private sector development response has been lower—a contrast attributed partly to the distinction between legal reform and practical implementation (Benhassine et al. 2009). That contrast (illustrated in figure 4.4) offers insight into a finding that is developed further below—that adding layers of reforms appears to be insufficient in

**FIGURE 4.3** The Middle East and North Africa has consistently ranked lower than other middle- to high-income regions on the Worldwide Governance Indicators, 2007–17

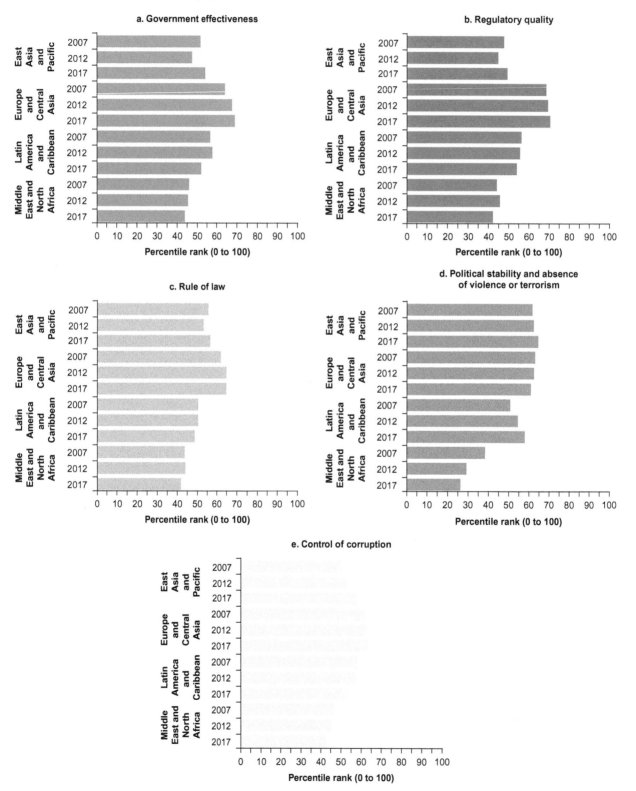

*Source:* World Governance Indicators Database, https://info.worldbank.org/governance/wgi/.

the Middle East and North Africa context, where some fundamental distortions remain unaddressed.

### History of the postcolonial development model

The development model most Middle East and North Africa countries pursued in the 20th century after independence from the British and French was both a reaction to, and in some ways a perpetuation of, the model pursued by colonial governments. Governments established social contracts that were framed as correcting for spatial disparities and widespread poverty maintained under colonial rule (Nabli et al. 2006). They were designed to depart from the colonial model, in which foreign private firms had lucrative deals to extract natural resources.

As such, core attributes of the new social contract across the region comprised (a) a shift from markets to states as key shapers of national economies; (b) a shift toward states to determine economic priorities; (c) a focus on redistribution through economic and social policy (and an assignment to the state of the provision of welfare and social services); and (d) the establishment of the political arena as an expression of national unity instead of as a platform for political contestation or a means for managing conflicting preferences (Nabli et al. 2006).

The implementation of this social contract was similar across the region, especially in Algeria, Egypt, Iraq, and the Syrian Arab Republic, and to a lesser extent in Jordan, Morocco, Tunisia, and the Republic of Yemen. It included single-party or ruling party governments, constitutions that established interventionist and redistributive principles, agrarian reform programs, centralization of professional associations and trade unions, and state provision of social services and subsidies.

To execute this new social contract, governments across the region took control of their natural resources from foreign firms (which had negotiated long concessions during World War II) (Mills and Alhashemi 2018).

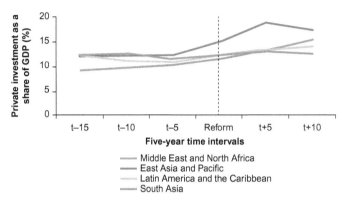

**FIGURE 4.4** **Private investment has responded less to reforms in the Middle East and North Africa than in other regions**

*Private investment (as % of GDP) in relation to reform episodes*

*Source:* Benhassine et al. 2009.
*Note:* Private investment rates are from the World Development Indicators Database, national accounts, and the International Monetary Fund and have been averaged over the five-year periods. Episodes of reforms are based on the Economic Freedom Index of the Fraser Institute (http://www.freetheworld.com), and a reform episode is defined as a five-year episode during which the 0–10 index permanently improved by at least one unit.

The new governments worked mostly through state-owned enterprises controlling oil, gas, phosphates, and other natural resources.

With revenues assured for the medium term from control of natural resources and a commitment to redistribution and social welfare, the region's governments pursued public sector job creation as a centerpiece of their development models. Natural resource and foreign aid rents limited the governments' needs for tax collection and therefore for active citizen participation in governance (Mills and Alhashemi 2018). Further, public sector employment limited the likelihood of citizen contestation against the government.

### Legacy of spatially biased policies and development

Although their stated objectives were to change the colonial development model and redistribute to the needy, the legacy of spatially biased systems inherited from colonial rule persisted in most countries of the Middle East and North Africa (Mills and Alhashemi 2018). National administrations and fiscal systems were spatially biased toward capital cities and coastal metropolises. Colonial rulers had focused on resource extraction in less connected areas and focused the investments on the coast with little to no representation of local interests. That system was maintained or mirrored after independence.

Regions that felt taken advantage of have increasingly risen in protest in a form of resource regionalism that mirrors resource nationalism (Mills and Alhashemi 2018). These lagging regions where resource extraction has been heavy include southern Algeria, southern and interior Tunisia, eastern and northeastern Syria, and the interior of Oman. And although some company towns in these regions represent enclaves of development, even urban centers in resource-rich areas often lag behind their national peers. Such cities include Basra and Kirkuk in Iraq, Assaluyeh in the Islamic Republic of Iran, Gafsa in Tunisia, and Khourigba in Morocco.

Instead of correcting the biases in their fiscal and administrative structures that reinforced spatial disparities, the region's governments sought to overcompensate for them with spatially targeted industrial policies. The industrial policies were largely vertical, focusing both on specific industries or sectors and on regions. Policies cultivated industries in specific sectors, while spatially targeted industrial policies were oriented toward distributing jobs and services to lagging regions. More than in comparator regions, the Middle East and North Africa governments pursued vertical (sector and spatially targeted) industrial policy instead of horizontal industrial policy (Nabli et al. 2006).

More generally, most of the region's governments seemed to perceive industrial policies, including subsidies, as a necessary part of industrial development because of the externalities of their instruments of redistribution and because of their heavy reliance on natural resource revenues and foreign aid. Price controls in the Middle East and North Africa divorced prices from production costs, and the region's governments pursued compensatory measures accordingly. Given the focus from the 1950s onward on food subsidization, the agriculture sector received large subsidies, trade protection, and other incentives for production.

Historically, while a stated pillar of government development models in the Middle East and North Africa has been to redistribute development gains to needier populations, their choice of vertical instead of horizontal industrial policies is consistent with pursuit of control. Vertical policies have concentrated winners and diffused losers and therefore help secure government power bases. In contrast, horizontal policies that are not industry- or territory-specific have diffuse benefits, concentrated losses, and often longer time frames for impact. So, they can be perceived as less politically rewarding. Given the initial orientation to reward a limited few at the expense of many, shifts from vertical to horizontal instruments have become increasingly difficult to make because insider economic actors are resilient to reforms. Reforms often reorganize opportunities for rent seeking rather than eliminating them (Nabli et al. 2006).

## Middle East and North Africa governments intervene in markets to shape economic geography

Across several countries in the Middle East and North Africa, there is a tension between governments facilitating and planning for organic growth, akin to historical city development, and adopting what they perceive as more modern approaches to enabling housing development and managing the location and nature of development. As outlined in chapter 1, informal development across many countries in the Middle East and North Africa mirrors medieval city development and features the compact development that many industrialized countries aspire to today.

However, in the Middle East and North Africa, this compact, mixed-use development had been regarded as problematic for much of the past several decades. Planners across several countries aspired to develop cities with an orientation they perceived as more modern—that is, as new cities with large new developments and zoning that separates uses. In the process, they have in many instances created neighborhoods and cities that were not desired by citizens and firms, while a large share of their citizens and firms chose an informal route that better responded to their needs. This section outlines the approaches many of the region's governments have taken to overregulate physical development and expansion at all spatial scales.

## Within cities, centralized and fragmented ownership and management distort land markets

Fragmented and opaque central government control of land as well as dysfunctional land markets have contributed to fragmented and underused supply-driven development. Well-functioning land markets positively support equity and efficiency in several ways. For example, they can transfer land from less to more productive activities and thus increase productivity. Also, transferable land rights make it possible to get jobs that are not land-intensive, increasing the labor pool for nonfarm activities. Additionally, land rights incentivize investments by providing certainty that investments will provide benefits even if investors do not personally use the land. Furthermore, well-functioning land markets undergird equity, providing certainty to those owning the land where dwellings are located (Deininger 2003).

*How state controls have led to fragmented development*

However, land markets in Middle East and North Africa's cities are mostly incomplete and inefficient, driven in part by centralized and fragmented ownership and management. In Egypt, for example, as chapter 1 described, most of the population is concentrated in a small portion (about 5 percent) of the country, and the remaining land is mainly desert that is publicly owned and, for the most part, undeveloped. To develop these vast state lands, Egypt has in the past

few decades relied on independent sectoral authorities affiliated with the ministries of agriculture, irrigation, tourism, housing, industry, and defense, which have been given control over large areas outside of the Zimam (the boundary of historically surveyed agricultural lands that are subject to the land tax). This has created segmented and isolated land markets driven by administrative fiat and supply-side considerations.

The sectoral authorities responsible for developing industry, tourism, housing, and new urban communities and for agriculture and land reclamation control more than 5 million feddans of public land (2.1 million hectares), equivalent to 2.5 percent of Egypt's territory and about half of the land area occupied by Egypt's 80 million inhabitants (World Bank 2012). Moreover, less than 10 percent of urban land and property in Egypt is registered, owing to cumbersome and complex procedures prone to rent seeking plus a backlog of an estimated 19 million disputes to be settled. There are already 12 million inhabitants living in informal areas of Greater Cairo.

Israel offers one of the most extreme examples by which state control of cities introduces inefficiencies and reduces productivity and well-being. Since 1967, Israel has been implementing a broad range of policies aimed at controlling the movement of populations in the West Bank and Gaza, causing fragmentation of the urban fabric in these territories. These policies include roadblocks, checkpoints, residency requirements, Israeli-only highways, and the separation wall. This strategy has severely affected the quality of daily life for many citizens by increasing unemployment, poverty, home demolitions, and business failures and therefore causing a major decline in GDP and average income (UN-Habitat 2012). Zoning, planning, and land classification policies are all enforced by various Israeli administrative departments with little attention to the efficiency of the urban system in the West Bank and Gaza.

Two important occupation phenomena have had far-reaching consequences: First, the creation of the seam zone adjacent to the separation wall will separate 50,000 Arab residents (living in 38 villages and towns) from the rest of the West Bank and separate 60,000 people living in East Jerusalem from their families and places of employment. Second, the division of the West Bank into three areas (A, B, and C) will result in further fragmentation. Areas A and B are mainly built-up areas, while area C constitutes 60 percent of the West Bank area. However, Israeli authorities have been thwarting development and built-up expansion in those areas despite provisions of the Oslo Accords (UN-Habitat 2012).[4]

In Morocco, a cumbersome and opaque land regulatory environment has contributed to lower-density cities. Moroccan cities face land challenges mainly around the complexity and cumbersomeness of legal provisions, the multiplicity of land tenure, and the weakness in the proportion of registered real estate (about 10 percent in rural municipalities).

An analysis carried out in Morocco at the level of the Greater Casablanca, Rabat-Salé-Témara, and Greater Marrakech regions for 2010–16 reveals the extent to which physical fragmentation is associated with declining urban densities (Lall et al. 2019). The dropout between urban sprawl and population growth was considerable: the growth rate of urbanized areas was more than 5 times that of demography in Marrakech (12.25 percent and 2.21 percent, respectively); more than 3 times for the whole Rabat-Salé-Témara region (5.85 percent and 1.96 percent); and more than 1.7 times for Greater Casablanca (2.78 percent and 1.64 percent).

*How regulatory schemes have increased informality*

Onerous building and zoning regulations are creating a mismatch between the location of jobs and formal housing, and in turn, demand is being met through informality. Chapter 1 highlighted how holes in the formal urban fabric are being "stitched" by informal sector activity that

can more freely respond to market forces. This subsection outlines the way in which onerous building and zoning regulations reinforce this duality.

Several countries restrict floor area ratios and thus limit the formal supply of residential and commercial units in their cities. In Tunisia, for example, the default height limit is three stories in residential areas, and this standard is often applied to unplanned developments as well. In theory, urban master plans can assign higher density to registered plots within planned areas. But that is restricted to large plots, and the cumbersome application process involves many steps and stakeholders.

In several Middle East and North Africa countries, inefficient and outdated zoning regulations and building codes discourage efficient land use and contribute to low-density, high-cost housing developments. In Jordan, only 30 percent of households can afford houses larger than 100 square meters without spending more that 30 percent of their monthly income (World Bank 2018b). These high costs are driven by a shortage of land and inefficient use of land due to inefficient zoning regulations and building codes.

Where formal housing costs are unaffordable and supply is restricted, a large share of urban populations opts to live in informal settlements. Between 2004 and 2015, half of Amman's new housing units were permitted before construction, more than 14 percent were registered after completion, and 37 percent are still unpermitted (World Bank 2018b). In most of Jordan's governorates, fewer than 30 percent of the new housing units have a building permit (30 percent in Maan, 26 percent in Kerak, 24 percent in Irbid, 23 percent in Madaba, 21 percent in Tafila, 19 percent in Zarqa, 11 percent in Mafraq, 10 percent in Jerash, and 8 percent in Ajlun). In those governorates, Jordanians have been building unlicensed housing units without. In Aqaba, the housing permit regulation is better followed, with 61 percent of the new housing units permitted before construction (box 4.1).

BOX 4.1    **The process for building a housing unit in Jordan**

In *Doing Business 2018*, Jordan ranked 72nd of 190 countries in registering property and 110th in issuing construction permits (World Bank 2018a). On average, national-level building permits require 62 days to be issued. (In Greater Amman, it can take up to four months, because the auditing bureau has only seven representatives for the entire city.) Typically, housing development follows these steps: In areas zoned for urban use, land is subdivided and sold. The owner (developer or individual) then consults with the municipality on the land-use options and may have to pay "improvement taxes" if the use has been changed from residential to commercial.

Land-use changes as well as amendments on the building terms for each land plot are frequent, and as a result, consultations with the authorities before any development are necessary. Subsequently, the owner seeks approvals from several referral agencies such as the Jordanian Engineers' Association, the Civil Defense Department (CDD), and Ministry of Tourism and Antiquities as well as from utility providers before applying for a building permit at the Greater Amman Municipality (GAM). Additional clearances may be required by other referral agencies (Public Security Department) and GAM units (Traffic Control Department or Special Projects Department) depending on project type and complexity. Once the structure is complete and third-party inspectors from GAM and CDD have cleared the project, a completion or occupancy permit, issued by the municipality to occupy the building, is necessary to get utility connections (electricity and water).

The owner bears the cost of bringing the trunk infrastructure from the nearest available network to the site, which can be very high (JD 300 per electricity pole at 30-meter intervals). The land owner must pay a building tax of JD 0.75 per square meter to the municipality and build an underground safe space or "refuge area" not smaller than 10 percent of the surface. The new municipal law adopted in 2015 includes a JD 150 fine per square meter built in contravention in order to push citizens and builders to follow zoning and building norms, including parking lots.

*Source:* World Bank 2018b.

## Within countries, interventions to move jobs and people have had limited success

New cities, zones, and spatially distortive industrial regulation are some of the mechanisms governments in the Middle East and North Africa have used to shape economic geography. The motivations for these interventions vary by country but comprise several major drivers. The first is the desire to move jobs to places where they are lacking and people are in need. To do so, countries in the Maghreb and Mashreq subregions have deployed investment incentives and a range of zones facilitating the relocation and new development of economic activity. The second is a desire to leverage unused land. In some cases, the focus is to create a new growth engine (such as Neom in Saudi Arabia), and in others, it is to correct for major challenges in existing cities (such as Egypt's new capital city).

Despite good intentions, the evidence that investment incentives have helped generate substantial jobs in targeted areas in the region's countries is limited. For example, Syria tried to influence the location of private sector investment by subsidizing specific sectors in some cities. During the early 2000s, it focused on supporting the textile and clothing sectors, incentivizing the clustering of relevant manufacturing firms. These policies were implemented without a private sector demand assessment, and there is no evidence that these policies increased efficiency or benefited Syria's economy (Chahoud 2011).

The recent history of new city development in several Middle East and North Africa countries has shown the high cost and often limited returns to noncontiguous city development. An estimate of the direct costs of developing these cities in Saudi Arabia and Egypt (outlined below) reveals the enormous outlays by the region's governments to build new desert cities. The low occupancy of most of these cities relative to projections reveals that they are not delivering the returns expected.

Although zones—industrial, economic, and free—could be a useful way to offer the suite of services and infrastructure needed for certain types of economic activity to develop, the limited success of these zones across the region demonstrates that location always matters. For example, Egypt has used industrial zones and new towns to divert firms and people from major cities and toward less-developed areas. As a result, however, access to markets has been a major impediment to their success and utilization. Of 139 industrial zones created from 1975 to 2012, almost all were in desert locations disconnected from agglomerations (Sims 2015). They are far from input sources and services, and markets find it difficult to mobilize and retain a large enough labor force. Manufacturing firms in industrial estates commonly provide bus transport for workers who must travel long distances, adding to recurrent costs. In some governorates where concerted efforts were made, occupancy rates of these zones are less than 25 percent of developed capacity.

In some cases where governments built zones in distant locations and observed limited occupancy, they attempted to create new towns around the zones for people to live in and agglomerations to develop. Egypt created planned new towns in three waves. Eight cities in the late 1970s and early 1980s were planned as major industrial towns with industrial zones (Sims 2015). They were disconnected from existing agglomerations but within reasonable freight distances to major ports and Cairo's agglomeration in Egypt's north. Nine more new towns were constructed in a similar area between 1982 and 1995, five of which were in Greater Cairo. A final wave of new towns was established since 2000, concentrated in Upper (southern) Egypt, where access to international markets and local agglomerations is much weaker.

But because of high housing costs and poor housing policies, few workers settled in the new towns, with vacancies in newer public housing units exceeding 50 percent (Sims 2015). The result is huge fleets of buses shuttling workers daily from the Cairo agglomeration and other urban centers to the new towns. Employment growth has also been low. The largest five industrial zones in new towns together employ fewer than 300,000 workers, and the contribution of the remaining new towns has been minimal. Overall, government-sanctioned industrial estates in Egypt's new towns and governates by 2006 had space for 2.5 million workers but hosted just 483,000 jobs. By comparison, in 2009, there were a total of 1.8 million workers in registered factories[5] outside formal industrial zones, mainly within current urban agglomerations (World Bank 2012).

## Across countries, resistance to regional cooperation constrains trade

The Middle East and North Africa's poor record on regional cooperation is somewhat surprising. There are no good structural reasons for it. The region has a history of intensive trading relations going back centuries. Like Latin America, it is bound by a common language and similar culture.[6] Its endowments should make it far more economically vibrant. Like East Asia, the region has abundant and increasingly well-educated labor. Like Eastern Europe and Central Asia, it is rich in resources. With the European Union (EU) to the north and the GCC within its region, it has nearby sources of capital. The region also has a favorable geography. It is close to the world's largest economy—the EU's single market—and located on major trade routes to the rising markets of East Asia and to the continent with the fastest growing population, Africa. There are few major physical barriers dividing the region, and no Middle East and North Africa country is landlocked.

Clearly, the region is fragmented because of history and policy, not geography (Malik and Awadallah 2013). Several factors have put the brakes on regional integration: conflict, political economy (vested interests), and the recent broader backlash against trade and globalization.

The trade barriers put in place over several decades by the region's governments constrain trade and are difficult to remove. Significant tariff and nontariff trade barriers mean that there is low complementarity between these economies: many countries produce the same things their neighbors produce. Removing these protections will affect a country's less-competitive sectors. A sudden opening of markets could cause severe adjustment shocks, including employment losses. In principle, the gains reaped by more competitive sectors should enable compensation for the losers and the creation of new job opportunities. But in practice, adjustment is rarely smooth. In many industrialized countries, those that lost from globalization did not have the right skills to switch to industries that gained.[7] The industries that lost and gained also often varied in different parts of the country, making job switching more difficult. These concerns do not void the case for greater integration, but they need to be taken seriously by policy makers, especially in countries with weak institutions and underdeveloped social safety nets.

Conflict—both violent and political, driven by a range of frictions—constrains cross-border trade. Territorial disputes reduce beneficial trade between neighbors. Conflict leading to military confrontation raises the cost. For instance, development economist Paul Collier estimated in 2003 that a typical civil war imposes costs of about US$64 billion and that civil wars' annual average cost far exceeds total development aid (Collier 2003).

Before 2011, Turkey and five Levant countries (Egypt, Iraq, Jordan, Lebanon, and Syria) pursued the establishment of the Levant Economic Zone.[8] The agreement would have considerably deepened trade integration between the countries not just by reducing tariffs but also by liberalizing transport and services trade and by imposing reforms that would have made the participating economies more competitive. With

the onset of the Arab Spring and the conflicts in Syria and Iraq, these regional integration efforts came to a halt. Syria and Iraq directly lost 14–16 percent of per capita welfare because of war, with neighboring countries losing 1–1.5 percent. If the forgone benefits of regional trade integration are included, the costs for Syria and Iraq almost double to 23 percent and 28 percent, respectively, and rise to 10 percent for Egypt and 9 percent for Jordan. Such estimates are obviously tentative, but conflict undoubtedly imposes high costs on Middle East and North Africa economies. It is difficult to see how deeper regional integration can be achieved without lasting peace and security.

## Government interventions cause varying magnitudes of spatial distortion in the Middle East and North Africa

Governments in the Middle East and North Africa and beyond have a spectrum of intervention options they can leverage to address constraints to development across space. These interventions may introduce spatial distortions (figure 4.5). From the most to the least spatially distortive, government interventions can (a) influence the exact location of economic activities (place-based interventions); (b) influence access to opportunities for people (people-based interventions); or (c) reduce distortions that constrain markets through broad-based national interventions (institution-based interventions).

This section analyzes government expenditure distribution in select Middle East and North Africa countries and in comparable countries with a focus on understanding the extent to which they intervene in spatially distortive manners. Characteristics such as GDP per capita, population size, and level of development were used to define the set of benchmark countries. Moreover, regional balance was sought in the choice of comparators, so they include countries from the East Asia and Pacific, Sub-Saharan Africa, and Europe and Central Asia regions. Although the analysis looks at snapshots in

FIGURE 4.5  **Government interventions can create varying degrees of spatial distortion**

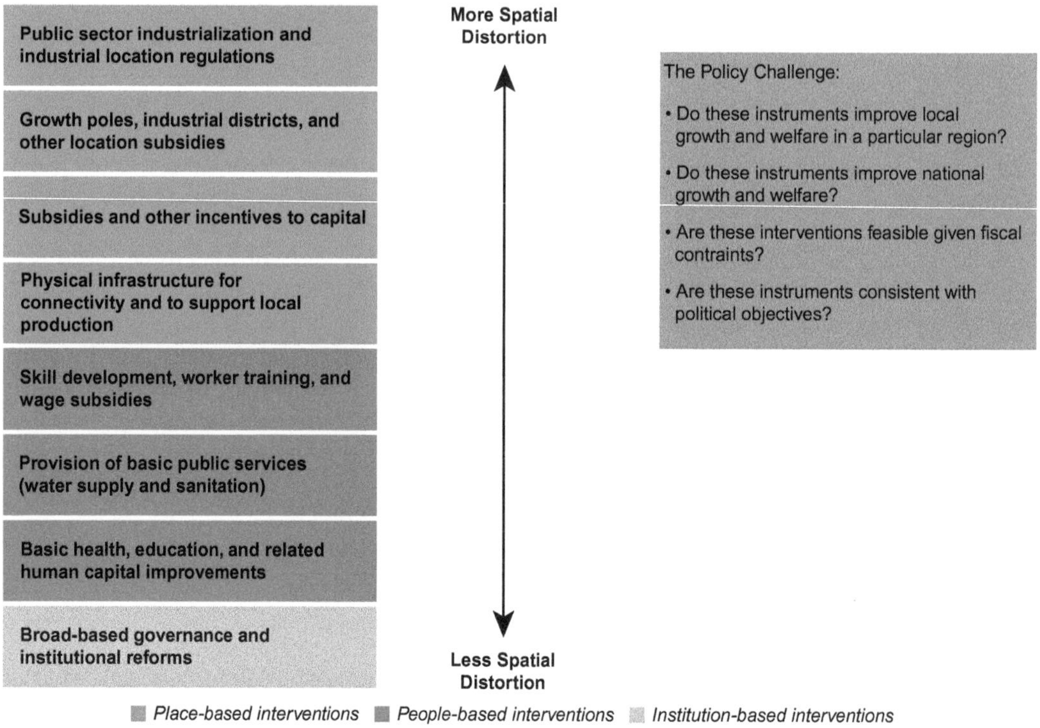

Public sector industrialization and industrial location regulations

Growth poles, industrial districts, and other location subsidies

Subsidies and other incentives to capital

Physical infrastructure for connectivity and to support local production

Skill development, worker training, and wage subsidies

Provision of basic public services (water supply and sanitation)

Basic health, education, and related human capital improvements

Broad-based governance and institutional reforms

**More Spatial Distortion**

**Less Spatial Distortion**

The Policy Challenge:

• Do these instruments improve local growth and welfare in a particular region?

• Do these instruments improve national growth and welfare?

• Are these interventions feasible given fiscal constraints?

• Are these instruments consistent with political objectives?

■ *Place-based interventions*  ■ *People-based interventions*  ▨ *Institution-based interventions*

*Source:* Lall 2009. ©World Bank. Further permission required for reuse.

time and relies on different data sources with some variation in coverage, the findings offer a preliminary indication of broader trends and should be interpreted as such.

## Most benchmark countries allocate the largest shares of government expenditure to developing human capital—and low shares to place-based interventions

Data for benchmark countries were obtained from the International Monetary Fund's (IMF) Classification of Functions of Government (COFOG) in the Government Finance Statistics (GFS) system.[9] General government units around the world can opt in to follow this classification and publish their expenses in the GFS system.[10] In the GFS database, COFOG adds both current and capital expenditures, executed on each of the functional categories by the general

government units of the central, regional, and local levels of government,[11] excluding public corporations. Expenditure data include budgetary and extrabudgetary expenses only for nonmarket activities (box 4.2).[12]

Government functions are classified in 10 broad categories, which are then disaggregated into 69 subcategories. (Data availability in this database also influenced the choice of comparator countries.) The methodology used to obtain a spatial perspective of the government expenditure distribution was to assign each of the 69 subcategories into one of the eight spatial dimensions shown in figure 4.6,[13] where the spectrum ranges from the least spatially distortive (broad-based governance and institutional reforms) to the most spatially distortive (public sector industrialization and industrial location regulations). For example, expenditure on law courts, one of the 69 subcategories, is classified within broad-based governance and institutional reforms.[14]

## BOX 4.2 **The IMF Government Finance Statistics database**

Data in the IMF's General Finance Statistics (GFS) system comprise general government expenditures, excluding those related to public corporations. The GFS system covers all entities that affect fiscal policies, which are usually implemented by entities focused on the economic functions of government, such as a government ministry, and not on market activities (figure B4.2.1). In addition to those entities, however, fiscal policy may be undertaken by government-owned or controlled enterprises that engage primarily in commercial activities. These enterprises, such as the central bank or national railroad, which are referred to as public corporations, are not considered part of the general government in the GFS system.

When a unit sells some or all of its output, it can be difficult to decide whether to classify the unit as either a government unit, a public corporation, or a public quasi corporation. In general, the decision is based on whether the unit sells its output at market prices. Any unit that sells all or almost all of its output at market prices is a corporation or quasi corporation, and all other units are government units. With public units, however, market prices are not always easy to identify.

The GFS system classifies expenditures of the general government by function in 10 broader categories, disaggregating them further into 69 subcategories according to the OECD classification published by the United Nations Statistical Division. Table B4.2.1 was extracted from the *Government Finance Statistics Manual 2014*, which describes in more detail each of the four-digit categories listed below.

**FIGURE B4.2.1** **The public sector and its main components**

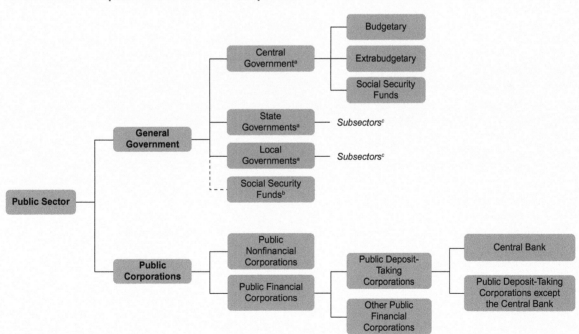

*Source:* IMF 2014, 20.
a. Includes social security funds.
b. Alternatively, social security funds can be combined into a separate subsector, as shown in the box with dashed lines.
c. Budgetary units, extrabudgetary units, and social security funds may also exist in state and local governments.

*box continues next page*

BOX 4.2  **The IMF Government Finance Statistics database** *(continued)*

TABLE B4.2.1  **Classification of expenditure, by government function, within divisions and groups**

| 7 | **Total expenditure** |
|---|---|
| **701** | **General public services** |
| 7011 | Executive and legislative organs, financial and fiscal affairs, external affairs |
| 7012 | Foreign economic aid |
| 7013 | General services |
| 7014 | Basic research |
| 7015 | R&D General public services |
| 7016 | General public services n.e.c |
| 7017 | Public debt transactions |
| 7018 | Transfers of a general character between different levels of government |
| **702** | **Defense** |
| 7021 | Military defense |
| 7022 | Civil defense |
| 7023 | Foreign military aid |
| 7024 | R&D Defense |
| 7025 | Defense n.e.c. |
| **703** | **Public order and safety** |
| 7031 | Police services |
| 7032 | Fire protection services |
| 7033 | Law courts |
| 7034 | Prisons |
| 7035 | R&D Public order and safety |
| 7036 | Public order and safety n.e.c. |
| **704** | **Economic affairs** |
| 7041 | General economic, commercial, and labor affairs |
| 7042 | Agriculture, forestry, fishing, and hunting |
| 7043 | Fuel and energy |
| 7044 | Mining, manufacturing, and construction |
| 7045 | Transport |
| 7046 | Communication |
| 7047 | Other industries |
| 7048 | R&D Economic affairs |
| 7049 | Economic affairs n.e.c. |
| **705** | **Environmental protection** |
| 7051 | Waste management |
| 7052 | Waste water management |
| 7053 | Pollution abatement |
| 7054 | Protection of biodiversity and landscape |
| 7055 | R&D Environmental protection |
| 7056 | Environmental protection n.e.c. |

| **706** | **Housing and community amenities** |
|---|---|
| 7061 | Housing development |
| 7062 | Community development |
| 7063 | Water supply |
| 7064 | Street lighting |
| 7065 | R&D Housing and community amenities |
| 7066 | Housing and community amenities n.e.c. |
| **707** | **Health** |
| 7071 | Medical products, appliances, and equipment |
| 7072 | Outpatient services |
| 7073 | Hospital services |
| 7074 | Public health services |
| 7075 | R&D Health |
| 7076 | Health n.e.c. |
| **708** | **Recreation, culture, and religion** |
| 7081 | Recreational and sporting services |
| 7082 | Cultural services |
| 7083 | Broadcasting and publishing services |
| 7084 | Religious and other community services |
| 7085 | R&D Recreation, culture, and religion |
| 7086 | Recreation, culture, and religion n.e.c. |
| **709** | **Education** |
| 7091 | Pre-primary and primary education |
| 7092 | Secondary education |
| 7093 | Postsecondary nontertiary education |
| 7094 | Tertiary education |
| 7095 | Education not definable by level |
| 7096 | Subsidiary services to education |
| 7097 | R&D Education |
| 7098 | Education n.e.c. |
| **710** | **Social protection** |
| 7101 | Sickness and disability |
| 7102 | Old age |
| 7103 | Survivors |
| 7104 | Family and children |
| 7105 | Unemployment |
| 7106 | Housing |
| 7107 | Social exclusion n.e.c. |
| 7108 | R&D Social protection |
| 7109 | Social protection n.e.c. |

*Source:* IMF 2014, 143.
*Note:* R&D = research and development. n.e.c. = not otherwise classified.

**FIGURE 4.6**  **Distribution and changes in government expenditures of comparator countries reflect priorities through a spatial lens**

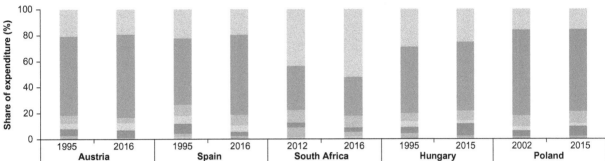

*Institution-based interventions*

▨ 1. Broad-based governance and
institutional reforms

*People-based interventions*

▨ 2. Basic health, education, and related human capital improvements    ▨ 3. Provision of basic public services

▨ 4. Skill development, worker training, wage subsidies

*Place-based interventions*

■ 5. Physical infrastructure for connectivity and to support local production    ▨ 6. Subsidies and other incentives to capital

▨ 7. Growth poles, industrial districts, other location subsidies    ▨ 8. Public sector industrialization and industrial location regulations

*Source:* Government Finance Statistics (GFS) database, International Monetary Fund.
*Note:* The period considered for each country uses the oldest and most recent years available in the GFS database. For specific percentages by country, category, and year, see table 4A.1 and table 4A.2.

Most of the governments, except for South Africa, allocate the largest share of public expenditure to developing human capital (figure 4.6). They are investing more than 60 percent on people-based policies (such as skill development and worker training, basic public services, and health and education), with Spain investing the most in 2016: 75 percent of public expenditure.

South Africa invested a higher percentage in institutions (broad-based governance and institutional reforms) than the other countries, and it also directed a high share of public expenditures toward people-based policies. South Africa allocated 52 percent of its budget to categories that relate to improving regulations. This is expected in low- to middle-income countries where there is still room for structural reforms.

Benchmark countries spent less than 15 percent of their budgets on place-based interventions, with less than 2 percent on the most spatially distortive ones. Hungary has the highest percentage among comparators with a total of 12 percent, followed by Poland with 10 percent. Excluding South Africa, infrastructure is the category of place-based interventions to which comparators assigned the highest allocations.

Over time, the share allocated toward people-based and institution-based interventions remained stable or increased (figure 4.6; also see annex 2A, table 2A.3), as follows:[15]

- *In Spain,* the government reduced by more than half its investment on infrastructure between 1995 and 2016 while increasing its human capital-related expenditures. This may be the case because right after joining the EU in 1986, Spain invested heavily in connective infrastructure.
- *In Austria,* on the other hand, the government reduced by 2 percent its expenditure on institutions between 1995 and 2016 while increasing by 3 percent expenses on people-based interventions.
- *In South Africa,* the government reduced its expenditures on place-based interventions and people-based interventions to allocate 8 percent more of its budget on institutions between 2012 and 2016. South Africa has been investing during recent years in enabling an environment for trade and businesses.

- *In Hungary,* between 1995 and 2015, the government decided to invest less in institutions, while increasing by 2 percent its expenditure on people-based and 3 percent on place-based interventions. This could be the case because, during the 1990s, Hungary needed to invest in institutions as part of its post-Soviet Union transition.
- *In Poland,* expenditures represented the only exception in our benchmark cases. The government increased its expenditure on place-based interventions from 2002 to 2015 by 4 percent, presumably a result of its increased focus on regional development policy.

### Government expenditure allocations in the Middle East and North Africa differ greatly from those in comparator countries

Based on our indicative analysis, government expenditure allocations in the Middle East and North Africa appear strikingly different from comparator country allocations.[16] One country from each subregion in the Middle East and North Africa was chosen for a deeper analysis (box 4.3): Morocco (from the Maghreb subregion), Jordan (from the Mashreq subregion), and Saudi Arabia (from the GCC subregion), including additional countries where data were more readily available,[17] such as no Egypt and Tunisia. (For details on why other countries in the region were excluded from a deeper analysis, see annex 4D.)

Results of the expenditure distribution analysis[18] are as follows (as shown in figure 4.7, figure 4.8, and table 4.1; also see annex 2A, table 2A.3):

- *Spatially distortive expenditures* in Morocco represent about 77 percent of government's expenditure in 2017, and in Tunisia, about 50 percent, while in benchmark countries, the percentage allocation of public expenditures to spatially distortive interventions was consistently below 15 percent.

---

BOX 4.3 **Government expenditure data for a subset of Middle East and North Africa countries**

Unlike the analysis for comparator countries, no comparable and comprehensive data source exists that classified all government expenditures in a given time period for Middle East and North Africa countries (except for partial data for the United Arab Emirates in the IMF GFS database). Instead, country-specific sources for this information were analyzed and details on the scope of each are outlined below and in footnotes to the figures included in this subsection. As such, in this section, the analysis offers a snapshot at one point in time. It may vary from the medium term distribution pattern for these countries but offers an illustration of how funds were distributed in each case country.

#### Morocco

The national budget in Morocco is split between the state budget and public enterprises and establishments.

The state budget is divided into five categories, where autonomously managed state services and special funds are special entities that have some flexibility in their budgetary allocations.

In 2017, 69 percent of the state budget was allocated through the general budget, which the team decided to zoom in on for the spatial analysis using the Law of Finance of 2017, which ministries are obliged to follow but which may differ from actual expenditure.[a] Moreover, data on expenditures of public establishments and enterprises are also included in the spatial analysis to give a more robust view of total government expenditures in Morocco.

#### Tunisia

The Government of Tunisia also votes on and approves annual expenditures through annual finance laws. Tunisian finance laws use the nation's five-year

*box continues next page*

BOX 4.3   **Government expenditure data for a subset of Middle East and North Africa countries**
*(continued)*

development plans as reference for their yearly expenditures. Expenditures listed in the finance laws include expenditures of state-owned enterprises and public agencies and authorities. This is a binding document for all public expenses. However, data in the Finance Law of 2017 were in some cases ambiguously categorized or lacked the detail needed for the primary analysis. As such, we did not rely on data from the Finance Law for the primary analysis, but we did analyze it as part of a robustness check. For this robustness check, we also integrated World Bank's Open Budgets Portal (BOOST).

Instead, the primary analysis is based on Tunisia's overarching five-year development strategy. The most recent five-year plan in Tunisia, the Development Plan 2016–20, is used for the data allocation in our primary analysis in this chapter. This plan listed 262 projects (divided into 16 sectors) that Tunisia plans to focus on during that period (and which are used in the spatial classification described in the main chapter text) at the national and at the governorate levels.[b] The plan includes expenditures of state-owned enterprises and public agencies and authorities. The Tunisia analysis in this chapter drawing from the five-year plan is the only one that spans more than one year.

### Egypt

The analysis for Egypt draws from multiple sources. National public expenditures are executed by the general government, by economic authorities, and by the public business sector. However, there is no document that includes the three different sectors or entities. General government expenses, also called *on-budget* expenses, can be found in the financial statements published by the country. The financial statement for 2018–19 was used for the analysis in this chapter.[c]

Economic authorities and public business sector are the entities performing the *off-budget* expenses. The off-budget expenditures in Egypt are more than twice the on-budget expenditures. Our analysis incorporates the expenditures of the 48 economic authorities that execute off-budget expenditures. They represent 14 sectors: agriculture and irrigation; industrial; mineral wealth and petroleum; electricity and power; transport; communications and aviation; trade and supply; financial and economic; housing and construction; health services; religious and public forces; culture and media; tourism; and social security and social affairs.

The only data we do not include in the analysis are those of the public business sector, within which there are 18 holding companies under Public Business Sector Companies Law No. 203 (of which 8 report to the Ministry of Public Business Sector and the other 10 to various line ministries); 2 companies under the General Companies Law (Telecom Egypt and Electricity Holding Company); and 4 corporations under Public Sector Law 97 (3 state-owned banks in addition to the Arab Contractors Company). We did not include them because financial data for the 24 companies were not readily available. However, based on data we obtained on the capital expenditures of a subset of 13 of these companies, we found that their total represented less than 1 percent of total expenditures (on- and off-budget).

### Jordan

Data used for Jordan are the "Summary of Functional Classifications for Estimated Public Expenditures According to Functional Divisions and Groups for the Fiscal Year 2018" in the Law No. (1) for the Year 2018, of the General Budget Law for the Fiscal Year 2018.

### Saudi Arabia

For Saudi Arabia and all other GCC countries, granular data are not publicly available. Instead, we synthesized the relevant orientations in Saudi Arabia's Ninth Development Plan 2010–2014 and analyzed budgetary allocations to new cities from publicly available documentation.

a. Morocco's recent Finance Law does not provide budget data for some categories (such as health services and most religious activities in the "General Budget" segment) and for some spatially distortive interventions (such as funding of roads within "Public Establishments and Enterprise"). These exclusions could result in overestimation of the allocations for other sections and underestimations of the allocations for "Basic Health, Education, and Related Human Capital Improvements" and "Physical Infrastructure for Connectivity."
b. The 20 sectors are agriculture, fishing, and water resources; industries; information and communication technology (ICT); transportation; roads and bridges; housing and urban development; environmental protection; education; higher education and scientific research; job readiness; employment; culture; health; women, family, and the elderly; finance; public employment, governance, and corruption; communal investment; rehabilitation and housing integration programs; regional development programs; and programs for inclusive development.
c. On-budget data for Egypt are available only at the aggregated level among nine functional categories: public services; public safety; economic affairs; environmental protection; housing and social infrastructure; health; youth, culture, and religion; education; and social protection. This limits our ability to complete the same analysis for Egypt as we have done for the focus countries of this analysis.

FIGURE 4.7 **Government expenditure distribution in selected Middle East and North Africa countries show priorities through a spatial lens for one year**

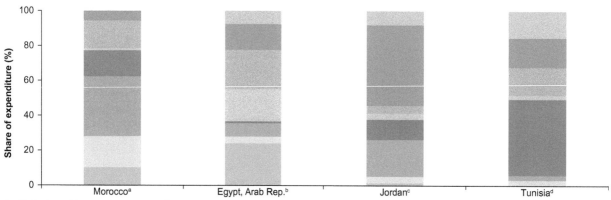

*Institution-based interventions*
  1. Broad-based governance and institutional reforms

*People-based interventions*
  2. Basic health, education, and related human capital improvements    3. Provision of basic public services
  4. Skill development, worker training, wage subsidies

*Place-based interventions*
  5. Physical infrastructure for connectivity and to support local production    6. Subsidies and other incentives to capital
  7. Growth poles, industrial districts, other location subsidies    8. Public sector industrialization and industrial location regulations

*Sources:* Government data (as described in notes below).
*Note:* For specific percentages by country, category, and year, see table 4A.3.
a. For Morocco, the information source is the 2017 Finance Law, specifically the "General Budget" and the "Public Establishments and Enterprises" segments.
b. For Egypt, the Financial Statement 2018–19 was used for on-budget data, and the total expenses of the 48 economic authorities were retrieved from their 2016–17 financial statements from the Ministry of Finance website.
c. For Jordan, the information source is "Capital and Current Expenses" classified by all line ministries, reported by the General Budget Department of the Ministry of Finance.
d. The Tunisia analysis draws from the most recent five-year plan, the Development Plan 2016–20.

FIGURE 4.8 **Government expenditure distribution in selected Middle East and North Africa countries, by spatial category, differs greatly from international comparators**

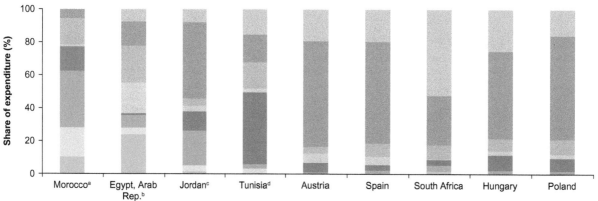

*Institution-based interventions*
  1. Broad-based governance and institutional reforms

*People-based interventions*
  2. Basic health, education, and related human capital improvements    3. Provision of basic public services
  4. Skill development, worker training, wage subsidies

*Place-based interventions*
  5. Physical infrastructure for connectivity and to support local production    6. Subsidies and other incentives to capital
  7. Growth poles, industrial districts, other location subsidies    8. Public sector industrialization and industrial location regulations

*Source:* Government Finance Statistics (GFS) database, International Monetary Fund; government data for Middle East and North Africa countries (as described in notes below).
a. For Morocco, the information source is the 2017 Finance Law, specifically the "General Budget" and the "Public Establishments and Enterprises" segments.
b. For Egypt, the Financial Statement 2018–19 was used for on-budget data, and the total expenses of the 48 economic authorities were retrieved from their 2016–17 financial statements from the Ministry of Finance website.
c. For Jordan, the information source is "Capital and Current Expenses (2018)," classified by all line ministries, reported by the General Budget Department of the Ministry of Finance.
d. The Tunisia analysis draws from the most recent five-year plan, the Development Plan 2016–20.

TABLE 4.1   **On average, comparator countries invest more in people- and institution-based interventions, and less in place-based interventions, than do Middle East and North Africa countries**
*Average percentage of government expenditure*

| Intervention category | Comparator countries[a] | Middle East and North Africa countries[b] |
| --- | --- | --- |
| Institution-based interventions | 27 | 8 |
| People-based interventions | 65 | 42 |
| Place-based interventions | 9 | 50 |

*Source:* Government Finance Statistics (GFS) database, International Monetary Fund; government data for Middle East and North Africa countries (as described below).
a. Comparator countries are Austria, Hungary, Poland, and South Africa.
b. Middle East and North Africa countries are the Arab Republic of Egypt, Jordan, Morocco, and Tunisia. For Egypt, the Financial Statement 2018–19 was used for on-budget data, and the total expenses of the 48 economic authorities were retrieved from their 2016–17 financial statements from the Ministry of Finance website. For Jordan, the information source is "Capital and Current Expenses (2018)," classified by all line ministries, reported by the General Budget Department of the Ministry of Finance. For Morocco, the information source is the 2017 Finance Law, specifically the "General Budget" and the "Public Establishments and Enterprises" segments. The Tunisia analysis draws from the most recent five-year plan, the Development Plan 2016–20.

- *Expenditures on institutions* represent less than 1 percent of public expenditures in Morocco and only 15 percent in Tunisia in the year studied, while comparator countries' share of expenditures range from 16 percent (in Poland) to 52 percent (in South Africa).
- *People-based policies* represent 22 percent of public expenditure allocation in Morocco and 35 percent in Tunisia. While Tunisia seems to allocate more resources toward skill development, basic public services, and basic health and education, this allocation reflects a sharp difference from benchmark countries. In the European Union comparators, this allocation is around 74 percent (Austria and Poland) and 75 percent (Spain).
- *Expenditures on basic health and education* showed the greatest gap with the benchmark countries within the people-based expenditure allocations.

## Country analyses

*Saudi Arabia*

Although detailed budget data are not publicly available for Saudi Arabia, an analysis of the nation's Ninth Development Plan 2010–2014 and its National Spatial Strategy reveals the weight the government places on balanced territorial development. The Ninth Development Plan 2010–2014 outlines the nation's development orientations across the range of sectoral and subnational dimensions. It explains that the nation has historically striven for balanced territorial development with a focus on infrastructure provision, taking regional potential into consideration (MEP 2010).

The regional development focus has aimed to reduce internal migration to large cities and to redirect economic activities to areas that appear to have insufficient demand for economic activities. The plan elaborates broad priorities for achieving better territorial balance and references leveraging investment grants oriented toward lagging regions as established through the Council of Ministers' Resolution No. 359 of 2008. The National Spatial Strategy is anchored around development corridors and growth centers.

A key pillar of Saudi territorial development policy is the development of new cities. Our analysis reveals the estimated expenditure to deliver eight new cities (table 4.2). These large outlays follow the establishment of predecessor new desert cities.

TABLE 4.2  **New cities in Saudi Arabia's development plan and spatial strategy**

| City | Start date | Anticipated completion date | Total estimated cost (US$, millions) | Surface area (km²) | Region | Location | Target population | Current population | Industries | Type of development |
|---|---|---|---|---|---|---|---|---|---|---|
| King Abdullah Economic City | 2005 | 2020 | 88,000 | 168 | Makkah | 90 km north of Jeddah | 2 million | 10,000 | Heavy industries, residential, recreational | Leapfrog |
| Jazan Economic City | 2009 | 2030 | 13,200 | 103 | Jizan | 100 km north of Jazan | 300,000 | 0 | Energy, residential; light industry; air and land transportation hub | Leapfrog |
| Al Faisaliah City | 2017 | 2050 | 246,400 | 2,450 | Makkah | From the Haram Boundary to the Red Sea Coast | 5.6 million residents and 10 million hajj visitors | 0 | Residential, industrial, diplomatic quarters, resorts, yacht club, hajj accommodations | Leapfrog |
| Neom | 2017 | 2025 | 500,000 | 26,500 | Tabuk | West of Tabuk with 468 km of Red Sea coastline | — | 0 | Biotech, food, advanced manufacturing, media, education, tourism, sports, energy, and water | Leapfrog |
| Red Sea Project | 2018 | 2022 | 6,160 | — | Madinah | 50 Red Sea islands; 100 km north of Yanbu | — | 0 | Luxury tourism | Leapfrog |
| Qiddiya Entertainment City | 2018 | 2022 (Phase 1) 2035 (Phase 2) | 6,160 | 334 | Riyadh | 40 km west of Riyadh | 1.5 million visitors (Phase 1); 17 million (Phase 2) | — | Recreation, entertainment, theme parks | Leapfrog |
| Prince Abdulaziz Bin Mousaed Economic City (PABMEC) | 2006 | 2025 | 6,160 | — | Ha'il | 8 km North of Ha'il | 140,000 | 0 | Agriculture, residential, industrial, transportation services, logistics, educational services, agricultural services, industrial and mining services, recreational services | Leapfrog |
| Al-Madinah's Knowledge Economic City | 2009 | 2024 | 6,600 | 4.8 | Madinah | 5 km east of Madinah | 150,000 | 0 | Religious tourism, shopping, medical facilities, residential | Contiguous |

*Sources:* World Bank estimates from the following data sources: Economic Cities Authority (2018) database on economic cities; Saudi Projects Network (2018) project database; King Abdullah Economic City official website (2018) Annual Report; Qiddiya official website (2018) press release on the establishment of Qiddiya Investment Company; Clyde and Co. (2016) Tax Incentives in the Kingdom of Saudi Arabia; Sports Venue Business (2018) interview with Almamoun Alshingiti, executive director of development, Qiddiya Investment Company; Gulf Business (2018), "Saudi Hires Ex-Canary Wharf Exec for Red Sea Tourism Project." May 28; Sabq Online (2017), "Change in the Leadership of PAMBEC Creates New Opportunities."

*Note:* km = kilometers. km² = square kilometers. — = unavailable.

TABLE 4.3  **Spatial classification of Tunisia's Finance Law 2017**

| Policy option | Share of total expenditure (%) |
|---|---|
| 1. Broad-based governance and institutional reforms | 5 |
| 2. Basic health, education, and related human capital improvements | 32 |
| 3. Provision of basic public services | 5 |
| 4. Skill development, worker training, wage subsidies | 5 |
| 5. Physical infrastructure for connectivity and to support local production | 25 |
| 6. Subsidies and other incentives to capital | 3 |
| 7. Growth poles, industrial districts, other location subsidies | 4 |
| 8. Public sector industrialization and industrial location regulations | 21 |

*Note:* Classification excludes expenses related to salaries and categories that lacked enough information to classify in one of the eight categories (other subsidies).

## Tunisia

### Robustness check

To check the extent to which the distribution of spending categories is consistent with the foregoing analysis, we analyzed the expenses of Finance Law 2017 within the eight categories (table 4.3).

Before the classification, two special cases were excluded: First, salaries were excluded. In Tunisia, 53 percent of total expenses are related to salaries. Of the international comparators, South Africa has the highest allocation of expenses on salaries, with about 35 percent, far below Tunisia. Poland, Spain, Hungary, and Austria have even lower shares, ranging from 26 percent to 21 percent.

Second, 32 percent of Tunisia's total budget could not be classified in the categories for lack of information or because of ambiguous categories. Among the remaining expenses, Tunisia's inclination toward spatially distortive interventions is confirmed, with 53 percent of total expenses allocated within the space-based categories (5 to 8) and only 5 percent toward broad-based governance and institutional reforms.

### Subsidies

Tunisia's Finance Law of 2017 allocated 26 percent of the total budget to subsidies, with 19 percent toward current expenses and 7 percent toward capital expenditures—the same as the average for 2013–17 (figure 4.9). Governments in general categorize their expenses as subsidies when they are direct

FIGURE 4.9  **Subsidies made up 23–31 percent of Tunisia's yearly budget, with the greater share linked to current expenditure, 2013–17**

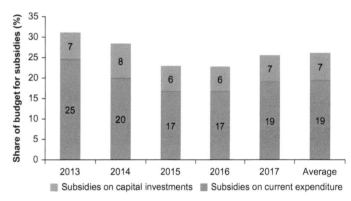

*Source:* Tunisia's Finance Law of 2017; data from World Bank's Open Budgets Portal (BOOST).

(such as cash transfers to producers to boost an economic sector or to promote employment for people with disabilities) or indirect (such as a tax relief in the form of payable tax credit for enterprises or a price reduction for health services) to influence the level of production, prices, or the profits of market and nonmarket enterprises.[19] Subsidies go to producers, not final consumers. In the case of Tunisia, as in most countries, indirect subsidies could not be readily quantified.

In 2017, 24 percent of the total budget in Tunisia was allocated to subsidies in four categories. First was public intervention expenditure by program, which contributed 95 percent of total subsidies on current expenditures. The other three contributed 87 percent of subsidies toward capital expenditures: interventions in the economy

FIGURE 4.10   **Subsidies on current expenditures, representing 19 percent of Tunisia's total budget, are mainly for place-based interventions**
*Percentage of total subsidies on current expenditures*

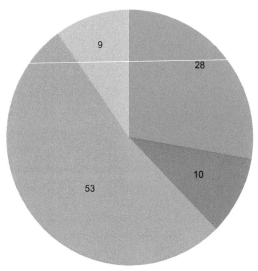

2. Basic health, education, and related human capital improvements

5. Physical infrastructure for connectivity and to support local production

6. Subsidies and other incentives to capital

7. Growth poles, industrial districts, other location subsidies

*Sources:* Tunisia's Finance Law of 2017; data from World Bank's Open Budgets Portal (BOOST).

FIGURE 4.11   **Subsidies on capital expenditures, representing 7 percent of Tunisia's total budget, are less focused than current expenditures on place-based interventions**
*Percentage of total subsidies on capital expenditures*

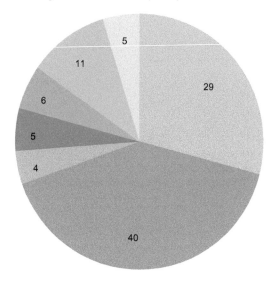

1. Broad-based governance and institutional reforms

2. Basic health, education, and related human capital improvements

3. Provision of basic public services

5. Physical infrastructure for connectivity and to support local production

6. Subsidies and other incentives to capital

7. Growth poles, industrial districts, other location subsidies

8. Public sector industrialization and industrial location regulations

*Sources:* Tunisia's Finance Law of 2017; data from World Bank's Open Budgets Portal (BOOST).

(47 percent), interventions in the social field (28 percent), and investment in services and infrastructure (11 percent).

Using the same spatial lens as before, we can identify how spatially distortive direct subsidies are in Tunisia.[20] In 2017, 95 percent of total subsidies on current expenditures were allocated to a category called "public intervention expenditure by program," of which 75 percent were focused on place-based interventions (categories 5, 6, and 7), while only 25 percent were focused on people-based interventions (figure 4.10).

Almost half of total subsidies on current expenses are for food support and market control (34 percent) and energy (14 percent), which are classified as subsidies and other incentives to capital (category 6), while 18 percent is split in half between truck transport (category 5) and local affairs (category 7).[21]

Analyzing the three capital expenditure categories, subsidies are less spatially distortive than current expenses. Twenty-six percent of total subsidies on capital expenses are on place-based interventions, while 44 percent are on people-based interventions, and 29 percent on institution-based interventions (figure 4.11). Forty percent of the subsidies are focused on housing and buildings for social support (basic health, education, and related human capital improvements), while the 29 percent on institutional interventions is split between grants to Tunisian Bank of Solidarity, a National Advertising Program, and a Program for Regional Development.

However, as noted above, subsidies on capital investments only represent 7 percent of the total budget, whereas subsidies on current investments represent 19 percent.

Moreover, indirect subsidies are targeted to the richest people in Tunisia, leaving those in need further behind. Table 4.4

TABLE 4.4 **Concentration shares of indirect subsidies in Tunisia, by income decile, 2010**

| Decile | Indirect subsidies (%) |
|--------|------------------------|
| 1 | 5.2 |
| 2 | 6.5 |
| 3 | 7.6 |
| 4 | 8.3 |
| 5 | 8.7 |
| 6 | 9.3 |
| 7 | 10.7 |
| 8 | 11.8 |
| 9 | 13.7 |
| 10 | 18.3 |

*Source:* Jouini et al. 2017, using data from 2010 Tunisia National Survey of Consumption and Household Living Standards (latest available).
*Note:* Calculations from Commitment to Equity (CEQ) Institute's "Tunisia Master Workbook 2015," where 1st decile is the poorest and 10th decile is the richest. "Indirect subsidies" are energy, food, and other general or targeted price subsidies.

shows the concentration share of indirect subsidies in each income decile of the population. Accounting for 2.3 percent of government spending in 2010, indirect subsidies were directed to the rich: the bottom 20 percent of the population received only 11.7 percent, and the richest 10 percent received 18.3 percent.

*Egypt*

As mentioned in box 4.3, government expenditures in Egypt include on-budget and off-budget expenditures. On-budget data, however, are available only at the aggregated level among nine functional categories.[22] This limits our ability to complete the same analysis for Egypt as for Jordan, Saudi Arabia, and Tunisia—the focus countries of this analysis.

Approximately 59 percent of the off-budget expenditure assigned to economic authorities goes to place-based interventions, with 42 percent on direct intervention in public sector industrialization and industrial location regulations (category 8). Table 4.5, panel a, shows the

TABLE 4.5 **Off-budget economic authorities in Egypt are highly spatially distortive**

| a. Including public sector social insurance fund (% of expenditure) | | | |
|---|---|---|---|
| Spatial category | Current | Capital | Total |
| 1. Broad-based governance and institutional reforms | 0 | 6 | 2 |
| 2. Basic health, education, and related human capital improvements | 1 | 1 | 1 |
| 3. Provision of basic public services | 3 | 8 | 5 |
| 4. Skill development, worker training, wage subsidies | 36 | 25 | 33 |
| 5. Physical infrastructure for connectivity and to support local production | 1 | 2 | 2 |
| 6. Subsidies and other incentives to capital | 9 | 7 | 8 |
| 7. Growth poles, industrial districts, other location subsidies | 5 | 12 | 7 |
| 8. Public sector industrialization and industrial location regulations | 44 | 39 | 42 |
| b. Without public sector social insurance fund (% of expenditure) | | | |
| Spatial category | Current | Capital | Total |
| 1. Broad-based governance and institutional reforms | 0 | 7 | 3 |
| 2. Basic health, education, and related human capital improvements | 2 | 1 | 2 |
| 3. Provision of basic public services | 4 | 10 | 6 |
| 4. Skill development, worker training, wage subsidies | 15 | 6 | 12 |
| 5. Physical infrastructure for connectivity and to support local production | 2 | 3 | 2 |
| 6. Subsidies and other incentives to capital | 12 | 8 | 11 |
| 7. Growth poles, industrial districts, other location subsidies | 7 | 15 | 9 |
| 8. Public sector industrialization and industrial location regulations | 58 | 49 | 55 |

*Source:* 2016–17 financial statements for each economic authority, Ministry of Finance of Egypt.

skewedness of off-budget expenditure in Egypt toward spatially distortive policies. Moreover, a large share of category 4 (skill development, worker training, wage subsidies) is due to government incentives to public sector employees, where the social insurance fund for employees in the governmental sector accounts for 24 percent of total off-budget expenditure. If we remove the social insurance expenditure, numbers skew even more toward spatially distortive interventions (table 4.5, panel b), accounting for 78 percent of total off-budget expenditure. As noted earlier, Egypt is one of the Middle East and North Africa countries with the highest share of public employment, hindering private sector activity.

In both on-budget and off-budget data from economic authorities, 37 percent of the national budget is allocated toward place-based policies (table 4.6). However, as mentioned before, public business sector expenditures are not included in the off-budget data.

*Jordan*

The current expenditures and capital expenditures of all Jordanian line ministries for 2018 were classified within the eight spatial categories (table 4.7). As in the Tunisian example, three categories were excluded from the analysis:

- *Public sector wages, salaries, and social security contributions*, which stood at 58 percent
- *Use of goods and services by line ministries*, including security, cleaning, and other contracts, which accounted for 23 percent (also including subsidies and grants to a wide range of uncategorizable

TABLE 4.6 **On-budget and off-budget expenditure by economic authorities in Egypt, by spatial category**
*Percentage of annual expenditure*

| Spatial category | On-budget | Off-budget | Total |
|---|---|---|---|
| 1. Broad-based governance and institutional reforms | 43 | 2 | 8 |
| 2. Basic health, education, and related human capital improvements | 21 | 1 | 13 |
| 3. Provision of basic public services | 31 | 5 | 23 |
| 4. Skill development, worker training, wage subsidies | 0 | 33 | 19 |
| 5. Physical infrastructure for connectivity and to support local production | 0 | 2 | 1 |
| 6. Subsidies and other incentives to capital | 5 | 8 | 8 |
| 7. Growth poles, industrial districts, other location subsidies | 0 | 7 | 4 |
| 8. Public sector industrialization and industrial location regulations | 0 | 42 | 24 |

*Source:* Ministry of Finance of Egypt.
*Note:* For Egypt, the Financial Statement 2018–19 was used for on-budget data, and the total expenses of the 48 economic authorities were retrieved from their 2016–17 financial statements from the Ministry of Finance website. Percentages within each type of budget (on-budget and off-budget) consider only its own category. The "Total" column considers both. The off-budget data shares include the public sector social insurance fund.

TABLE 4.7 **Jordanian public expenditures, by spatial category, 2018**

| Policy option | Share of total expenditure (%) |
|---|---|
| 1. Broad-based governance and institutional reforms | 8 |
| 2. Basic health, education, and related human capital improvements | 46 |
| 3. Provision of basic public services | 4 |
| 4. Skill development, worker training, wage subsidies | 4 |
| 5. Physical infrastructure for connectivity and to support local production | 12 |
| 6. Subsidies and other incentives to capital | 21 |
| 7. Growth poles, industrial districts, other location subsidies | 4 |
| 8. Public sector industrialization and industrial location regulations | 1 |

*Source:* "Capital and Current Expenses (2018)," classified by line ministry, General Budget Department of the Ministry of Finance, Hashemite Kingdom of Jordan.

administrative committees such as Jordan Motor Sports Committee, political party subsidies, and the Joint Jerusalem Fund subsidies)

• *Military spending and nuclear energy projects*, which accounted for 0.2 percent of total expenditures.

Excluding those categories, public expenditures fall from about JD 9 billion to about JD 1.7 billion, of which 38 percent fall into spatially distortive interventions, 54 percent into people-based interventions, and approximately 8 percent into institution-based interventions.

Distinguishing capital expenditures and current expenditures provides a clearer picture of the state's spatial intervention. Of capital expenditures, 56 percent go toward spatially distorting policies. Of the capital expenditures going toward people-based

**FIGURE 4.12  Jordanian current public expenditures, by spatial category, 2018**

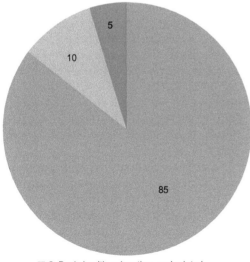

- 2. Basic health, education, and related human capital improvements
- 4. Skill development, worker training, wage subsidies
- 6. Subsidies and other incentives to capital

*Source:* "Summary of Functional Classifications for Estimated Public Expenditures According to Functional Divisions and Groups for the Fiscal Year 2018," Law No. (1) for the Year 2018, General Budget Law for the Fiscal Year 2018, Hashemite Kingdom of Jordan.
*Note:* Chart excludes spatial categories 1, 3, 5, 7, and 8 because their value is less than 1 percent.

policies, the majority goes for building schools, hospitals, and other social amenities in regional governorates.

The vast majority of current expenditures in Jordan (85 percent) goes toward basic health, education, and related human capital improvements, standing at about JD 500 million (figure 4.12). Within that category, 93 percent is funneled toward six organizations: Social Aids for the Royal Hashemite Court, Cash Subsidies under the Ministry of Finance, Jordanian Government Universities subsidies under the Ministry of Education and Scientific Research, the Kidney Failure Fund and Civil Health Insurance Fund under the Ministry of Health, and the National Aid Fund under the Ministry of Social Development.

## Implications and persistence of governments' approach to shaping markets in the Middle East and North Africa

Limitations on competition and an emphasis on spatially distortive territorial development policies in the Middle East and North Africa have created a high fiscal burden with limited results. At the city level, the new-city orientation of several of the region's governments has resulted in the development of many expensive and unproductive new cities and zones at the expense of enabling existing centers of growth to thrive.

A mainstay of Egypt's overarching development vision for several centuries—and now part of the "Egypt Vision 2030" strategy—has been a model whereby Egypt leverages its desert land to create new cities for growth (Sims 2015). An analysis of the government's fiscal year 2015–16 budget by a nongovernmental organization, 10 Tooba Collective, found that about 30 percent of the nation's built environment budget was allocated to new cities and zones (which host about 2 percent of the nation's population), and about 29 percent of the budget was allocated to existing cities and towns (which host roughly 98 percent of the nation's population) (Sims 2015). Although it is not possible to access GDP data for new cities and zones in Egypt, an analysis of 23 new cities established between 1979 and 2000 found that despite a projected population of over 20 million Egyptians, the 2006 population was 783,103, representing less than 4 percent of projected population. Several new cities were completely unoccupied several decades after their development (Sims 2015).

Although the vast majority of the desert zones and cities have been underoccupied or unoccupied, the government of Egypt has announced a scaling-up of its new zone and city development over the past half decade. The Industrial Development Authority, which is responsible for most zones in Egypt, announced in 2017 that it would assign 60 million square meters of industrial zone space between 2017 and 2020 (Sims 2015). It had assigned 11 million square meters during 2006–15 and another 11 million square meters in 2016. In April 2017, the Minister of Trade and Industry announced the establishment of new zones in all seven governorates of Upper Egypt, one of the country's most lagging regions. Meanwhile, the occupancy rates of existing zones is low: the average in Qena Governorate was 14 percent in 2016, and the average in Sohag Governorate was 34 percent (World Bank 2016). In addition, over the past four years, the Ministry of Housing announced 12 new cities (Sims 2015).

At the within-country level, most Middle East and North Africa countries offer considerable investment incentives to firms that locate in high-priority regions identified by governments. Those incentives cost governments and deliver limited numbers of jobs in lagging regions. In Tunisia, the priority of a territory is negatively associated with its development level and is viewed as territorial affirmative action—a subsidy for firms to create jobs in regions that otherwise have an undersupply. In some cases, those incentives could be perceived as both a means of showing attention to regions in relative need and also perhaps as a way of shifting competition away from economic hubs that are home to firms that governments want to protect from competition. In Tunisia, firms benefiting from those incentives have located in a band parallel to the western coastline in the zones bordering leading areas and distant from the areas of weak economic activity. Worse yet, many of the success cases—foreign and domestic firms, notably Benetton, that relocated to Tunisia's lagging regions to benefit from those incentives—closed their operations as soon as their subsidies expired (World Bank 2018c).

As with new cities and zones, several of the region's governments are expanding their use of incentives and transfers for investments in lagging regions, with few changes to their approach despite evidence of limited results. In Tunisia after the Jasmine Revolution, the government revised the Investment Incentive Code, which governs regional subsidies, to further distinguish between degree of need, and it increased its allocation of subsidies. Also, in response to the worsening conditions in lagging regions after the Jasmine Revolution, the government increased the volume of financing it assigned to the Regional Development Program—a transfer program established several decades ago to support regional development.

At the cross-country level, many governments' concerns about undermining their local firms—and thus the insiders supporting their administrations—have led them to maintain barriers to trade and hence also the barriers to increasing revenues from greater international market access. The low level of international trade observed in the Middle East and North Africa relative to comparator regions affects overall economic development and spatial development in two ways: First, it reduces the demand for production and for the further development of the system of cities in the region's countries. Second, some border areas that would otherwise be thriving are relatively depressed or preoccupied with informal activity because of the hard formal borders they face.

Despite the limited impact of their primary territorial development interventions, several of the region's governments continue to take the same approach to territorial development for several reasons. First, despite limited economic returns to their spatial bets, some groups receive them. Investors that receive no-cost or low-cost access to land that will appreciate in value benefit from new city and zone policies. Likewise, investors that benefit from generous locational subsidies have an interest in sustained and even augmented subsidies linked to their location choices. Regarding international trade, there will be strong support for regional integration when local elites, especially the business community, see opportunities from enhanced trade and interaction. There will be little support, or outright obstructionism, if they benefit from the status quo (Malik and Awadallah 2013). Even though fragmentation of regional markets means that companies forgo benefits from scale and agglomeration, in many countries, they gain from high levels of monopoly power in their domestic markets. As long as market entry is restricted and political patronage serves incumbents, there will not be a sizable constituency for greater openness. A high degree of state ownership; resource rents that reduce reform pressures; and rents from licensing, quotas, contracts, or preferential access to land further reduce efficiency and international competitiveness (Diwan, Keefer, and Schiffbauer 2015; Gatti et al. 2013). It will thus be difficult to initiate greater regional integration and related reforms without finding ways to

overcome the resistance from influential rent-seeking beneficiaries of the status quo. Since these cases represent situations of concentrated winners and diffuse losers, the pressure on governments to sustain these interventions is high.

Second, it can be easier to start fresh than to fix an existing challenge. In the case of desert development policies in Egypt, Saudi Arabia, the United Arab Emirates, and others, decision makers advocate for developing new cities and zones as a way of navigating around rather than working through constraints to growth. They pitch new city and zone development as ways to develop new centers of growth that are unfettered by poor planning and informal development.

Third, concrete information is scarce on the relative successes and failures of territorial development policies in the region. In general, it is difficult to accurately quantify the impact of different territorial development policies. In the Middle East and North Africa context, this methodological challenge is exacerbated by the paucity of data and accurate information about the costs, benefits, and trade-offs of various development interventions.

Fourth, there is always hope. Some territorial development experiments in the region have succeeded—such as Dubai, Tangier, and Marrakesh—which have inspired decision makers elsewhere to attempt to replicate their successes. What separates the success stories from the larger number of relative failures are natural geography advantages (as in Dubai and Tangier); a focus on reinforcing market demand and organically and contiguously expanding development; up-front efforts to make the business environment extremely welcoming; and coordinated efforts and high-level vision and support to deliver these projects. Few of the territorial efforts have met these requirements.

## Annex 4A Disaggregation of government expenditure, by government level, for each of the comparator countries

TABLE 4A.1    **Disaggregation of government expenditure for comparator countries, by spatial category**

| a. Spain | |
|---|---|
| Spatial category | Share of public expenditure (%) |
| 1. Broad-based governance and institutional reforms | 45 |
| 2. Basic health, education, and related human capital improvements | 42 |
| 3. Provision of basic public services | 5 |
| 4. Skill development, worker training, wage subsidies | 5 |
| 5. Physical infrastructure for connectivity and to support local production | 1 |
| 6. Subsidies and other incentives to capital | 1 |
| 7. Growth poles, industrial districts, other location subsidies | 0 |
| 8. Public sector industrialization and industrial location regulations | 0.2 |

| b. South Africa | |
|---|---|
| Spatial category | Share of public expenditure (%) |
| 1. Broad-based governance and institutional reforms | 59 |
| 2. Basic health, education, and related human capital improvements | 22 |
| 3. Provision of basic public services | 11 |
| 4. Skill development, worker training, wage subsidies | 1 |
| 5. Physical infrastructure for connectivity and to support local production | 4 |
| 6. Subsidies and other incentives to capital | 3 |
| 7. Growth poles, industrial districts, other location subsidies | 0 |
| 8. Public sector industrialization and industrial location regulations | 2 |

| c. Hungary and Poland | | |
|---|---|---|
| Spatial category | Hungary (share of public expenditure, %) | Poland (share of public expenditure, %) |
| 1. Broad-based governance and institutional reforms | 24 | 15 |
| 2. Basic health, education, and related human capital improvements | 58 | 69 |
| 3. Provision of basic public services | 5 | 8 |
| 4. Skill development, worker training, wage subsidies | 3 | 2 |
| 5. Physical infrastructure for connectivity and to support local production | 8 | 4 |
| 6. Subsidies and other incentives to capital | 2 | 1 |
| 7. Growth poles, industrial districts, other location subsidies | 0 | 0 |
| 8. Public sector industrialization and industrial location regulations | 0.4 | 0.2 |

Source: Government Finance Statistics (GFS) database 2015, International Monetary Fund.

In addition, data to show changes over a 10-year period among benchmark countries were obtained from the International Monetary Fund's (IMF) Classification of Functions of Government (COFOG) in the Government Finance Statistics (GFS) system (table 4A.2). These changes are shown graphically in figure 4.6.

Several Middle East and North Africa countries were further analyzed concerning their government expenditures in the same eight spatial areas relative to those in the comparator countries (table 4A.3). The expenditure distribution analysis revealed striking differences with the comparator countries—toward more spatially

TABLE 4A.2 **Distribution and changes in government expenditures by comparator countries through a spatial lens**
*Percentage of government expenditure*

| | Austria | | Spain | | South Africa | | Hungary | | Poland | |
|---|---|---|---|---|---|---|---|---|---|---|
| Category | 1995 | 2016 | 1995 | 2016 | 2012 | 2016 | 1995 | 2015 | 2002 | 2015 |
| 1. Broad-based governance and institutional reforms | 21 | 19 | 22 | 20 | 44 | 52 | 29 | 25 | 16 | 16 |
| 2. Basic health, education, and related human capital improvements | 61 | 64 | 51 | 62 | 34 | 30 | 51 | 53 | 66 | 63 |
| 3. Provision of basic public services | 6 | 4 | 9 | 8 | 9 | 8 | 6 | 7 | 9 | 9 |
| 4. Skill development, worker training, wage subsidies | 4 | 6 | 6 | 5 | 1 | 1 | 5 | 2 | 3 | 2 |
| 5. Physical infrastructure for connectivity and to support local production | 5 | 6 | 8 | 3 | 3 | 3 | 5 | 9 | 5 | 8 |
| 6. Subsidies and other incentives to capital | 3 | 1 | 2 | 2 | 8 | 4 | 4 | 2 | 1 | 2 |
| 7. Growth poles, industrial districts, other location subsidies[a] | — | — | — | — | — | — | — | — | — | — |
| 8. Public sector industrialization and industrial location regulations | 0.2 | 0.4 | 1.9 | 0.5 | 1.2 | 1.8 | 0.1 | 0.5 | 0.2 | 0.3 |

*Source:* Government Finance Statistics (GFS) database, International Monetary Fund.
*Note:* — = not available. The period considered for each country uses the oldest and most recent years available in the IMF database. Expenditures on foreign aid are excluded from the analysis.
a. None of the functions listed in the Classification of Functions of Government (COFOG) of the GFS system were classified in "7. Growth poles, industrial districts, other location subsidies." This could be driven by the IMF database exclusion of public corporations, which underestimates potential market activities undertaken by comparator countries, such as growth poles and industrial districts.

TABLE 4A.3 **Expenditure distribution in the Middle East and North Africa is highly weighted toward spatially distortive policies**
*Percentage of government expenditure*

| Policy option | Morocco[a] | Egypt, Arab Rep.[b] | Jordan[c] | Tunisia[d] |
|---|---|---|---|---|
| 1. Broad-based governance and institutional reforms | 0.2 | 8 | 8 | 15 |
| 2. Basic health, education, and related human capital improvements | 5 | 15 | 46 | 17 |
| 3. Provision of basic public services | 16 | 23 | 4 | 16 |
| 4. Skill development, worker training, wage subsidies | 1 | 19 | 4 | 2 |
| 5. Physical infrastructure for connectivity and to support local production | 15 | 1 | 12 | 44 |
| 6. Subsidies and other incentives to capital | 34 | 8 | 21 | 3 |
| 7. Growth poles, industrial districts, other location subsidies | 18 | 4 | 4 | 3 |
| 8. Public sector industrialization and industrial location regulations | 10 | 24 | 1 | 0.1 |

*Sources:* Government data (as described in notes below).
a. For Morocco, the information source is the 2017 Finance Law, specifically the "General Budget" and the "Public Establishments and Enterprises" segments.
b. For Egypt, the Financial Statement 2018–19 was used for on-budget data, and the total expenses of the 48 economic authorities were retrieved from their 2016–17 financial statements from the Ministry of Finance website.
c. For Jordan, the information source is "Capital and Current Expenses (2018)," classified by all line ministries, reported by the General Budget Department of the Ministry of Finance.
d. The Tunisia analysis draws from the most recent five-year plan, the Development Plan 2016–20.

distortive policies. This distribution is shown graphically in figure 4.7.

## Annex 4B Disclaimers regarding the classification of government expenditures

Table 4B.1 lists several disclaimers concerning the classifications of each of the government functions published either by the International Monetary Fund or by each of the countries into the eight spatial categories.

Further, differences in government dissemination of expenditure data has meant that we do not have one standardized means for accessing expenditure information.

TABLE 4B.1   **Difficulties in classification of spatial categories of government expenditures**

| Spatial category | Difficulty |
|---|---|
| 1. Broad-based governance and institutional reforms | Regulatory reforms are not always explicitly spatially blind. |
| 2. Basic health, education, and related human capital improvements | Housing is classified in this category because this expenditure is usually oriented toward addressing people's basic needs. However, expenditures linked to "new communities," as in Egypt, are considered spatially distortive, hence placed within category 8. |
| 3. Provision of basic public services | Some basic services can be provided to foster economic activity in a region, which is not clear from the description. |
| 4. Skill development, worker training, wage subsidies | Splitting worker training from standard education is not always straightforward. |
| 5. Physical infrastructure for connectivity and to support local production | No difficulties noted. |
| 6. Subsidies and other incentives to capital | Spatial policies are difficult to identify specifically if they are undertaken by other entities within the central government. They can be hidden from explicit government functions. Moreover, subsidies can be implicit within projects, making it difficult to disaggregate budget by specific activity. |
| 7. Growth poles, industrial districts, other location subsidies | |
| 8. Public sector industrialization and industrial location regulations | |

## Annex 4C Classification of the IMF database

TABLE 4C.1   **Classification of subcategories of the IMF Government Finance Statistics (GFS) database into eight spatial categories**

| Government functions in IMF database | Spatial category, by number |
|---|---|
| A.  *Expenditure on general public services* | |
| Expenditure on executive, legislative, fiscal, and external affairs | 1. Broad-based governance and institutional reforms |
| Expenditure on foreign economic aid | Excluded from the analysis. |
| Expenditure on general public services | 1. Broad-based governance and institutional reforms |
| Expenditure on basic research | 1. Broad-based governance and institutional reforms |
| Expenditure on general public services research and development | 1. Broad-based governance and institutional reforms |
| Expenditure on general public services not elsewhere classified | 1. Broad-based governance and institutional reforms |
| Expenditure on public debt transactions | 1. Broad-based governance and institutional reforms |
| Transfers between different levels of government | 1. Broad-based governance and institutional reforms |
| B.  *Expenditure on defense* | |
| Expenditure on military defense | 3. Provision of basic public services |
| Expenditure on civil defense | 3. Provision of basic public services |
| Expenditure on foreign military aid | Excluded from the analysis. |
| Expenditure on defense research and development | 1. Broad-based governance and institutional reforms |
| Expenditure on defense not elsewhere classified | 3. Provision of basic public services |
| C.  *Expenditure on public order and safety* | |
| Expenditure on police services | 3. Provision of basic public services |
| Expenditure on fire protection services | 3. Provision of basic public services |
| Expenditure on law courts | 1. Broad-based governance and institutional reforms |
| Expenditure on prisons | 1. Broad-based governance and institutional reforms |
| Expenditure on public order and safety research and development | 1. Broad-based governance and institutional reforms |
| Expenditure on public order and safety not elsewhere classified | 3. Provision of basic public services |
| D.  *Expenditure on economic affairs* | |
| Expenditure on economic, commercial, and labor affairs | 1. Broad-based governance and institutional reforms |
| Expenditure on agriculture, fishing, forestry, and hunting | 6. Subsidies and other incentives to capital |
| Expenditure on fuel and energy | 6. Subsidies and other incentives to capital |
| Expenditure on mining, manufacturing, and construction | 6. Subsidies and other incentives to capital |
| Expenditure on transport | 5. Physical infrastructure for connectivity and to support local production |
| Expenditure on communication | 3. Provision of basic public services |

*table continues next page*

**TABLE 4C.1**  **Classification of subcategories of the IMF Government Finance Statistics (GFS) database into eight spatial categories** *(continued)*

| Government functions in IMF database | Spatial category, by number |
|---|---|
| Expenditure on other industries | 8. Public sector industrialization and industrial location regulations |
| Expenditure on economic affairs research and development | 1. Broad-based governance and institutional reforms |
| Expenditure on economic affairs not elsewhere classified | 6. Subsidies and other incentives to capital |
| *E. Expenditure on environmental protection* | |
| Expenditure on waste management | 3. Provision of basic public services |
| Expenditure on wastewater management | 3. Provision of basic public services |
| Expenditure on pollution abatement | 3. Provision of basic public services |
| Expenditure on biodiversity and landscape protection | 3. Provision of basic public services |
| Expenditure on environmental protection research and development | 1. Broad-based governance and institutional reforms |
| Expenditure on environmental protection not elsewhere classified | 3. Provision of basic public services |
| *F. Expenditure on housing and community amenities* | |
| Expenditure on housing development | 2. Basic health, education, and related human capital improvements |
| Expenditure on community development | 8. Public sector industrialization and industrial location regulations |
| Expenditure on water supply | 3. Provision of basic public services |
| Expenditure on street lighting | 3. Provision of basic public services |
| Expenditure on housing and community amenities research and development | 1. Broad-based governance and institutional reforms |
| Expenditure on housing and community amenities not elsewhere classified | 2. Basic health, education, and related human capital improvements |
| *G. Expenditure on health* | |
| Expenditure on medical products, appliances, and equipment | 2. Basic health, education, and related human capital improvements |
| Expenditure on outpatient services | 2. Basic health, education, and related human capital improvements |
| Expenditure on hospital services | 2. Basic health, education, and related human capital improvements |
| Expenditure on public health services | 2. Basic health, education, and related human capital improvements |
| Expenditure on health research and development | 1. Broad-based governance and institutional reforms |
| Expenditure on health not elsewhere classified | 2. Basic health, education, and related human capital improvements |
| *H. Expenditure on recreation, culture, and religion* | |
| Expenditure on recreational and sporting services | 2. Basic health, education, and related human capital improvements |
| Expenditure on cultural services | 2. Basic health, education, and related human capital improvements |
| Expenditure on broadcasting and publishing | 2. Basic health, education, and related human capital improvements |
| Expenditure on religious and community services | 2. Basic health, education, and related human capital improvements |
| Expenditure on recreation, culture, and religion research and development | 1. Broad-based governance and institutional reforms |
| Expenditure on recreation, culture, and religion not elsewhere classified | 1. Broad-based governance and institutional reforms |
| *I. Expenditure on education* | |
| Expenditure on preprimary and primary education | 2. Basic health, education, and related human capital improvements |
| Expenditure on secondary education | 2. Basic health, education, and related human capital improvements |
| Expenditure on postsecondary nontertiary education | 2. Basic health, education, and related human capital improvements |
| Expenditure on tertiary education | 2. Basic health, education, and related human capital improvements |
| Expenditure on education not definable by level | 4. Skill development, worker training, wage subsidies |
| Expenditure on subsidiary services to education | 2. Basic health, education, and related human capital improvements |
| Expenditure on education research and development | 1. Broad-based governance and institutional reforms |
| Expenditure on education not elsewhere classified | 2. Basic health, education, and related human capital improvements |
| *J. Expenditure on social protection* | |
| Expenditure on sickness and disability | 2. Basic health, education, and related human capital improvements |
| Expenditure on old age | 2. Basic health, education, and related human capital improvements |
| Expenditure on survivors | 2. Basic health, education, and related human capital improvements |
| Expenditure on family and children | 2. Basic health, education, and related human capital improvements |
| Expenditure on unemployment | 4. Skill development, worker training, wage subsidies |
| Expenditure on housing | 2. Basic health, education, and related human capital improvements |
| Expenditure on social exclusion not elsewhere classified | 4. Skill development, worker training, wage subsidies |
| Expenditure on social protection research and development | 1. Broad-based governance and institutional reforms |
| Expenditure on social protection not elsewhere classified | 1. Broad-based governance and institutional reforms |

TABLE 4D.1 **Estimated shares of public expenditures, by category, in Lebanon, the Republic of Yemen, and Iraq**
*Percentage of public expenditure*

| Policy option | Lebanon | Yemen, Rep. | Iraq |
|---|---|---|---|
| 1. Broad-based governance and institutional reforms | 2 | 43 | 14 |
| 2. Basic health, education, and related human capital improvements | 12 | 11 | 29 |
| 3. Provision of basic public services | 38 | 21 | 20 |
| 4. Skill development, worker training, wage subsidies | 1 | 17 | 2 |
| 5. Physical infrastructure for connectivity and to support local production | 34 | 0.4 | 0 |
| 6. Subsidies and other incentives to capital | 14 | 8 | 22 |
| 7. Growth poles, industrial districts, other location subsidies | 1 | 0 | 1 |
| 8. Public sector industrialization and industrial location regulations | 0.2 | 0.03 | 11 |

*Sources:* Harake and Kostopoulos 2018; National Budget 2013, Republic of Yemen; Citizens Budget 2018, Iraqi Ministry of Finance.

## Annex 4D Reasons for excluding other Middle East and North Africa countries from the spatial analysis of government expenditures

Middle East and North Africa countries considered in the analysis of this chapter were included because of the availability of sectoral data on government expenditures. For countries such as Lebanon, Iraq, and the Republic of Yemen, publicly accessible data were not available at a level of disaggregation sufficient to provide a robust analysis and compare with the rest of the region and comparator countries. We include information on these three countries below.

To the authors' knowledge, Lebanon does not have a national budget. The team reviewed a list of projects that Lebanon intends to invest in, as reviewed in the World Bank's assessment of the country's Capital Investment Plan (Harake and Kostopoulos 2018). Given the limitations of this data, we did not include our analysis of it in the chapter; however, we reflect the distribution of projects based on our spatial classification criteria (table 4D.1). Another source that could have been used is the lagging regions report produced by the Lebanese Center for Policy Studies, which has data on the actual expenditure, by district, of the Council for Development and Reconstruction as of September 2017 (Atallah et al. 2018). However, this expenditure represents a partial picture of the total expenditure executed in Lebanon, and using it would mislead the reader.

Data on Iraq and the Republic of Yemen are highly aggregated, so the classification shown in the table 4D.1 should be considered with caution. For the Republic of Yemen, we used data classified by function in the National Budget 2013, which only has a three-digit classification used by the IMF. For Iraq, we used data published in the Citizen Budget 2018, albeit with few functional categories.

No detailed data on expenditures are available for Algeria, Djibouti, Libya, West Bank and Gaza, and the GCC countries.

## Notes

1. The Gulf Cooperation Council (GCC) countries are Bahrain, Kuwait, Oman, Qatar, Saudi Arabia, and the United Arab Emirates.
2. This score includes the GCC countries, which average a GCI score of 4.75. Excluding the GCC subregion results in an average score of 3.93.
3. The 2017–18 index considers 137 countries, with 66 countries scoring higher than 4.28 and 93 countries higher than 3.93 (Schwab 2017).
4. The Oslo Accords, a set of agreements signed by the government of Israel and the leadership of the Palestine Liberation Organization (PLO), were ratified in 1993 (Oslo I) and 1995 (Oslo 2). Under the Accords, the PLO agreed to formally recognize the state of Israel, and Israel in turn allowed for limited self-governance in West Bank and Gaza.
5. "Registered factories" refers to those registered with Egypt's Industrial Development Authority (IDA).
6. Exceptions are Israel and the Islamic Republic of Iran.

7. See, for instance, the "China shock" debate in the United States (Autor, Dorn, and Hanson 2016).

8. For the analysis underlying the following estimates, see Ianchovichina and Ivanic (2014).

9. The only country from the Middle East and North Africa in the IMF database is the United Arab Emirates, but its data are not disaggregated by specific function, making the spatial classification unmeaningful. Moreover, the only Latin America country in the IMF database with disaggregated data is El Salvador, which is not comparable with most Middle East and North Africa countries.

10. Government units include all nonmarket nonprofit institutions that are controlled and mainly financed by the government, including budgetary and extrabudgetary data.

11. General government expenditure includes those performed by the central, state, and local governments, including any social security fund in the administrative organization of the country. Annex 4C includes the spatial classification of expenditure by each level of government, including social security funds at the central level. There were no disaggregated data for Austria.

12. Extrabudgetary entities are those with individual budgets not fully covered by the main (or general) budget (such as road transportation or nonmarket production of health and education services).

13. It is important to highlight that this classification is subjective and that each of the 69 subcategories may contain more than one of the 8 spatial categories; however, this exercise offers a general sense of the degree of spatial distortion introduced by government expenditures. Additional disclaimers, by spatial category, as well as specific percentages by country and category are shown in annex 4B.

14. The classification of each of the 69 subcategories is listed in annex 4C.

15. The period considered for each country uses the oldest and most recent years available in the IMF database.

16. An important difference between the IMF database and the analysis of the countries in the Middle East and North Africa is that the IMF database excludes public corporations, which are highly relevant to understand the government's expenditure in the Middle East and North Africa region. This means that allocation of expenses in comparator countries may be underestimating shares in place-based interventions, while the expenses in the Middle East and North Africa will be considering them. It is also crucial to highlight that public corporations in the region are focused not only on place-based policies but also on people-based policies, diminishing the potential bias toward place-based policies.

17. With the exception of the United Arab Emirates, which is included in GFS but for which there are significant data gaps that render developing an allocation profile unfeasible currently. Although the definition of the expenditure profile of GFS countries using our territorial development spectrum is imperfect, doing so for Middle East and North Africa countries based on national instruments for planning and budgeting is also imperfect. We will make accessible the files within which we assigned line items to territorial intervention categories, and we will engage in consultations in Middle East and North Africa countries to ground-truth the categorizations.

18. The analysis of MENA countries is based on one year of analysis and for the most recent year for which complete data were available. Patterns observed may be the result of specificities in spending in the given year (or five years in the case of Tunisia).

19. Countries may differ on how to classify specific types of subsidies or expenses.

20. To classify functions of subsidies by spatial dimension, only the four categories mentioned above are considered. Moreover, within these four categories, only subsidies that accounted for more than 5 percent of the total subsidies by category are included.

21. Although subsidies for primary products and transport were established in the 1990s, the energy subsidy was introduced for the first time in 2003 to promote the competitiveness of the private sector and support the purchasing power of the middle class because of increases in energy prices in the international market.

22. The nine functional categories on on-budget data for Egypt are public services; public safety; economic affairs; environmental protection; housing and social infrastructure; health; youth, culture, and religion; education; and social protection.

# References

Atallah, Sami, Daniel Garrote Sánchez, Nizar Hassan, Dima Mahdi, and Jana Mourad. 2018. "Introductory Chapter: Analytical Framework for Improving Urban Resilience in Lebanon's Districts Impacted by the Syrian Refugee Crisis." Unpublished report, Lebanese Center for Policy Studies, Beirut.

Autor, D. H., D. Dorn, and G. H. Hanson. 2016. "The China Shock: Learning from Labor-Market Adjustment to Large Changes in Trade." *Annual Review of Economics* 8 (1): 205–40.

Benhassine, Najy, Youssef Saadani Hassani, Philip E. Keefer, Andrew H. W. Stone, and Sameh Naguib Wahba. 2009. *From Privilege to Competition: Unlocking Private-led Growth in the Middle East and North Africa*. MENA Development Report. Washington, DC: World Bank.

Chahoud, T. 2011. "Syria's Industrial Policy." Working paper, German Development Institute (DIE), Bonn.

Collier, Paul. 2003. *Breaking the Conflict Trap: Civil War and Development Policy*. Washington, DC: World Bank; New York: and Oxford University Press.

Deininger, Klaus. 2003. *Land Policies for Growth and Poverty Reduction*. World Bank Policy Research Report. Washington, DC: World Bank; Oxford: Oxford University Press.

Diwan, I., P. Keefer, and M. Schiffbauer. 2015. "Pyramid Capitalism: Political Connections, Regulation, and Firm Productivity in Egypt." Policy Research Working Paper 7354, World Bank, Washington, DC.

Gatti, R., M. Morgandi, S. Brodmann, D. Angel-Urdinola, J. M. Moreno, D. Marotta, M. Schiffbauer, and E. Mata Lorenzo. 2013. *Jobs for Shared Prosperity: Time for Action in the Middle East and North Africa*. Washington, DC: World Bank.

Harake, Wissam, and Christos Kostopoulos. 2018. "Strategic Assessment: A Capital Investment Plan for Lebanon—Investment Opportunities and Reforms." Working Paper, Report No. 124819, World Bank, Washington, DC.

Ianchovichina, Elena, and Maros Ivanic. 2014. "Economic Effects of the Syrian War and the Spread of the Islamic State on the Levant." Policy Research Working Paper 7135, World Bank, Washington, DC.

IMF (International Monetary Fund). 2014. *Government Finance Statistics Manual 2014*. Washington, DC: IMF.

Jouini, N., N. Lustig, A. Moummi, and A. Shimeles. 2017. "Fiscal Incidence and Poverty Reduction: Evidence from Tunisia." Economics Working Paper 1710, Tulane University, New Orleans, LA.

Lall, Somik V. 2009. "Territorial Development Policy: A Practitioner's Guide." Report No. 70398, World Bank, Washington, DC.

Lall, Somik, Ayah Mahgoub, Augustin Maria, Anastasia Touati, and Jose Luis Acero. 2019. "Leveraging Urbanization to Promote a New Growth Model While Reducing Territorial Disparities in Morocco." Urban and Regional Development Policy Note, Report No. 137850, World Bank, Washington, DC.

Malik, A., and B. Awadallah. 2013. "The Economics of the Arab Spring." *World Development* 45: 296–313.

MEP (Ministry of Economy and Planning, Kingdom of Saudi Arabia). 2010. "Regional Development." In "Ninth Development Plan (2010–2014)," 209–22. Ministry of Economy and Planning, Kingdom of Saudi Arabia, Riyadh.

Mills, R., and F. Alhashemi. 2018. "Resource Regionalism in the Middle East and North Africa: Rich Lands, Neglected People." Brookings Doha Center Analysis Paper 20, Brookings Institution, Washington, DC.

Nabli, M. K., J. Keller, C. Nassif, and C. Silva-Jáuregui. 2006. "The Political Economy of Industrial Policy in the Middle East and North Africa." Working Paper, Report No. 116424. World Bank, Washington, DC.

Rijkers, B., C. Freund, and A. Nucifora. 2014. "All in the Family: State Capture in Tunisia." Policy Research Working Paper 6810, World Bank, Washington, DC.

Schiffbauer, M., A. Sy, S. Hussain, H. Sahnoun, and P. Keefer. 2015. *Jobs or Privileges: Unleashing the Employment Potential of the Middle East and North Africa*. MENA Development Report. Washington, DC: World Bank.

Schwab, Klaus, ed. 2017. *The Global Competitiveness Report 2017–2018*. Geneva: World Economic Forum.

Sims, D. 2015. *Egypt's Desert Dreams: Development or Disaster?* Oxford: Oxford University Press.

UN-Habitat (United Nations Human Settlement Programme). 2012. *The State of Arab Cities 2012: Challenges of Urban Transition.* Nairobi, Kenya: UN-Habitat.

WEF (World Economic Forum) and World Bank. 2018. "The Arab World Competitiveness Report 2018." Insight Report, World Economic Forum (WEF), Geneva.

World Bank. 2012. "Arab Republic of Egypt: Reshaping Egypt's Economic Geography: Domestic Integration as a Development Platform." Report No. 71289-EG, World Bank, Washington, DC.

———. 2016. "Upper Egypt Local Development Program-for-Results Project." Project Appraisal Document, Report No. 108094, World Bank, Washington, DC.

———. 2017a. *Doing Business Regional Profile 2017: Middle East and North Africa.* Washington, DC: World Bank.

———. 2017b. *Doing Business 2017: Equal Opportunity for All.* Washington, DC: World Bank.

———. 2018a. *Doing Business 2018: Reforming to Create Jobs.* Washington, DC: World Bank.

———. 2018b. "Jordan Housing Sector Review." Technical Note, Report No. AUS0000232, World Bank, Washington, DC.

———. 2018c. "Policy note on How Tunisia Can Leverage Its Regions in a Differentiated Manner for Shared Prosperity." Project 159072, World Bank, Washington, DC.

# Centralized Government: Contributor to Economic Geography | 5

As chapter 2 documented, many countries in the Middle East and North Africa suffer large spatial disparities in government service delivery, outcomes for citizens, and citizen satisfaction. This chapter explains how excessive centralization in government planning and provision of services has contributed to spatial inequality, exacerbating poor outcomes for citizens in the region's lagging areas.

In the Middle East and North Africa, many governments have sought convergence in living standards through the provision of jobs and public services. The development strategies and national plans of most of these countries emphasize enhancing welfare, improving quality and efficiency of service delivery, and increasing equality—as outlined in the Vision 2030 strategies recently released by Algeria, the Arab Republic of Egypt, Iraq, Qatar, and the United Arab Emirates. Moreover, recent national plans or government programs for Jordan, Morocco, Saudi Arabia, and Tunisia specifically highlight the importance of reducing spatial imbalances in living standards, including through improved delivery of public services. This is in line with citizen priorities: recent perception data confirms that at multiple spatial scales, citizens in the Middle East and North Africa believe it to be the top priority for their states to

enable job creation and provide public services, with some evidence that this preference is especially pronounced in rural areas and low-income households.

However, the policies that the region's governments deploy to meet these objectives are characterized by excessive centralization of resources, decision making, and service delivery mechanisms. This is true of policies pursuing *convergence in access to basic services* (primarily through top-down allocation and planning of public investment); *convergence in service quality* (mainly through centralized service delivery mechanisms); and, as discussed in chapter 4, *convergence in consumption levels* (typically through massive public employment in lieu of poverty-targeted social protection).

These policies closely reflect the "distinctively interventionist and redistributive" social contracts established in the region's countries after independence, which have been marked by (a) a preference for state planning over free-market outcomes; (b) the rise of a centralized, hierarchal bureaucracy or administration; and (c) a preference for redistribution, with the state perceived as responsible for providing welfare and social services including, to a great extent, employment (Yousef 2004).

This distinctively top-down approach to welfare planning and delivery is reinforcing spatial disparity. Drawing on empirical research and country-specific analytical work within the Middle East and North Africa, this chapter shows that these centralizing policies are spatially biased. They encourage a vertically unbalanced flow of resources and decision making at the national level, combined with insufficient development of human, financial, and technical capacity to respond to citizens' needs for delivery of quality services at the local level—particularly in lagging areas. Effectively meeting citizens' demands for jobs and services therefore requires moving from the monumental to the incremental—away from top-heavy, state-centric models and toward more locally grounded, people-centric approaches to investment planning, service delivery, and accountability.

## What do citizens expect of the state in the Middle East and North Africa?

What citizens expect of the state in the Middle East and North Africa varies spatially but with a clear preference for socioeconomic policies, particularly in rural areas. Subnational perception data from the 2016 Arab Barometer show that when asked to describe the essential characteristics of democracy, respondents in the surveyed Middle East and North Africa economies[1] overwhelmingly value functions to improve their socioeconomic well-being (narrowing the gap between rich and poor, providing basic necessities and jobs for all, and providing quality public services) over characteristics reflecting political freedoms and fair institutions.

On average, in the full sample of almost 9,000 people in seven economies, 48 percent of respondents agreed that government enablement of job opportunities for all is an essential characteristic of democracy, compared with only 28 percent for government provision of quality public services, 26 percent for free and fair elections, and 16 percent for freedom of speech (figure 5.1, panel a). This general ranking of preferences holds in both urban and rural areas (figure 5.1, panel b), and the preference for government enablement or provision of both job opportunities and public services is particularly pronounced in the rural areas of most countries (figure 5.2).

**FIGURE 5.1** **Respondents in surveyed Middle East and North Africa economies identified functions to improve socioeconomic well-being as the most essential characteristics of democracy**
*Percentage of respondents selecting answers in multiple-choice format*

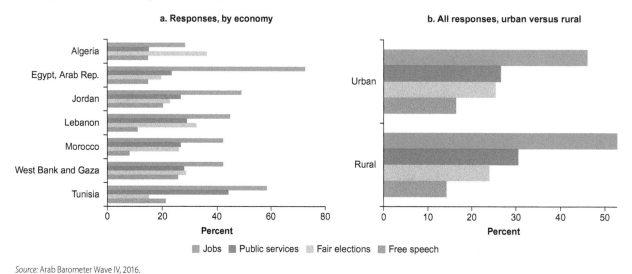

*Source:* Arab Barometer Wave IV, 2016.
*Note:* Percentages add up to more than 100 because they reflect respondents' selection of one statement from each of four sets of answers to the question (Wave IV, no. 515): "If you have to choose only one from each of the four sets of statements that I am going to read, which one would you choose as the most essential characteristics of a democracy?" Categories shown summarize each choice described.

**FIGURE 5.2** **Rural respondents were more likely to cite government's role in job creation and public service provision as essential characteristics of democracy**
*Percentage of respondents selecting answers in multiple-choice format*

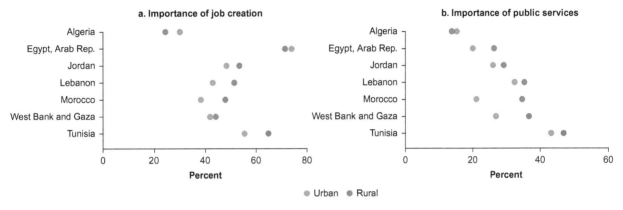

*Source:* Arab Barometer Wave IV, 2016.
*Note:* Preferences reflect respondents' selection of one statement from each of four sets of answers to the question (Wave IV, no. 515): "If you have to choose only one from each of the four sets of statements that I am going to read, which one would you choose as the most essential characteristics of a democracy?" Categories shown summarize each choice described.

Between the two priorities, there is a clear preference for government's role in enabling job creation over public service provision at the subnational level, which is potentially more pronounced in low-income households. In most governorates of Algeria, Jordan, Lebanon, Morocco, and West Bank and Gaza,[2] a greater proportion of respondents name government's role in job creation over government provision of quality public services as an essential characteristic of democracy (figure 5.3). For most countries, this preference appears to be slightly more pronounced when considering only households in financial difficulty, although this finding should be treated with caution given the low number of survey respondents in this category.[3]

## Centralized government responses reinforce spatial bias, undermining instead of encouraging convergence

As chapter 2 documented, authorities in the region have struggled to uphold their end of this redistributive social contract, suggesting that their policy menu needs to be revised. This chapter does not negate the importance of redistribution but argues that convergence

objectives have been pursued in spatially biased ways that limit achievement of the objective.

This section analyzes the policies that Middle East and North Africa governments have used to uphold their end of the social contract, focusing on efforts to encourage (a) *convergence in access to basic services* (for which the dominant strategy has been top-down allocation and planning of public investment), and (b) *convergence in service quality* (mainly pursued through centralized mechanisms of service delivery). The section presents evidence that these policies are characterized by excessive centralization of capacity, resources, and decision-making processes, which undermine convergence objectives by reinforcing spatial disparities.

### Centralized response 1: Top-down allocation and planning of public capital investments results in fragmented or uncoordinated development

To assess the robustness of the Arab Barometer data analyzed in this section, we analyzed World Values Survey (WVS) data for Middle East and

# FIGURE 5.3 Across Middle East and North Africa economies, subnational surveys also show a preference for governments' role in job creation over public service delivery

*Percentage of respondents selecting answers in multiple-choice format*

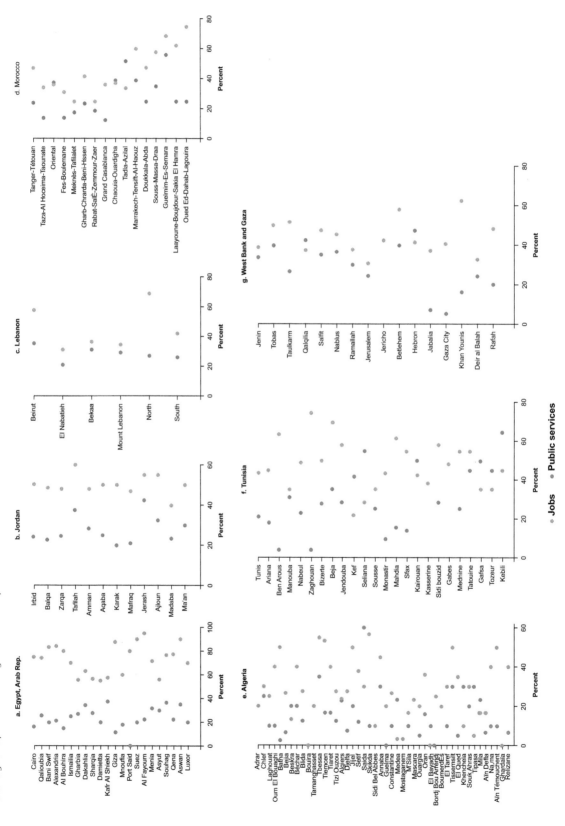

a. Egypt, Arab Rep.

b. Jordan

c. Lebanon

d. Morocco

e. Algeria

f. Tunisia

g. West Bank and Gaza

● Jobs   ● Public services

*Source:* Arab Barometer Wave IV, 2016.

*Note:* Preferences reflect respondents' selection of one statement from each of four sets of answers to the question (Wave IV, no. 515): "If you have to choose only one from each of the four sets of statements that I am going to read, which one would you choose as the most essential characteristics of a democracy?" Categories shown summarize each choice described.

**Comparing Arab Barometer and World Values Survey responses on government's role**

The WVS Wave 6 (2010–14) collected data about what people consider "the most important aims of the country" (figure B5.1.1). It appears that people consider economic growth, by far, to be the main objective that their countries and governments should pursue. This corroborates the strong weight given by Arab Barometer respondents to their governments' responsibility in enabling economic development (that is, jobs). Unfortunately, neither the subregional data nor the urban versus rural segmentation is available from the WVS for the Middle East and North Africa countries, so we cannot compare subnational results with the Arab Barometer.

**FIGURE B5.1.1   WVS respondents from most Middle East and North Africa economies identified economic growth as the country's "most important" goal**
*Percentage of respondents selecting answers in multiple-choice format*

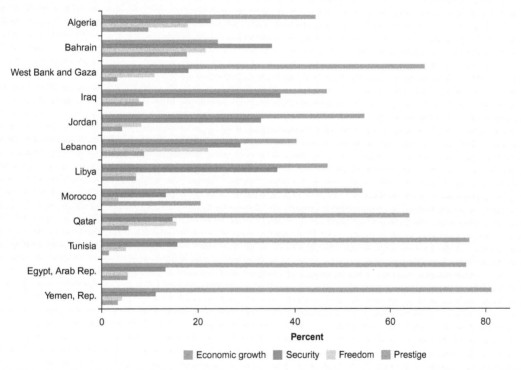

*Sources:* World Values Survey Wave 6 (2010–14 and 2015 datasets), World Values Survey Association 2015, http://www.worldvaluessurvey.org/WVSDocumentationWV6.jsp.
*Note:* WVS = World Values Survey. Respondents selected from several choices in WVS Wave 6, question no. V60: "People sometimes talk about what the aims of this country should be for the next 10 years.... Would you please say which one of these you, yourself, consider the most important?" Categories shown summarize each aim described.

North Africa economies. Although it does not include a question identical to the one analyzed from the Arab Barometer, an analysis of somewhat comparable questions and answers from the WVS reveal consistent perceptions (box 5.1).

The governments of the Middle East and North Africa have made sizable public capital investments in recent years as a key tool for pursuing convergence in access to basic services. Chapter 4 documents a functional imbalance between government spending on infrastructure (especially place based) and spending on human capital (social services) in the region's countries relative to comparator economies.

Indeed, sizable public infrastructure investments have been a hallmark of several of the region's governments in recent years, including recent major infrastructure projects in Egypt and megaprojects in Saudi Arabia. This focus on infrastructure is prevalent even in the social services, with recent evidence showing that the education budgets of many of these countries heavily emphasize capital investments (such as construction of new schools, rehabilitation and expansion of existing facilities, or procurement of school equipment) rather than other learning inputs. Qatar, Kuwait, Morocco, and Lebanon respectively allocate 24 percent, 21 percent, 13 percent, and 13 percent of public education spending to capital investment—much higher shares than the Organisation for Economic Co-operation and Development (OECD) average of 7.6 percent (World Bank 2018d).

Yet in most countries in the region, decisions regarding the geographic allocation of investment expenditure are made by sectoral ministries within the central government, with little agency left to subnational governments. For example, in Egypt in 2016, local administration expenditures on nonfinancial assets for local development activities represented only 3 percent of total local administration spending, reflecting that most local investment expenditure in Egypt is decided and implemented by central government agencies (Amin 2016). Likewise, in Jordan, sectoral investments are generally planned at the central level with limited attention to optimizing those investments across sectors or applying a territorial planning framework (World Bank 2018a). Even in Tunisia, which has decentralized greater decision-making authority to local administrations, five-year municipal development plans make up the sum of all municipal investment programs but account for only 10 percent of total investment in urban infrastructure. The remaining 90 percent is based on national development plans financed and implemented directly by line ministries and state-owned service enterprises. This can lead to sectorally fragmented or uncoordinated investment planning and funding decisions, without an integrated view of regional and local priorities for socioeconomic development.

A related challenge is that the region's governments have tended to proliferate rather than consolidate their subnational government units, hindering their ability to take on a coherent spatial and regional development planning role. In Saudi Arabia, for example, the historic region of Hejaz is now split between four governates. Iraq similarly took a much simpler preindependence structure and multiplied the number of governates. Lebanon is an extreme case, with more than 1,100 municipalities (*baladiyat*) and some 53 unions of municipalities, many of which have fewer than 10 member municipalities. The small size of these subnational units, their lack of local identity, and their upward-facing accountability pose significant obstacles to their viability as socioeconomic layers and removes what would otherwise be logical counterparts for spatially oriented interventions.

## Centralized response 2: Service delivery mechanisms favor primate cities, especially political capitals

In the pursuit of convergence in service quality, most Middle East and North Africa countries have committed to decentralize authority for service delivery to local bodies. Internationally, local authorities such as municipalities and city councils are commonly made responsible for delivering basic services to citizens, and they are generally viewed as the first and best contact points between the citizenry and the government apparatus.

The "International Guidelines on Decentralisation and Access to Basic Services for All," approved by the Governing Council of the United Nations Human Settlement Programme (UN-Habitat) in 2007 and 2009, outline an international consensus that the decentralization of responsibilities, policy management, decision-making authority, and sufficient resources to local authorities are requirements for effective and sustainable service delivery (UN-Habitat 2009). Several Middle East and North Africa countries have recently made important advances in implementing a decentralization agenda—including Lebanon and Tunisia, which both held long-awaited local elections in 2018.

Nonetheless, local government systems in the region remain mostly deconcentrated rather than decentralized,[4] mirroring the excessive concentration of the region's urban systems. Chapters 1–3 of the report documented how territorial development in the Middle East and North Africa is characterized by economic and demographic primacy of the main city (spatial fragmentation within the urban system). This is the legacy of the political economy and administrative arrangements of the Ottoman Empire, which concentrated public services and tax revenues in capitals and neglected lagging regions (World Bank 2011). Subsequently, colonial powers developed metropolis- and export-oriented economies that encouraged coastal agglomeration and hindered the development of effective administrative institutions (Brixi, Lust, and Woolcock 2015). This is especially the case in the Mashreq subregion, where the excessive urban primacy and underdevelopment of secondary cities seem to have been predominantly the consequence of political bias (as further discussed in chapter 3).[5]

High population growth, migration-driven rapid urbanization, nondemocratic and centralized political government, and colonial history have all been identified as factors driving further urban concentration (Faraji 2016). Politically centralized regimes in low- and middle-income countries tend to provide better services and safety in the capital city and give more attention to that local population. As such, there is evidence that migrants settling in the primate city come not only from rural areas but also from small towns and medium-size cities (El-Din Haseeb 2012). As highlighted by Henderson (2002), primate cities that are also political capitals are on average 25 percent bigger than primate cities not concentrating political power.

The legacy of this centralized structure of service provision and decision making is still visible in the region's public administrations today, particularly in the Mashreq subregion. The public administration system is highly centralized in most of the region, with deconcentrated units of the central government providing some services directly (particularly health and education), while basic services are provided by field offices of line ministries or governorates, districts, and municipalities (UCLG 2010). Although local governments are usually run by elected councils, they typically have limited authority over the services they are mandated to provide. Their role mostly consists in carrying out service delivery decisions made by the central government and performing limited functions such as library and park services, street paving, street lighting, and garbage collection (UCLG 2010). Figure 5.4 summarizes the territorial governance structure typical of the different Middle East and North Africa subregions. The fiscal decentralization indexes calculated by Ivanyna and Shah (2012) suggest that the Mashreq subregion is significantly less decentralized than the Maghreb subregion, particularly in the cases of Egypt, Iraq, Jordan, and the Syrian Arab Republic, as further shown in chapter 3.

These decentralization patterns have resulted in a general mismatch between fiscal centralization and functional devolution of responsibility for delivering basic services. Two common metrics of decentralization in cross-country comparisons are the relationship of subnational revenues and expenditures to national totals. Central transfers continue to be the main source of local finance, and the share of local expenditures in total government spending remains low (figure 5.5). As a result, municipalities run perennial operational deficits. Where they exist, the various local taxes, fees, and permits that constitute the bulk of local revenues cover a small portion of the budget and go almost entirely to salaries and operations and maintenance. Municipalities have little flexibility in adjusting the rates and mechanisms for levying fees for public services to reflect the real costs of service provision.

**FIGURE 5.4** **The subregions of the Middle East and North Africa represent a spectrum in the degree of decentralization**

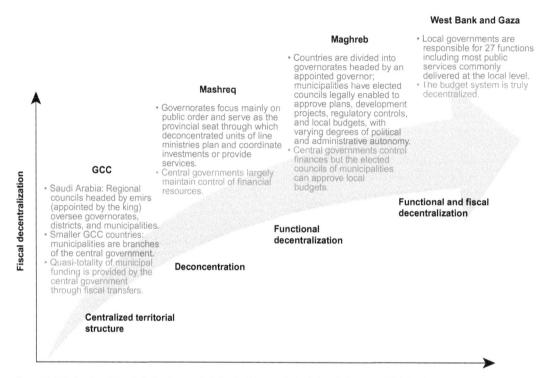

*Source:* World Bank review of decentralization literature, including fiscal decentralization indexes by Ivanyna and Shah (2012).
*Note:* GCC = Gulf Cooperation Council, comprising Bahrain, Kuwait, Oman, Qatar, Saudi Arabia, and the United Arab Emirates. Maghreb includes Algeria, Libya, Morocco, and Tunisia. Mashreq includes the Arab Republic of Egypt, Iraq, Jordan, Lebanon, and the Syrian Arab Republic. Among the notable exceptions to these categorizations, the United Arab Emirates has a significant degree of fiscal decentralization.

The reliance on central transfers to cover local deficits and finance capital projects makes funding local initiatives and projects a pervasive problem. The main exception to this in the region is West Bank and Gaza, where 90 percent of property taxes (collected directly in Gaza or indirectly through the Palestinian National Authority in the West Bank) go to municipalities, which in turn depend on central transfers for only 15 percent of their total revenue (World Bank 2017c). Maghreb countries, particularly Morocco, also tend to have somewhat greater financial autonomy at the local government level—including some extent of commercial subnational borrowing.

This highly centralized administrative structure has led to uneven spatial development. The implication of this centralizing approach for spatial disparity is confirmed by econometric analyses of spatial imbalances in the Middle East and North Africa compared with other world regions. World Bank (2011) presents statistical evidence that countries with centralizing governance characteristics tend to follow a more spatially concentrated development path.

In related research, Kremer, Mijiyawa, and Whitmore (2012) find a strong negative correlation between (a) a political rights index, in which the Middle East and North Africa ranks lower than other world regions; and (b) a spatial agglomeration index (an indicator of the concentration of economic activities, which the authors use as a proxy measure for spatial imbalances), in which the Middle East and North Africa ranks higher than other regions. This research concludes that an increase in political rights and a greater sharing of political accountability

FIGURE 5.5 **The fiscal decentralization of subnational governments in the Middle East and North Africa remains low compared with OECD countries**

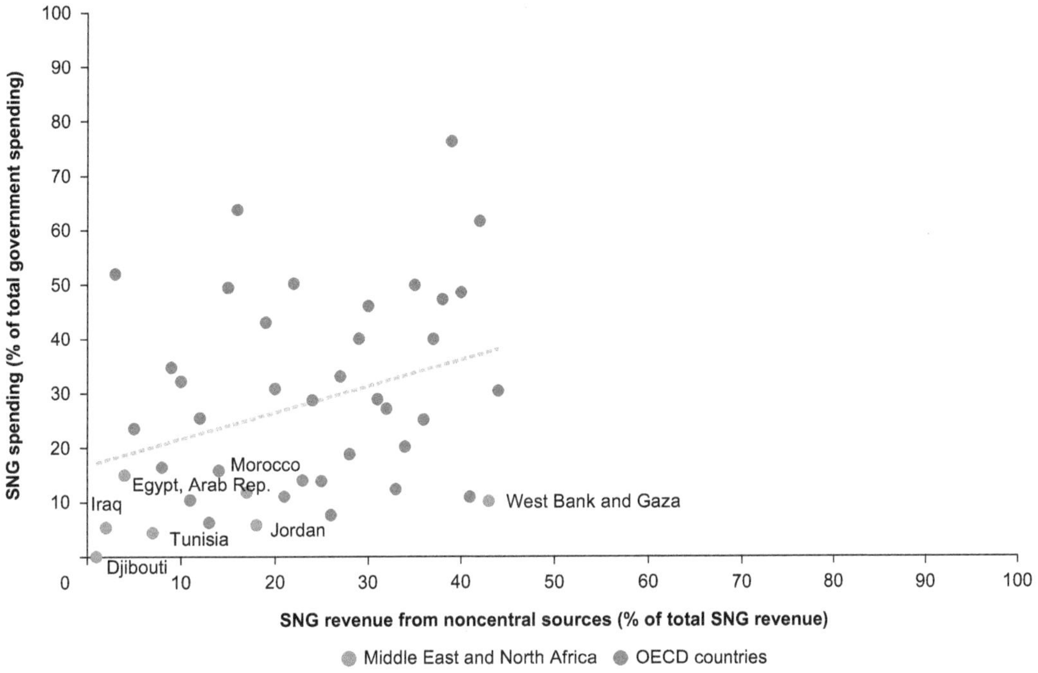

*Sources:* OECD.Stat database 2015 (https://stats.oecd.org/) and 2014–18 World Bank country reports.
*Note:* Figure shows each country's (a) share of subnational expenditure in total national expenditure, in relation to (b) its share of total subnational revenue from sources other than central transfers. OECD = Organisation for Economic Co-operation and Development. SNG = subnational government.

across a territory favors a reduction in spatial imbalances (World Bank 2011).

Of course, not all spatial imbalances are negative. Indeed, one of the major intellectual contributions of *World Development Report 2009: Reshaping Economic Geography* was the argument that dispersing production more broadly does not foster prosperity (World Bank 2009). However, this uneven spatial development is concerning because it contributes to spatial disparities in living standards, as the next section discusses.

## Decentralization has complex implications for spatial disparity

Theoretically, the transfer of decision-making authority and resources to lower levels of government has a potentially ambiguous effect on spatial disparity. On the one hand, Oates (2005) suggests that this will improve allocative efficiency by better matching public spending to differentiated needs across the territory and can also increase service quality by fostering competition among local governments. This is the basis of the subsidiarity principle that governs European Union competences, whereby decisions on social and political issues should be made at the most immediate (or local) level that enables their resolution. The logic is that lower tiers of government can often better identify needs of their citizens and firms and be more adept at designing, delivering, and coordinating than myriad central government agencies. The theoretical argument in favor of decentralization also centers on its potential to improve the quality, transparency, and responsiveness of local governance by bringing government closer to the people (Ivanya and Shah 2012).

On the other hand, to the extent that more prosperous and productive regions are better equipped to plan and use resources, placing this authority at a lower level could undermine the redistributive role of the state and exacerbate territorial imbalances (Prud'homme 1995). Decentralization may thus allow inequalities to develop or become reinforced in the absence of proper accountability frameworks and incentives.

Internationally, empirical studies suggest that at middle-to-high income levels and in the presence of a sufficiently strong public sector, decentralization tends to reduce territorial disparities. In a rich review of the relevant literature, Martinez-Vazquez, Lago-Peñas, and Sacchi (2017) conclude that despite the mixed evidence of any direct impact of decentralization on poverty or income inequality, "the evidence is quite robust" regarding its impact on geographical and interregional disparities, with decentralization generally contributing to regional convergence and more equal access to services. Econometric analysis by Rodríguez-Pose and Ezcurra (2010) indicates that the net effects depend on economic and political circumstances. In particular, the decentralization of resources and decision making to subnational governments is most likely to reduce territorial inequalities in middle- to high-income countries and when the state has greater capacity to redistribute financial resources across regions (that is, a larger public sector). However, in low-income countries where the state has a lower redistributive capacity (a smaller public sector), decentralization is found to increase regional inequalities. Econometric analysis by Lessmann (2012) also finds that the positive effects of decentralization are conditional on a country's level of development, with a positive relationship at higher country income levels.

The implications of these findings for the Middle East and North Africa vary by level of country income and degree of fragility. Although the Rodríguez-Pose and Ezcurra (2010) study includes none of the region's countries in its sample, its findings suggest that decentralization may have beneficial effects on spatial disparity for the higher-income countries in the region, particularly considering that the public sector in the Middle East and North Africa is large by international standards and has significant redistributive capacity. This also implies, however, that the positive effects of decentralization on spatial inequalities will be weaker in the region's low-income countries and when redistributive mechanisms are poorly designed. The implications also differ for countries struggling with separatist conflict and profound governance challenges, such as Iraq, Libya, and the Republic of Yemen, where administrative decentralization has potential to reduce conflict and improve service delivery but should be handled with care to avoid reinforcing separatist tendencies (box 5.2).

With these nuances in mind, this chapter does not make a specific policy recommendation regarding administrative or fiscal decentralization. It focuses instead on analyzing the extent to which the region's top-down decision-making structures and centralized service delivery mechanisms have contributed to the spatial disparities documented in chapters 1–3 of the report.

## Spatial bias 1: Budget processes may result in unpredictable and regressive subnational resource transfers

The budget processes governing sectoral and subnational resource allocations for public investment in the Middle East and North Africa commonly lack transparency and predictability, potentially skewing resource flows toward areas with greater bargaining power. Several econometric studies from the OECD find that political bias in the territorial allocation of central government grants across regions is stronger as equalization systems become weaker and less transparent (Pitlik, Schneider, and Strotmann 2006; Simon-Cosano, Lago-Peñas, and Vaquero 2013).

To safeguard against political bias and allow local governments greater predictability in resource flows, guidance from the OECD (2013), the World Bank (Boadway

## BOX 5.2    Handling decentralization in fragile environments

In an empirical analysis of the relationship between decentralization and secessionism across 30 countries, Brancati (2006) finds that decentralization is generally beneficial in reducing conflict, by bringing services closer to the people, but that it can also increase conflict indirectly by reinforcing ethnic and regional identities.

On one hand, stronger subnational governments can improve service delivery if the state is absent or otherwise constrained. For example, in West Bank and Gaza, local government units (LGUs) have gained paramount importance in local service provision in the presence of a greatly constrained central authority, and their role has grown with the increasing political and geographical fragmentation over the past two decades (World Bank 2016b). In the Republic of Yemen, the success of Marib province has reignited discussion on the potential of developing a functional decentralized governance system based on building local institutions' capacity through a local-first approach (Baron 2018; World Bank 2017a). Commentators on Libya and Syria have also suggested the usefulness of shifting power from the center to local authorities during the reconstruction

and state-building process to rebuild state legitimacy, help integrate communities, and allow for elite accommodations across ethnic groups. This is in line with empirical findings from Alesina and Spolaore (2003), who find there is a potential role for decentralization in alleviating secessionist pressures (Martinez-Vazquez, Lago-Peñas, and Sacchi 2017).

On the other hand, poorly implemented decentralization reform can establish the foundation for secession. A recent report from the Brookings Institution suggests that this may be the case in Iraq, where the recent dramatic push for decentralization of functions to the local level is combined with low local capacity and poorly designed resource revenue-sharing arrangements that give too much legitimacy to local claims from resource-rich provinces. The authors explain that decentralization "is only as effective as the political and administrative power-sharing arrangements between the central and subnational governments in a given country" and should therefore be combined with other policies targeting spatial inequality at a national level, such as investment in human capital and improving governance and the business climate (Mills and Alhashemi 2018, 19).

and Shah 2007), and UN-Habitat (2009) recommend that intergovernmental grant systems should be timely, transparent, and predictable. A lack of clear allocation criteria, on the other hand, can lead to suboptimal spatial and economic outcomes. The Egyptian system illustrates how weaknesses in the subnational budget process can reinforce spatial disparity on several fronts (box 5.3) because of "the phenomenal fragmentation in planning and budgeting" that produces "a lack of accountability for the outcomes of public spending" and implicitly favors geographic areas with higher bargaining power (World Bank 2012, 2).

Even in countries that apply formulas for the subnational allocation of central government resources, these are commonly oriented by default toward leading areas (based on an area's population or natural resource revenues). Subnational resource

transfers from the central government to local administrations are commonplace in many high-income and low- to middle-income countries and have been used primarily for equalization purposes, as incentives for good performance, or as pass-through payments for a centrally mandated expenditure. International experience and empirical research show that such fiscal equalization schemes can indeed "deliver smaller spatial economic disparities across regions" (Henkel, Seidel, and Suedekum 2018, 2).

However, such formulas can also have an uneven spatial incidence that reinforces territorial imbalances. For example, in Iraq, central government budget allocations to governorates are based primarily upon past spending, population, and a petrodollar formula. The resulting allocations are a disincentive to economizing and skew resources

BOX 5.3    **Spatial bias in Egypt's subnational fiscal architecture**

Lack of transparency and predictability in Egypt's territorial budget allocation process reinforces spatial disparity in the following ways:

- The system uses no official formula or consistently applied set of criteria for making resource allocation decisions, so it serves no clear redistributive function.
- All horizontal and vertical resource allocations are determined through individual negotiations between the Ministry of Finance and each of the 324 budget entities,[a] meaning that subnational entities with little bargaining power or negotiating skills—such as potentially those in lagging areas—may suffer lower resource allocations.
- Budgeting takes place throughout the fiscal year under ad hoc circumstances, which prevents the parliament from recognizing and discussing the geographical allocation of budgeting.
- Deconcentrated implementing agencies can change the spatial location of any assigned project with only the approval of the minister of planning.

New efforts are under way to reform the country's subnational fiscal architecture as part of an ongoing engagement between the World Bank and the government of Egypt. The local investment planning process is undergoing a revision to introduce multiyear planning, clarify functional assignments between the governorate and district levels, and introduce formula-based allocations by the Ministries of Planning and Local Development to allocate funds to and between governorates and districts in a more fair, transparent, and predictable manner. With support from the World Bank, the government is piloting these changes even before codifying them through its integrated Economic Development in Lagging Regions Program, which the World Bank is supporting through the Upper Egypt Local Development Program-for-Results Project.

a. These budget entities include line ministries and service delivery authorities at the central government level and governorate-level sectoral departments within each governorate.

away from lagging governorates that tend to be less populated: the correlation between a governorate's share of investment budget and poverty rate is –0.125, and the correlation between a governorate's poverty rate and its population is –0.15. The use of the petrodollar formula also rewards wealthier governorates—such as Basra and Karkouk, which have poverty rates of 14 percent and 9 percent, respectively (below the governorate average of 21 percent in 2012 based on the national poverty line)—resulting in significant horizontal disparities in resource allocations (World Bank 2016a).

Indeed, a recent Brookings Institution report finds that the use of natural resource endowments as a basis for revenue sharing is widespread in the Middle East and North Africa's fiscal transfer mechanisms and tends to reinforce resource regionalism and fuel separatist tensions (whereby resource-rich regions demand to retain further benefits from locally generated revenues). The report recommends that governments target spatial

inequalities at the national level rather than through redistributive mechanisms that explicitly reward resource-rich regions and perpetuate resource reliance (Mills and Alhashemi 2018).

The excessively centralized, and sometimes spatially blind, allocation of central government resources for capital investment can directly enhance spatial disparity. The case of Lebanon is illustrative. Overall, public investment in infrastructure in Lebanon has been low and skewed more toward the most developed districts, even after controlling for population. In per capita terms for 2017, the districts of Batroun, Beirut, Chouf, Jbeil, and Marjaayoun received the highest investments made by the Council for Development and Reconstruction (a national agency, reporting directly to the prime minister, that is responsible for planning and coordinating donor funding and financing for rebuilding infrastructure at the national and local level). Among those districts, only Marjaayoun can be considered a disadvantaged region, and its relatively higher investment per capita is primarily driven by one big sewerage and wastewater project of a relatively short duration.

On the other hand, there was limited investment in more peripheral districts such as Bint Jbeil, Jezzine, and Nabatiyeh in the South; Baalbeck and Rachaya in the Bekaa; and Akkar in the North. The spatial distribution of public investment per capita leads to similar levels of disparity. Public investment therefore does not have a redistributive nature, and the infrastructure gap between leading and lagging districts could actually be increasing (Atallah et al. 2018).

On an encouraging note, several of the region's countries have reformed their subnational fiscal transfer frameworks toward the use of needs- and performance-based formulas that also consider the economic and fiscal capabilities of individual regions. For example, Jordan's system of grants to municipalities is reported to be clear, simple, and predictable: Article 23 of the Law on Municipalities provides guidelines for the distribution of total government revenue that include elements that tend to correct spatial disparities, including distance from the center of the municipality to Amman, nominal gross domestic product (GDP) index, and municipal spending needs.

In Morocco, financial transfers to municipalities are carried out through a value added tax (VAT) designated account[6] with explicit equalization objectives that are generally fulfilled (World Bank 2017b). The impact of such transfers can be further enhanced by making greater use of incentive structures, so that municipalities are incentivized to build their technical capacity, financial sustainability, and service delivery performance to access the funds.

Such conditional transfers based on local government performance have been successfully implemented by the Urban Development and Local Government Program (UDLGP) in Tunisia and the Municipal Development Program in West Bank and Gaza. These programs are typically paired with a capacity-building element that helps underperforming local authorities get up to speed and hence keep existing capacity gaps from becoming entrenched. These experiences are contributing to improved financial sustainability and management practices in local governments and illustrate how a country's subnational fiscal architecture can be designed to become a powerful tool for improving access to basic services territorially.

## Spatial bias 2: Human resource capacity gaps create uneven quality of investment planning and execution

Several countries display significant regional imbalances in terms of local government staffing and human resource capacity that disproportionately affect lagging areas. This is exemplified by the case of Tunisia. The explanatory role played by spatial bias in human resource allocation is confirmed by a 2018 study on public employment in the country's local governments, which finds regional imbalances in staffing and human resource capacity between northern and coastal municipalities and between interior and rural ones (World Bank 2018c). Approximately 67 percent of local governments lacked a qualified engineer, 75 percent lacked an architect on their payrolls, and 24 municipalities lacked a qualified administrative or financial director within their administration. In total, the analysis estimated that more than 1,100 staff would need to be hired to ensure that each of these key managerial and technical functions is filled by at least one staff member in all local governments. To address these gaps, the government of Tunisia has begun piloting the use of financial incentives to encourage staffing mobility to local governments in lagging areas.

These capacity gaps translate into uneven planning and execution among local governments. Indeed, in many countries, the systematic mismatch of planned budget and executed budget "tends to nullify the usefulness of budget planning and the prioritization of expenditures" (World Bank 2016b, 104). In Jordan, few local authorities seem to prepare and regularly update local development and investment plans, with the result that capital expenditure allocations are often made on an ad hoc basis without a coherent strategic vision and only limited citizen engagement or public participation (World Bank 2018a). In Morocco, the limited capacity of municipalities to execute their investment budgets represents a major constraint to local service delivery, with municipalities often executing less than 50 percent of their investment plans (World Bank 2018b).

Execution capacity also tends to be lower in lagging areas: a 2017 internal analysis of a survey of local government infrastructure quality in Tunisia finds that the execution rate of infrastructure projects was advancing faster in coastal (leading) areas, with 50 percent of projects from communes' 2016 annual investment plans completed and another 25 percent under way, compared with 40 percent and 33 percent respectively in interior (lagging) areas (World Bank 2017d). Execution of the annual investment plans also tended to be higher in intermediary cities (10,000–50,000 hectares) than in small towns.

### Spatial bias 3: Weak financial capacity and fiscal autonomy of local governments drive service delivery disparities

Additionally, the revenue-raising capabilities of municipalities are unevenly distributed, with weaker fiscal autonomy in smaller municipalities and lagging areas. In Jordan, the ability of municipalities to raise own-source revenues is directly related to their size. The 2 municipalities of Greater Irbid and Greater Zarqa mobilize almost three-quarters (74 percent) of their revenues from own sources, whereas the next 8 municipalities in population size split their reliance about 50-50, and the remaining 86 municipalities mobilize only 20 percent, heavily relying on intergovernmental transfers for the rest of their funding (Timofeev and Wallace 2017).

Likewise, in Lebanon, deep-dive analyses of municipal finances in two lagging regions (Akkar and Minnieh-Dannieh) find that, compared with the national average, these districts suffer from a small tax base (because of small populations in each municipality) and low revenues compared with the national average (Atallah et al. 2018). Because of the weakness of their independent direct revenues, the municipalities have very limited autonomy from the central government, because they depend on highly volatile transfers.

Geographic gaps in municipal revenue mobilization potential can thereby exacerbate spatial disparity in the quality of services. In the case of Lebanon, below-average municipal revenues in the lagging Akkar and Minnieh-Dannieh regions "severely hinders the capacity of municipalities to provide necessary public services for which they are responsible" (Atallah et al. 2018). This is consistent with econometric findings from multiple low- to middle-income, emerging, and high-income economies showing that decentralization improves the efficiency of public service delivery but only given sufficient *expenditure* decentralization accompanied by sufficient *revenue* decentralization (Sow and Razafimahefa 2015).

In the Middle East and North Africa, spatial inequalities in access to basic services appear to be particularly high in some of the region's most fiscally centralized countries, particularly when considering multiple deprivations and service quality. A 2016 World Bank report on access to opportunities in the region concludes that when opportunity is defined as access to a bundle of basic services, or when the quality of services is taken into account, location of residence explains more than half the variation in access to opportunity, "with spatial advantages accruing to capital cities and large metropolitan areas that coincide with poles of economic activity" (Krishnan et al. 2016, 49). That these differences are particularly high in the Mashreq subregion supports the idea that excessive centralization may lead to spatially biased outcomes.

Improving the fiscal autonomy of local governments can therefore be a powerful tool to correct spatial disparities in service delivery. In West Bank and Gaza, a recent household survey shows that, even when ruling out differences due to size and location, "fiscal capacity can be identified as one, if not the strongest driver of local government performance" in access, quality, and reliability of local service delivery (World Bank 2017c). Economic models using proxy indicators of fiscal sustainability (satisfactory collection efficiency and own revenue sources as well as a basic surplus in both operational and enterprise budgets) yield positive and statistically significant coefficients. Municipalities with satisfactory collection efficiency and own revenue sources average a 5.6 higher performance score, and municipalities with a surplus in operational and enterprise budgets perform on average 5.4 points higher.

Per capita revenues are strongly associated with higher LGU performance in West Bank and Gaza, and an even stronger relationship exists between per capita expenditures and LGU performance. Furthermore, the geographic variation in LGU performance scores is closely linked to various measures of "lagginess"—household wealth, remoteness from governorate, and poverty—suggesting that improving local capacity to mobilize and manage resources, particularly in lagging areas, can have a significant impact on reducing spatial disparities, assuming this is feasible given socioeconomic conditions in these territories.

In Saudi Arabia, increasing the own-source revenues of municipalities has become a key performance indicator of the recently adopted National Transformation Program (KSA 2016a), reflecting the importance of this issue in achieving the kingdom's vision of "providing world-class government services which effectively and efficiently meet the needs of our citizens" (KSA 2016b, 7).

## Spatial bias 4: Excessive central government decision-making dilutes local accountability

Highly centralized decision making on service provision impedes service quality by reducing the agency and accountability of local service providers, particularly in the social services. Specifically, in education, decentralization of decision making to lower administrative units such as governorates, school districts, or individual schools has been the topic of reform efforts internationally. Evidence from the Programme for International Student Assessment (PISA) suggests that with proper support and accountability mechanisms, enhancing district and school autonomy in core managerial responsibilities can improve student performance, notably by aligning teacher and parent incentives. Additionally, schools with more autonomy over teaching content, student assessment, and resource allocation tend to perform better than those with less autonomy (OECD 2011). By contrast, the Middle East and North Africa's education systems are overly centralized.

In the region's countries that participated in the 2015 PISA, teachers were found to have far less decision-making responsibility than those in OECD countries, and most decisions are made at the central level, often resulting in a mismatch between school needs and service delivery (World Bank 2018d). In some cases, such as Egypt, attempts to decentralize decision making over education have not been accompanied by the necessary resources to implement decisions. Elsewhere, efforts have shifted administrative responsibilities to lower levels without any agency to effect change in choosing teachers, tailoring the curriculum, or learning approaches to different needs—for example, half-day school days in rural areas or different languages of instruction for refugee communities, which can be particularly relevant for enhancing learning in lagging areas or neighborhoods.

An exception to this pattern is the United Arab Emirates, where there are clearly demarcated roles between the central ministry and different emirates in delivering educational services, with reportedly better outcomes (World Bank 2018d). This is in line with empirical research analyzing the impact of decentralization on educational outcomes. Decentralization also has a positive impact on health outcomes, although the relationship is weaker than with education (Martinez-Vazquez, Lago-Peñas, and Sacchi 2017).

The limited autonomy of local governments over service delivery decisions also undermines local accountability. This externalization of decision making (concentration of authority in the central government) can distance citizens from local government officials, who do not hold the answer to their problems. As expressed by a local council member interviewed in the Republic of Yemen, "I exhaust all efforts in serving and helping the citizens, but I am helpless when there is no response [from the state]" (Brixi, Lust, and Woolcock 2015, 218).

To the extent that local governments in lagging areas are particularly removed from the decision-making apparatus of the central government, inhabitants of these regions may feel less heard. According to a 2012 dataset on perceptions of service delivery and government performance among urban youth in Tunisia, the largest proportions of youth reporting dissatisfaction with municipal officers came from the (lagging) Center West and the North West subregions, where only 26 percent of respondents believed that municipalities listen to residents of their districts (World Bank 2014). Percentages were higher in the coastal (leading) subregions such as the North East (47 percent).

This distancing can be detrimental in several ways: it can lead citizens in less well-off areas to disengage from the state or lower their expectations (potentially worsening spatial disparity because of reduced bottom-up pressure from lagging areas) and ultimately to lose trust in the state. On the other hand, greater input from local officials—regarding both local priority setting and local administration—has the potential to result in a higher-performing public sector, where local administrative units spend their resources more efficiently and effectively and where local officials are better positioned to deliver responsive public services to citizens.

Investing in citizen-centric modes of service delivery, with a greater emphasis on local accountability, can therefore help improve the quality and reliability of service delivery in lagging areas. International analysis shows that robust mechanisms of social accountability, transparency, and feedback have the potential to improve the quality and equity of service delivery as well as to engage citizens in behavioral change that can be critical in improving outcomes (Schott 2014).

Similarly, comparative analyses of local successes in service delivery in the Middle East and North Africa highlight the importance of autonomy, accountability relationships, and local participation (Brixi, Lust, and Woolcock 2015). This is backed up empirically by data from a 2017 World Bank Local Government Performance Assessment (LGPA) in the West Bank and Gaza, which found that regardless of an LGU's size and location or the institutional arrangement for service provision, the quality and reliability of services was higher for local governments that performed better on responsiveness and accountability metrics (World Bank 2017c). Local governments with the highest shares of households reporting that their LGU was "very responsive" to citizen concerns and complaints scored 16.4 points higher on average than other local governments on an LGU Performance Index (100-point scale) measuring the quality, reliability, and access to local services.

## Efforts to move from state-centric to citizen-centric approaches vary across the region

This chapter has documented spatial biases arising from the excessive centralization of government planning and service provision in the Middle East and North Africa. As they fine-tune the decentralization agendas currently taking shape across the region (box 5.4), the region's governments should carefully consider the spatial implications of alternative policy options.

The discussion in this chapter would suggest focusing on introducing more balance into the vertical flow of resources and decision making at the national level,

**BOX 5.4**  **Recent advances in implementing decentralization agendas across the Middle East and North Africa, by region**

### Maghreb subregion

*In Tunisia,* 2018 was a particularly eventful year, witnessing the first local elections since the 2010–11 Jasmine Revolution and the long-awaited adoption of a local government organic code. These developments fit into the broader decentralization agenda set into motion by the Constitution of 2014: the involvement of different ministries (in committees) to define key communal competences; the creation of a new Ministry of Local Affairs in 2016; and the restructuring of the local government fund allocation system, including the introduction of an allocation formula-based performance transfer.

*In Morocco,* based on the reforms introduced by the Constitution of 2011 and subsequent organic laws, the government has launched an ambitious reform program aiming to consolidate both (a) *decentralization* through the "advanced regionalization" project (which includes, among other things, the consolidation of the country's territory into fewer regions with expanded competencies and financial resources); and (b) *deconcentration* through a Deconcentration Charter.

*In Algeria,* the government is currently developing a national "Vision 2035" policy document, which affirms a willingness to deepen the country's decentralization process and the active role of regions and territories in the country's economic development. Additionally, a local government organic law was adopted in 2012 that suggests significant changes in administrative structures and public governance, although it has since suffered from severe implementation challenges.

*In Egypt,* a country with a long history of strong central government, a proposed local administration bill calls for greater fiscal and administrative decentralization, seeking the establishment of separate budgets at the different local administrative levels and the expansion of local government responsibilities for revenue collection and investment planning. The local administration bill seeks to establish a central government committee to set criteria for central transfers and design a framework for program-based budgeting across different government levels.

### Mashreq subregion

*In Lebanon,* the first municipal elections since 2010 were held in May 2016. The country has a dual system of governance consisting of deconcentrated authorities at the regional level and decentralized authorities at the local level, represented by more than 1,100 municipalities.

*In Jordan,* local political elections were held for the first time in August 2017 for provincial councils, municipal councils, local councils, mayoralties, and the Amman Secretariat, which governs the capital. A Fiscal Decentralization Unit was established in the Ministry of Finance, with a detailed, phased fiscal decentralization plan developed for 2017–19. These measures include providing revenue equalization grants through fiscal transfers from central government fuel tax collections and allocating development budgets to governorates, in line with Objective 2 of the Jordan Economic Growth Plan 2018–22, which sets forth the government's vision to "achieve developmental balance, reduce disparity and distribute development revenues fairly" (EPC 2018, 26).

*In Iraq,* although responsibility for basic service delivery has historically been almost exclusively in central government ministries, a strong push by the prime minister throughout 2015 has moved devolution forward, building on the provisions of the Constitution of 2005 and Law 19 (2013), which identified eight sector ministries for which some functions and responsibilities were expected to be transferred to the governorates within a two-year time frame. However, this legal and policy framework is yet to be followed through with efficient implementation.

*In Syria,* even before the civil war, the country's governance structure was highly centralized, with decision-making power over security, political, budgetary, and judicial issues in the hands of the government. Although decentralization has often been proposed as a solution to the conflict in the ongoing peace negotiations, no agreement has been reached.

### Other economies

*In the Republic of Yemen,* an ambitious Local Authority Law was adopted in 2000 to establish a framework for a

*box continues next page*

decentralized local government system based on 22 governorates and 333 districts, each with directly elected local councils. Although local councils were established to devolve power and encourage local participation in service delivery, the form of decentralization in the Republic of Yemen is a mix of deconcentration and devolution, with national ministries continuing to play a major role, and with the strong involvement of nonstate actors. These hybrid service delivery arrangements are complicated by the ongoing civil war.

*Even in Djibouti,* a small state, a decentralization process was initiated in 2006 and has achieved some progress, including the holding of regular local elections, the establishment of local councils, the devolution of some tax collection authority to the local level

through a 2017 finance law, and creation in 2016 of a ministry in charge of implementing a national decentralization action plan.

*In West Bank and Gaza,* as a result of increasing political and geographical fragmentation, LGUs have gained paramount importance in providing services to the local population, particularly in areas where the relatively central government is politically, geographically, and fiscally constrained.

*In the GCC subregion,* particularly in Saudi Arabia, there is recent evidence of government priorities moving toward placing greater responsibility and resources at subnational levels, in line with national objectives of correcting spatial imbalances.

combined with greater development of human, financial, and technical capacity to respond to citizens' needs and deliver quality services at the local level (particularly in lagging areas). Whether or not these reforms are couched within a decentralization framework, the focus should be on (a) enhancing the state's ability to better connect with the demands of the citizenry by delivering services in an accountable and responsive manner, and (b) correcting sources of spatial bias.

## Concluding remarks

Effectively meeting citizens' demands for quality public services requires shifting from the monumental to the incremental: away from top-heavy, state-centric planning and delivery of services toward placing greater agency, capacity, and resources at the local level. Enabling subnational governments to provide services at the local level is a key part of this agenda.

Although Ligthart and van Oudheusden (2015) find that decentralization increases

trust in government and in other political institutions, placing administrative functions at lower levels of government does not necessarily go hand in hand with greater political autonomy or downward accountability at the local level. Shifting decision making and accountability to subnational government might facilitate greater allocative and productive efficiency, but resources allocated to subnational governments should come with agreements to ensure that local initiatives improve national welfare along with local welfare. Likewise, feedback mechanisms and accountability loops between citizens and local service providers need to be established so that the service providers are responsive to the needs of lagging areas and tailored to local realities.

More attention must be paid to supporting effective governance arrangements that engage citizens at all stages of development planning, investment prioritization, and feedback on service delivery performance. Specific recommendations on developing citizen-centric modes of service delivery are discussed in chapter 6.

## Notes

1. The Arab Barometer public opinion surveys in Wave IV (2016–17) were conducted in the following seven Arab economies: Algeria, Egypt, Jordan, Lebanon, Morocco, Tunisia, and West Bank and Gaza. For more information, see the website: https://www.arabbarometer.org/waves/arab-barometer-wave-iv/.
2. The Arab Barometer refers to West Bank and Gaza as "Palestine."
3. Arab Barometer Wave IV (2016–17), Question 1016, asks respondents to select which of several statements best describes their household income in terms of how well (or with how much difficulty) their income covers their expenses.
4. "Decentralization" refers to the transfer of political, fiscal, and administrative powers from the central government to lower levels of government (through downwardly accountable actors, such as elected local authorities), whereas "deconcentration" refers to the transfer of administrative responsibility for specific functions to lower levels within the central government bureaucracy (which are part of the central government and upwardly accountable to it).
5. The Mashreq subregion comprises Egypt, Iraq, Jordan, Lebanon, and the Syrian Arab Republic. The Maghreb subregion comprises Algeria, Libya, Morocco, and Tunisia.
6. The CAS TVA (Compte d'Affectation Spéciale – Part des Collectivités locales dans la taxe sur la Valeur ajoutée) includes 30 percent of national VAT revenue as well as contributions from line ministries and public foundations.

## References

Alesina, A., and E. Spolaore. 2003. *The Size of Nations*. Cambridge, MA: MIT Press.

Amin, Khaled. 2016. Unpublished technical paper for the Upper Egypt Local Development Program-for-Results Project, World Bank, Washington, DC.

Atallah, Sami, Daniel Garrote Sánchez, Nizar Hassan, Dima Mahdi, and Jana Mourad. 2018. "Introductory Chapter: Analytical Framework for Improving Urban Resilience in Lebanon's Districts Impacted by the Syrian Refugee Crisis." Unpublished report, Lebanese Center for Policy Studies, Beirut.

Baron, Adam. 2018. "The Marib Paradox: How One Province Succeeds in the Midst of Yemen's War." Policy Brief, European Council on Foreign Relations, Berlin.

Boadway, Robin, and Anwar Shah, eds. 2007. *Intergovernmental Fiscal Transfers: Principles and Practice*. Public Sector and Accountability Series. Washington, DC: World Bank.

Brancati, Dawn. 2006. "Decentralization: Fueling the Fire or Dampening the Flames of Ethnic Conflict and Secessionism?" *International Organization* 60 (Summer 2006): 651–85.

Brixi, Hana, Ellen Lust, and Michael Woolcock. 2015. *Trust, Voice, and Incentives: Learning from Local Success Stories in Service Delivery in the Middle East and North Africa*. Washington, DC: World Bank.

El-Din Haseeb, K. 2012. *The Future of the Arab Nation: Challenges and Options*. Abingdon, U.K.: Routledge.

EPC (Economic Policy Council, Jordan). 2018. "Jordan Economic Growth Plan 2018–2022." EPC, Hashemite Kingdom of Jordan, Amman.

Faraji, S. 2016. "Urban Primacy in Urban System of Developing Countries: Its Causes and Consequences." *Human Research in Rehabilitation* 6 (1): 34–45.

Henderson, V. 2002. "Urbanisation in Developing Countries." *World Bank Research Observer* 17 (1): 89–112.

Henkel, Marcel, Tobias Seidel, and Jens Suedekum. 2018. "Fiscal Transfers in the Spatial Economy." CESifo Working Paper Series 7012, CESifo Group, Munich, Germany.

Ivanyna, M., and A. Shah. 2012. "How Close is Your Government to Its People? Worldwide Indicators on Localization and Decentralization." Policy Research Working Paper 6138, World Bank, Washington, DC.

Kremer, Alexander, Abdoul'ganiou Mijiyawa, and Loic Whitmore. 2012. "Does MENA's Governance Lead to Spatial Agglomeration?" *Middle East Development Journal* 4 (2): 1–23.

Krishnan, Nandini, Gabriel Lara Ibarra, Ambar Narayan, Sailesh Tiwari, and Tara Vishwanath. 2016. *Uneven Odds, Unequal Outcomes: Inequality of Opportunity in the Middle East and North Africa*. Directions in Development Series. Washington, DC: World Bank.

KSA (Kingdom of Saudi Arabia). 2016a. "National Transformation Program: Delivery Plan, 2018–2020." Planning document, KSA, Riyadh.

———. 2016b. "Vision 2030 Kingdom of Saudi Arabia." Council of Economic and Development Affairs of Saudi Arabia, KSA, Riyadh.

Lessmann, C. 2012. "Regional Inequality and Decentralization: An Empirical Analysis." *Environment and Planning* 44 (A): 1363–88.

Ligthart, J. E., and P. van Oudheusden. 2015. "In Government We Trust: The Role of Fiscal Decentralization." *European Journal of Political Economy* 37: 116–28.

Martinez-Vazquez, Jorge, Santiago Lago-Peñas, and Agnese Sacchi. 2017. "The Impact of Fiscal Decentralization: A Survey." *Journal of Economic Surveys* 31 (4): 1095–129.

Mills, Robin, and Fatema Alhashemi. 2018. "Resource Regionalism in the Middle East and North Africa: Rich Lands, Neglected People." Brookings Doha Center Analysis Paper No. 20, Brookings Institution, Washington, DC.

Oates, W. 2005. "Toward a Second-Generation Theory of Fiscal Federalism." *International Tax and Public Finance* 12 (4): 349–73.

OECD (Organisation for Economic Co-operation and Development). 2011. "School Autonomy and Accountability: Are They Related to Student Performance?" PISA in Focus Note 2011/9, OECD Publishing, Paris.

———. 2013. *Fiscal Federalism 2014: Making Decentralisation Work.* Paris: OECD Publishing.

Pitlik, Hans, Friedrich Schneider, and Harald Strotmann. 2006. "Legislative Malapportionment and the Politicization of Germany's Intergovernmental Transfer System." *Public Finance Review* 34 (6): 637–62.

Prud'homme, R. 1995. "The Dangers of Decentralization." *World Bank Research Observer* 10 (2): 201–20.

Rodríguez-Pose, Andrés, and Roberto Ezcurra. 2010. "Does Decentralization Matter for Regional Disparities? A Cross-Country Analysis." *Journal of Economic Geography* 10 (5): 619–44.

Schott, Berenike. 2014. "Institutionalizing Citizen Engagement in Local Governance: Tunisia." Citizen Engagement in MENA Case Note Series No. 1, World Bank, Washington, DC.

Simon-Cosano, Pablo, Santiago Lago-Peñas, and Alberto Vaquero. 2013. "On the Political Determinants of Intergovernmental Grants in Decentralized Countries: The Case of Spain." *Publius: The Journal of Federalism* 44 (1): 135–56.

Sow, Moussé, and Ivohasina F. Razafimahefa. 2015. "Fiscal Decentralization and the Efficiency of Public Service Delivery." Working Paper WP/15/59, International Monetary Fund, Washington, DC.

Timofeev, Andrey, and Sally Wallace. 2017. "An Assessment of the Subnational Fiscal Framework in Jordan." Draft Paper, International Center for Public Policy, Andrew Young School of Policy Studies at Georgia State University, Atlanta, GA.

UCLG (United Cities and Local Governments). 2010. *Local Government Finance: The Challenges of the 21st Century.* Second Global Report on Decentralization and Local Democracy (GOLD II). Cheltenham, U.K.: Edward Elgar Publishing.

UN-Habitat (United Nations Human Settlements Programme). 2009. *International Guidelines on Decentralisation and Access to Basic Services for All.* Nairobi, Kenya: UN–Habitat.

World Bank. 2009. *World Development Report 2009: Reshaping Economic Geography.* Washington, DC: World Bank.

———. 2011. *Poor Places, Thriving People: How the Middle East and North Africa Can Rise Above Spatial Disparities.* MENA Development Report. Washington, DC: World Bank.

———. 2012. "Arab Republic of Egypt: Reshaping Egypt's Economic Geography: Domestic Integration as a Development Platform." 2 vols. Report No. 71249, World Bank, Washington, DC.

———. 2014. "Tunisia Urbanization Review: Reclaiming the Glory of Carthage." Report of the Partnership for Sustainable Urbanization, Collaboration for Development (C4D) platform, World Bank, Washington, DC.

———. 2016a. "Republic of Iraq: Decentralization and Subnational Service Delivery in Iraq: Status and Way Forward. Working Paper, Report No. AUS17063, World Bank, Washington, DC.

———. 2016b. "West Bank and Gaza: Public Expenditure Review of the Palestinian Authority: Towards Enhanced Public Finance Management and Improved Fiscal Sustainability." Report No. ACS18454, World Bank, Washington, DC.

———. 2017a. "Inclusive Service Delivery: Yemen Policy Note 4." Working Paper, Report No. 120534, World Bank, Washington, DC.

———. 2017b. "Making Urbanization Work for Growth and Shared Prosperity in Morocco." Urban and Regional Development Policy Note, World Bank, Washington, DC.

———. 2017c. "The Performance of Palestinian Local Governments: An Assessment of Service Delivery Outcomes and Performance Drivers in the West Bank and Gaza." Report No. ACS22456, World Bank, Washington, DC.

———. 2018a. "Jordan—Urban and Municipal Program for Balanced and Inclusive Growth: Concept State Program Information Document (PID)." Concept Note, Report No. PIDC151796, World Bank, Washington, DC.

———. 2018b. "Maroc: Donner aux villes les moyens financiers de relever les défis de l'urbanisation." [Morocco: Give cities the financial means to meet the challenges of urbanization]. Thematic Note, Report No. 131221, World Bank, Washington, DC.

———. 2018c. "Tunisia—Urban Development and Local Governance Program Project: Additional Financing." Program-for-Results Information Document (PID), Report No. 125729, World Bank, Washington, DC.

———. 2018d. "Unleashing the Potential of Education in the Middle East and North Africa." MENA education flagship draft for decision meeting, World Bank, Washington, DC.

Yousef, Tarik M. 2004. "Development, Growth and Policy Reform in the Middle East and North Africa since 1950." *Journal of Economic Perspectives* 18 (3): 91–116.

# Five Steps for Enabling Growth through Thriving Cities and Towns in the Middle East and North Africa  6

The preceding chapters have shown that in the Middle East and North Africa, most governments have been oriented toward equalizing endowments across places using hard investment, infrastructure, and investment subsidies. Development strategies, particularly targeting lagging areas, emphasize hard infrastructure. But efforts to equalize endowments in the absence of reforms that relax institutional constraints to growth have resulted in high-cost, low-return development strategies. Efforts to enhance endowments could enable greater growth and produce the resources needed to finance more spatially inclusive development, but for infrastructure and other hard investments to pay off, complementary interventions will be necessary to address the institutional constraints to growth.

Designing and operationalizing institutional reforms to this end in the Middle East and North Africa is difficult. Political economy, institutional, social, and financial constraints make many bold, ideal reforms unfeasible in many contexts in the region; pursuing these alone may risk more harmful isomorphic mimicry[1] or simply the continuation of today's ineffective approaches.

However, while governments strive toward ideal policies and outcomes, there is

also potential to make important progress through more feasible "scaffolding" reforms—policies that help address barriers to wholesale reforms by offering a transitional path to better outcomes. This scaffolding may appear to be a second-best approach when the range of binding constraints are not taken into account, but it may constitute a first-best option when binding constraints and more complex policy goals are considered. As certain constraints are relaxed during the transition, the returns to other reforms may also change, meaning that careful thought as to the sequencing and coordination of reforms is important.

This chapter therefore puts forward options for a transitional path to unlock the potential of cities, people, and regions in the Middle East and North Africa. The region's cities have underperformed as engines of national growth, job creation, and social inclusion, but reforms within cities—as well as connections between cities and the global markets able to fuel their growth—can raise their performance.

The transitional path must also unlock people's potential by delivering globally competitive skills that grant access to better jobs and places and by directly addressing welfare disparities. A transition that develops the potential of all subregions requires a more appropriate tailoring of policy to the needs and potentials of each place, supported by local governments with the capacity to plan and deliver reforms in a manner sensitive to these local conditions. Taking these agendas together, a key insight is that economic growth, social inclusion, and regional equity are not mutually exclusive but can be supported by the same set of reforms.

## Transitional Step 1: Adopt new, evidence-based criteria to guide spatial interventions

Earlier chapters have highlighted something of a paradox in spatial development across the Middle East and North Africa: There have been heavy public investments, incentives, and regulations to direct firms to lagging, less-developed regions instead of leading cities. However, as also documented earlier, these have often failed to deliver better outcomes for those regions, with leading cities retaining stronger productivity, firm density, public services, business environments, and wages relative to workers' skills.

This is partially explained by the economic advantages of leading cities, such as agglomeration economies and any natural advantages. However, uneven accountability across places may also play a role: capital cities tend to host the government and main power base, encouraging greater sensitivity to local needs, while lagging regions often face weak structures for representation and accountability as well as lower local government capacity. As a result, investments in lagging regions are often highly visible but tokenistic, failing to address the key local bottlenecks or opportunities.

This transitional step presents a framework for more effective strategies to support lagging regions, while Transitional Step 2 concerns higher-level policies to improve the accountability and performance of local government.

## Adopt a framework for effective policies in lagging areas

Three dimensions are key to understanding the success and failure of regional development policies across the Middle East and North Africa: density, distance, and divisions (World Bank 2009). One of the most important factors for productive firms and workers is access to large, diverse markets. This market access is affected by the combination of

- *Density,* referring to the concentration of economic activity and people in the location (such as a large, dense city);
- *Distance,* referring to access to external markets (either domestic or abroad), such as through transport networks and proximity; and
- *Divisions,* referring to additional divisions—such as language barriers, conflicts, or ethnic divisions—that may fragment markets despite physical connectivity or density and hence require an additional, tailored response.

This market access cannot be equalized across space. Density arises because agglomeration economies cluster economic activity in space—implying, in turn, that other places have relatively low density and that the overall economic landscape is "lumpy." What's more, the value of proximity increases the returns to the scale of dense places, creating a certain momentum to density and consequently a challenge to reverse it and spread jobs and production more evenly across space. Reflecting this dynamic, as shown in chapter 1, spatial concentration in the Middle East and North Africa strongly reflects historical agglomerations.

As for distance, natural advantages (such as coasts and borders) and the costs of extending connective infrastructure also ensure inequality in connectivity to external markets. And divisions within populations can result in marginalization of certain groups; such groups may require further interventions to overcome division.

*Tailor policies according to the local mix of density and distance*

Territorial policies should try to raise market access in appropriate ways while also being sensitive to each place's degree of market access and attendant economic and social potential. Policies with high returns in a dense and well-connected place may have no, or negative, impacts in an isolated, sparse location. Meanwhile, locally dense but poorly connected locations may have different needs. This basic idea can inform a framework for more evidence-based policy making.

### Lagging regions with low market access

In regions with low market access—including low local density and weak external connectivity—policy should prioritize addressing institutional bottlenecks and the quality of basic services. Sparse, isolated locations have both weak local markets and weak connectivity to other markets, limiting their productive efficiency and attractiveness to investors. Investments in heavy productive or connective infrastructure often have low returns given low demand from either the small local population or from external investors.

The provision of basic services and core institutional functions are priorities, however, being the foundations for both quality of life and private sector development. Strengthening the local business environment and related institutions can remove barriers to whatever private sector job creation potential is present. National institutional functions like progressive taxation, transfers, and social services are also critical to redistribute the gains of economic concentration elsewhere to these less advantaged areas and ensure universal basic service provision—which not only contributes to human welfare directly but also equips people with better human capital to pursue income opportunities across space, addressing the challenges of "stuck" people discussed in chapter 2.

Governments across the Middle East and North Africa have committed themselves to

pursuing spatial equity in living standards. Recent national plans or government programs for Jordan, Morocco, Saudi Arabia, and Tunisia specifically highlight the importance of reducing such imbalances. The development strategies and national plans of most of the region's countries echo the priorities of enhancing welfare, improving quality and efficiency of service delivery, and increasing equality across regions. The objectives and pillars of the Vision 2030 strategies recently released by Algeria, the Arab Republic of Egypt, Iraq, Qatar, and the United Arab Emirates all emphasize these aspects.

However, sparse, isolated, and otherwise lagging areas would benefit from strengthened attention and tailored approaches to deliver equity in basic services and institutions. The provision of more basic services and infrastructure (such as sanitation, education, and access to rural markets) has outsize impacts on quality of life and economic dynamism in places where their initial provision was low—although, even here, it must be tailored to demand and affordability (Agénor, Nabli, and Yousef 2005).

In addition, although service delivery is a priority everywhere, its challenges and appropriate solutions manifest differently in different locations.[2] Remote rural areas may require more novel "last mile" solutions to service delivery (box 6.1), whereas certain dense urban areas require highly adaptive systems to accommodate rapid population changes. It is important to disaggregate statistics about delivery and outcomes across places to identify pockets of higher deprivation or stress, set an agenda for regional convergence, and identify the tailored local policies required for convergence. This should consider that the biggest challenge for service delivery across the Middle East and North Africa concerns quality rather than access to services: frequent blackouts, shortage of medical supplies, ineffective pedagogy, widespread absenteeism of doctors and teachers, and so on.

BOX 6.1 **Spatially sensitive "last mile" education provision**

Sparse rural areas of the Middle East and North Africa face challenges of small scale and high transport costs, challenging their ability to deliver basic services to all citizens, such as quality basic education. Spatially tailored solutions may be required to achieve universal targets in service delivery, as demonstrated in international examples of solutions to deliver basic education in such locations.

School clustering leverages economies of scale between small schools. In the Catalonia region of Spain, clustered schools share teachers who travel between the different rural schools in the cluster. Each cluster is coordinated by a common management body, including a cluster principal. This system helps overcome the high costs of specialized teachers in rural areas (World Bank 2016a). In the Middle East and North Africa, school clustering could address the serious shortage of male science and math teachers in rural areas.

In other isolated areas (such as mountainous areas of Bhutan), boarding becomes increasingly common at higher levels of education, at which schools require a certain scale to teach specialized subjects, and students are mature enough to thrive while living away from home.

### Lagging but dense regions with higher market access

Compared with a sparser area, a lagging region with a large, dense population has relatively strong local market access, raising its potential productivity. Given this, it is important to diagnose the remaining bottlenecks to stronger growth and job creation. These may include institutional weaknesses and human capital, as in sparse lagging areas. However, these locations also often lag because of their dislocation from external markets, such as leading domestic cities or global markets that might otherwise offer strong opportunities for trade and growth. If so, investments in connectivity to mitigate the effects of distance from markets can be transformative.

To avoid adverse consequences, however, connective investments must be tailored to local demand and density. It is important to avoid overinvestment not matched by demand, which not only has low returns but also creates stranded assets whose high recurrent operations and maintenance costs often fall on the targeted area. Diagnostics must also assess whether connectivity is indeed the binding constraint to local productivity. This is essential because connectivity operates in two directions—improving the target location's access to markets to sell products but also exposing the location to greater competition from outside (box 6.2). Broadly speaking, sectors that were already competing with imports from other locations, and failing to export elsewhere, tend to struggle under this greater competition and may decline, while sectors that were already "exporting" to the connected locations tend to benefit from this improved access and hence grow. A lagging area with few competitive exporting sectors compared with import-competing sectors can decline absolutely following a connective investment (Duranton and Venables 2018).

### Avoid reliance on high-stakes, place-based interventions

Certain policies place particularly high bets on the productive potential of a targeted location, investing a large amount in fixed immobile capital or tax incentives. These policies include industrial parks, special economic zones (SEZs), generous regional tax incentives, or industrial location directives and land-use policies forcing sectors to the target location. In the Middle East and North Africa, governments have sometimes invested heavily in such capital-intensive place-based policies in lagging areas that lack the underlying conditions for success. This may be motivated by the urgency of local need such as persistent local challenges of unemployment or poverty,

BOX 6.2    **Do cheap land and labor create opportunities for lagging regions?**

Strategies to promote industry in lagging regions often assume that firms can be attracted by cheap local land, labor, and so on. The assumption is that local prices will adjust to compensate for weaknesses in the local economy. However, local prices do not simply adjust to meet demand, because many factors of importance to firms can move from the lagging area, in search of higher returns elsewhere. Low local wages, for example, attract firms but also repel workers, who may relocate to leading areas where returns to their skills are higher. Finance and machinery can also typically relocate in search of higher prices. Thus, rather than factor prices simply adjusting to competitive levels in lagging regions, the supply of factors may also fall, allowing absolute decline in the local economy (Duranton and Venables 2018).

Opportunities for lagging and disadvantaged areas remain, however, thanks to immobile factors.

The price of factors that *cannot* move across space will adjust according to demand. This includes costs of land, preexisting built structures like buildings and infrastructure, and any less-mobile labor (such as workers who are less educated or who face divisions preventing migration such as language barriers, lack of social networks across space, cultural norms, and so on). Disadvantaged areas will likely struggle to grow industries that rely heavily on mobile assets like skilled workers, but they are more likely to have a competitive edge in sectors that are intensive in more immobile factors—such as agriculture and low-skill activities. Relatedly, as documented in *World Development Report 2009*, as land and unskilled labor prices climb in leading cities, the opportunities for secondary or lagging areas to benefit from spillover growth often increase as cheap land and unskilled labor become relatively more important to firms (World Bank 2009).

---

divisions that prevent people from accessing opportunities elsewhere (stuck people), regional risks to national stability or security, and so on. It may also stem from more political motivations—such as a squeaky wheel syndrome whereby a region of largely historical importance retains an outsize voice in the national government today.

Sometimes strategies to spread jobs and growth to lagging regions are criticized as inefficient because of their relatively small direct impacts. However, appraisals should not overlook the indirect effects of such policies on outcomes of concern (such as unemployment, poverty, stability, and security).

However, even considering indirect impacts, these investments have rarely met their objectives in locations that lack strong market access in the form of both major local agglomerations (proximity to dynamic cities) and strong connectivity to international export markets. Similarly, impacts have been poor when hard place-based investments are not complemented by the building blocks mentioned earlier: institutions, basic infrastructure and services, and human capital.

In general, outcomes would be improved by reduced reliance on these high-stakes, place-based policies. Such policies can instead be mobilized as a final nudge once the targeted location's underlying competitiveness is secured through more foundational institutional reforms, local agglomeration economies, and external connectivity (figure 6.1).

The components of figure 6.1 should be understood as building blocks. Even in a place with a high agglomeration of firms and people, capital-intensive place-based industrial policies (as described above) are likely to fail without the foundations of strong institutions, adequate human capital, and strong connectivity to markets for their products. Likewise, if connectivity to a large market is delivered to a place that lacks quality institutions and human capital, then, as discussed above, the outcome may be increased importation of goods and services without parallel exports and hence the gradual loss of people and firms to the larger market. Effective policies for the development of lagging areas are both multidimensional and properly sequenced.

FIGURE 6.1    **Framework for effective spatial policy in the Middle East and North Africa, from foundations to final steps**

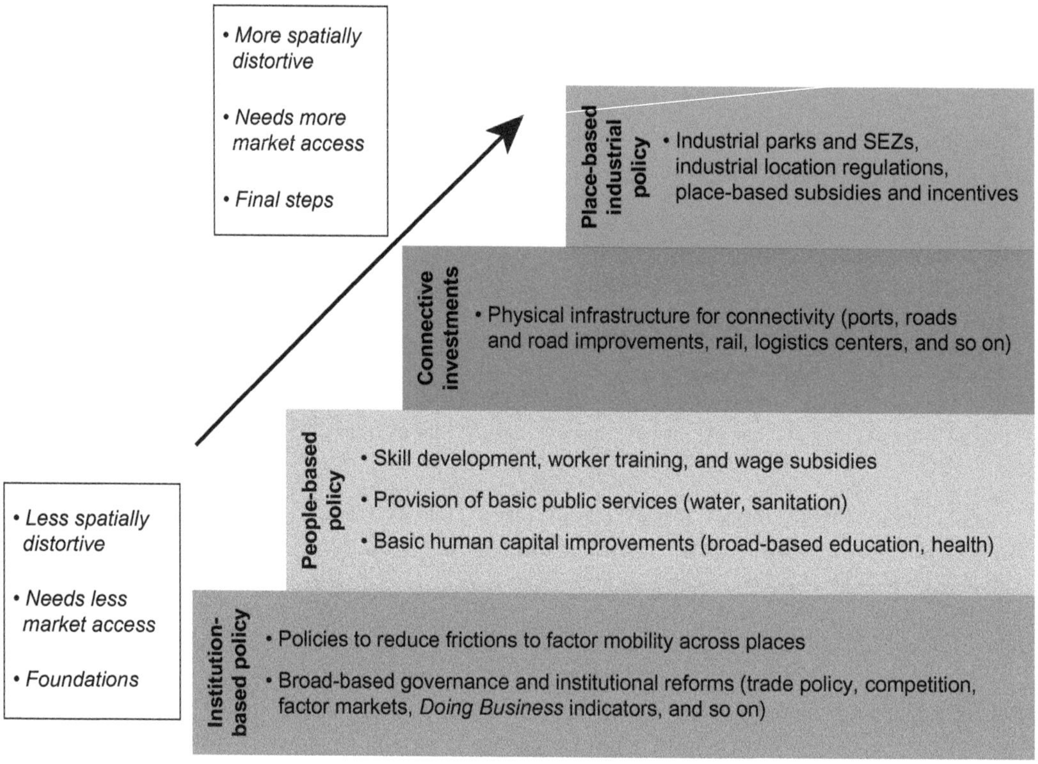

Source: Adapted from World Bank 2009.
Note: SEZs = special economic zones.

## Improve the outcomes of place-based policies

The above framework recommends a sequential approach to support lagging areas, differentiated by the market access and productive potential of each place. Three principles can help to identify strategies that avoid the common pitfalls of place-based policies and successfully tap the available local potential: (a) account for complements, (b) coordinate across places, and (c) focus on market failures.

### Account for complements

When investment is not flowing into a region, it is typically the result of not one but several disadvantages. The need for multiple factors to be in place in a location can create a weakest-link problem, where the absence of just one critical factor (such as security, access to external markets, or the ability to obtain land or a business license) prevents private investment despite heavy public investments in some dimensions of competitiveness. Chapter 4 discussed this problem, documenting particularly low returns to infrastructure investments in the Middle East and North Africa, likely because infrastructure is planned without important complements that address the remaining weakest links.

The importance of complementarities and the risk of weakest links often leads policy makers to consider big-push efforts for lagging areas, investing heavily across multiple areas to ensure that every possible complement is accounted for. However, successful big pushes were not indiscriminate, place-blind programs to spark investment by fiat. Instead, they were often oriented around a big local opportunity and addressed precise bottlenecks preventing its realization. For instance, arguably the most celebrated big push—the Tennessee Valley Authority (TVA) programs in the United States after the

Great Depression—focused on exploiting the potential for cheap local hydropower due to powerful local rivers and booming national industrialization as well as on managing attendant risks and constraints (flooding, barriers to navigation of the rivers, and environmental degradation of farmland). The wider package of complements came in behind this more strategic, focused push to heighten impacts.

Big pushes can also demand huge spending levels to see returns; even granted positive effects, their cost-effectiveness is often questionable. The TVA cost approximately

10 percent of local income for several years, while the greatest poverty reduction in the region was in fact attributable to a more natural process of urbanization (Duranton and Venables 2018). The case of the Tanger Mediterranean Port (Tanger-Med) in Morocco tells a similar story, where a big push strategically targeted a big opportunity—modernizing the port to connect Tangier to international markets—and complementary investments addressed the remaining bottlenecks revealed by consultations with the local business community (box 6.3).

---

BOX 6.3   **Big bottleneck or big opportunity: Targeted place-based policies in Afghanistan and Morocco**

### One big bottleneck in Afghanistan: Security

Afghanistan has considered constructing special economic zones (SEZs) in former military air bases. This fragile and conflict-affected state enjoys good access to power and a well-connected location, but of course, security and gaps in infrastructure have been major concerns. The military bases had been particularly well serviced with infrastructure and could also provide a more secure environment for firms. In this way, the SEZ construction targets a precise remaining major bottleneck.

### One big opportunity in Morocco: Tanger-Med Port

Nestled on the Strait of Gibraltar, Tangier occupies a strategic location for international trade and valuable shipping routes, but it had been neglected for many years and was relatively peripheral to the Moroccan economy by the late 1990s.

Aiming to support stronger development in northern Morocco, the government undertook a range of national reforms and local development efforts to capitalize on Tangier's potential, centered on opening Tangier to international trade while developing local productive capacities. Central to this was the development of the Tanger Mediterranean Port (Tanger-Med) in 2002 at a cost of €1 billion (Ducruet, Mohamed-Chérif, and Cherfaoui 2011), complemented by national reforms including free trade agreements, open skies agreements for airline travel, and relaxed investment and visa regimes.

Between 2005 and 2012, Tangier created new jobs three times as fast as Morocco as a whole. The manufacturing sector enjoyed 28 percent employment growth from 2002 to 2004 and an annual increase of investment of 13.2 percent. The strategy has also supported a deepening of backward linkages, diversification of the

local and regional economy (including strengthening tourism), and increased production in manufacturing-intensive sectors such as the automotive industry (Ducruet, Mohamed-Chérif, and Cherfaoui 2011). Given the increase of employment, a new city between Tangier and Tétouan is being developed, with investment committed for housing developments.

Such success is rare among regional development efforts, so what made the difference in Tangier?

- *The project centered on a big untapped opportunity*: access to international markets.
- *Closely informed by the private sector, the project was effectively coordinated* between the relevant public and private stakeholders. A strong public-private partnership known as the Tanger-Med Special Agency (TMSA) instilled collaboration across private and public actors throughout the development of the strategy and coordinated the actions of various government agencies. Further, regional government actors built their own communication and feedback loops between private and public actors throughout the life cycle of implementation.
- *The resulting strategy was multidimensional*, addressing not only the port but also the essential complements for its success. These included national reforms promoting liberalized trade, investment, and migration; national transport infrastructure for roads and rail; local free trade zones for industry and logistics; training and education of the local workforce; city regeneration through activities such as improved water supply and waste management, protection of green spaces, cultural heritage, and beaches; and modernization of the old port for cruise ships.

*Sources:* Bismil 2018; Kulenovic 2015.

The examples of the TVA and Tanger-Med highlight the positive side of the weakest-link problem: in a lagging area with major latent advantages, an intervention that diagnoses and closely targets the remaining bottlenecks can unlock disproportionately large benefits. Overall, the importance of complementarities often entails high discontinuities in the impacts of place-based policies, with the chance of no returns to heavy investments when weakest links are not addressed but also the opportunity for transformation with the right intervention targeted at the remaining big bottleneck and opportunity.

One low-risk, high-return approach to the delivery of complements is to better coordinate existing activities. Different line ministries and national, regional, and local governments should coordinate their activities locally to better exploit complementarities between investments (box 6.4). For example, if an industrial zone is planned, it should be easily accessible from good highways and well serviced by power by the time of completion, and so industrial zone, power, and highway plans should be coordinated. Addressing local human capital deficits may require coordination on school reform, housing and social support, internet connectivity, and so on.

*Ensure horizontal coordination*

Coordination across localities is also essential to optimize returns to place-based policy. For a local leader, a policy is effective if it brings jobs and investment to that leader's own locality at reasonable costs to the local government. However, despite these positive local impacts, a policy or investment may worsen outcomes for another competing place. Consider, for instance, offering tax incentives that attract firms from one region to another: this benefits the implementing locality but harms the city from which firms and people leave. And if the implementing locality is a less efficient place for those firms to produce, it also harms overall job creation and growth nationally.

Without coordination across local governments, their individual efforts at local economic development can become a race to the bottom—a costly fiscal competition in spending and taxes to attract firms to their locations that entails high waste on a national level. An uncoordinated strategy where each locality tries to attract the most and best firms can also impede the development of agglomerations by scattering firms' incentives across space. Thus, overall, when place-based policies are combined, they often lead to a national framework with considerable wastage and inconsistency as well as missed opportunities to work together to develop scale and specialization across places. There is a need to reconcile agendas across subnational units, and between subnational and national governments, so that all pull in the same direction in the country's best interests. Transitional Step 2 discusses practical options for such coordination.

---

**BOX 6.4**  **Industrial zones in Egypt: Suffering a lack of density and complements**

Egypt's industrial zones have often provided subsidized land to industry, but many lack the complements needed for productivity. Several of Egypt's industrial zones were not located on major roads to connect them to local markets or ports, which implies that zones will either remain poorly accessible or entail high costs to retroactively connect them to markets.

Some of the roads between Cairo and industrial zones in the "new towns" built in the deserts surrounding Greater Cairo were also inadequately planned, meaning that routes from Cairo to the towns are seriously congested. The industrial zones have also often lacked adequate infrastructure to complement the cheap land, because of coordination failures between agencies. Finally, investment facilitation services—standard in industrial zones worldwide and important to their success—are limited in Egypt's zones.

*Sources:* Sims 2015; World Bank 2016b.

*Address market failures*

Strategies for local economic development should focus on addressing market failures, simply because private firms will independently pursue a productive opportunity unless market failures are present. Many types of market failures can reduce local investment, including the following:

- *"First mover" problems* preventing the creation of new agglomerations
- *Gaps in factor markets* such as problems in property transfer, credit, and business registration

- *Coordination problems* impeding the private provision of shared infrastructure
- *Negative externalities* such as congestion and pollution in major cities
- *Incomplete information markets,* preventing investor or household knowledge about local potential.

The first mover problem implies that, to attract firms to lagging areas, governments have a role in coordinating expectations about where new firm clusters will develop (box 6.5). The importance of agglomeration economies means that many firms would not

---

### BOX 6.5 How the dynamics of large investors can justify government intervention

**Large investors in economic theory**

Private investments that are large relative to the local economy can drive up local factor prices (such as the costs of land and immobile labor). This benefits local owners of those factors (local landowners and immobile workers who enjoy higher wages), but it reduces the investor's own profits. Because some benefits of the investment are social and do not benefit the investor, some such investments can be forgone despite being socially beneficial.

In these circumstances, final-straw improvements that nudge the large investor just over the private profit threshold can have large social impacts: they unlock the previously forgone net social benefit as well as the newly available private marginal benefit to the investor. These impacts are demonstrated econometrically by Duranton and Venables (2018).

This potential creates a role for government to attract marginal large investors by capturing and returning a portion of the social benefits to the investor. An obvious case is a subsidy or tax incentive, though other mechanisms could involve local infrastructure or skills training relevant to the firm. However, correctly calibrating these mechanisms is challenging, and governments must always be wary of the risks of simply subsidizing uncompetitive, unsustainable industries, or as above, engaging in a destructive race to the bottom across localities.

**Large investors in practice: Hawassa Industrial Park, Ethiopia**

The example of Hawassa Industrial Park (HIP) in Ethiopia illustrates how a government might overcome first mover problems by attracting a catalytic large investor—in this case, Phillips-van Heusen (PVH), the world's second

largest apparel company. The government worked closely with PVH to identify areas of mutual interest and delivered them to create an attractive environment for PVH in the new Hawassa Industrial Park (HIP). They included

- *Demonstrating government commitment* by raising capital, building facilities fast, and delivering world-class factories with high environmental standards as agreed;
- *Delivering strong access to international markets* (particularly important for the fashion industry), including through the enterprise bargaining agreement (EBA), the 10-year extension of the African Growth and Opportunity Act (AGOA), streamlined customs procedures, extension of the new Djibouti–Addis Ababa rail line to Hawassa,[a] and improvement of the Addis Ababa–Kenya highway on which Hawassa lies;
- *Exploiting abundant hydropower* to undercut regional competitors in electricity price and reliability (electricity being a major cost in the garment industry);
- *Complementing the large pool of local labor* with employee selection and training programs run jointly by PVH, the government, and donors; and
- *Offering tax holidays,* described as "icing on the cake" rather than a key element.

Thanks to PVH's investment, 18 foreign and 5 domestic supplier companies have already committed to follow it to HIP, and more are expected. The park was inaugurated in July 2016 and is planned to create 60,000 direct jobs on US$1 billion in export sales.

*Source:* Adapted from Duranton and Venables 2018.
a. Hawassa is also referred to as Awasa or Awassa.

move to an underdeveloped lagging area without assurance that others would join them. This creates a first mover problem, which can cement existing agglomerations even where new agglomerations may be more efficient. Governments can help assure firms and households that others will move, such as by coordinating investors, addressing local bottlenecks, and publicizing these efforts; updating local plans and branding; attracting catalytic large private investors around whom other firms may coordinate; and so on.

Smaller shifts in agglomerations are easier to support than large ones. For example, Egypt's new towns performed far better when close to Cairo than in brand new, isolated desert locations. Another example would be encouraging the consolidation of an existing industrial cluster on better land within the same city or in a nearby satellite town.

Tax incentives and other subsidies are often used to attract investment to priority locations, citing first mover justifications among others. However, Gaubert (2018) and others have shown that tax incentives are typically low priorities for firms deciding where to locate, compared with factors more fundamental to productivity like market access and trade facilitation; basic infrastructure; and reliable, strong institutions. This means, in turn, that the exemptions and subsidies needed to attract firms are often very high. In addition, firms that chose a location because of tax incentives, rather than its broader suitability, tend to be less complementary to the local economy and create weak local spillovers (Gaubert 2018).

If used at all—in line with the earlier framework—evidence-based spatial-policy tax incentives or subsidies should be a final nudge to bring investors to an already competitive location. Tax incentives also need to be coordinated across localities given the risk of "beggar thy neighbor" tax competition and footloose firms that drive down the margin of social benefits by shopping for the best incentive package from each subnational government.

## Transitional Step 2: Devolve greater functional authority and resources for local revenue generation and service provision to local governments

Chapter 5 argued that to improve outcomes across the Middle East and North Africa's regions—particularly its lagging regions—there is a need to move "from the monumental to the incremental—away from top-heavy, state-centric models and toward more locally grounded, people-centric approaches" through the strengthening and empowerment of local government.

### Strengthen the capacity and effectiveness of local governance

This speaks to the importance of regional development policy that is sensitive to local needs. However, this local sensitivity is often in tension with two other essential qualities of effective local governance: scale economies and capacity, on the one hand, and horizontal coordination across locations on the other (Bahl 2008).

*Sensitivity to local needs.* Given the importance of sensitivity to local needs, the principle of *subsidiarity* asserts that government functions should be decentralized to the most local level available unless there is a particular argument for their allocation to higher levels. Whereas planning has often been disconnected from realities on the ground in the Middle East and North Africa, taking better advantage of local governments' proximity to the population can improve information about local needs and strengthen planning through better channels of accountability and feedback. Local populations and circumstances are also generally more homogeneous, enabling more tailored policies. Smaller local governments may also avoid the diseconomies of scale associated with the larger and more complex bureaucracies of many central governments, such as blocked channels of communication, a lack of agility, onerous procedures, and slow decision making and responsiveness. These factors give reason to move from highly centralized governance in many regional contexts.

*Scale and capacity.* However, more-local authorities tend to suffer capacity and efficiency challenges due to their small scale. This is particularly so in the Middle East and North Africa, where many local authorities have been subdivided (resulting in very low scale) and suffer from historic underresourcing and weak institutional frameworks. Small-scale authorities have less capacity to hire skilled and specialized staff (as documented in chapter 5) or to invest in thorough research and planning processes. In addition, certain public functions (such as major hospitals, universities, railways, or industrial zones) are only efficient when undertaken at scale (given a need for specialized inputs or large capital investments and other fixed costs), making provision by small local units inefficient and infeasible.

*Coordination of external effects.* Small local authorities may also fail to properly manage the external effects of their actions, to the detriment of wider regional and national development. Investments, policies, economic activities, and so on in one area often have external impacts on other areas. Some are positive—such as when a district that hosts a vibrant city benefits surrounding districts as a source of jobs and services.

Others are negative—such as pollution, congestion, or a race to the bottom in local tax competition. In either case, fragmented local authorities without dedicated coordination frameworks often fail to control negative spillovers or jointly develop shared assets and may engage in wasteful "beggar thy neighbor" competition.

As argued in chapter 5, in contrast to the principle of subsidiarity, the default in many Middle East and North Africa governments (particularly in the Gulf Cooperation Council [GCC] and Mashreq subregions) is the centralization of political, administrative, and financial powers and structures—leading to planning that lacks adequate sensitivity to local needs and conditions. This has been problematic for efforts aimed at local economic development, for example, which requires sensitivity to local conditions to address the key local bottlenecks, as noted earlier.

Decentralization, however, needs to be sensitive to how scale economies and coordination challenges affect local governments and the functions they must perform. Effective decentralization is often therefore both incremental and asymmetric, tailored to the varying capacities and needs of different localities. Decentralization efforts also need to improve scale and capacity, coordination, and local accountability structures (box 6.6).

---

**BOX 6.6**   **Instruments to improve scale and coordination among local governments**

### Vertical coordination: France's State-Region Plan Contracts

In France, binding contracts between regions and the central government promote effective region-led planning while aligning efforts of the local and central government. State-Region Plan Contracts (CPERs) have been implemented in France since the mid-1980s. These are five- to seven-year agreements between the national government and the regions (the highest level of local government) to deliver the region's highest-priority development projects.

CPERs are coordination tools: they do not make new resources available; rather, preexisting resources (from the region and the state) are aligned around the priorities set. The central government delineates broad categories of projects that are eligible for CPERs, within which regional governments propose their own priority projects, increasing the coherence and complementarity of regional plans. The national and regional governments legally engage jointly to deliver the projects, agreeing on their financing, delivery modalities and agencies, beneficiaries, selection criteria, and results indicators. CPERs can also coordinate

*box continues next page*

actors beyond the regional and central governments—such as sectoral line ministries, national transport agencies, cross-regional bodies, and subregional bodies (such as metropolitan areas or nature areas)—that often cosign CPERs.

Contracts between states and regions give the regions considerable responsibility to deliver on the agreed-upon goals: the regions must contribute a large part of plans' financing, and if implementation of any contracted project is not begun within 18 months, it is cancelled automatically.

Overall, CPERs promote strong bottom-up planning sensitive to local needs while aligning efforts and resources among national and regional actors. Other countries have since adopted similar systems inspired by this model, such as Colombia's *contratos plans*. An innovation of the *contratos plans* is that several local authorities can cooperate to sign the same state-region contract.

### Horizontal coordination for broad local planning and management: England's combined authorities

In England, groups of local authorities can submit proposals to form joint combined authorities. These exist above the level of the local authorities and are often formed to improve the management of major cities and their surrounding metro and rural areas, which otherwise spill across administrative boundaries. Combined authorities conduct functions benefiting from shared planning across the region, such as regional economic planning, overseeing regional transit services, and investing in innovation hubs or industrial parks. Based on their needs and performance, combined authorities negotiate for incrementally greater decentralized powers and responsibilities, through a sustained dialogue with the central government.

### Horizontal coordination for narrow functions: France's EPCI and Finland's municipal coordination

The different functions local governments must perform often have geographies, not aligned with administrative boundaries, such as those of a district, region, or city. For example, a particular group of scattered municipalities hosting heritage sites may benefit from collaboration for preservation and tourism promotion; a different group along a river basin may benefit from collaboration for environmental management,

irrigation, river-based trade facilitation, and economic development initiatives; and a final group may consist of municipalities within a city as well as a wider catchment area (such as the commuting span) not within the city boundaries. Because spillovers and coordination needs do not always align with administrative boundaries and vary with the geography of each function, local governments in the Middle East and North Africa may benefit from instruments for flexible and function-specific collaboration or coordination.

An example is the French public institution of intercommunal cooperation (Établissement Public de Coopération Intercommunale, EPCI)—a flexible instrument through which municipalities can collaborate to perform either a single narrow function (such as local water supply) or broader functions (such as city management or, for a more rural area, complementary environmental, tourism, training, and social and economic development activities).

Finland's municipalities play the major role in local administration in Finland but suffer from very low scale, which motivated a 2005 reform—the Project to Restructure Local Government and Services (PARAS)—to raise the scale of local governance. For example, municipalities are responsible for the design, provision, and oversight of all health and social care.[a] Yet in 2008, the average municipality had just 4,700 inhabitants. Demographic and migration pressures added to the pressures on municipal services and finances, with several municipalities facing declining working-age populations alongside an increased number of elderly requiring care. The PARAS reform encouraged municipalities to merge and cooperate to achieve greater scale economies to meet these mounting challenges. Mergers were voluntary but encouraged through large financial incentives.

Through these voluntary mergers, the number of municipalities fell from 444 in 2005 to 320 by 2015. In addition, it is compulsory for municipalities to form joint bodies to finance and manage certain functions requiring major scale economies—including universities, central hospitals, disabled people's services, and regional councils. Cooperation on other aspects of service provision is optional. Overall, joint municipal bodies have been popular, with each municipality a member of approximately 5–10 intermunicipal bodies.

*Source:* World Bank 2019.
a. "The Kainuu Regional Experiment," Ageing Studio (2010) Dossier, Helsinki Design Lab archive, http://helsinkidesignlab.org/dossiers/ageing/kainuu.html.

Regarding capacity, local authorities must be properly resourced to carry out their decentralized functions. This includes own-source revenues, and central-to-local transfers. Relevant areas for fiscal decentralization include increasing local governments' control over fees to cover service costs and decentralizing land and property tax regimes and administration. Central-to-local government transfers also require greater transparency, predictability, and more equitable formulas, particularly in the Mashreq subregion. As argued in chapter 5, transparency and predictability are important to counteract spatial biases in spending and outcomes, while in many cases, formulas also need revision to reduce the bias toward resource-rich locations and better target poverty in lagging regions.

However, financial resources alone are insufficient. Many local governments fail to spend and execute the limited budgets they possess. Any reform should clarify the division of responsibilities for each level of government and otherwise coordinate the local and national activities affecting each region.

Overall, expanding the scale of local governance may be important in the Middle East and North Africa, where authorities have been highly fragmented. This can be achieved through consolidation (reducing the number of local governments, as by incentivizing local governments to merge) as well as through coordination between authorities. The latter might involve incentivizing local authorities to form joint bodies, either for larger tasks such as metropolitan management and regional planning or for narrower service-delivery tasks (for example, Finland's requirement that municipalities cooperate to jointly deliver services subject to large-scale economies).

## Ensure local accountability for service delivery

Service delivery challenges in the Middle East and North Africa's local governments are not purely technical but intertwined with the domestic political economy. The link between local governments and their residents and businesses is not always functional. Many of the region's governments have been pursuing relevant reforms, such as the adoption of transparent and performance-based recruitment and pay systems. The process of building accountability is complex, however, and transitional measures may be required to improve the quality of local service delivery while it is developed.

An alternative source of accountability is between residents and private sector organizations. In a competitive market, clients can directly hold private providers accountable through their purchasing choices. Private providers may also address gaps in capacity and financing. However, the private sector requires proper government oversight and regulation, as illustrated in two examples from the Republic of Yemen and Kenya (box 6.7).

Community management and monitoring can also hold frontline delivery agents directly to account. For example, the School and District Development Program in Jordan has supported community-managed schools through appointment of a domain leader who uses input from stakeholders (parents, students, and teachers) to design the school improvement plan and submit it to the local education council. The program has resulted in better learning outcomes (Brixi, Lust, and Woolcock 2015), as have school monitoring programs in Egypt and Morocco (Beddies et al. 2011).

Citizen participation can also improve local government performance through both accountability and information channels. Incorporating the opinions of residents and businesses may take time and require extra resources up front but can help ensure that service provision has the desired impacts. Local businesses, for example, usually know very well what infrastructural bottlenecks are hindering their daily operations, such as lack of road connectivity or stable electricity supply (Australian Embassy and Asia Foundation 2016).

---

**Government-regulated private sector service delivery in the Republic of Yemen and Kenya**

**A partnership for water delivery in the Republic of Yemen**

In the Republic of Yemen, a considerable water supply gap is being filled by private wells and water tanker trucks. Typically, urban or peri-urban wells sell water to tankers, which then deliver the water to urban households. However, this arrangement raises serious questions about water quality, pricing, and sustainable water resource management.

The World Bank has implemented a pilot program to create a private partnership with water tankers in Sana'a. In this program, private tanker trucks sign a contract with local water corporations and deliver water from wellfields managed by local water corporations to customers at affordable prices. This approach helps increase supply and raise scale economies, brings down costs, and serves as an entry point to more sustainable use of water resources while also developing more effective regulation of water quality (World Bank 2017a, 2017b).

**A franchise model for clinics in Kenya**

In Kenya, the Child and Family Wellness Clinic has implemented a franchise model since 1997. The model provides clinic and pharmacy franchises with business incentives to both comply with regulations and provide high-quality, affordable health services (World Bank 2017c). Private clinics or pharmacies in the network have access to a cost-effective drug and medical equipment supply chain as well as incentives to retain customers, while regulations require all participating clinics to follow standardized medical procedures.

## Transitional Step 3: Step away from credentialist education and toward schooling that cultivates globally tradable skills

Citizens of the Middle East and North Africa will benefit most from trade integration if they possess the skills to compete for and secure high-quality jobs in a global marketplace. Human capital is also critical for the knowledge spillovers responsible for much of the dynamism and productivity of cities as well as to empower people in sparse and lagging areas to migrate to opportunities.

However, as documented in chapter 2, the region's citizens underperform in the technical and problem-solving skills required to be competitive in global labor markets. A World Bank flagship report on education in the Middle East has diagnosed four underlying tensions that need to be addressed to improve outcomes in the region on the scale required (El-Kogali and Krafft 2019):

- *Credentials and skills:* Greater employer demand for skills can raise students', parents', and other stakeholders' demand for education that confers those skills. Raising demand for education may require policy makers to address barriers to private sector job creation, such as by reducing the dominance of public employment and addressing the disparity in wages and conditions between the public and private sectors. In addition, exam reform to ensure that test scores better reflect skills can make paper credentials a better signal of real skills for employers.

- *Discipline and inquiry:* Curriculum reform and teacher training are needed to raise students' engagement (and reduce passivity) as well as to ensure that memorization of facts (dominant in many systems) is properly complemented by critical thinking and other skills.

- *Tradition and modernity:* In certain Middle East and North Africa countries (such as Jordan and Kuwait), such curriculum reforms have received deep criticism—for reflecting imported values and undermining national character or religious identity. Reforms should not import foreign systems but rather assess the effectiveness of current teaching in conferring the desired opportunities to the next generation and incrementally adjust accordingly.

- *Control and autonomy:* A greater decentralization of authority to schools and teachers can potentially increase local ownership while also addressing challenges of low innovation, adaptation, and motivation in schools. Global evidence shows that assigning greater local authority to schools and teachers tends to raise outcomes but must be complemented by adequate local capacity, resources, and accountability, reflecting the broader lesson of Transitional Step 2.

Building out from these underlying tensions, the report offers specific practical recommendations: (a) closing the spatial and demographic gaps in educational access and outcomes; (b) targeting preprimary enrollment; (c) focusing on foundational learning skills; (d) improving teacher performance; and (e) engaging the private sector to increase work-relevant skills.

*Closing gaps in educational access and outcomes.* Human capital outcomes—and their returns on the labor market—are not equal across regions, neighborhoods, classes, and genders. A focus is needed on diagnosing these disparities and tailoring policy to address them. Subnational variations in educational inputs and human capital outcomes should be systematically monitored and used to inform targeted investments for regional convergence, thus helping to ensure that regardless of where people are born, they can access productive opportunities and quality of life.

The Middle East and North Africa also displays above-average disparity in educational outcomes between richer and poorer students as well as high gender disparity. (Girls far outperform boys in many of the region's countries, but men nonetheless enjoy better returns to education in terms of access to job opportunities.)[3]

*Targeting preprimary enrollment.* Preprimary education is key to prepare students to learn in primary school. A priority is to address the region's low preprimary enrollment (30 percent gross, on average). The United Arab Emirates has demonstrated one reform path, targeting universal enrollment in its UAE Vision 2021, and is now on track to achieve 95 percent enrollment by 2021, complemented by investments in quality improvements.

*Focusing on foundational skills.* Standardized tests for literacy (such as the Early Grade Reading Assessment, or EGRA) and mathematics (such as the Trends in International Mathematics and Science Study, or TIMSS) show that students in the Middle East and North Africa tend to greatly underperform their global counterparts on core skills. An urgent focus on these foundational skills is needed in the first three years of school.

This agenda would be supported by aligning preprimary and primary education to ensure that children arrive in primary school ready to learn (also done in the United Arab Emirates) and to support students who are transitioning from local languages and dialects to Modern Standard Arabic. To sustain learning at higher levels, where instruction of certain subjects may be in English or French, many students will also need to develop a stronger foundation in these languages at the primary level.

*Improving teacher performance.* Shortcomings in teacher skills and pedagogy can be addressed through large strategic investments in professional development and by introducing greater sensitivity to pedagogical skills (over credentials) in teacher recruitment and promotion. Professional development should raise teachers' focus on inquiry and skills over discipline and examinations (to complement curricula reforms) and address teachers' own skill gaps, such as foreign language skills.

In addition, teacher motivation and accountability suffer from the centralization of hiring, firing, and promotion decisions; decentralizing autonomy over these decisions to schools may result in better incentives for performance and effort (through recognition and promotions) and better ability to manage poor behavior such as absenteeism. This devolution of responsibilities may benefit from complementary activities (such as training and the provision of frameworks and guidance) to raise schools' and districts' capacity to manage resources, staffing, curricula, and so on (Mansuri and Rao 2013).

*Increasing work-relevant skills.* Greater interaction between the school system and the private sector can improve the relevance of schooling and the school-to-work transition. Workplace training (such as apprenticeships, technical training, and internships for university students) can be employed to increase students' employability after graduation. In Tunisia, for example, introducing an entrepreneurship track that combines business training with personal coaching helped to reshape the business skills of university students (Valerio, Parton, and Robb 2014). Building partnerships between schools and the private sector can also close information gaps between the labor market and education by consulting on curriculums, providing internships and vocational training curricula, hosting job fairs, or providing career counseling (Gatti et al. 2013).

## Transitional Step 4: Renew the focus on nurturing urban agglomerations by streamlining land transfer procedures and relaxing zoning regulations in existing cities, lowering the regulatory barriers to their redevelopment

Much of the rapid growth and poverty reduction of the past century has taken place in, and been shepherded by, cities. Well-managed cities offer large, well-connected markets—for products, services, labor, jobs, and ideas—to firms and residents. This connectivity can greatly reduce the costs of a huge range of transactions, raising efficiency and productivity. Dense markets in turn enable firms to produce at scale and with higher specialization, two dynamics that are fundamental to productivity, economic growth, and job creation. Given the productivity-enhancing effect of cities, the concentration of firms and people in cities is not only beneficial for growth and inclusion but also inevitable.

The Middle East and North Africa is no exception. A high concentration of the region's population, and its poor, live in cities, where productivity and income opportunities are higher. However, chapters 1–4, outlined how several of the region's cities may be underperforming relative to their potential.

Modernist planning ideals have left cities fragmented internally and disconnected from the global economy. These modernist ideals are observed in the government-led development of new sites fragmented from the main, "messy" urban fabric and in regulations outlawing market-appropriate housing and commercial developments. The disjunction between top-down visions and standards and bottom-up market demand and purchasing power has been accompanied, on the one hand, by underused, expensive developments—such as the largely uninhabited new towns of Egypt, Morocco, Saudi Arabia, and the United Arab Emirates (for instance, Abu Dhabi's Masdar City)—and, on the other hand, by the proliferation of informality as stifled markets try to breathe.

These planning practices tend to raise the costs and reduce the connectivity of the Middle East and North Africa's cities, limit the exploitation of productive opportunities at a cost to job creation, and prevent the market from meeting households' needs. As a result, large numbers of residents unable to meet the elevated costs are forced into informal homes and jobs, where a vicious cycle of poverty and social segregation follows. Weak connectivity, high costs of living and doing business, and heavy restrictions on productive activities prevent scarce urban land from being used most productively, reduce efficiency and job creation, and leave the region's cities less able to break into global tradables and stuck in a model of "consumption cities."

How can these patterns be reversed? An important strategy is to move away from modernist planning ideals and work with private sector demand for positive urban density. This does not demand an acceptance of urban chaos; indeed, disorderly informal housing and jobs have been the result of planning that is out of sync with demand. Rather, it means supporting a market-led urban density and affordability that creates space in the formal economy for lower-income residents and firms and ensures their access to the basic services required for their productivity and well-being. The role of the government versus the private sector would be adjusted, with governments identifying and getting behind emerging density and demand to provide the complementary public goods and services that support productivity and avert the downsides of density such as congestion, pollution, contagion, and crime. Specifically, this reorientation would include the following:

- *Reviewing city master plans* to encourage market-led density, connectivity, and affordability
- *Diagnosing and shedding unnecessary, distortive, or infeasible planning codes and regulations* (such as building standards, industrial location directives, and zoning regulations) that may be stifling affordability, densification, productivity, and adaptability of the city
- *Prioritizing in situ upgrading of basic neighborhood and trunk infrastructure* in the urban core instead of focusing predominantly on greenfield development—ensuring that current neighborhoods have proper infrastructure for sanitation, floodproofing, street lighting, waste collection, and so on, as well as diagnosing the need for bus lanes, improved junctions, and wider traffic management
- *Identifying and planning the urban expansion area* and addressing incentives that encourage sprawl (such as more relaxed regulations in peripheral versus central areas and low central area attractiveness) while undergoing basic grid planning to ensure that any further expansion is orderly.

An ideal response may involve clarification of land and property ownership as well as wholesale reforms to land and property registration and transactions, building permitting, and business licensing. However, this will be a lengthy process for many countries, testing institutional capacities, while in others, vested interests and broader political sensitivities may pose insurmountable barriers to meaningful reform and modernization.[4]

Where the complete modernization of factor markets is unrealistic, important gains can nonetheless be made through incremental scaffolding reforms that lay the foundations for later modernization or tackle the most harmful bottlenecks. For example, land and property market modernization can be approached in bite-size chunks, such as first digitizing the existing cadaster and updating records incrementally, beginning with priority locations such as major commercial and industrial areas or important urban neighborhoods. Attaching more demanding land and property tax obligations to land and property ownership claims can also encourage owners themselves to clarify ownership.

Where broader reforms are not attainable, countries and regions have also used industrial parks and SEZs to create pockets of better-functioning land and property markets and wider business environment institutions. Others have forgone these benefits by applying the same or even more stringent regulations within industrial parks and hence failing to create attractive pockets of well-functioning institutions.

Although Transitional Step 4 focuses on city-level reforms, they will not alone create the growth and job creation needed in the Middle East and North Africa. Also key will be delivering more effective support to lagging areas (Transitional Step 1); making city management more responsive and effective (Transitional Step 2); strengthening human capital so workers are globally competitive (Transitional Step 3); and opening cities to the large global and regional markets that can sustainably fuel their growth (Transitional Step 5).

## Transitional Step 5: Expand market access for cities by thinning the "thick borders" that inhibit mobility across the Middle East and North Africa for both regional trade and migration

At present, the concentration of people and firms in the Middle East and North Africa's leading cities is unmatched by those cities' integration into larger external markets, because "thick borders" restrict critical input and output flows throughout the region (as examined in chapter 3). Yet regional and global integration—and the market access this brings—will be crucial to the economic dynamism of these cities.

Globally, firm and industry value chains are now increasingly spread across countries because of the falling costs of transport, communication, and data transfer. Manufacturing, but increasingly also services, has become more about specialized tasks within global or regional value chains than about finished products. This interindustry and intraindustry trade (rather than trade in final goods) is what has increased tremendously over the past half century, especially in East Asia, North America, and Western Europe. An example is the consumer technology cluster in East Asia, where China has done most of the assembly but high-tech inputs come from Japan or the Republic of Korea and some lower-tech ones from Southeast Asia (box 6.8).

### A country typology offers a general framework for market integration

Despite the formidable barriers to similar regional integration in the Middle East and North Africa, the stakes are too high to abandon efforts. A precondition for participation in these cross-national production networks has been countries' willingness to open their markets for inputs and outputs and reduce barriers to trade and to capital and labor flows.

*World Development Report 2009: Reshaping Economic Geography* outlined a framework to understand priorities for integration with external markets. Its starting point delineated three types of countries based on their relationships with world markets and large emerging markets (World Bank 2009):

- *Type 1 countries* are close to the leading world markets such as North America, Europe, and East Asia. Most of the Middle East and North Africa countries belong to this type, such as North African countries with European and global access via seaports.

- *Type 2 countries* have large emerging markets nearby but are far from world markets. These include the countries neighboring Brazil, China, India, the Russian Federation, and South Africa. Middle East and North Africa countries with relatively large neighboring economies can, with similar considerations, implement policies to tap into the growth potential of their dominant neighbor. This may apply, for example, to the Islamic Republic of Iran, Iraq, and the Syrian Arab Republic with respect to Turkey.

- *Type 3 countries* are in regions far from world markets and also lack large local emerging markets. These regions include Central Africa, Central Asia, East Africa, West Africa, and the small Pacific islands. The category also includes countries affected by conflicts or otherwise politically fragmented from world markets, as experienced in many Middle East and North Africa countries and regions. For instance, although Syria adjoins Turkey, its civil war has greatly reduced the chance to trade, and hence Syria is arguably temporarily in this third type. Likewise, the Republic of Yemen would fall into this category because conflict has fragmented it from trade opportunities.

*Type 1 countries: Align institutional reforms with international market standards*

The greatest opportunities come from the largest global markets. Where these are accessible (in Type 1 countries), the priority is

**BOX 6.8    How special economic zones supported China's incremental integration into global markets**

In the 1970s, the Chinese government had resolved to experiment with greater openness to global trade and free market institutions. Rather than liberalizing the entire economy—which was politically and institutionally infeasible at the time—China approached this process incrementally and experimentally. An early step was the introduction of four special economic zones (SEZs) in 1980, strategically located along the southeastern coast (Shenzhen, Zhuhai, and Shantou in Guangdong Province and Xiamen in Fujian Province) at China's gateway to the global economy (map B6.8.1, left panel).

Following the early success of these SEZs, 14 cities along the coast began to accept overseas investment in 1984, and the island of Hainan was assigned SEZ status in 1988 (map B6.8.1, middle panel). Around the same time, the coastal belt around the Yangtze and Pearl River Deltas and the Xiamen-Zhangzhou-Quanzhou Triangle in south Fujian Province opened for business with the world. In the early 1990s, the government opened another 11 border cities and 6 ports along the Yangtze River (map B6.8.1, right panel).

The developments reflected a strategy of incremental liberalization of ever-expanding pockets of the economy, building on positive experiences, which may offer lessons for challenging cases in the Middle East and North Africa where full liberalization is infeasible.

Several countries have tried to replicate China's success but misinterpreted its success factors and merely placed cookie-cutter, infrastructure-heavy economic zones in targeted lagging regions. China's strategy succeeded because it closely targeted a specific and major binding constraint in the local economy (being closed to foreign investment and featuring illiberal economic institutions) and located the SEZs in places with strong access to global markets. China's accompanying economic boom and significant poverty reduction have been intensely concentrated in these advantaged coastal locations, while sparsely populated inland places remain much less economically dynamic.

MAP B6.8.1    **China gradually increased special economic zones from 1980 through the 1990s**

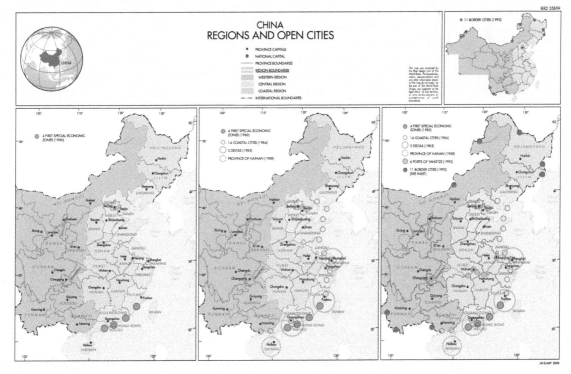

*Sources:* IBRD 35899, January 2008; World Bank 2009.

to align domestic institutions and regulations with the standards of the international market.

Countries close to world markets have a geographical advantage because multinational enterprises look to extend their supply chains to countries peripheral to the main markets served. These investors look, above all, for effective and transparent institutions and regulations, good and stable governance, a stable macroeconomy, and any relevant trade agreements. Therefore, such foundational institutional reforms are critical to unlock potential in such countries. This approach can be seen in the Middle East and North Africa, such as in select sectors in Morocco and Tunisia that integrated into global production chains via institutional reforms such as improved governance and alignment of quality standards and certification.

### Type 2 countries: Align infrastructure and regulations with large neighboring markets

Middle East and North Africa countries with a large neighboring market (Type 2) may wish to target integration with that neighbor. The largest regional markets are relatively well placed to attract global investment and can form hubs for regional supply chains, into which neighbors can be integrated through connective infrastructure, regulatory alignment, and broader trade and diplomatic agreements. This approach may be a priority for countries in the region with relatively low gross domestic product (GDP) and foreign investment but whose neighbors are well integrated in global supply chains, such as the countries bordering Turkey: the Islamic Republic of Iran, Iraq, and the Syrian Arab Republic.

However, regional integration among the region's countries is a complement, rather than an alternative, to deeper integration with other world regions. The Middle East and North Africa lacks a single dominant, reliable anchor economy in the region to serve as the gateway to international markets (in the way Western Europe served this role for Eastern Europe after 1990 or as

Japan and later Korea linked up with China and other Asian neighbors). Regional integration is important to compensate for the relatively small size of individual countries' economies and scaling-up capacity; to improve specialization and scale across the region; and to strengthen the Middle East and North Africa's basis to trade with the world. With this regional integration, the Middle East and North Africa can particularly benefit from nearby Europe as an important final market and source of capital and know-how.

### Type 3 countries: Take advantage of global and regional incentive mechanisms

For countries far from major global markets and lacking a large, dynamic neighbor—the Type 3 countries—more targeted incentives may be necessary. For example, the European Union has a compensating mechanism to finance infrastructure and other development projects in less-developed and slow-growth regions, spreading the gains from more-advanced regions. Other incentive mechanisms might include direct aid and preferential market access.

Although Middle East and North Africa countries have relatively good proximity to large markets in Europe, current or historic conflict and other divisions have nonetheless often isolated countries from opportunities to trade (as seen recently in Iraq, Libya, Syria, and the Republic of Yemen). More broadly, not all countries that pursue regional integration benefit equally, although practically all have raised their economic fortunes. Where the political willingness exists to compensate those that fell relatively behind, regional integration can generate the resources to do so. Thus, regional economies most strongly positioned to gain from global trade may benefit from also supporting less-advantaged regional counterparts through investments in infrastructure, human capital development, and institutional strengthening that can both further regional integration and raise those countries' gains from trade.

## Small steps toward trade integration could bring immediate benefits

In the Middle East and North Africa, an ideal, comprehensive, and resilient regional trade agreement and infrastructure network is unlikely. However, smaller steps—which neighboring countries, or groups of them, can implement—can provide immediate benefits and move countries along the transition path to greater long-term integration. Informed by this framework, governments could consider a pragmatic strategy of incremental improvements comprising three elements:

- *Institutional reforms* that enable economic actors to take advantage of cross-border economic opportunities would include efficient customs procedures, regulatory harmonization, migration regimes, and broad business environment reforms.
- *Incremental improvements to the physical infrastructure* for trade would focus on borders, transport and energy, and information and communication technology (ICT).
- *Appropriate incentives* take into consideration that not all participants in a regional agreement will benefit equally from it. Certain forms of compensation or offsetting benefits will often be necessary.

*Reform institutional functions to unlock cross-border opportunities*

Physical trunk infrastructure to connect markets, while helpful, is rarely the binding constraint on regional trade in the Middle East and North Africa. Rather, institutional reform is required to enable and facilitate the exchange of goods, services, capital, people, and ideas; address risks; and strengthen economic fundamentals to ensure that a country's outputs are indeed internationally competitive.

*Logistics sector improvements.* Greater competition in infrastructure service provision may be important to increase goods trade efficiency in areas such as port operation (to reduce container dwell times), transport services (to reduce hauling costs), and

power markets. Weak logistics sectors appear to be a major institutional barrier to regional integration in the Middle East and North Africa (box 6.9).

In many contexts, the mechanisms to track shipments are not available; customs procedures require many documents and checkpoints; customs clearance information is not shared between border agencies, even within the same country; customs regulations are not coordinated across borders; international standards of customs procedures are not adopted; and bribery and other kinds of corruption are widespread in border crossings. There is also underutilization of ICT, which could complement these deeper reforms to raise the efficiency of procedures (as seen in Tunisia's and Morocco's recent online goods clearance systems, Tunisia TradeNet [TTN] and the BADR e-payment system, respectively) (Kulenovic 2015). Finally, state monopolies of the logistics sector in most of the region's countries have undermined incentives to reform.

*Regulatory harmonization.* While liberalization of the logistics sector can improve efficiency, more incremental efficiency improvements can also shepherd substantial progress without overstretching institutions. Incremental, technocratic reforms to address these challenges—such as streamlining customs procedures, harmonizing customs regulations across borders, and upgrading logistics services—have the potential to reduce delays, costs, and poor reliability (Rouis and Tabor 2013). Morocco provides a positive example, supporting the development of logistics zones that overcame broader weaknesses in the sector (in Casablanca, Tangier, and elsewhere); removing regulations deterring foreign direct investment (FDI) in the logistics sector; and establishing new customs regimes suitable for logistics activities (Rouis and Tabor 2013).

The case of China's SEZs (discussed earlier in box 6.8) also showed how institutions can be strengthened in pockets of the economy as scaffolding when wholesale reform across the economy was unattainable. The Democratic Republic of Congo and

## BOX 6.9 Logistics, more than infrastructure, impedes trade in the Middle East and North Africa

Middle East and North Africa countries tend to fall behind less in infrastructure quality than in areas of logistics quality, international shipping, and the quality of customs services. The poor quality of trade support services—such as customs procedures, trucking, warehousing, or freight forwarding—increases trade costs substantially.

The World Bank's 2018 Logistics Performance Index (LPI) summarized these elements for 160 countries around the world. The Gulf Cooperation Council (GCC) countries and Israel ranked relatively high across these logistics indicators, followed by Egypt and the Islamic Republic of Iran (table B6.9.1).[a] Most

other countries in the region ranked in the middle or lower portions of the LPI: Three Maghreb states (Algeria, Morocco, and Tunisia) ranked between 105 and 117. Two Mashreq states (Syria and Iraq) as well as the Republic of Yemen and Libya came in the lowest in the region, ranking between 138 and 154.

Among the non-GCC countries, the Islamic Republic of Iran, Djibouti, and Egypt achieved the greatest improvements in their LPI scores between 2010 and 2018 (figure B6.9.1, panel a). On the customs quality indicator, Egypt, the Islamic Republic of Iran, Israel, and Jordan raised their scores the most (figure B6.9.1, panel b).

TABLE B6.9.1  **Logistics Performance Index (LPI) rankings of Middle East and North Africa countries, 2018**

| Country | Overall LPI rank | Customs | Infrastructure | International shipments | Logistics quality and competence | Tracking and tracing | Timeliness |
|---|---|---|---|---|---|---|---|
| United Arab Emirates | 11 | 15 | 10 | 5 | 13 | 13 | 4 |
| Qatar | 30 | 38 | 27 | 9 | 31 | 30 | 36 |
| Israel | 37 | 29 | 28 | 75 | 34 | 32 | 48 |
| Oman | 43 | 44 | 39 | 36 | 49 | 66 | 29 |
| Saudi Arabia | 55 | 66 | 43 | 56 | 57 | 46 | 67 |
| Bahrain | 59 | 63 | 68 | 55 | 58 | 60 | 68 |
| Kuwait | 63 | 56 | 45 | 98 | 67 | 96 | 59 |
| Iran, Islamic Rep. | 64 | 71 | 63 | 79 | 62 | 85 | 60 |
| Egypt, Arab Rep. | 67 | 77 | 58 | 73 | 63 | 89 | 74 |
| Lebanon | 79 | 106 | 73 | 70 | 104 | 74 | 77 |
| Jordan | 84 | 88 | 70 | 119 | 93 | 84 | 76 |
| Djibouti | 90 | 113 | 60 | 118 | 135 | 72 | 85 |
| Tunisia | 105 | 107 | 133 | 115 | 123 | 71 | 70 |
| Morocco | 109 | 115 | 93 | 103 | 101 | 112 | 114 |
| Algeria | 117 | 138 | 96 | 122 | 113 | 103 | 124 |
| Syrian Arab Republic | 138 | 154 | 82 | 126 | 124 | 128 | 148 |
| Yemen, Rep. | 140 | 104 | 131 | 141 | 131 | 146 | 151 |
| Iraq | 147 | 153 | 140 | 131 | 159 | 144 | 129 |
| Libya | 154 | 149 | 115 | 159 | 153 | 160 | 123 |
| Mid. East & N. Africa avg. | *84* | *89* | *72* | *89* | *88* | *85* | *81* |

*Source:* World Bank Logistics Performance Index (LPI) 2018.
*Note:* The 2018 LPI covered 160 countries globally. No data were available for West Bank and Gaza. Shading designates global quintiles, from light blue (highest) to dark orange (lowest).

*box continues next page*

BOX 6.9    **Logistics, more than infrastructure, impedes trade in the Middle East and North Africa**
*(continued)*

FIGURE B6.9.1    **Among the Middle East and North Africa countries, about half improved their logistics performance between 2010 and 2018**

*Source:* World Bank Logistics Performance Index (LPI) 2010 and 2018.
*Note:* Countries are arranged in order of most to least improvement on the LPI, which covered 160 countries globally in 2018. No data were available for West Bank and Gaza. For Morocco, the 2010 and 2012 scores were used.

a. The Gulf Cooperation Council (GCC) countries are Bahrain, Kuwait, Oman, Qatar, Saudi Arabia, and the United Arab Emirates. The Mashreq subregion comprises the Arab Republic of Egypt, Iraq, Jordan, Lebanon, the Syrian Arab Republic, and West Bank and Gaza. The Maghreb subregion comprises Algeria, Libya, Morocco, and Tunisia.

Rwanda offer other examples of scaffolding: they created pockets of liberalized trade and movement between border towns through a novel visa and small traders' regime (box 6.10).

Customs reforms are most effective when harmonized between neighbors (ECA 2015). Certain governments in the region have created a national agency to promote coordination of border control services within the country (for example, the Moroccan Agency for Logistics Development). Similar institutions might usefully work with neighbors and wider regional partners to fast-track harmonization.

*Migration-related reforms.* Chapter 3 also emphasized institutional barriers to services trade and the movement of people, which limits not just services trade directly but also the exchange of ideas and know-how and the establishment of stronger social and business networks across borders. Reforms in this area are particularly important in the Middle East and North Africa, given the size of services sectors and remittances in the region's economies.

Reforms include aligning domestic regulations that license service providers across borders (such as mutual recognition agreements for professional bodies of architects,

---

**BOX 6.10**  **Scaffolding for cross-border trade and migration in the Great Lakes Region**

The Rwanda–Democratic Republic of Congo border cuts between the twin cities of Goma (Democratic Republic of Congo) and Rubavu (Rwanda) in the north, and between Bukavu (Democratic Republic of Congo) and Rusizi (Rwanda) in the south. These cities sit at the edge of eastern Democratic Republic of Congo's troubled Kivu provinces, the epicenter of major conflicts and illicit activities for decades.

However, an innovative regime facilitates fluid, small-scale, cross-border trade and migration between the cities. For example, in 2018, an estimated 90,000 people crossed the Goma–Rubavu border each day, predominantly to trade small volumes of items such as fresh produce, meat, clothes, or water but also for services trade like accessing a bank, barbers, or restaurant, and for social purposes.

The key to fluid trade across this challenging border has been the Economic Community of the Great Lakes Countries (CEPGL) protocol. Through this initiative, residents of each border city can use their voter or national IDs to obtain a *jeton* card, enabling free travel into the cross-border town (not beyond the town's limits) without any further documentation. Additional inexpensive passes are available to travel farther into each country without a passport for a limited number of days per trip and cumulative days per year. For purposes of small trade, the CEPGL is complemented by a directive that simplifies procedures and reduces tariffs (to 5 percent) for agricultural consignments under US$500 or 60 kilograms. Rwanda has recently also introduced electronic border gates,

allowing nationals to simply scan their ID cards and pass through a turnstile to enter Goma.

In theory, the CEPGL is also complemented by the Common Market for Eastern and Southern Africa's Simplified Trade Regime, allowing small traders (identified by their membership in an association issuing IDs) to trade goods up to US$2,000 in value from a harmonized list of products (agreed to bilaterally) without any tariff or nontariff barriers. However, in practice, because of poor communication about the Simplified Trade Regime on both sides as well as particularly weak institutions in the Democratic Republic of Congo, this provision is little known or accessed by traders. For instance, traders may face checks and irregular taxes and fees from up to 17 agencies on the Democratic Republic of Congo side (only 5 of the agencies are permitted to be present).

Studies have found, however, that despite such hurdles, the intense border trade has created important livelihood opportunities for low-income people in each border city, particularly women, who form the majority of traders. It also fills important gaps in access to goods and services, particularly for the Democratic Republic of Congo, such as trade of water during cuts, food supplies, and access to more modern banking facilities. There is also evidence the scheme has improved social relations, with 40 percent of traders reporting new social invitations from across the border since they began trading.

*Sources:* Mwanabiningo 2015; Vanguard Economics 2018.

accountants, lawyers, and so on), reducing barriers to FDI in services, reducing visa requirements, and removing barriers to the flow of information. These would be complemented by developing more competitive human capital able to create and take advantage of the opportunities beyond low-value-added services trade.

*Broad business environment reforms.* Unblocking trade between the Middle East and North Africa's countries will yield only muted benefits if the underlying bottlenecks to private sector development, competition, and diversification are not also addressed. The well-documented institutional bottlenecks include preferential treatment of favored firms, other regulations that constrain competition and entry, high shares of government employment, dominance of natural resource rents in exports, and firm subsidies that impose a large fiscal burden without benefiting the poor. For example, firm-level data indicate that the region's exporting firms are no more productive than firms that do not export, while there is a large and significant productivity premium for manufacturing firms that import (Francis and Schweiger 2017).

This situation is consistent with the existence of barriers and privileged access affecting imports and exports. For example, cities are unlikely to benefit from lower tariffs on intermediate inputs if favored importers control distribution and would simply capture the savings (Hoekman 2016). Similarly, even with tariff and nontariff barriers, energy trade is unlikely to take off without addressing energy subsidies and price controls.

Chapter 3 also noted that despite high capital openness, regional capital flows are low, in part because of underlying institutional weaknesses. In addition, it noted that meaningful digital integration in the region is hampered by such underlying barriers as low human capital and restrictions on the exchange of information (for example, media controls).

During the recent decline of oil prices, many of the region's countries started to reform their energy sectors. Reducing subsidies and setting tariffs high enough to recover costs is important, yet politically and technically complicated, and reform has often failed because of strong political protests. The Islamic Republic of Iran achieved temporary success in removing a large energy subsidy. The government introduced highly publicized compensatory mechanisms, including mass cash transfers, and held frequent dialogues and campaigns with citizens to gain favor for the reforms (Salehi-Isfahani 2011). Although this suggests ingredients of success, the reform also struggled over the long term in the context of international sanctions and high inflation, and political challenges arose to focusing cash transfers only on the poorest to manage affordability.

*Improve the regional infrastructure for trade*

Infrastructure that connects places to markets can shape the fortunes of cities and regions. Better-connected areas offer greater access to markets, typically encouraging densification and elevated investment. However, as noted in Transitional Step 1, for infrastructure to benefit the local economy, it should be within the framework of a multidimensional strategy that addresses complementary constraints to competitiveness. These include the business environment and trade institutions, basic public services, and human capital to ensure that corridors are attractive sites for investment, not merely recipients of final imports or flyover towns.

A concrete vision for a regional network of development corridors, and an assessment of its benefits, could help create greater support for closer integration in the Middle East and North Africa. Other regions have pursued integration through such strategic regional visions as the Trans-European Transport Network (TEN-T) to improve connectivity across the continent, especially between Eastern and Western Europe (complemented by the regulatory harmonization of the European Union)[5] and China's Belt and Road

Initiative, connecting China not just within Asia but as far as Europe and Africa.

Academic research has made considerable progress in evaluating the benefits of such initiatives at both the national level and for places within countries.[6] A comprehensive assessment of a regional integration strategy could estimate the potential gains from overcoming integration barriers as well as the geographical and distributional impacts within each country. Some of the specific transport infrastructure improvements that could be evaluated include the following (Rouis and Tabor 2013):

- *Enabling road traffic from Egypt to Jordan and Saudi Arabia,* which currently relies on ferry service, by opening a 15-kilometer corridor through Israel
- *Facilitating cross-border trade in the Mashreq subregion* (Iraq, Israel, Jordan, Lebanon, and Syria), in part to encourage economies of scale in port operations and shipping services, which are now scattered across seven medium-size ports
- *Expanding rail connections from Saudi Arabia to Jordan* and beyond as well as to other Gulf countries
- *Improving rail connections from the Islamic Republic of Iran to Turkey,* including building the missing rail link around Lake Van, which currently requires a ferry to cross
- *Better leveraging border free-trade zones,* such as that between Tunisia and Libya, for incremental integration.

Infrastructure does not only concern roads and railways. Infrastructure and complementary reforms affecting regional energy trade may be particularly transformative. National power generation capacity is generally small in the Middle East and North Africa, while energy demand is projected to increase by 50–60 percent in the region between 2018 and 2048.[7] Even with potentially large efficiency increases, the energy supply will need to expand. Integration of energy networks and increased trade can make these supply increases more affordable.

Larger systems improve capacity utilization and supply reliability even while reducing required reserve margins, because trends in daily and seasonal supply and demand tend to vary across countries and subnational regions. This becomes even more important as the share of intermittent renewable power sources increases. For instance, high renewable energy shares in Europe would not be possible without the ability to trade electricity among countries. All of these benefits result in greater reliability and lower prices for end users.

Several power grid interconnection schemes already exist or are planned in the Middle East and North Africa:

- *In the Maghreb subregion,* Algeria, Morocco, and Tunisia are interconnected, with Morocco also connected to the pan-European transmission network via Spain.
- *In the Mashreq subregion,* the interconnection involves eight countries (including Turkey).
- *In the GCC subregion,* the interconnection involves six countries.

A vision for a pan-Arab electricity network exists (World Bank 2013). It proposes a parallel process of strengthening the infrastructure and expanding trade while also building the institutional, legal, and policy framework. The result would be (a) full interconnection between the three subregions and any countries not yet included in one of these; (b) additional connections to other countries in Europe, Africa, and Asia; and (c) open access to the transmission network with full wholesale competition. Electricity trade would be overseen by a regional market operator that would also ensure functioning of financial markets as required for effective trading. Many steps will be necessary to achieve this vision. Initial scaffolding actions could begin today to strengthen existing networks and gradually expand connections to new participants and interconnections between the networks as reforms in individual countries allow.

*Design incentives to share the gains from integration*

Integration will benefit the region overall, but particular people or places may gain less or even be harmed. Regional integration can increase the concentration of economic activity, exacerbating inequality within or across countries despite the overall gains. Some past regional integration agreements have failed in part because of the perception of unequal gains.[8] Gains should be great enough that those who gain from regional integration can compensate those who do not or who become worse off.[9] However, orchestrating such redistribution is not straightforward.

Domestically, such compensation requires that governments capture some of the gains of trade and use them to benefit, for example, people in isolated lagging areas who may see an out-migration of firms to newly connected regions. Redistributive policies are far more complex at an international level. Only the European Union has extensive mechanisms for redistributing resources across countries through several structural and investment funds.[10] Such mechanisms require far closer international agreements than seem feasible in the Middle East and North Africa in the foreseeable future.

Instead, agreements more limited in geographic and substantive scope would constitute important transitional steps for regional integration. For example, a larger, more influential nation may be the most ready to benefit from openness, the most likely able to make concessions in return, and hence the most able to lead the financing of regional infrastructure or offer the greatest concessions in regional institutional reforms.[11] Alternatively, countries that benefit from increased economic activity around a modernized regional port might in turn offer their neighbors greater access to their market to sell agricultural goods or allow greater labor inflows. Such narrow agreements have been successful even between countries and regions that otherwise have strained relations; an example is the Indus Water Treaty between India and Pakistan, which has held up throughout many decades of tense relations.

## Concluding remarks

Rather than representing new development objectives, the transitional steps set forth in this chapter offer opportunities for governments in the Middle East and North Africa to pursue their same final objectives with greater efficacy. In concluding, we illustrate how the above considerations may inform more effective strategies to meet a range of possible policy objectives.

### Create jobs for youth

If the government's aim is to create jobs for young people, the first lesson is that large cities with strong market access offer the greatest potential for doing so. How can cities then deliver these jobs? This is the concern of Transitional Steps 1, 2, and 3: unlocking the potential for private job creation in cities through

- *Proper public investment* in the fundamentals for growth and reduced regulation that stifles private investment;
- *Connections between cities and world markets* as sources of growth, particularly by deepening regional integration; and
- *Preparation of young people,* ensuring they are equipped not only with paper credentials but also with globally tradable skills.

Where social divisions affecting certain youth (such as language or cultural barriers between their home and the leading city) prevent migration to leading cities and thus make local cities more relevant, Transitional Steps 2 and 3 provide guidance on how to better support local job creation in spite of the challenges.

### Decongest a leading city

If policy makers are concerned by what economist Edward Glaeser has termed the "downsides of density" and wish to decongest a leading city (for example, a capital city), consider three key complementary approaches:

- *Address the negative externalities in the city itself* (which are unlikely to recede of their own accord because of strong demand for major cities) by investing in transport and other basic infrastructure and regulating negative externalities like pollution and traffic, as discussed in Transitional Step 4.
- *Unlock any latent potential in alternative locations for firms and people* that offer strong access to national and international markets and have already signaled demand by attracting households and firms. Such places may include the urban expansion area of a main city, fast-growing satellite towns, or highly accessible secondary cities. Opportunities in these alternative locations can be unlocked through the same urban reforms as well as better local governance (Transitional Step 5) while observing the warnings and principles of Transitional Step 2.
- *Address gaps in welfare and human capital* in lagging areas. This can prevent residents from leaving prematurely before urban opportunities are available while also equipping residents with stronger human capital to tap into opportunities that do arise locally or in cities.

### Revive a particular lagging area

If the aim is to revive a particular lagging area, it is important to recognize the challenges of such efforts (given path dependency and any underlying disadvantages that explain the place's underperformance) and to build on whatever advantages and potential are already there. This means identifying existing centers of density and market access (such as major regional cities, ports, transit corridors, and so on) that might serve as poles of growth for the area and ensuring connectivity to external markets (through soft and hard reforms) as a minimum. This high accessibility is the most common source of "one big opportunity" for an area, but complementary factors may include fixed assets such as tourism heritage.

Beyond building on the area's existing potential, it is essential to diagnose the key local bottlenecks to greater productivity, including through engagement with the local business community and residents, and to carefully target development strategies to address these bottlenecks. Strategies that are sensitive in this way to local needs and opportunities and properly coordinated in the lagging area can be particularly encouraged by strengthening the role—while building the capacity and accountability—of local governments.

### Launch an effective SEZ

Regional policies should avoid the mistake of assuming that SEZs are the solution to their problem. However, an SEZ may be justified, such as to serve as a second best pocket of liberal trade and investment in a more restrictive regime. If an SEZ is planned, how can its chances of success be optimized?

- First, zones should be in locations with strong access to international markets and must offer the essential soft complements such as appropriate openness, ease of doing business, trade facilitation, and so on. This may require liberalization of relevant trade services.
- The intention of benefiting the local market should be remembered; hence, zones should be placed close to existing population centers with relevant capacities and should facilitate supply chain linkages and technology transfer.
- Unhelpful competition between subnational authorities should be avoided, and opportunities for authorities to coordinate to develop a shared zone with greater agglomeration economies should be explored.
- Weaknesses in local governance that risk undermining the reliability of infrastructure and quality of business services should be addressed (or compensated for, such as through private management of the zone).

- Given large uncertainty about the potential of the zone or wider region, feedback loops should be built in and frictions to the transformation of land, buildings, and productive activities in the zone reduced to allow competition between firms and sectors and to help zones adapt as competencies and advantages evolve.

## Notes

1. Andrews, Pritchett, and Woolcock (2017) define "isomorphic mimicry" as the tendency of governments to mimic other governments' successes in ways that often conflate form and function. This mimicry leads to a situation where "looks like" substitutes for "does"; that is, governments look capable after the mimicry but are not actually more capable. Isomorphic mimicry may explain why countries fail to build real capability even after years of policy and reform engagement and billions of dollars of capacity-building work—especially where public sectors have become closed to novelty but open to (and supportive of) agenda conformity.
2. While remote, rural areas of the region have the largest share of households lacking access to basic services, dense urban areas often host the largest number of households suffering poor service delivery, and certain areas face particular demand shocks from internally displaced persons and refugees.
3. For example, girls outperform boys in mathematics, engineering, and computer information in many Middle East and North Africa countries, but they are underrepresented in the booming technology sector (El-Alfi and Boutros 2018).
4. For example, the World Bank report, "Reshaping Egypt's Economic Geography," notes that Egypt's land and property system would ideally undergo a complete overhaul but that such a process has been attempted several times and failed because of entrenched systems and institutions as well as the sheer scale of the challenge (World Bank 2012).
5. "Infrastructure and Investment," Mobility and Transport, European Commission website: https://ec.europa.eu/transport/themes/infrastructure_en.
6. For a review, see Roberts et al. (2018).
7. *International Energy Outlook 2017* projects that energy use will increase during 2018–48 by 56 percent in the Middle East and by 63 percent in Africa (EIA 2017).
8. Examples are Central America in the 1960s and East Africa in 1970s (World Bank 2009).
9. This principle is the so-called Kaldor-Hicks criterion, as discussed in Donaldson (2015).
10. "European Structural and Investment Funds," EU Regional and Urban Development, European Commission website: http://ec.europa.eu/regional_policy/en/funding/.
11. For a discussion, see chapter 9 in World Bank (2009).

## References

Agénor, P.-R., M. K. Nabli, and T. M. Yousef. 2005. "Public Infrastructure and Private Investment in the Middle East and North Africa." Policy Research Working Paper 3661, World Bank, Washington, DC.

Andrews, Matt, Lant Pritchett, and Michael Woolcock. 2017. "Looking Like a State: The Seduction of Isomorphic Mimicry." In *Building State Capability: Evidence, Analysis, Action*, edited by Matt Andrews, Lant Pritchett, and Michael Woolcock, 29–52. Oxford: Oxford University Press.

Australian Embassy and Asia Foundation. 2016. "Coordinating Roads and Infrastructure Investments for Development (CR+ID): Working Towards More Strategic and Sound Local Public Investments." Coalitions for Change project note, Asia Foundation, San Francisco.

Bahl, R. 2008. "The Pillars of Fiscal Decentralization." CAF Working Paper 2008/07, CAF (Corporacion Andina de Fomento)–Development Bank of Latin America, Caracas, Venezuela, RB.

Beddies, Sabine, Mariana Felicio, Gabriel Dedu, Fatou Fall, and Caroline Vagneron. 2011. "MENA Local Service Delivery Initiative: Promoting Social Accountability and Demand for Good Governance." Arab World Brief No. 3, Report No. 69347, World Bank, Washington, DC.

Bismil, Farmanullah. 2018. "The Future of Special Economic Zones in Afghanistan: How Does the Trump Administration's New South Asia Strategy Change the Plan for Establishing SEZs in Afghanistan?" *The Diplomat*, June 6.

Brixi, H., E. Lust, and M. Woolcock. 2015. *Trust, Voice, and Incentives: Learning from Local Success Stories in Service Delivery in the Middle East and North Africa*. Washington, DC: World Bank.

Donaldson, D. 2015. "The Gains from Market Integration." *Annual Review of Economics* 7 (1): 619–47.

Ducruet, César, Fatima Zohra Mohamed-Chérif, and Najib Cherfaoui. 2011. "Maghreb Port Cities in Transition: The Case of Tangier." *PORTUSplus* 1 (1).

Duranton, Gilles, and Anthony Venables. 2018. "Place-Based Policies for Development." NBER Working Paper 24562, National Bureau of Economic Research, Cambridge, MA. doi:10.3386/w24562.

ECA (United Nations Economic Commission for Africa). 2015. "International Transport and Trade Facilitation in North Africa." Publication CEA-AN/PUB/14/1, Subregional Office for North Africa, ECA, Rabat, Morocco.

EIA (U.S. Energy Information Administration). 2017. "International Energy Outlook 2017." Publication No. IEO2017, EIA, Washington, DC.

El-Alfi, Ahmed, and Iris Boutros. 2018. "What Tech Can Do for Arab Women." *The Cairo Review of Global Affairs* 31 (Fall 2018).

El-Kogali, Safaa El Tayeb, and Caroline Krafft, eds. 2019. *Expectations and Aspirations: A New Framework for Education in the Middle East and North Africa*. Washington, DC: World Bank.

Francis, D. C., and H. Schweiger. 2017. "Not So Different from Non-Traders: Trade Premia in the Middle East and North Africa." *Economics of Transition* 25 (2): 185–238.

Gatti, R., M. Morgandi, R. Grun, S. Brodmann, D. Angel-Urdinola, J. M. Moreno, D. Marotta, M. Schiffbauer, and E. Mata Lorenzo. 2013. *Jobs for Shared Prosperity: Time for Action in the Middle East and North Africa*. Washington, DC: World Bank.

Gaubert, C. 2018. "Firm Sorting and Agglomeration." NBER Working Paper 24478, National Bureau of Economic Research, Cambridge, MA.

Hoekman, B. 2016. "Intraregional Trade: Potential Catalyst for Growth in the Middle East." Policy Paper 2016-1, Middle East Institute, Washington, DC.

Kulenovic, Z. Joe. 2015. "Tangier, Morocco: Success on the Strait of Gibraltar." *Private Sector Development Blog*, November 25. https://blogs.worldbank.org/psd/tangier-morocco-success-strait-gibraltar.

Mansuri, Ghazala, and Vijayendra Rao. 2013. *Localizing Development: Does Participation Work?* World Bank Policy Research Report. Washington, DC: World Bank.

Mwanabiningo, Nene Morisho. 2015. *Deriving Maximum Benefit from Small-Scale Cross-Border Trade between DRC and Rwanda*. London: International Alert; Nairobi: TradeMark East Africa.

Redding, Stephen J., and Esteban Rossi-Hansberg. 2016. "Quantitative Spatial Economics." NBER Working Paper 22655, National Bureau of Economic Research, Cambridge, MA.

Roberts, M., M. Melecky, T. Bougna, and Y. Xu. 2018. "Transport Corridors and Their Wider Economic Benefits: A Critical Review of the Literature." Policy Research Working Paper 8302, World Bank, Washington, DC.

Rouis, Mustapha, and Steven R. Tabor. 2013. *Regional Economic Integration in the Middle East and North Africa: Beyond Trade Reform*. Directions in Development Series. Washington, DC: World Bank.

Salehi-Isfahani, Djavad. 2011. "Iran: Subsidy Reform amid Regional Turmoil." Op-Ed, March 3, Brookings Institution, Washington, DC. https://www.brookings.edu/opinions/iran-subsidy-reform-amid-regional-turmoil/.

Sims, D. 2015. *Egypt's Desert Dreams: Development or Disaster?* Oxford: Oxford University Press.

Valerio, Alexandria, Brent Parton, and Alicia Robb. 2014. *Entrepreneurship Education and Training Programs around the World: Dimensions for Success*. Directions in Development Series. Washington, DC: World Bank.

Vanguard Economics. 2018. "Democratic Republic of Congo Borderlands Report." Report, Vanguard Economics, Kigali, Rwanda.

World Bank. 2009. *World Development Report 2009: Reshaping Economic Geography*. Washington, DC: World Bank.

———. 2012. "Arab Republic of Egypt: Reshaping Egypt's Economic Geography: Domestic Integration as a Development Platform." Report No. 71289-EG, World Bank, Washington, DC.

————. 2013. "Middle East and North Africa Integration of Electricity Networks in the Arab World: Regional Market Structure and Design." Energy study, Report No. ACS7124, World Bank, Washington, DC.

————. 2016a. "Hashemite Kingdom of Jordan: Education Sector Public Expenditure Review." Report No. ACS18935, World Bank, Washington, DC.

————. 2016b. "Upper Egypt Local Development Program-for-Results Project." Project Appraisal Document, Report No. 108094, World Bank, Washington, DC.

————. 2017a. "Dire Straits: The Crisis Surrounding Poverty, Conflict, and Water in the Republic of Yemen." WASH Poverty Diagnostic Series, Report No. 11711, World Bank, Washington, DC.

————. 2017b. "Inclusive Service Delivery: Yemen Policy Note 4." Working Paper, Report No. 120534, World Bank, Washington, DC.

————. 2017c. "Opportunities for Improving Urban Service Delivery in South Sudan: A Tale of Two Cities. Part I: Service Delivery Status Report." World Bank, Washington, DC. doi:10.1596/29199.

————. 2019. "Territorial Development in Support of NDS 2030." Reimbursable Advisory Services (RAS) paper for the Croatia 2030 National Development Strategy (NDS), World Bank, Washington, DC.